D1093886

THE LUTHERAN PAROCHIAL SCHOOL
DATES, DOCUMENTS, EVENTS, PEOPLE

THE
LUTHERAN
PAROCHIAL
SCHOOL

Dates, Documents, Events, People

Wayne E. Schmidt

Concordia Seminary Publications

The Lutheran Parochial School
Dates, Documents, Events, People
By Wayne E. Schmidt

ISBN 0-911770-73-9

Printed by Sheridan Books, Chelsea, Michigan

To my wife, Bonnie, and in recognition
of the dedicated Christian service of her
and my Lutheran parochial school teachers
and those of our children, Jonathan and Tara.

CONTENTS

Acknowledgments

The idea to write a treatise on the history of the Lutheran parochial school in the arrangement of the following pages goes back to a book authored by Edward A. Krug in 1966. Krug was the present author's doctoral advisor at the University of Wisconsin in Madison and taught, in addition to a number of electives, a required undergraduate course called "School and Society." An educational historian, Krug structured his "School and Society" course around a framework of dates and eventually put his analysis of the events of those dates into a Harper and Row publication entitled *Salient Dates in American Education: 1635-1964*. The present writer has found that little volume a handy guidebook from which to gain an acquaintance with a number of important events in the history of education in the United States and has long felt that the same kind of annotated calendar would be useful for acquiring a perspective on the history of the Lutheran Christian day school in America. The undersigned acknowledges his indebtedness, therefore, to the late Edward A. Krug, not only for a book idea but also for the example which the latter set as a classroom professor and academic advisor.

Various kinds of written materials were necessary for the writing of *The Lutheran Parochial School: Dates, Documents, Events, People*. These materials included *Proceedings* of conventions of The Lutheran Church—Missouri Synod (LCMS), the Wisconsin Evangelical Lutheran Synod (WELS), and the Evangelical Lutheran Synodical Conference of North America. Past periodical literature produced in both the

Missouri and Wisconsin Synods made it possible to discover what people were saying about certain events at the time those episodes were taking place. In addition, institutional and other types of histories also had to be consulted. The library of Concordia Seminary in St. Louis—a campus on which the author has both lived and worked—had many of the needed resources. The staff of the library was always most helpful when assistance was needed and went to the trouble on several occasions of obtaining through inter-library loan things which were not in the Concordia collection. That kind of service was much appreciated.

Concordia Historical Institute, located on the campus of Concordia Seminary, was a second valuable source for information pertinent to the study of Lutheran educational history. The Institute's collection of reading books for Lutheran schools, for example, cannot be matched in any other place. That collection was absolutely necessary for the writing of the present book's section under the date 1926. As the archival repository for The Lutheran Church—Missouri Synod, Concordia Historical Institute also houses certain types of reference materials and historical resources not found in lending libraries. The Institute's holdings were consulted frequently.

The archival collection of the Wisconsin Evangelical Lutheran Synod has not been as extensively developed as that of The Lutheran Church—Missouri Synod. Norbert Manthe, who as a volunteer was doing pioneer work in the organizing of Wisconsin's archives at the time of the writing of the present book, was able to provide information, however, on what was available in the WELS archives. He also supplied the undersigned with surplus copies and photocopies of materials from that collection.

Since German was the language used in both the Wisconsin and Missouri Synods in their early history, synodical documents from that time are in German. Unless otherwise noted, the translations into English of excerpts from documents which exist only in the German are those of the present author. A small study grant and the appointment of a graduate research fellow—both provided by Concordia Seminary—helped the undersigned to locate and examine these and other documents.

Of inestimable value in the entire project was the assistance of Debbie Roediger in the secretarial services office of Concordia Seminary. In addition to her many duties for other Concordia faculty members, she found the time to type and retype the author's handwritten manuscript and to make it ready for submission to the publisher. The author is deeply indebted to Miss Roediger for her expert word-processing skills and her cheerful willingness to make alteration upon alteration over a period of several years.

A final word of thanks to my wife for her help and patience during the writing of the book and to seminary colleague Robert Rosin, editor of Concordia Seminary Publications and to his wife, Laine Rosin. The editorial hands and eyes of the latter two have brought *The Lutheran Parochial School: Dates, Documents, Events, People* into the form you now see.

The school pictures on the title page are from the files of St. John's Lutheran School, Amelith Road, in Bay City, Michigan, St. Peter's Lutheran School in Fond du Lac, Wisconsin, the elementary Lutheran school attended by the author, and Green Park Lutheran School in St. Louis, Missouri. The photos are used by permission.

Wayne E. Schmidt

INTRODUCTION

Lutheran elementary and secondary schools have been part of the American educational scene for a long time. When immigrants came from Europe they brought with them their parish school traditions. Many of the parochial schools which nineteenth-century German Lutheran immigrants established in the United States offered courses of study comparable to those of the public schools of the day in the areas where the church schools were located. Other parish schools, however, were little more than part-time religious instruction centers which sought to prepare the rising generation primarily for the rite of confirmation and full membership in the Lutheran church. Since Lutherans emphasized the private use of Holy Scriptures, family devotional reading, and religious instruction in the home, the teaching of reading and writing attached itself naturally to even the most unpretentious church school. Instruction in basic literacy was considered to be part of a parish school program. Before the enactment of compulsory school attendance laws, and even after such legislation, the limited education of these confirmation-type parish schools was often the only kind of schooling that some Lutheran children received.

The gradual development of the American public school into a more comprehensive institution and the increasing requirements placed upon schools of all types by state legislatures had a dual effect on the parochial school movement. Many Lutheran parishes abandoned altogether the concept of a parochial school in which common schooling was offered in conjunction with religious instruction and within the framework of the confession of the church. Such parishes chose to confine themselves to religious and confirmation instruction only and left the general aspects of elementary education to the public school. Other Lutherans, however, were unwilling to go that route and embarked instead upon a course of action which sought to preserve the comprehensive parochial school in American education.

Two sizable contemporary American Lutheran church bodies which have continued to maintain a system of Lutheran parochial schools at both the elementary and secondary levels are The Lutheran Church—Missouri Synod and the Wisconsin Evangelical Lutheran Synod. Both of these church bodies are represented throughout the United States and have international connections as well. Both synods operate colleges for the training and certifying of Lutheran school teachers and both have executive officers at the synodical level to guide and support the parochial school movement in their respective synods. The Lutheran Church—Missouri Synod with a membership of 2,594,358 and 6,172 congregations[1] reports a total of 997 elementary schools and 65 secondary schools.[2] The Wisconsin Evangelical Lutheran Synod has a membership of 411,295 in 1,235 congregations[3] and includes 366 elementary and 21 secondary schools in its statistics.[4]

---

[1] The Lutheran Church–Missouri Synod, *The Lutheran Annual* (St. Louis: Concordia Publishing House, 1998), 402.

[2] Department of School Ministry, *Statistical Report Summary 1997-98* (St. Louis: The Lutheran Church–Missouri Synod), 12. The elementary school figure does not include preschools or early childhood centers.

[3] Wisconsin Ev. Lutheran Synod, *Statistical Report* (Milwaukee: Wisconsin Ev. Lutheran Synod, 1997), 2.

[4] Commission on Parish Schools, *School Statistics 1997-98* (Milwaukee: The Wisconsin Evangelical Lutheran Synod, December 1, 1997), 3, 18. The elementary school figure does not include preschools or early childhood centers.

For a period of 90 years The Lutheran Church—Missouri Synod and the Wisconsin Evangelical Lutheran Synod were members of a Lutheran federation known as the Evangelical Lutheran Synodical Conference of North America. Although the Synodical Conference no longer exists, while it was functioning it fostered the cause of Lutheran parochial schools and devoted time periodically in convention to a discussion of matters pertaining to such schools. Both the Missouri and the Wisconsin Synods experienced theological conflicts in the twentieth century which resulted in the loss of some churches. A number of congregations which severed their Missouri and Wisconsin synodical ties had been operating parish schools and continued to do so in new or realigned ecclesiastical fellowships. The small Evangelical Lutheran Synod, which was a part of the Synodical Conference for about 45 years, also encourages the establishment of Lutheran parochial schools. It is The Lutheran Church—Missouri Synod and the Wisconsin Evangelical Lutheran Synod, however, which have the most comprehensive network of full-time elementary and secondary schools and synodical offices to promote this type of education.

Both synods were founded by German Lutheran immigrants in the mid-nineteenth century and in that way have a common background. The two school systems also originated in the nineteenth century and are indebted for their present vigor to people, events, and thinking of the past. *The Lutheran Parochial School: Dates, Documents, Events, People* seeks to trace some of that past and does so by providing a general framework within which to become acquainted with Lutheran parochial school history. The book is set up chronologically and highlights specific years in which something noteworthy in the history of the Lutheran parochial school movement took place. The years chosen for annotated comment are admittedly selective and represent only a small portion of what might be considered important in the unfolding story of full-time common schooling in Lutheran parishes. Other years, together with the people and events of them, could be added to the list to give a more detailed and comprehensive picture of the subject in hand. The present volume intends merely to provide an overview, however, and considers the selected dates as helpful markers for that task.

A primary purpose of *The Lutheran Parochial School: Dates, Documents, Events, People* is to make available a resource for college and seminary courses in the history of Lutheran education and American Lutheranism. Those who are preparing themselves for professional service in Lutheran church bodies which maintain parochial schools should be able to use the book with profit in order to gain an understanding of the origin and purposes of such schools. In-service Lutheran teachers, administrators, and parish pastors may also find the book instructive and informative. And, finally, it is hoped that *The Lutheran Parochial School* will serve other readers who might have an interest in the history which lies behind today's full-time Lutheran elementary and secondary schools in the United States. A knowledge of that history is not without its own worth and the study of it can be fascinating besides.

✠ ✠ ✠ 1524 ✠ ✠ ✠

Martin Luther

To the Councilmen of All Cities in Germany That They Establish and Maintain Christian Schools

Martin Luther's approach to the subject of schools is important in the history of public schools as well as in the history of Lutheran parochial schools. The reason lies in the fact that church and state were so intimately joined together in Luther's day that he was able to expect a state-established and -operated school to work in total harmony with the church and actively to support and promote the educational goals of the church. For Luther the school was an agency of both church and state. For that reason, one might justifiably link the development of both the Lutheran parochial school and the modern public school to some of Luther's thinking.

Luther himself did not write extensively on the subject of schools, and the implementation of his ideas, even in his own day, was left to his assistants. In his open letter of 1520 *To the Christian Nobility of the German Nation Concerning the Reform of the Christian Estate* he had included a few comments on what ought to be going on in schools,[1] and in 1523 he had said a bit

---

[1] Martin Luther, "To the Christian Nobility of the German Nation Concerning the Reform of the Christian Estate" (1520), *Luther's Works*, American Edition, vol. 44, *The Christian in Society I*, ed. James Atkinson, trans. Charles M. Jacobs (Philadelphia: Fortress, 1966), 204-7.

also about the funding and supervision of common schools.[2] It was not until 1524, however, that he addressed the school issue in a treatise completely devoted to the subject of education, the document entitled *To the Councilmen of All Cities in Germany That They Establish and Maintain Christian Schools.*[3] This work and the treatise *A Sermon on Keeping Children in School* (1530)[4] are Luther's major writings on school matters.

To the Councilmen . . . That They Establish and Maintain Christian Schools deals with educational matters in very broad terms. One is well-advised not to read more specifics into it than are there, lest features of school and curricular organization not specifically mentioned by Luther be attributed to him. Johannes Bugenhagen and Philip Melanchthon were Luther's two co-workers who drew up early designs for community schools. They and other sixteenth-century church leaders authored the well-known church and school regulations (*Kirchenordnungen* and *Schulordnungen*) which organized church and school life in the century of the Lutheran Reformation. It is in these documents that the details of school programs are put into place. The general designs rest on Luther's theoretical discussions, of course, but the details may not necessarily be his, for his two major treatises speak only in general terms and do not spell out specifics.

---

[2] Martin Luther, "Ordinance of a Common Chest, Preface" (1523), *Luther's Works*, American Edition, vol. 45, *The Christian in Society II*, ed. Walther I. Brandt, trans. Albert T. W. Steinhaeuser (Philadelphia: Muhlenberg, 1962), 188-89.

[3] Martin Luther, "To the Councilmen of All Cities in Germany That They Establish and Maintain Christian Schools" (1524), *Luther's Works*, American Edition, vol. 45, *The Christian in Society II*, ed. Walther I. Brandt, trans. Albert T. W. Steinhaeuser (Philadelphia: Muhlenberg, 1962), 339-78.

[4] Martin Luther, "A Sermon on Keeping Children in School" (1530), *Luther's Works*, American Edition, vol. 46, *The Christian in Society III*, ed. Robert C. Schultz, trans. Charles M. Jacobs (Philadelphia: Fortress, 1967), 207-58.

It was not for a lack of things to do that Luther enlisted his pen twice in the interest of schools. Educational institutions were becoming victims of some unfortunate circumstances. As monks and nuns who had become adherents of the Lutheran Reformation began to leave their orders, the schools which these people had heretofore been operating ceased to exist. The property of the monasteries and religious foundations was confiscated by secular authorities but was not always then used for the school purposes which had been served earlier. Since such property represented no small amount of wealth, the acquisition of it was inviting, and Luther in 1523 complained about the "mad scramble for the assets of such vacated foundations" and the "greedy bellies" which grabbed such ecclesiastical foundations and then claimed that Luther himself had put them up to it.[5] The occasion for the letter *To the Councilmen* was Luther's concern that "schools are everywhere being left to go to wrack and ruin."[6]

Since the general populace was not convinced of the value of schools and the type of education offered in them Luther felt that it was necessary to explain and defend the purposes of schools. He had no use, of course, for much of what had gone on in the universities and monasteries in the period prior to the Reformation, and he did not hesitate to label such schools "asses' stalls and devil's training centers."[7] Nonetheless, he did feel that schools at all levels could redirect their purposes and that educational institutions were absolutely necessary for the well-being of humanity. He proceeded in *To the Councilmen*, therefore, to argue the school case on two grounds. Schools were necessary, first, for the contribution which they made to

---

[5] Martin Luther, "Ordinance of a Common Chest," *Luther's Works*, 45:170.

[6] Martin Luther, "To the Councilmen," *Luther's Works*, 45:348.

[7] Ibid., 352.

"the spiritual realm and the salvation of souls."[8] Schools, in other words, were to serve the church and its religious aims. Second, schools were necessary if temporal government was to survive and function.[9] Without schools, orderly and good government would cease to exist. These are the arguments which Luther employed in *To the Councilmen* to encourage the establishment and maintenance of schools in Germany.

The first part of the essay, which deals with the spiritual benefit of schools, includes a lengthy discussion on the necessity of teaching Latin, Greek, and Hebrew in schools. "We will not long preserve the gospel without the languages," Luther wrote,[10] and although he granted that simple preachers could proclaim "faith and the gospel . . . without a knowledge of the languages," he also maintained that "such preaching is flat and tame; people finally become weary and bored with it, and it falls to the ground."[11] The schools which Luther had in mind in this treatise were those which taught Latin, Greek, and Hebrew. He considered those languages essential for the welfare of the spiritual estate and attributed the corruption which he perceived in the Roman Catholic Church to a neglect especially of the two biblical languages, Greek and Hebrew. He argued that the devil opposed schools which taught those languages because "the devil smelled a rat, and perceived that if the languages were revived, a hole would be knocked in his kingdom which he could not easily stop up again."[12] "In proportion then as we value the gospel, let us zealously hold to the languages."[13]

---

[8] Ibid., 367.
[9] Ibid.
[10] Ibid., 360.
[11] Ibid., 365.
[12] Ibid., 358.
[13] Ibid., 359.

It becomes apparent from this that Luther was not urging the councilmen to establish and maintain a comprehensive system of German vernacular schools. This does not mean that he was opposed to such schools and what they did, but it is decidedly not the institution which he was promoting in his address of 1524. Luther was speaking about schools for the young as well as for the more advanced student, but in both cases he had language and liberal arts schools in mind. His extensive treatment of the ecclesiastical value of the languages for use by the professional theologian demonstrates that he is advancing the cause of a classical school for both young and old. Students who were especially gifted and had the potential for becoming very able theological leaders were to be permitted to go to school longer than the ordinary student. It was expected that some, both men and women, might be dedicated to a life of study,[14] but the schools attended even at an early age were Latin language schools. That is the kind of institution which the councilmen were being exhorted to establish and maintain.

Although it might seem a bit unusual to the analyst of contemporary curriculum practice, Luther did not have a different kind of school in mind when he pleaded for an educational system in order to maintain good temporal government. The second part of his essay recommended that the classical language school be the training ground for boys who would eventually enter positions of secular authority in government and for girls who would have to know how to manage their households well.[15] The Reformer's reasons for espousing schools of this type for future government authorities are not difficult to detect. Latin was still in common use in government business. That, however, was not Luther's only reason for recommending the teaching of that language. He was a humanist in the sense that he felt history and literature

---

[14] Ibid., 371.
[15] Ibid., 368.

informed and enabled a person to see beyond his own local environment. Since the literature of western culture in the sixteenth century was in Latin and Greek and not in vernacular tongues, Luther was convinced that only through the teaching of Latin and Greek classics could schools produce competent, good, and enlightened rulers.[16] In *To the Councilmen* there was no emphasis, therefore, upon the establishment of a universal system of vernacular schools even at the elementary level.

Although Luther made it clear in his essay that the public welfare was at stake in the school issue, he was also theologian enough to recognize that the Bible, too, spoke on the matter of training the young. He drew upon biblical imperatives, therefore, in his endeavor to motivate the German states to establish schools. The seat of responsibility for the instruction of the young in Holy Scripture is clear. Parents have it. For that reason it was necessary for Luther to demonstrate how the duty for training the rising generation moved from the home to the state.

In approaching this matter he granted that the Bible speaks directly only about parental instruction of the young. In fact, he himself raised the objection which a councilman might present after he had heard Luther's biblical argumentation which urges parents to instruct their children: "Ah, you say, but all that is spoken to the parents; what business is it of councilmen and the authorities?"[17] The transfer of responsibility, according to Luther, came about for three reasons.

First, the state must assume responsibility because parents have neglected their duty. Parents, Luther said, are like the ostrich: "They deal cruelly with their young. They are content to have laid the eggs and brought children into the world; beyond this they will do nothing more."[18] For that reason, someone else would have to discharge the God-given responsibility to

---

[16] Ibid., 368-69.

[17] Ibid., 354.

[18] Ibid., 355.

educate the young. It is interesting to note that Luther was appealing to the city councilmen rather than princes and lords because he felt that the latter were too busy with "sleigh riding, drinking . . . and important functions in cellar, kitchen, and bedroom."[19] Both parental and princely neglect had made it necessary for the city fathers to take upon themselves the obligations to educate Germany's young for the spiritual and temporal well-being of the nation.

Second, Luther maintained that parents could not educate their children because parents were academically unfitted for the task. When one considers the kind of school which Luther was advocating, a school which taught Latin and Greek, it is obvious that most sixteenth-century parents were hardly equipped for the teaching assignment. Although basic literacy might have been more common among the population than is sometimes assumed, many parents would have been hard-pressed to teach even the vernacular well. Latin, Greek, and Hebrew were obviously out of the question, and that was what Luther expected to be taught in the schools he was promoting in *To the Councilmen*. In fact, he did not hesitate to chide the religious group known as the Waldensian Brethren for their neglect of those languages.[20]

Third, Luther recognized what some advocates of home schooling sometimes overlook. It takes a lot of time to educate children at home, time which parents don't always have. Private tutors, of course, were not uncommon in Luther's day, but he understood that most parents lacked the financial resources to engage such tutors.[21] Since Luther was recommending an educational program built upon the foundation of Latin and Greek, a private tutor even for the young would have to have been an individual of no mean scholarly achievement. The cost

---

[19] Ibid., 368.

[20] Ibid., 365-66.

[21] Ibid., 355.

of engaging such tutors was obviously prohibitive for the common man. For that reason, a publicly supported school system was necessary so that church and state would be able to tap the potential intellectual resources among the children of the general populace.

The rather erudite kind of schooling which Luther was proposing would seem to suggest that students would have to spend much time in the classroom. It is not only a contemporary observer who might draw such an inference. The sixteenth-century parent was also apparently ready to arrive at the same kind of conclusion, for Luther anticipated the argument against his school proposal when he wrote: "So you say, 'But who can thus spare his children and train them all to be young gentlemen? There is work for them to do at home.' "[22] In answer to the objection, Luther replied that he was expecting a boy to attend classes only one or two hours per day and then go home to work and learn a trade. Girls, he was certain, could surely find one hour in the day for such schooling and still take care of their duties at home.[23] Luther was advocating only minimal classroom time even for the kind of education which he envisioned.

Although the time a student was expected to be in school was not anticipated to be excessive, the academic and financial resources necessary to establish and maintain the kind of school system proposed would not be insignificant. From where would the money come? From where would the teachers come? Luther saw no problem on either score. Since people were no longer "obliged to waste a great deal of money and property on indulgences, masses, vigils, endowments, bequests, anniversaries, mendicant friars, brotherhoods, pilgrimages, and similar nonsense,"[24] the populace would and should be able to

---

[22] Ibid., 370.

[23] Ibid.

[24] Ibid., 351.

contribute toward schools. With a supply of teachers there was also no problem because "we have today the finest and most learned group of men, adorned with languages and all the arts who could also render real service . . . as instructors of the young."[25] The availability of qualified teachers was more than a fortunate circumstance; it was a mandate for action:

> Now that God has so richly blessed us . . . and provided us with so many men able to instruct and train our youth aright, it is surely imperative that we not throw his blessing to the winds and let him knock in vain. He is standing at the door; happy are we who open to him! He is calling us; blessed is he who answers him! If we turn a deaf ear and he should pass us by, who will bring him back again?[26]

The resources were there; the time was ripe for action.

To complement the work of schools and teachers, libraries were also essential, a fact not overlooked in Luther's exhortation to the councilmen. Libraries, in his opinion, had degenerated over the centuries into collections of worthless books. The kinds of books which Luther recommended reflect the nature of the school system the Reformer was advocating. Bibles in Latin, Greek, Hebrew, German, and any other languages and Bible commentaries in Greek, Hebrew, and Latin were deemed basic to a book collection. Works in Latin and Greek covering the liberal arts, law, and medicine and authored by pagan as well as Christian writers were to find their way into the stacks. The German people, in the mind of Luther, needed schools to insure that the young were taught the Holy Scriptures, the languages in which these Scriptures were

---

[25] Ibid.

[26] Ibid., 352.

originally written and later commented on, and the various liberal arts which contribute to the well-being of a Christian society. Libraries were essential adjuncts to that kind of educational enterprise.

Martin Luther's contributions to the body of formal literature on the subject of education are not extensive. He took pen in hand when he became alarmed at the decline and deterioration of school programs in the early period of the Reformation. In his 1524 address *To the Councilmen of All Cities in Germany That They Establish and Maintain Christian Schools* he appealed to municipal authorities to reverse the downward trend. He called for a system of schools operated and supported by secular authority and built upon Christian principles and the foundation of the classical languages. The schools were to be there for both boys and girls and were to serve the interests of church and state at the same time. In keeping with the close ties which existed between church and state in his day, the type of school which he was recommending could in today's language be called both public and parochial.

Suggested for Further Reading

Luther, Martin. "To the Councilmen of All Cities in Germany That They Establish and Maintain Christian Schools." *Luther's Works*, American Edition. Vol. 45, *The Christian in Society II*, ed. Walther I. Brandt, trans. Albert T. W. Steinhaeuser, 339-78. Philadelphia: Muhlenberg, 1962.

✤✤✤ 1528 (A) ✤✤✤

Philip Melanchthon and Martin Luther

Instructions for the Visitors of Parish Pastors in Electoral Saxony

Two documents which appeared in the year 1528 were destined to have long-lasting and far-reaching effects on the design of German schools. The one document was drawn up by Luther's scholarly co-worker Philip Melanchthon. It included a preface by Luther and was later also edited by him. It is usually included, therefore, in editions of *Luther's Works* under the title *Instructions for the Visitors of Parish Pastors in Electoral Saxony*.

The second document came from the pen of another of Luther's co-workers, Johannes Bugenhagen. Its purpose was similar to that of the Saxon *Visitation Articles* composed by Melanchthon and Luther. It sought to provide guidelines for parish and public school life in the city of Braunschweig, even as the aforementioned *Visitation Articles* were to serve the same purpose in electoral Saxony. Bugenhagen's guide is usually referred to simply as the *Braunschweig Kirchenordnung* (Church Ordinance for Braunschweig) of 1528.

These two guides were influential because they became models for a large number of similar codes written by different authors for various cities, towns, and states in sixteenth-century Germany. This genre of literature has come to be known as the *Kirchenordnungen* (Church Regulations) and *Schulordnungen*

(School Regulations) in German political and ecclesiastical life. Several such sets of ordinances had appeared in Lutheran areas before 1528, but the two done by Melanchthon (Luther) and Bugenhagen served as guides for later church and school regulations which continued to appear in the sixteenth century. That is part of the significance of the 1528 documents.

Instructions for the regulation of church life did not originate with the Protestant Reformation. Guidelines for ecclesiastical and school life had been in existence prior to that time. The large effort in this direction during the Reformation century arises out of the ecclesiastical and political confusion which came about in Germany as a result of the Protestant Revolt. Religious houses were abandoned or left with few inhabitants. Political rulers confiscated property formerly owned by religious groups, and parish pastors together with their parishioners did not always have a full understanding of the new theology and how to order church life under it. This caused Luther as early as 1525 to urge the Elector of Saxony to make provision for a visitation of the clergy and churches in his realm. When the visitation was ready to take place in Saxony, Melanchthon drew up the *Instructions for the Visitors of Parish Pastors in Electoral Saxony*. His *Visitation Articles* of 1528, endorsed by Luther and further edited by the Reformer in 1538, were regularly drawn upon by other authors of subsequent ecclesiastical constitutions.

What is it which makes church ordinances important in school history? To answer that question it is necessary to understand the scope of these church regulations. Although no uniform arrangement is followed in the various orders, a large variety of topics is regularly addressed. The first part of the ordinance is usually devoted to a presentation of doctrinal matters. Thus, for example, the 1528 *Articles* deal with theological subjects such as the Ten Commandments, Baptism, and Prayer. The same document also outlines procedures for daily worship and gives advice on what pastors should teach people about the institution of marriage. There are, in addition, regulatory instructions dealing with how pastors are to conduct themselves and how they are to be supervised. Finally, the *Visitation Articles* include a plan for schools. Although school regulations would in the course of time exist independent of church regulations and in that context become more detailed, a section on school organization was regularly a part of the *Kirchenordnungen* (Church Ordinances) which appeared during the Reformation century.

In the *Visitation Articles* Melanchthon outlined the program for a Latin grammar school. He made it clear that only Latin was to be taught in the schools: "In the first place the schoolmasters are to be concerned about teaching the children Latin only, not German or Greek or Hebrew."[1] There is no provision in the *Articles* for any kind of German school. Even the classroom conversation was to be Latin: "The pupils shall also be required to speak Latin. The schoolmaster himself, as far as possible, should speak only Latin with the pupils so that they become accustomed to and are encouraged in this practice."[2] The only reference to the use of German in the educational process appears in the requirement that the pupils memorize a number of easy Psalms. The titles of these Psalms were given in the vernacular,[3] from which one might conclude that German was used in certain aspects of religious instruction. The students were very likely expected to be able to recite the Lord's Prayer, the Creed, and the Ten Commandments in German and use German in worship.

---

[1] Martin Luther, "Instructions for the Visitors of Parish Pastors in Electoral Saxony" (1528), *Luther's Works*, American Edition, vol. 40, *Church and Ministry II*, trans. and ed. Conrad Bergendoff (Philadelphia: Muhlenberg, 1958), 315.

[2] Ibid., 320.

[3] Ibid., 319.

The curriculum of the *Visitation Articles* had three major foci: religion, Latin, and music. The music was religiously functional since Matins and Vespers were to be conducted daily in the churches, and if there was a school in conjunction with a church, these offices would have been choral.[4] Major traditional chants and hymns were to be included in Matins and Vespers, both of which might or might not have a sermon.[5] The German and Latin languages would have been employed in these services, although the Latin works studied in school were not primarily ecclesiastical works but the writings of classical authors like Cicero, Vergil, Ovid, and Terence. Melanchthon's school was a Latin school in the strictest sense of the term. Latin grammar was taught; Latin authors were read; Latin conversation was to prevail. And this school was not just Melanchthon's; it was Luther's as well, the kind of school which he had promoted in his 1524 exhortation *To the Councilmen of All Cities in Germany* and in his 1530 *Sermon on Keeping Children in School.*

Suggested for Further Reading

Luther, Martin. "Instruction for the Visitors of Parish Pastors in Electoral Saxony." *Luther's Works*, American Edition. Vol. 40, *Church and Ministry II*, trans. and ed. Conrad Bergendoff, 263-320. Philadelphia: Muhlenberg, 1958.

Meyer, Carl S. "Philip Melanchthon." In *A History of Religious Educators*, ed. Elmer L. Towns, 144-60. Grand Rapids: Baker, 1975.

---

[4] Ibid., 307.
[5] Ibid.

✠ ✠ ✠ 1528 (B) ✠ ✠ ✠

Johannes Bugenhagen

Church Ordinance for Braunschweig (Brunswick)

Philip Melanchthon, for a number of reasons, is the best-known co-worker of Martin Luther. In school matters Melanchthon is usually regarded as the major Reformation era spokesman. He has been called the "Praeceptor Germaniae" (the teacher of Germany) and is deserving of the title. His classical bent, so evident in the Saxon *Visitation Articles*, left an indelible imprint upon German secondary schools for several centuries. The celebrated German *Gymnasium* with its classical language foundations had its roots in Melanchthon's sixteenth-century school plans, and he corresponded with no fewer than 56 cities regarding the funding and conduct of educational programs. His influence upon the schools of Germany and Lutheran schools brought from that country to the United States is considerable.

A co-worker of both Luther and Melanchthon not quite so well-known is Johannes Bugenhagen. He, too, was a major consultant in the field of education in the Reformation era. In fact, his name appears on fully as many sixteenth-century school plans as does that of Melanchthon. The striking thing about Bugenhagen's approach to school organization is his inclusion, even in his earliest plan, of provisions for elementary German language schools. Whether he did this because of a stronger philosophical commitment to that kind of school or because such schools had been developed more extensively in earlier times in the communities which he advised than in other places need not be debated. The fact is that while the Melanchthon-Luther Saxon *Visitation Articles* of 1528 made no specific mention of German elementary schools, Bugenhagen's 1528 *Church Ordinance for Braunschweig*[1] did make provision for that type of institution. From the point of view of Lutheran elementary school history Bugenhagen's German language schools are notable, for in them one sees the beginnings of the Lutheran parish type school in which basic vernacular literacy, rudimentary computational skills, singing, and religion were taught.

Lutheran doctrine on the authority of Scripture and the universal priesthood of all believers accounted in part for the development of vernacular schools in Germany. If Scripture is authoritative in spiritual matters, as Lutherans taught, and if, as Lutherans also hold, all Christians are priests before God, then the laity will be expected and encouraged to read the Bible. For that reason, Luther put the Old and the New Testaments into the German language. The availability of the Bible in that language and the expectation that the common people use Holy Scripture on their own and not be dependent upon an interpreter gave impetus to the establishment and maintenance of vernacular schools for the purpose of teaching reading. Reformation principles and achievements contributed positively to the advancement of universal schooling to teach basic reading ability in one's own language.

Vernacular schools themselves had existed prior to the time of the Reformation and were part of a rather complex educational scene of church, municipal, and private schools which had come out of the medieval centuries. A major force in the development of these schools in Germany and elsewhere

---

[1] The English name for Braunschweig is Brunswick.

was the desire on the part of the emerging business class to have their children read, write, and do simple arithmetic. This was practical learning and, in the minds of those engaged in business operations, far more useful than the Latin grammar schools operated by both the church and a number of municipalities. Some of these vernacular schools might have been town schools, but many were also private ventures taught by itinerant teachers. Boys and girls alike attended these schools and learned to read and write in their native tongue. Although vernacular schools were educational stepchildren, the institutions were popular. Bugenhagen chose not to ignore these popular schools, made provisions for them already in 1528 in his *Church Ordinance for Braunschweig*, and set something of a pattern for the later German *Volksschule* (people's school) which remained attached to church and state for many years to come.

Mention of Bugenhagen's recognition of the value of vernacular schools in church and state life should not leave the incorrect impression that such institutions received major attention in his school plans. Quite the opposite is the case. Considering the length and detail of the school regulations in Bugenhagen's 1528 Braunschweig document, one would have to admit that the proposals for the German language schools are hardly a major part of the whole plan. The classical Latin grammar school of Luther and Melanchthon received the most comprehensive treatment. In a low-German edition of the Braunschweig ordinance,[2] arrangements for the classical language school take up a little more than seven pages of text. The German schools are handled in two short paragraphs,

---

[2] Hans Lietzmann, ed., *Johannes Bugenhagens Braunschweiger Kirchenordnung 1528* (Bonn: A. Marcus und E. Weber's Verlag, 1912), 26-34. An English translation of parts of this section of the Brunswick ordinance appears in *Early Protestant Educators* by Frederick Eby (New York and London: McGraw-Hill, 1931), 193-206.

about one-fourth of a page. In fact, Bugenhagen had more to say about schools for girls than for German elementary schools in general. Bugenhagen's educational emphasis was still that of Luther and Melanchthon, a classical language school to equip the rising generation for service in church and state.

By making official arrangements for the vernacular school, Bugenhagen was also being a realist. The German language reading and writing schools in pre-Reformation times in many cases had been administered by neither church nor state. School administration of that kind the reformers were not willing to countenance. A number of ordinances, that for Braunschweig included, specifically stated that the so-called *Winkelschulen* (corner schools, i.e., small private schools), which would have taught basic vernacular literacy, were illegal. Recognizing the popularity of such schools and perhaps also the need for them, Bugenhagen provided for their functions in the municipal system of education. This removed any excuse for the establishment and use of *Winkelschulen* and avoided any educational, religious, or political problems which might conceivably have arisen in such private school classrooms.

It was more than administrative practicality, however, which prompted Bugenhagen to organize vernacular elementary schools. His concern was for schools which would reach all of the young with the biblical message. Like Luther, Bugenhagen spoke about schools for both boys and girls. The introduction to the school section of his Braunschweig church ordinance also made it clear that parental responsibility to provide Christian education for the young had its foundation in the sacrament of Holy Baptism. Parents, according to Bugenhagen, do not discharge their duties properly just by bringing their children to the font.[3] Nurture in the Christian faith must continue, and for this schools were deemed

---

[3] Lietzmann, 23-26.

necessary, schools which would be available to all, boys and girls, rich and poor, schools which would teach the language of the people and employ it as the medium of instruction.

The *Braunschweig Ordinance* did not provide for an extensive curriculum in the proposed German schools. There were to be only two schoolmasters for these schools in Brunswick, in contrast to the no fewer than seven teachers for the two Latin schools.[4] The two teachers had the mandate "to teach their children at certain times something good from the word of God, the ten commandments, the creed, the Lord's prayer, concerning the two sacraments instituted by Christ, with short explanation, and Christian song."[5] More than that was not mentioned, although it was noted that pupils were not expected to remain as long in the German school as in the Latin school.

Except for the specific note that "the girls need to learn only to read," the curriculum of the girls' schools, to be conducted close to home and by women, was the same as that of the elementary German schools.[6] One would assume from that comment about the girls that something more was very likely included in the German school for boys. The additions were perhaps things like arithmetic and writing since skills in these subjects had previously been taught in vernacular schools and were useful in the management of one's personal business affairs. The major emphasis, however, was upon religious instruction and sacred song, a curricular emphasis which continued to remain strong into the early twentieth century in Lutheran schools in both Germany and the United States.

---

[4] Frederick Eby, *Early Protestant Educators* (New York and London: McGraw-Hill, 1931), 195, 204.

[5] Ibid., 204.

[6] Ibid., 204-6.

In Bugenhagen's outline for religious instruction there was one other feature which deserves a word of comment. Christian doctrine in pre-Reformation times was taught under three headings, namely, the Ten Commandments, the Creed, and the Lord's Prayer or under the last two of these three. This was popularly known as the Catechism. The *Visitation Articles* of 1528, for example, refer in the section on worship to the practice of preaching on these parts of the Christian faith.[7] Bugenhagen, in his school regulation, added the two sacraments to the commonly known three parts of instruction and did this not only for the German and girls' schools but in his general remarks on school curriculum as well. His code anticipated two major divisions of Luther's Small Catechism which was soon to appear and which has remained a primary instruction tool for Lutheran youth even to this day. Whether the sacramental note was Bugenhagen's contribution to Lutheran instructional materials or whether it was the result of his association with Luther while the latter was planning the Small Catechism makes little difference. The point is that Bugenhagen, who did much more than Luther in designing specific school plans, made sacramental teaching a part of basic instruction in an early and influential school code. This pedagogical approach is consistent with Lutheranism's dual emphasis upon both Word and Sacrament in theology.

Religious goals were of prime importance for Bugenhagen also in the Latin schools which he recommended for the city of Brunswick. Schoolmasters were not only to be scholars but were to understand the Gospel of Christ and at times read to the older students from the Latin Scriptures. In Brunswick there were to be two Latin schools, to each of which a cantor

---

[7] Martin Luther, "Instructions for the Visitors of Parish Pastors in Electoral Saxony" (1528), *Luther's Works*, American Edition, vol. 40, *Church and Ministry II*, trans. and ed. Conrad Bergendoff (Philadelphia: Muhlenberg, 1958), 308.

was attached to teach children how to sing. The songs, sung in both Latin and German, were intended as Melanchthon had ordered in the *Visitation Articles* for use in the church's worship services. In a section of the *Church Ordinance for Braunschweig* dealing with stipends of various sorts in the Latin schools Bugenhagen also referred to the practice of having children sing at funerals and church weddings, evidence of how the school music program was to serve the religious life of school and community. Music in the schools was expected to be ecclesiastically functional.

The Latin instruction to be offered at Braunschweig was to follow the Saxon program of studies outlined by Melanchthon. Bugenhagen referred to the Melanchthon document by name, made a few comments on specific items applicable to the Braunschweig situation in each of the three divisions of the school, and then added a few provisions for the teaching of Greek and Hebrew at the secondary level.[8] When all was said and done, the Bugenhagen school order for Braunschweig created and organized primarily a Latin grammar school in which the Bible, religion, Latin and Greek language and literature, Hebrew, and church song were the major ingredients. Vernacular schools were not forgotten but were not at this point in history of primary importance in the minds of the framers of school constitutions.

A review of the Braunschweig school regulations would not be complete without a few comments about Johannes Bugenhagen himself. A man of considerable ability, Bugenhagen stood side by side with Luther and Melanchthon to give leadership to the Lutheran community in both doctrine and practice. A nineteenth-century German church encyclopedia notes that Luther has been called the prophet of the Reformation, Melanchthon the professor of the

---

[8] Eby, 199-201.

Reformation, and Bugenhagen the pastor of the Reformation.[9] It was in Wittenberg that Bugenhagen served as pastor, counting among his parishioners none other than Luther himself. Having organized parish life in that community, Bugenhagen became a resource person to provide guidelines for church organization elsewhere.

Luther's junior by two years, Bugenhagen had come to Wittenberg in the year 1521, matriculating at the university at the age of 35. He had been ordained into the priesthood in 1509 and had been attracted to the Reformation through Luther's writings. Coming from the Low-German-speaking region of Pomerania, Bugenhagen easily gathered other Pomeranian students around himself for group study. His presentations to these students on the Psalms became so popular that others were drawn to them, with the result that university approval was granted for him to lecture in public.[10]

When a pastor was needed in 1522 for St. Mary's church in Wittenberg Luther rather arbitrarily proclaimed Bugenhagen pastor.[11] He spent his career in the Wittenberg parish, although he could have accepted administrative posts in other places, the university in Copenhagen being among them. It is from this base in Wittenberg that Bugenhagen assisted others with the reorganization of their parish life. He spent four months in Braunschweig in 1528 on the *Kirchenordnung* there and then moved on to Hamburg for another eight months to frame the *Church Ordinance* of 1529 in that city. He was either the prime

---

[9] Carl Meusel, ed., *Kirchliches Handlexikon,* vol. 1 (Leipzig: Verlag von Justus Naumann, 1887), s.v. "Bugenhagen," 597.

[10] Maurice E. Schild, "John Bugenhagen. Theological Existence and Practice," *Lutheran Theological Journal* (Lutheran Church of Australia) 19 (May 1985): 3.

[11] Heinrich Bornkamm, *Luther in Mid-Career 1521-1530,* trans. E. Theodore Bachman (Philadelphia: Fortress, 1983), 273-74.

author or an assistant for similar documents in other communities.[12]

It was an active life which Bugenhagen lived in the cause of the Reformation. As pastor at St. Mary's, he preached regularly—at times apparently at some length;[13] he produced commentaries on biblical books; he was involved in the production of a Low-German translation of the Bible which came out shortly before Luther's High-German edition; he compiled a Passion History which even present-day Lutherans use in worship during Lent; and he wrote constitutions which organized church and school life. In all of his activities Bugenhagen was interested in the effective communication of the spiritual message of the Reformation to the general populace. As a pastor he concerned himself extensively with matters of school curriculum, design, and administration, and of this the school regulations in the *Church Ordinance for Braunschweig* (Brunswick) are good evidence.

Suggested for Further Reading

Eby, Frederick. *Early Protestant Educators*, 193-206. New York and London: McGraw Hill, 1931.

Schild, Maurice E. "John Bugenhagen. Theological Existence and Practice." *Lutheran Theological Journal* (Lutheran Church of Australia) 19 (May 1985): 2-11.

---

[12] Schild, 7.

[13] Luther thought highly of the content of Bugenhagen's sermons but was critical of their length. Martin Luther, *Luther's Works*, American Edition, vol. 54, *Table Talk*, trans. and ed. Theodore G. Tappert (Philadelphia: Fortress, 1967), 214, 393, 428. See also Wilhelm Pauck, *The Heritage of the Reformation*, Revised and Enlarged Edition (n.p.: The Free Press of Glencoe, Inc., 1961), 128.

✦✦✦ 1530 ✦✦✦

Martin Luther

A Sermon on Keeping Children in School

Martin Luther, in his 1524 address *To the Councilmen of All Cities in Germany*, had urged that municipal authorities establish and maintain schools. Philip Melanchthon, Johannes Bugenhagen, and others served as resource persons to help various cities organize and regulate church and school life in their respective communities. Comprehensive as the church and school regulations drawn up by these men were, such constitutions in and of themselves did not always create flourishing educational systems. Schools need students to be successful. Surprising as it may seem, parents were apparently not sending their children in large numbers to the schools which the reformers were so actively promoting. In fact, statistical information at the university level makes it very clear that enrollments in the schools of higher education were plummeting rapidly during the 1520s. The University of Erfurt, for example, reported an enrollment of 311 in 1521 and 14 in 1527; the University of Leipzig enrolled 340 in 1521 and 81 in 1526; student enrollments at Wittenberg dropped from 245 in 1521 to 73 in 1527.[1] Social and political upheaval in Germany during the 1520s lay behind some of the decline in university

---

[1] John E. Wise, *The History of Education* (New York: Sheed and Ward, 1964), 203, n. 4.

enrollments, but other factors were very likely involved as well.

Luther's treatise entitled *A Sermon on Keeping Children in School*, written in 1530, points out that enrollment declines had affected more than the universities.[2] Parents were not sending their children to the schools which Luther had urged the cities to establish and maintain. Recognizing this state of affairs, the Reformer sought to correct the situation by composing a sermon, dedicated to Lazarus Spengler, a government official in the city of Nürnberg, and intended for preachers "here and there to the effect that they should exhort people to keep their children in school."[3] Luther's strategy was to exhort preachers, who in turn were to charge their hearers to exercise proper parental responsibility by sending their children to school.

Luther's hortatory tone in this sermon was anything but mild as he tried to get at the root of the problem. In essence, he did battle on three fronts. He remained convinced of his position of 1524 that the school issue was a battle with Satan himself, for the latter was seen as an enemy of Christian education. In the second place, Luther felt that parents were indifferent to the value of a classical education. And, finally, he maintained that a world of commerce and business had sown the seeds of materialism and a desire only to make money.

That the war was seen as an engagement with Satan becomes apparent already from the dedicatory letter to Spengler and the introduction to the pastors and preachers. Although Luther felt that conditions were not too bad in Nürnberg, he warned, nonetheless, that "it is hardly likely that in so great a city with such a large population the devil will not

---

[2] Martin Luther, "A Sermon on Keeping Children in School" (1530), *Luther's Works*, American Edition, vol. 46, *The Christian in Society III*, ed. Robert E. Schultz, trans. Charles M. Jacobs (Philadelphia: Fortress, 1967), 234.

[3] Ibid., 213.

try his arts and tempt some to despise the word of God and the schools."[4] Even where things were going tolerably well an admonition to be on guard was not deemed inappropriate.

Although Luther perceived Nürnberg as being something of an exception to the general rule of deterioration, he remarked that the pastors and preachers were able with their own eyes to see

> how that wretch of a Satan is now attacking us on all sides with force and guile. He is afflicting us in every way he can to destroy the holy gospel and the kingdom of God. . . . He deludes and deceives the common people so that they are not willing to keep their children in school or expose them to instruction.[5]

And even as the treatise began with an attack on Satan, so it closed. Noting that governments compel citizens to carry guns and fight wars, with reference to the function of schools and the duty of sending children to them, Luther concluded by saying:

> Here there is a worse war on, a war with the very devil, who is out to secretly sap the strength of the cities and principalities, emptying them of their able persons until he has bored out the pith and left only an empty shell of useless people whom he can manipulate and toy with as he will.[6]

---

[4] Ibid.

[5] Ibid., 217.

[6] Ibid., 257.

Satan was held to be the enemy who wanted children kept out of the schools which the reformers were seeking to have established.

The indifference of parents to the value of schools was a second concern of Luther. He attributed such indifference also partially to the devil, for parents who were not sending their children to the schools which God had provided were exhibiting, according to Luther, "the great and shameful ingratitude into which the devil is so craftily leading them."[7] Luther felt that this ingratitude was deserving of God's fiercest anger, for those who refused to send their children to school were chided most sternly:

> Ought not God to be angry over this? Ought not famine to come? Ought not pestilence . . . find us out? Ought not blind, fierce, and savage tyrants come to power? Ought not war and contention arise? . . . Indeed, it would not be surprising if God were to open the doors and windows of hell and pelt and shower us with nothing but devils, or let brimstone and hell-fire rain down from heaven and inundate us . . . in the abyss of hell, like Sodom and Gomorrah.[8]

The indifferent were admonished, therefore, to reflect upon God's numerous temporal and spiritual blessings and out of gratitude for such gifts to send their children to school.

In addition to a general attitude of indifference toward the use of schools and the spiritual attacks of Satan which Luther felt he had to combat, there was still a third front on which he engaged with the forces of opposition in the school matter. He suspected that parents were more interested in having their

---

[7] Ibid., 218.

[8] Ibid., 254.

offspring learn how to conduct a business and get rich than they were in giving their children an intellectually stimulating education. Although Luther understood human nature well and was very likely correct in his assessment of parents to a large degree at least, he might nevertheless not have recognized that a new age was bringing about an inevitable change in educational practices. His was the school of Latin and Greek. The new direction was toward vernacular schools, and it might well be that parental indifference toward the use of Reformation-type schools and a desire to teach that which would equip a person for business stemmed partially from a legitimate dissatisfaction with educational practices which were not quite in touch with the times. Societal and economic forces somewhat unrelated to the Reformation movement itself were beginning to have an impact upon sixteenth-century parents and their regard for the kinds of schools which the Lutheran reformers were advocating.

Luther, however, saw only the one issue at this point. Materialism and greed were deeply ingrained in the hearts and minds of people. "The run-of-the-mill miser," he wrote, "despises learning so deeply and says, 'Ha, if my son can read and write German, do arithmetic, that is enough. I am going to make a businessman of him.' "[9] Luther was a little less mild in his comments when in another place he was chiding parents for not wanting to educate their children for various kinds of governing positions: "We shamefully despise God when we begrudge our children this glorious and divine work (i.e., positions in civil government) and stick them instead in the exclusive service of the belly and of avarice, having them learn nothing but how to make a living, like hogs wallowing forever with their noses in the dunghill, and never training them for so

---

[9] Ibid., 251.

worthy an estate and office."[10] Luther had little respect for parents who neglected to send their children to the classical school because such an education was not considered necessary for making a living. He argued that parents owed it to their children to provide them with an education so that these children could serve others. An unwillingness to invest in such an education, he maintained, was the sign of a selfish and materialistic mentality, while a willingness to provide a broader education was a good work in the sight of God. Luther wanted pastors to impress this upon their parishioners and so added *A Sermon* to his earlier educational treatise.

Structurally, *A Sermon on Keeping Children in School* has two main parts similar to the two divisions of the essay *To the Councilmen*. In both documents Luther set forth the purposes he expected the schools to serve. They were the institutions in which church workers and various kinds of civil authorities were to be educated. Written for a different audience and at a different time, each document, however, has a color of its own. In *A Sermon* Luther strikes much harder at the conscience of his audience than he does in *To the Councilmen*. The reader is struck by the two fire-and-brimstone proclamations of law in *A Sermon*, one in each part of the treatise. A sample is in place.

Having exhorted parents to make wise investments by training their sons for church vocations, Luther then proceeded to show the consequences people might reap if they stubbornly refused to lend their children to the Lord:

> Suppose God were to address you on your deathbed, or at the Last Judgment, and say, "I was hungry, thirsty, a stranger, naked, sick, imprisoned, and you rendered me no service. For in that you have not done it to people on earth and to my kingdom or gospel, but have helped put

---

[10] Ibid., 241.

them down and allowed men's souls to perish, you have done this to me. For you could have helped. I gave you children and material means for this purpose, but you wantonly allowed me and my kingdom and the souls of men to suffer want and pine away—and you thereby served the devil and his kingdom instead of me and my kingdom. Well, let him be your reward. Go with him now into the abyss of hell."[11]

Similarly, having shown the honor which comes with civil service in the interest of humankind, Luther issued a word of warning to parents about their accountability to God if they would not provide the state with educated workers:

Now if you have a son who is able to learn, and you are in a position to keep him at it, but do not do so, if you go your way without even asking what is to become of worldly government and law and peace, then you are doing all in your power to oppose worldly authority, . . . like the devil himself. For you are taking from empire, principality, land, and city, a savior, comforter, cornerstone, helper, and deliverer. . . . What will God, who has given you child and property with which to serve him by keeping your son in his service, say to this? . . . Is not your heart terrified at this abominable abomination— your idolatry, despising of God?[12]

Although Luther argued for schools for the same reasons in both *To the Councilmen* (1524) and *A Sermon* (1530), he became far more vehement with his language in 1530. Perhaps he was disillusioned or at least disappointed, not having

---

[11] Ibid., 230.

[12] Ibid., 242-43.

anticipated that parents whose children were the beneficiaries of the schools would choose not to use them. Perhaps a rapid decline in school attendance was interpreted as a threatening crisis situation which demanded swift and vigorous action. In any case, Luther spared no words in 1530 as he sought to improve school attendance for the benefit of both church and state.

On the other hand, Luther's language was not just that of law. To motivate parents to educate their sons for the office of pastor, the Reformer spoke as well about the glorious work which a faithful pastor accomplishes in the discharge of his duties.

> A true pastor . . . contributes to the well-being of men in body and soul, in property and honor. . . . He also serves God. . . . For by his work and word there are maintained in this world the kingdom of God, the name and honor and glory of God, the true knowledge of God, the right faith and understanding of Christ, the fruits of the suffering and blood and death of Christ, the gifts and works and power of the Holy Spirit, the true and saving use of baptism and the sacrament, the right and pure teaching of the gospel, the right way of disciplining and crucifying the body, and much more.[13]

Luther considered the office of pastor a high calling and by praising it in his *Sermon on Keeping Children in School* sought to encourage parents to educate their sons for the office.

It should be understood that when Luther was speaking about ecclesiastical and civil service he had numerous functions in mind. Jurists and scholars were needed, he said, because they are preservers of law upon earth. Having said that,

---

[13] Ibid., 227-28.

he then proceeded to explain what he included in the term jurist: "Now when I speak of the jurists I mean . . . chancellors, clerks, judges, lawyers, notaries, and all who have to do with the legal side of government; also the counselors at the court, for they too work with law and exercise the function of jurists."[14] In short, he included all who functioned under emperor, king, prince, or municipal authority to maintain law and order and protect property and business as civil servants.

Church functions were similarly very broad and embraced a large variety of offices, more perhaps than are normally thought of today. Speaking about "the office of preaching and the service of the word and sacraments,"[15] Luther stated that "the work of pastors, teachers, preachers, lectors, priests (whom men call chaplains), sacristans, schoolmasters, and whatever other work belongs to these offices and persons"[16] are to be included in the ecclesiastical estate. He held teachers in especially high regard, remarking that "a diligent and upright schoolmaster or teacher . . . can never be adequately rewarded or repaid,"[17] and added: "If I could leave the preaching office and my other duties, or had to do so, there is no other office I would rather have than that of schoolmaster or teacher of boys; for I know that next to that of preaching, this is the best, greatest, and most useful office there is."[18] These statements of Luther on the importance of the teaching office and its relationship to the ecclesiastical estate were long remembered not only in Germany but also among Lutherans in the United States whenever and wherever the cause of Lutheran schools was being advanced on the American scene. As Lutheran

---

[14] Ibid., 240.

[15] Ibid., 220.

[16] Ibid.

[17] Ibid., 252-53.

[18] Ibid., 253.

church history unfolded, the parish school teacher became a major assistant to the parish pastor in both Germany and the United States. Luther's generous praise of the Christian teacher and his inclusion of this office among the ecclesiastical functions contributed in no small way to the high degree of respect which in subsequent history was often accorded the position of parochial school teacher in Lutheran parishes.

The schools which Luther was recommending and in which civic and ecclesiastical leaders were to be trained were not intended to be only for the wealthy. It was the Reformer's intent that the sons of the common people and the poor be educated for service in church and state,[19] the community having the responsibility to arrange for endowments to make it possible for the poor to attend school.[20] He was not ready to insist, of course, that all boys become pastors, preachers, or schoolmasters, but he was not worried about an oversupply, for he made the following novel suggestion: "Even though a boy who has studied Latin should afterward learn a trade and become a craftsman, he still stands as a ready reserve in case he should be needed as a pastor or in some other service of the word."[21] On the other hand, the need for educated people was seen to be great in both church and state,[22] and if further incentive was required to encourage education in pursuit of the pastoral office, it was to be noted that a "son can easily get as good a living from the preaching office as from a trade—unless of course you are thinking of great wealth."[23]

Luther was convinced that without competent leadership in church and state all of ordered society would fall into chaos

---

[19] Ibid., 231, 250.

[20] Ibid., 257.

[21] Ibid., 231.

[22] Ibid., 234, 244.

[23] Ibid., 236.

and destruction. The word of God would disappear, war and violence would replace peace and tranquility, and even the world of business would collapse.[24] For that reason, government was expected not only to support schools but also to compel children to attend the schools which were established.[25] This would assure a supply of government leaders who would rule not according to "the law of the fist but the law of the head."[26] This would enable ordinary pastors to use Latin fluently and provide theological scholars with competence in Greek and Hebrew, languages essential for a careful study of Holy Scripture.[27] The well-being of society— corporately and individually, spiritually and physically—was dependent, in the mind of Luther, on Christian schools. The type of school to which the sixteenth-century reformers gave particular attention was the classical Latin language school, and in *A Sermon on Keeping Children in School* Luther made it a matter of conscience for parents to send their children to that kind of educational institution.

Suggested for Further Reading

Luther, Martin. "A Sermon on Keeping Children in School." *Luther's Works*, American Edition. Vol. 46, *The Christian in Society III*, ed. Robert C. Schultz, trans. Charles M. Jacobs, 207-58. Philadelphia: Fortress, 1967.

---

[24] Ibid., 251-52.

[25] Ibid., 256.

[26] Ibid., 239.

[27] Ibid., 232.

✠✠✠ 1847 ✠✠✠

Constitution of the German Evangelical Lutheran Synod of Missouri, Ohio, and Other States

In the history of American Lutheranism the year 1847 is important because it marks the founding of what is known today as The Lutheran Church—Missouri Synod. The date is noteworthy in the history of Lutheran education because the founding constitution of the Missouri Synod addressed issues pertaining to education and Lutheran schools. Since this church body has promoted the Lutheran school movement throughout the synod's history and since The Lutheran Church—Missouri Synod still operates an extensive parochial school system, an examination of what the synod's first constitution had to say about schools and schooling is in place.

The Missouri Synod was organized by Lutheran immigrants whose settlement in the United States antedated the founding of the synod. The organizers of the church body came not only from Missouri but from several other midwestern states as well, a fact quite apparent from the very first name of the synod, the German Evangelical Lutheran Synod of Missouri, Ohio, and Other States. Once organized, the synod grew through the founding of new churches in various parts of the country and by accepting into the synodical membership congregations already in existence.

The voice of Lutherans in the state of Missouri was especially strong, however, in the shaping of the synod's doctrine and practice. In fact, even before the synod was founded, the Rev. C. F. W. Walther of St. Louis had begun the publication of *Der Lutheraner* (*The Lutheran*). This German Lutheran religious periodical, having appeared for the first time in 1844, had been somewhat instrumental in creating a desire for the formation of an alliance of conservative Lutherans in the United States. It was not that *Der Lutheraner* had as its major purpose the promotion of a multistate synodical structure but rather that the publication's theological stance began to attract a friendly audience beyond the state of Missouri. Walther and the German Lutheran immigrants who had come with him from Saxony in 1839 were seen as representatives of a staunchly confessional Lutheranism. The St. Louis clergyman was considered a spokesman for what was popularly known as "old Lutheranism" and with his periodical was nurturing the hope of others to bring together American Lutherans of this same persuasion. This desire achieved fruition with the formation in 1847 of the German Evangelical Lutheran Synod of Missouri, Ohio, and Other States.

School matters received attention in a number of ways in the first constitution of the new synod. Not the least of these was a concern about textbooks for use in Lutheran schools. This concern found expression in the very first article of the constitution which set down reasons for forming a synodical organization. One of the objectives of the synod was "the promotion of special church projects."[1] Among these were included the following publications: agenda, hymnal, Book of Concord, and schoolbooks. It becomes apparent that the schoolbooks referred to were more than basic religious instructional materials such as Bibles, Bible histories, catechisms, and the like, for reading books were specifically

---

[1] "Our First Synodical Constitution," *Concordia Historical Institute Quarterly*, 16 (April 1943): 3.

mentioned in the constitution's second article which established the "conditions under which a congregation may join Synod and remain a member."[2] Among these conditions were "the exclusive use of doctrinally pure church books and schoolbooks."[3] At this point the writers of the constitution explained with a parenthetical enumeration that they also included readers among the books which were to be "doctrinally pure."

The 1847 Missouri Synod constitution in no way outlined the form which the educational programs in member congregations were to take. The reading book designation, however, indicates that the framers of the constitution assumed a type of parish school which would also teach basic literacy. It was this kind of school that the German immigrants had known in their homeland. Schools in Germany were state sponsored, but state sponsorship regularly included church control of local elementary schools. Common schools, though public, were closely joined to the parish. The church shaped, directed, and monitored various aspects of local educational programs. In Germany church control of public elementary schooling was still taken as a given in the early 1800s, and German Lutherans in America's Midwest held to the view that the church had a responsibility for elementary education even in a new homeland where public schools existed but where church and state could not be mixed. The Lutheran parish school was the institution, therefore, in which religious instruction and general elementary education could be combined, with the church having control of the whole process. Unwilling to make a sharp distinction between the religious and secular in the schooling of the young, the founders of the German Evangelical Lutheran Synod of Missouri, Ohio, and Other States felt obligated to call

---

[2] Ibid.
[3] Ibid.

for orthodox reading books in synodical parish schools.
Children in Lutheran schools were expected to learn to read
from materials not inconsistent with Lutheran doctrine and
practice. And when the 1847 constitution was revised in 1854,
the term reading books (*Lesebücher*) was replaced with the
more inclusive term textbooks (*Lehrbücher*), suggesting that
the young church body felt a need already in its early history to
be concerned about more than just reading books. In both
cases, however, the constitutional statements made it clear that
the organizers of the Missouri Synod were expecting Lutheran
schools to be built next to Lutheran churches.

The term parochial school (*Gemeindeschule*) does not
appear in the 1847 constitution. In addition to the reference to
readers, however, there was among the conditions for
membership in the Synod a requirement which suggested a
parochial school for Lutheran educational purposes. Synodical
members, according to the constitution, obligated themselves
to furnish "the children of the congregation with Christian
school-instruction" (*mit christlicher Schulunterricht*). An
English rendition of this first constitution translates the words
christliche Schulunterricht (Christian school-instruction) with
Christian education,[4] a possibly misleading term because of the
rather broad meaning often attached to this expression in
current church life. The German word *Schulunterricht* is more
specific within the context of nineteenth-century German
American Lutheranism. The immigrants who were forming
congregations at that time knew little about Sunday school
programs but were well acquainted with the German
Volksschule (common school) in which reading, writing, and
arithmetic were taught together with religion in a school
closely attached to the church. It is reasonable to assume,
therefore, that the constitutional provision for the Christian

---

[4] Ibid.

education of the young (*Schulunterricht*) was a call for some type of parochial school arrangement and not for a Sunday school or some similar once-a-week kind of educational program.

At this point it should perhaps be noted that it is difficult to determine exactly what a parochial school was in the middle of the nineteenth century, for parochial schools could differ quite markedly from one another. There was no uniformity in length of school terms, for example—a not surprising situation when one considers that the same kind of disparity prevailed also among public schools. Compulsory education laws, which would eventually regulate schools and terms of instruction, were just being written at that time. Prior to the enactment of such laws, each school was something of a law unto itself and accountable only to its own constituency. Curriculum, therefore, was anything but standardized, and in parochial schools the staffing, too, differed from one school to another. Sometimes the pastor was the only teacher; sometimes there was a teacher who taught everything except the confirmation class; and in some cases schools were beginning to have more than one teacher. Regardless of the nature of the school, however, it was expected that the religious instruction of the young would take place in a somewhat formally constituted school setting which incorporated a certain amount of general learning together with the teaching of religion. These are the elements of Christian school-instruction (*christliche Schulunterricht*).

Although congregations which joined the Missouri Synod did not lose their autonomy, they did agree to a certain amount of synodical supervision. With reference to school matters, for example, the president of the Synod was to visit congregations and include in his report to the Synod whether he found that schoolbooks used in parish schools contained "anything contrary to the confession of the true faith."[5] Parish pastors were likewise required to make written reports to the synodical convention about conditions in their parishes. Among the items to be reported was the number of "school children of the members as well as those of non-members."[6] The reference to school children of non-members is worthy of note since it demonstrates that the framers of the constitution anticipated that parochial schools of the Synod would very likely reach beyond the confines of the sponsoring parish, a matter of interest to the Synod because of its concern for outreach and extension.

The constitution under which the Missouri Synod was organized reflects a desire for parish schools and a keen interest in the doctrinal purity and mission of these schools. The teachers, however, who taught in these schools were not empowered to vote at synodical conventions, for voting membership in the Synod was granted only to pastors whose congregations authorized them to vote and to lay delegates who were elected by member congregations. Teachers were given advisory membership status and have continued through the years in that kind of relationship to the voting members of the Synod. Needless to say, the arrangement has at times been something of an irritant to synodical teachers who have felt, especially as their numbers have grown, that their professional voice is not being heard in synodical actions, even though their work is deemed highly important in the Synod's mission.

Advisory membership status did not exclude teachers from supervision by the Synod, however. One of the responsibilities of the Synod, according to the first constitution, was "the supervision over the performance of the official duties on the

---

5 Ibid., 7.

6 Ibid., 14.

part of the pastors and teachers of Synod."[7] This supervisory role was affirmed in the constitution immediately after it was stated that the Synod was "to stand guard over the purity and unity of doctrine within the synodical circle, and to oppose false doctrine."[8] The proximity of these two constitutional items to one another makes it clear that Lutheran orthodoxy among those who were going to teach in Lutheran schools was a primary concern of the Synod. For that reason, there was also to be a "conscientious examination of candidates for the ministry and teaching profession."[9] Teachers, when they entered Lutheran school classrooms and while they were teaching in them, were expected to know Lutheran doctrine and practice and to teach in conformity with the same. The president of the Synod was to have an examining commission in conjunction with which he would "give each pastor, teacher, and candidate for the ministry or teaching profession an assignment on a theological or a pedagogical subject, which are to be submitted to the President and the respective members of the commission at least three months before the next session of Synod."[10] With these kinds of procedures the Missouri Synod hoped to discharge its supervisory responsibilities over pastors and teachers.

At the parish level pastors also had an examiner's role to perform for prospective teachers. The constitution stipulated that candidates for the teaching profession were "to be examined by the *pastor loci* [local pastor], who is to prepare for the candidate a detailed certificate for presentation before Synod."[11] The constitution then specified in which areas the

---

[7] Ibid., 5.

[8] Ibid.

[9] Ibid.

[10] Ibid., 15-16.

[11] Ibid., 9.

pastors were to examine teacher candidates. The list made it quite clear that religious instruction was of paramount importance in Lutheran elementary schools. Teacher candidates were to demonstrate that they had a "knowledge of the Bible and understanding of Scripture; Christian doctrine, with particular reference to the Symbolical Books, especially the two Catechisms of Luther; church and Reformation history."[12] In addition to that, the candidate was obligated both to write and conduct a catechism lesson. Having kept their eyes first and foremost upon the religious purposes of the school, the framers of the constitution then added the subjects German, arithmetic, penmanship, geography, history, and music to the fields in which prospective teachers were to be examined.

The expertise required of a Lutheran school teacher quite obviously demanded a special training program. The level of competence called for in theological areas plus proficiency in the German language meant that the kind of general teacher-training programs which might develop on the American school scene would not serve Lutheran school teacher candidates. If the German Evangelical Lutheran Synod of Missouri, Ohio, and Other States intended to be serious about the constitutionally stated requirements for parochial school teachers, the Synod itself would have to develop a teacher-training program.

There can be no doubt that the Synod did take itself seriously, for teacher preparation also received due attention in the first constitution. Recognizing, however, that the educational program desired and needed for the training of church workers had not been developed as yet, the Synod called upon capable pastors to "take it upon themselves to train suitable young people for service in the Church."[13] But matters

---

[12] Ibid.

[13] Ibid., 8.

were not to be left there, for it was "the duty of Synod to erect, support, and supervise institutions for the preparation of future pastors and teachers for service in the Church."[14] Provision was then made also for the funding of such institutions. Pastors and teachers who were members of the Synod were obligated to pay one dollar annually into the synodical treasury. Pastors were to invite their congregations to have free-will offerings for the benefit of the Synod. The monies which flowed into the synodical treasury were to be used, among other things, for the "founding and support of institutions for the preparation of future pastors and teachers."[15]

In this way the first constitution laid the basis for a synodical system of higher education to train church workers. Programs of instruction for the training of pastors developed first, but the need for the training of Lutheran teachers was also keenly felt. At first such training took place in schools where future pastors were taught. It was not long, however, before the Synod established a separate teacher training seminary and began what has grown into a major educational enterprise of The Lutheran Church—Missouri Synod, namely, college programs for the training of Lutheran school teachers. Synodically trained teachers for Lutheran schools was a goal of the founders of the Synod and has continued to be a matter of synodical concern. The need for Lutheran parochial school teachers to be conversant in German eventually gave way, of course, thus eliminating the linguistic aspect of Lutheran teacher training, but since elementary Lutheran school teachers are expected to conduct classes in religion the theological element in the preparation of Lutheran teachers has not come to an end. It continues to be a component in the certification of teachers for Lutheran schools.

---

[14] Ibid., 7.

[15] Ibid., 18.

One last observation still needs to be made about the first constitution and schools. It pertains to the constitutional provision that requires the "exclusive use of the German language in the synodical conventions."[16] The Synod was German and intended to remain so, at least for the time being. The steady flow of German immigrants to the midwestern regions of the United States continued to be a major factor in keeping midwestern German Lutheran synods Germanic throughout the nineteenth century. This affected the parochial schools in that they also continued to use and promote the German language. The cycle of events is most natural, for if the synodical language is German, the language of Sunday morning worship will be German. Since the parochial schools were adjuncts of the church, they had the obligation to make their students fluent in German so that these students could participate meaningfully in the church's worship and organizational life. German became the medium of instruction, not only for classes in religion but for other classes as well. The Missouri Synod, as well as the Wisconsin Synod which was founded three years later, continued to be active in the production of German books and materials for all of church and school life. The desire for things German was so strong that according to the proposed draft of the 1847 constitution candidates for the teaching profession were to be examined not only in German language ability but also in their knowledge of the mother country. The final draft of the constitution omitted the reference to the knowledge of the mother country but yielded in no way on the ability to use German fluently. This German heritage in the schools was not easily relinquished and remained a characteristic of many Lutheran parochial schools even into the first decade or two of the twentieth century, a situation which brought the church upon more than one

---

[16] Ibid., 4.

occasion into conflict with the forces of Americanism and even with the law.

The founders of the German Evangelical Lutheran Synod of Missouri, Ohio, and Other States were convinced that there was an intimate bond between church and school. Coming from a homeland in which these two agencies functioned closely together, the organizers of the Synod proceeded to draft a constitution which assumed that a Lutheran school would stand next to a Lutheran church. That constitution laid the foundation for a Lutheran parochial school system which was to develop into a major force in the private and denominational sector of American education.

Suggested for Further Reading

"Our First Constitution." *Concordia Historical Institute Quarterly* (St. Louis) 16 (April 1943): 1-18.

✤ ✤ ✤ 1864 ✤ ✤ ✤

Addison Teachers Seminary
Addison, Illinois

The desire of midwestern German Lutheran immigrants to establish parochial schools and to have in these schools Lutheran teachers who were conversant in the German language and able to give instruction in religion and the usual elementary school subjects demanded that the church itself give attention to teacher training. Some teachers had immigrated to the United States from Germany and so were fluent in the language of that country. Their numbers were not large, however, and they had not always been well-schooled in Lutheran theology. When qualified teachers were not available or when congregations were not large or affluent enough to support a teacher, pastors were expected to conduct parochial schools. As more congregations and schools were formed and as they grew in size, it soon became apparent that a synodical teacher-training program would be the only answer for an adequate supply of Lutheran teachers. A major and far-reaching step in that direction took place in 1864.

To meet the early needs of teachers, pastors sometimes gave private instruction to prospective candidates. Upon occasion, theological candidates taught school, and it had also been the hope of the Saxon Lutherans in Missouri that their theological college in Altenburg, and later in St. Louis, would prepare teachers as well. In Fort Wayne, Indiana, teacher training and pastoral training were combined in a joint curriculum at the practical theological seminary established in that city in 1846, one year before the founding of the German Evangelical Lutheran Synod of Missouri, Ohio, and Other States. Although this arrangement never produced many teachers in its 11-year existence, the program was the forerunner of a separate teacher-training department begun at the Fort Wayne school in 1857 and continued there until 1864.

The teacher-education department introduced at Fort Wayne in 1857 was to some extent also the outgrowth of a private teacher-training endeavor begun in Milwaukee, Wisconsin, in 1855. Three pastors and two teachers had combined their efforts to conduct a private Lutheran teachers seminary in that city and kept it in operation until 1857 when the new program was begun in Fort Wayne. Only four teachers were graduated from the Milwaukee institution, but the concept of establishing a separate school or department for training prospective Lutheran school teachers was certainly furthered by the Milwaukee undertaking. One of the pastors operating the Milwaukee school, the Rev. Philipp Fleischmann, was called to Fort Wayne to head the separate education department beginning there. Upon his acceptance of the call in 1857, the school in Milwaukee was closed, all efforts for the preparation of Lutheran school teachers having been consolidated in Fort Wayne, where the venture would remain under Fleischmann's direction until 1864.

In the year 1864, a new chapter was begun in the history of teacher training in The Lutheran Church—Missouri Synod. It was at that time that the Synod relocated its entire program for teacher education and developed a new campus specifically for that purpose in Addison, Illinois. This school continued to be the major source of supply for synodically-trained elementary school teachers until 1913, when the Addison Teachers Seminary was moved to a new campus in River Forest, Illinois, and became known as Concordia Teachers College, a name changed to Concordia College, River Forest, in 1979 and Concordia University in 1990.

The selection of Addison as the site for the new teachers college came upon the request of the Missouri Synod's Western District in which Addison was located. The memorial to the Synod stated a number of reasons for relocating in that city. Among these were the offer of the congregation in Addison to provide the necessary land without cost and the willingness of the Addison church and others in the area to subscribe to a large portion of the cost of erecting the necessary buildings. There was confidence, moreover, that the churches in the general area would provide foodstuffs in generous quantities and thus keep student boarding costs at a minimum. The move, it was further argued, would enable the congregations in and around Fort Wayne to distribute their special gifts for a boarding school to an institution which had only a ministerial-training program rather than two departments, one for teacher training and one for ministerial education. The conclusion of the Western District was that if the seminaries at Fort Wayne and St. Louis and teacher education could not be combined on one campus, then the transfer of teacher training to Addison would be a wise move.

The synodical convention committee which endorsed the petition of the Western District added some other considerations to support the relocation proposal. The committee felt, for example, that parishes in Wisconsin would also eventually supply the Addison school with various kinds of provisions for the college kitchen. In addition, the new location would be a central point for the meeting of teachers' conferences from Northern Illinois, Wisconsin, and parts of Michigan. And, finally, since it was expected that the teachers seminary would be located in the vicinity of one of the schools which the Addison congregation was conducting, future teachers would have the opportunity to observe experienced teachers in classrooms and do practice teaching under the supervision of such teachers, a hope which was not realized, however, until about 15 years later.

The Synod adopted the recommendation of the synodical convention floor committee, after amending the section of the committee's report which dealt with the local pastor's relationship to the new school. The committee had spoken about a "collegial working relationship with the seminary instructors" which the Addison pastor would have and of his "pastoral influence . . . upon the students."[1] At Fort Wayne, however, the pastor of the local congregation, Wilhelm Sihler, had exercised a more direct control over the activities of the Synod's school. Sihler had founded the Fort Wayne seminary a year before the Synod itself had been organized, and during his tenure as pastor at St. Paul's Lutheran Church in that city he also served as an instructor and president of the school. There apparently was concern that the new synodical institution in Addison would not have the same kind of pastoral supervision which Sihler had been able to exercise at Fort Wayne, for the convention committee recommending the relocation acknowledged that Sihler's supervision would be lost in the move and that "it is by no means to be denied that the institution requires adequate supervision at all times in order to preserve and foster the proper spirit."[2] The Synod wanted more than a "collegial working relationship" with the local pastor and proceeded at the convention, therefore, to appoint the Rev. A. G. C. Francke, pastor of Zion Lutheran Church in Addison, President of the Teachers Seminary (*Praeses des Schulseminars*). It was in this way that the Synod hoped to

---

[1] *Elfter Synodal-Bericht der allgemeinen deutschen evang.-luth. Synode von Missouri, Ohio u.a. Staaten vom Jahre 1863* (Eleventh Synodical Report of the German Evangelical Lutheran Synod of Missouri, Ohio, and Other States for the Year 1863), 77.

[2] Ibid.

retain the same kind of pastoral supervision of its teacher-training program that Sihler had exercised from his pastoral office in Fort Wayne.

Institutional oversight of a synodical school by a local pastor did not remove the need for some kind of faculty administrative head, however. The Rev. Philipp Fleischmann had served in this capacity at Fort Wayne since 1857 and was known as the Director of the teacher-training program, but in February of 1864, *Der Lutheraner* (The Lutheran) announced that Professor Fleischmann had submitted his resignation "because of the increasing weakness of his eyes."[3] This meant that a new director would have to be found for the school in Addison. The Synod was informed that nominations for the vacant professorship were in order and was invited to submit names of candidates for the position. The synodical constitution gave nominating privileges to an appointed board of electors, the school's faculty, and each congregation within the Synod. From a slate of five candidates, publicized in an April issue of *Der Lutheraner,* the board of electors on May 28, 1864, called the Rev. J. C. W. Lindemann as director and professor of the Addison Teachers Seminary, a call accepted by Lindemann in the summer of the same year.

Lindemann was only 37 years old when he assumed the directorship of the Synod's new teacher-training institution, but it was not ordained that he should have a long life. He did spend the remainder of his career, however, in the Addison post. That was a period of nearly 15 years, a span of time in itself not insignificant and in Lindemann's case years which turned out to be very productive and fruitful. Since the Synod's teacher-training program had in a sense come of age with a relocated campus and a separate set of new buildings, there came with the Addison directorship an opportunity to give a kind of direction

---

[3] Theodore J. Brohm, "Bekanntmachung" (Notice), *Der Lutheraner* (February 15, 1864): 95.

to the parochial school movement which very likely had not been able to take place before in Fort Wayne, where one senses that the teacher-education program was something of a stepchild enterprise. From his chair in Addison, the Director could speak with a better chance of being heard both inside and outside the Synod. In addition, Lindemann was clearly the Synod's choice for the position and through the power of his pen soon came to be recognized as a leading interpreter of the Lutheran parochial school movement among German-speaking Americans.

When Lindemann, as pastor in Cleveland, Ohio, and before his election, had seen the list of candidates published in the April 15, 1864, issue of *Der Lutheraner*, he wrote a letter relative to his nomination and possible selection as director at Addison to C. F. W. Walther.[4] The letter, in which the advice of Walther and others was being sought by Lindemann in the event that he should receive the call to Addison, reveals that the Cleveland pastor sensed that the board of electors was inclined to select him. Lindemann stated that should this happen, he was of the opinion that he would have to decline the call.[5] To support his position he set forth six reasons which he felt were compelling enough to lead him to this decision.

The first two reasons which Lindemann elaborated on dealt with Professor C. A. T. Selle, who with resigning Director Fleischmann was the only other full-time faculty member in the teacher-training program at Fort Wayne. Selle had not been nominated for the Addison directorate by the board of electors or by any congregation. He himself had apparently either persuaded the Fort Wayne faculty to nominate his personal friend, Pastor W. S. Stubnatzi, or had been able as the only instructor on the education staff to exercise the faculty

---

[4] Walther had been synodical president from 1847 to 1850 and would be elected again in 1864. He continued to serve as president until 1878.

[5] J. C. W. Lindemann to C. F. W. Walther, April 18, 1864, Manuscript Collection, Concordia Historical Institute, St. Louis.

nomination privilege himself. In any case, Lindemann seems to have felt that Selle had not been treated fairly when he was passed by and that Lindemann himself might not have been Selle's choice as teaching colleague and administrator at Addison. Besides a possible desire to avoid a situation which might have been ready-made for strained interpersonal relationships, Lindemann also held that Selle was more qualified for the position because of his age and experience at the school in Fort Wayne and that Selle was also as well equipped academically for the position as Lindemann. In addition, Lindemann was quick to point out that Selle was better qualified in music, a subject which the Cleveland pastor felt was an essential part of Lutheran parochial-school teacher training.[6]

The future director of the Addison school also added several personal reasons for intending to decline the call if it were extended to him. His wife's health made it desirable that she live near the church; in Addison their home would be two miles distant. He claimed that his own physical condition was not the best, a situation which led him to believe that he might not be able to meet the challenges and bear the strain of daily teaching and administration. To these personal considerations Lindemann also added that he was very content in his parish ministry. The pastoral office was one to which he had long aspired and he was reluctant to leave it, although he recognized that a professorship at Addison was a position from which one could exert a significant influence upon the schools within the Synod. In April 1864, Lindemann seemed, for a number of reasons, quite content to remain in Cleveland rather than move to Addison.[7]

The last argument which the leading candidate for the vacant directorate advanced for his inclination to decline a possible call was his personal conviction that he really lacked the

---

[6] Ibid.

[7] Ibid.

academic credentials for the position. To prove this to Walther, Lindemann briefly sketched his academic and professional career, noting in his letter that he had never attended a *Gymnasium* (German school for classical education at the secondary and junior college levels) and that his own training even for teaching had been minimal and gained to a large extent through experience.[8] Apparently Lindemann's reputation as a teacher was rather good, but he commented in his remarks to Walther that it does not follow that a person who himself can conduct school tolerably well will also be able to head an institution and educate others to be teachers. One senses that Lindemann felt keenly his lack of extensive formal education.

The Cleveland pastor had read the situation of his candidacy correctly. According to the June 1, 1864, issue of *Der Lutheraner*, he was chosen as director and professor of the Addison institution on May 28 by a 7 to 4 vote of the board of electors. Aware of the selection, C. F. W. Walther in a letter to Lindemann dated June 4 congratulated the latter on his having been called to the position and expressed the hope that he would accept the call.[9] In spite of the misgivings voiced in his April letter to Walther, Lindemann did accept the appointment and arrived in Addison in August of 1864. There he joined Professor Selle, the Fort Wayne faculty member who had not been nominated for the directorate and who had moved to Addison in July. Although the new buildings were not ready for use in September, Lindemann and Selle were able to begin a fall schedule of teaching in temporary quarters under rather primitive conditions. Thus, a Lutheran parochial school teachers college on a separate campus was born in The Lutheran Church—Missouri Synod.

---

[8] Ibid.

[9] C. F. W. Walther to J. C. W. Lindemann, *Briefe von C. F. W. Walther an seine Freunde, Synodalgenossen und Familienglieder* (Letters of C. F. W. Walther to His Friends, Synodical Colleagues, and Family Members), ed. L. Fuerbringer (St. Louis: Concordia, 1915), 203-4.

J. C. W. Lindemann and C. A. T. Selle both spent the remainder of their careers at the Addison teachers seminary, the former until his relatively early death at age 52 in 1879, the latter until his retirement in 1893 at the age of 74, five years before his death. Neither man brought extensive formal academic preparation to the professorship to which he was called. Both were ordained clergymen in the German Evangelical Lutheran Synod of Missouri, Ohio, and Other States, but their paths into the clergy ranks of that synod stands in rather marked contrast to the more scholarly theological training of some of the other early synodical leaders. Even the formal teacher training of these two men had been minimal, although teacher training in mid-nineteenth century Germany and the United States was by today's standards less than second-rate and really had no uniform pattern at all.

Lindemann's education had begun in his native Germany when he was six years old. He completed the upper elementary level of schooling at age 14 but was unable financially to attend a *Gymnasium*. He spent about six months in a practice-teaching kind of arrangement and another six months at a teachers seminary. That was the extent of his education when he came to the United States to teach school in Baltimore in the congregation of the Rev. F. K. D. Wyneken, early leader and second president of The Lutheran Church—Missouri Synod.

Having taught for a short time and having been encouraged by Wyneken to prepare for the ministry, Lindemann moved to Fort Wayne and spent a little over a year in study at the theological seminary there. He was then ordained in Cleveland, Ohio, and continued to serve in that city until he accepted the call to Addison, Illinois.[10] Lindemann's formal education for the office of both pastor and teacher spanned a less than two-

---

[10] For a brief biography of J. C. W. Lindemann, see A. C. Stellhorn, "J. C. W. Lindemann," *Concordia Historical Institute Quarterly*, 14 (October 1941): 65-92.

year period beyond upper elementary school. One can understand his apprehensions, therefore, when Lindemann wrote to Walther and said:

> My intellectual abilities are not sufficient to be able to execute the office of Seminary Director even to some extent in an emergency situation. I have not learned anything! . . . Through God's grace I do have the good intention to serve my neighbor in every possible way. Good intentions, however, can never compensate for the lack of a solid education.[11]

In spite of his assessment of himself, Lindemann's subsequent accomplishments make clear that what he lacked in formal schooling he more than made up for in personal study, zeal, and dedication. He was a leading force in the nineteenth-century Lutheran parochial school movement.

The academic credentials of Lindemann's colleague, C. A. T. Selle, were even less impressive. Selle, too, was a native of Germany, but he had not been able to pursue his education beyond elementary school. He taught school already at the age of 14 and immigrated to the United States when he was 18. In the United Stated he supported himself by manual labor and studied on his own. Eventually he was licensed to preach in the Ohio Synod, a Lutheran church body from which he separated himself because of the tolerance of Reformed theological positions in that fellowship. He became pastor of First St. Paul's Lutheran Church in Chicago and was a charter member of The Lutheran Church—Missouri Synod, which held its constituting convention at Selle's church in 1847. After two other pastorates Selle accepted the call to the teachers seminary in Fort Wayne and moved with that school when it was

---

[11] J. C. W. Lindemann to C. F. W. Walther, April 28, 1864, Manuscript Collection, Concordia Historical Institute, St. Louis.

relocated in Addison.[12] A brief sketch of his life makes it clear that beyond elementary schooling he was a self-trained man. The respect he gained as a church leader came as a result of personal study and faithful service.

Lest the meager academic credentials of the two mainstays on the faculty of the Addison Seminary in its early years suggest that the institution was hardly respectable, it must be remembered that mid-nineteenth-century educational practices cannot be judged in terms of contemporary standards. Elementary school curricula of that time were very modest and school terms often short, especially in rural areas and smaller communities. Basic literacy and elementary arithmetic skills were all that many elementary schools were expected to teach. In many cases, students attended school rather sporadically, being able to enroll in school sessions only as family resources and responsibilities permitted. On the moving frontier there was no elaborate system of public schools, and in the schools which did exist, teachers were not required to present extensive educational credentials.

Colleges of the time were unable to expect that matriculating students had gone to a secondary school, since such an institution was not at all readily available in many areas. It was common, therefore, for colleges to have preparatory departments. The Addison school, too, had such a department, but even the purpose of that seems to have been misunderstood,

---

[12] Upon the death of C. A. T. Selle, *Der Lutheraner*, official periodical of the Missouri Synod, published an account of the man's life in a series of 14 articles from May 31, 1898, until November 29, 1898. The series was apparently edited by C. A. Mennicke who wrote the last two portions which reported on the close of the life of the well-known professor. The first 12 articles are autobiographical and are written in the first person singular. "Lebenslauf des seligen Prof. C. A. T. Selle (Von ihm selbst beschrieben)" ("Life of the sainted Prof. C. A. T. Selle [as described by himself]"), *Der Lutheraner* 54 (1898): 92-94, 100-101, 108-9, 118-19, 127-28, 138-39, 148-49, 155-57, 164-65, 176-77, 184-85, 194-95, 204-5, 217-18.

for Director Lindemann had to plead that students should not be advised to come to Addison unless they had learned their ABCs. Like other schools, the Teachers Seminary at Addison admitted students with a variety of educational backgrounds. The school was not necessarily substandard; it was operating in an educational milieu quite different from today. The products of its school, moreover, were not expected to step into elementary schools with comprehensive curricula. A basic command of fundamental processes, a rudimentary knowledge of biblical facts and Lutheran doctrine, and some ability as a church musician were what was required of the Lutheran parochial school teacher. A faculty which by training and personal study, formal or informal, was able to bring students to moderate levels of achievement in these areas was able to discharge its duties satisfactorily. Lindemann and Selle both had the talent and ability to do that and were recognized as competent educators.

Theologically, the two men had also apparently proved themselves to the satisfaction of the church body they were serving, although here, too, their formal training had been minimal. Their backgrounds were not unique here either, for the education of the clergy in American Lutheran church life at that time was anything but standardized. Among the Germans in the Midwest there were, of course, some university-trained theologians, but there were also pastors who had been sent by German mission societies upon the completion of relatively short courses of study. In addition, there were those who entered the ministry by colloquy after a period of study with an experienced pastor. Certification standards today would ordinarily require more formal theological training for entry into the pastoral office than Lindemann or Selle had, but in their day the route into the ministry of the Lutheran church was more flexible, something possible perhaps when church bodies were smaller.

The dedication of the two men to their tasks at Addison is beyond question. They worked indefatigably and with minimal concern for their personal comfort. Especially in their first year at Addison they confronted circumstances which would easily have elicited the resignation of less determined and saintly men. A solid foundation was laid, however, and from this teachers seminary of the German Evangelical Lutheran Synod of Missouri, Ohio, and Other States there developed for The Lutheran Church—Missouri Synod a program of parochial-school teacher training which other institutions later followed.

The especially trying circumstance at the Addison school in its first term was the fact that the school's new building was not ready for occupancy in September when classes were scheduled to begin. This required the renting of a vacant two-story tavern which was inadequate for almost any purpose. The stairway to the second floor was unsafe, there were cracks in the walls, and some of the windows were broken. The stoves in the building malfunctioned under certain wind conditions and filled the rooms with suffocating smoke. For a dormitory, 20 of the students used the attic of the two-room house rented for Professor Selle. Living and learning conditions at the Missouri Synod's Addison teachers seminary tested the mettle of all in the initial term of that school's existence. Two weeks before Christmas, Director Lindemann was forced to suspend classes and arranged to have students housed in the homes of local members. When classes resumed in January, students and faculty were able to occupy the new building erected by the Synod and dedicated on December 28, 1864.

The opening enrollment in that first year, according to Lindemann's report in the October 1865 issue of the *Schulblatt* (School Journal), was 43. The educational backgrounds of the students varied considerably, and they ranged in age from the teens to the 30s. Designing a curriculum and organizing classes for such a varied student body was no small task. A class schedule for 1869 shows what kind of curriculum eventually evolved during the first years at Addison. The faculty in 1869 was composed of three men who were given the following individual assignments:

C. A. T. SELLE

Subject	Periods per week
Bible History	2
Symbolical Books	1
Geography	2
English	9
Piano	13
Total	27

KARL BRAUER

Singing	5
Violin	5
Piano	15
Organ	7
Music Theory	1
Total	33

J. C. W. LINDEMANN

Catechism	2
Introduction to the Bible	1
Memorization	2
Introduction to Education	1
Practical Catechetics	2
German	6
Arithmetic	4
History	1
Natural History	1
Penmanship (German and English)	4
Drawing	2
Total	26 [13]

---

[13] *Evangelisch-Lutherisches Schulblatt* (Evangelical Lutheran School Journal) (July 1869): 335. Also in Alfred J. Freitag, *College with a Cause* (River Forest: Concordia Teachers College, 1964), 48.

It is apparent from the above that the Addison faculty members had full teaching loads. Some of the subjects were designated for the two upper-level classes only, while others were taken by both preparatory and upper-level students. In some cases two or three sections of a class were offered, very likely to accommodate the different mastery levels of the enrolled students. All courses in the five-year program were required.

Although J. C. W. Lindemann was only 37 years old when he assumed the directorship at Addison, his tenure at the school came to an unexpected end with his early death at age 52. The entire front page of the February 1 issue of *Der Lutheraner*, official periodical of the Missouri Synod, was given over to an announcement of Lindemann's death and a heartfelt tribute to him by C. F. W. Walther, who had encouraged Lindemann to accept the Addison appointment 15 years earlier. Of the deceased director, Walther said

> A man . . . highly gifted and richly equipped with rare knowledge and wide experience, yet humble at heart; always ready to yield in matters that affected his person, but adamant and unyielding in matters pertaining to the Word and cause of God; burning in his zeal for the house of God, but forgetful of self and his personal benefits . . . a light, a salt, an ornament, a jewel of our church denomination. . . .[14]

The Rev. H. C. Schwan, recently elected president of the Synod and pastor under whom Lindemann had vicared in 1853, came from Cleveland to deliver the funeral sermon in the church at Addison. Schwan's sermon and that of the Illinois District president were printed in pamphlet form so that the discourses

---

[14] Translated by A. C. Stellhorn in "J. C. W. Lindemann," *Concordia Historical Institute Quarterly* 14 (October 1941): 90.

would be accessible to the synodical constituency. Availability of the publication was made known through the following announcement in the March 1 issue of *Der Lutheraner*:

> IN MEMORY OF THE SAINTED DIRECTOR J. C. W. LINDEMANN: **Address and sermon delivered at his funeral on January 20, 1879. With a portrait of the departed.** Proceeds to be used for the benefit of his surviving widow.

> This pamphlet of 16 pages needs no recommendation. . . . Who would not gladly want to have a striking picture of the sainted Director Lindemann? Who would not gladly want to read the words which were spoken at his funeral by the Honorable President of the Illinois District . . . and the Honorable President of the Synod . . . ? Who, moreover, would not gladly also want to make a small contribution to the surviving widow of the deserving man?[15]

In the days when synods were smaller, individuals in leadership positions were more easily recognized for their contributions to a synodical cause than their counterparts are in today's larger organizations. That very likely explains some of the rather emotional recognition accorded J. C. W. Lindemann in his day, but in fairness it must still be said that his type of dedication and energy in behalf of the Lutheran parochial school did rise well above the ordinary. The tributes paid to him upon the occasion of his unexpected and early death were deserved.

Lindemann's dedicated co-worker, C. A. T. Selle, assumed the role of acting president until a new director for the Addison school was selected. That choice fell on E. A. W. Krauss, a pastor in Germany. Born in 1851, he received his pre-university

---

[15] *Der Lutheraner*, March 1, 1879, 40.

training in a classical German *Gymnasium* and had studied
theology from 1869 to 1873 at the universities of Erlangen and
Leipzig. Upon the completion of his theological studies, he
came to the United States and served as pastor of a Missouri
Synod congregation in Cedarburg, Wisconsin. He stayed in this
country but a short time, returning to Germany in 1875. There
he served as pastor of a free church in Sperlingshof, Baden. He
was called to Addison in 1880 where, besides being director of
the institution, he also taught classes in religion and education.
He remained at Addison for 25 years and then accepted a call
to teach church history and theological propaedeutics at
Concordia Seminary in St. Louis. In 1915, on the occasion of
its 50th anniversary, the Wisconsin Synod's Northwestern
College at Watertown, Wisconsin, conferred upon Krauss the
Doctor of Theology degree. In that same year, the Missouri
Synod's Concordia Seminary awarded an honorary Ph.D.
degree to Northwestern's president, A. F. Ernst. The actions of
these two institutions attest to the cordial relationship which
existed in the early 20th century between those two Synodical
Conference synods so well-known for their advocacy of
Lutheran parochial schools.

A commendable amount of pioneering work took place at
the Addison Teachers Seminary under Director Lindemann, but
it was during the 25-year administration of Director Krauss that
the school really came of age. The enrollment at the school
increased considerably during that time. Faculty were added,
and the physical plant of the school was enlarged. Comments
on several of the developments are in place to give something
of an idea of the kinds of issues and problems which
confronted the Missouri Synod's teachers college at that time.

What kind of education is necessary in order to prepare
common school teachers for their profession? was a question
not infrequently asked in the public domain during the last
decades of the nineteenth century. A concern for adequate and

quality teacher education for prospective Lutheran school teachers was also felt in connection with the teachers seminary at Addison. The Synod began to address the issue first by setting minimum standards for entrance into the school's program. The following minimum requirements were presented to the 1881 synodical convention by Director Krauss and adopted by the Synod. For admission to the beginning class in the preparatory department at Addison an applicant was expected to demonstrate proficiency in the following areas:

Bible History

A knowledge of at least the following narratives: the Creation, the Fall into Sin, the Flood, the Patriarchs; in addition, a knowledge of the major details in the life of Jesus—an acquaintance, in short, with the narrative texts of the festivals of the church year—and a knowledge of the pericope concerning the Last Judgment.

Catechism

The applicant should know from memory Luther's Small Catechism from the Ten Commandments to the point of the Christian Questions.

German

The applicant must be able to read selections from the Second Reader fluently and with understanding. With respect to German grammar he should be able to recognize at least nouns, adjectives, and verbs, and be able to decline the noun together with a modifying adjective and conjugate the verb in the indicative in both the active and the passive voices. . . .

English

In English, it is expected of pupils coming from our schools that they be required to read a First Reader without difficulty and that they be able to understand and write its vocabulary correctly, just as the writing and spelling of the vocabulary in the First German Reader is required.

Arithmetic

In this area the entering student should not only be able to perform mechanically the four fundamental operations with concrete numbers but also be able to apply this skill to situations in ordinary life.

Music

In music the entering student should be able to sing alone and correctly such melodies as are sung almost every Sunday in his church ("All glory be to God on high," "Lord, help us ever to retain the Catechism's doctrine plain," "Lord Jesus Christ, be present now").[16] [17]

The prerequisites for admission listed above and adopted by the Missouri Synod in 1881 were asking no more of students

[16] *Synodal-Bericht der . . . Synode von Missouri . . .* (Synodical Report of . . . the Synod of Missouri . . .), 1881, 56-57. An English translation of these requirements also appears in the *Lutheran School Journal*, May 1932, 399-400.

[17] The English requirement applied only to entering students who had attended a Lutheran parochial school in the United States. For immigrant teachers from Germany the Addison faculty conducted a separate division from 1884 to 1888. This was a two-year program and included instruction in English, music, and Lutheran doctrine.

desiring to enter the Addison Teachers Seminary than that they have an elementary Lutheran parochial school education. The requirements were minimal and called for basic literacy in German, English, and arithmetic, an elementary knowledge of Bible history and Lutheran doctrine, and a beginning acquaintance with Lutheran hymnody. That such requirements had to be approved by a synodical convention would seem to indicate that the Synod's teachers seminary had been receiving applications or inquiries from prospective students who did not meet the standards being set and had perhaps even accepted some such applicants. It was necessary, therefore, to address admission standards before any other contemplated curricular upgrading could be considered. The adoption of a specific statement on prerequisites for admission took place early in the administration of E. A. W. Krauss, only one year, in fact, after his assuming the directorship at Addison. The problem was not newly discovered at that time, however, for Krauss' predecessor, J. C. W. Lindemann, as mentioned before, had requested early in the school's history that boys who still needed to learn their ABCs not be encouraged to make application to the preparatory department of the teachers seminary.

Another item long on the agenda at Addison and also finally resolved during the Krauss administration was the arrangement for practice teaching. When the synodical teacher-training program was moved to Addison in 1864, it was hoped that students would be able to observe an experienced teacher in the West District school of the local Zion Lutheran Church and do some practice teaching at that school. That plan didn't materialize until 1878 when students were finally given the opportunity to teach four one-half hours per week. That token practice teaching experience remained in effect until 1898 when a separate training school, attended primarily by children from the local Lutheran orphanage, was established in a classroom on campus. By 1901, however, a separate building for the practice school was erected, enabling the Board of Control to report to the 1902 synodical convention:

> We hope that we are bringing especially good news to the Honorable Synod when we report that the practice school now has its own home. . . . It is a building 55 x 30 feet and is, in our opinion, practicably furnished. . . . The school is equipped with individual desks for the children and with various sorts of necessary and useful teaching aids.[18]

It was during the Krauss administration that a gymnasium was also constructed, although that structure was built "without burdening the synodical treasury."[19] Such a building was not considered essential for a school in the 1890s and for that reason was not a top priority for synodical funding. The Board did report, however, that the gymnasium was dedicated "with great rejoicing" in November of 1895 and that "an abundant use of it" was anticipated. The building was called "Turnhalle" in German, which means that it was a place primarily for student gymnastic activities, some of which were required. It was not a gymnasium in today's sense of a building designed to accommodate interscholastic team sports with large numbers of spectators. The gymnasium together with a major academic building, a new dining hall and kitchen, and the separate practice school building were part of the physical expansion of the Addison campus during the 25-year tenure of E. A. W. Krauss.

When Director Krauss accepted a call to the faculty of Concordia Seminary in St. Louis in the fall of 1905, Theodore Brohm was appointed acting president of the Addison school

---

[18] *Synodal-Bericht der . . . Synode von Missouri . . .* (Synodical Report of . . . the Synod of Missouri . . .), 1902, 44.

[19] *Synodal-Bericht* (Synodical Report), 1896, 55.

and elected to the position permanently in March of 1906. He had been a faculty member at the school since 1879. Born in New York City, Brohm was graduated from Concordia Seminary in St. Louis in 1866. After additional study at New York University, he served as pastor of a congregation in Boston. In 1871, he joined the faculty of the Wisconsin Synod's Northwestern University (College) at Watertown, Wisconsin. E. E. Kowalke in his *Centennial Story* of Northwestern speaks of Brohm as an "able and popular teacher of English and science" at Northwestern.[20] Brohm stayed in Watertown until 1879 when he joined the faculty at Addison. Married to the daughter of a former professor at Concordia Seminary in St. Louis, Theodore Brohm was the brother-in-law of John Schaller who at the time of Brohm's selection as director at Addison was the president of the Wisconsin Synod's teacher-training college in New Ulm, Minnesota. The Brohm presidency was not a long one, lasting only until 1913 when the Addison Teachers Seminary was moved to River Forest, Illinois.

Talk of relocation was in the air already when Brohm became president at Addison, although the decision to move the school was not made until the 1911 synodical convention. While the possibility of relocation was being talked about, the Synod was reluctant, of course, to allocate funds for needed improvements and expansion on the Addison campus. Two developments which did take place at that time, however, are especially worthy of note. One was curricular and affected the Synod's teacher training school at Seward, Nebraska, as well as at Addison. The other involved the local parish in Addison, Zion Lutheran Church, and was, in a sense, the precursor of something which later developed in River Forest in 1929 when

---

[20] E. E. Kowalke, *Centennial Story* (Watertown, WI: Northwestern College, 1965), 124-25.

Grace Lutheran Church of Oak Park, Illinois, relocated so as to be adjacent to the Synod's teachers college.

The curricular change which occurred at Addison during Theodore Brohm's presidency was major in that it expanded the length of the synodical teacher-education program by a year. Since the founding of the school in 1864, teacher education at Addison had been a five-year course of study. Three of these years were considered preparatory to the more specifically professional orientation of the last two years of the curriculum. By resolution of the Synod in 1908, an additional year was added to the preparatory department at Addison as well as at Seward, the Synod's second teachers seminary which had been established as a preparatory school in 1894 and expanded into a full teacher training institution in 1906. This action was consistent with what was happening in American teacher education generally, namely, requiring a four-year high school diploma as a prerequisite for admission to programs of professional teacher education.

Before the addition of a sixth year of study during the Brohm administration, another event affecting the lives of students at Addison had also taken place. The teachers seminary was located near a satellite school of the local Lutheran church, but the church building itself was two and one-half miles distant from the college campus. Students from 1864 to 1893 had to walk that distance for Sunday morning worship. In 1893, arrangements were made with Zion Lutheran Church, the local parish, to conduct Sunday morning services also in the college chapel. Zion's pastor alternated Sundays with professors in conducting worship there. In 1905, however, the Synod had requested that another church be established nearer the campus. Zion was receptive to the suggestion and assisted in the founding of the new church by releasing a sizable number of its own members to help with the organizing of a congregation closer to the Synod's teachers college.

Known as St. Paul's Lutheran Church, the congregation dedicated its new building in 1907, thus providing a more convenient church home for the approximately 200 students at the college.

These students were not served by the new church for too long, however, for Lutheran school teacher training came to an end in Addison, Illinois, in 1913, when the German Evangelical Lutheran Synod of Missouri, Ohio, and Other States moved its Addison program to River Forest. In the 49 years of parochial school teacher education at Addison, three men had held the position of Director of the Synod's Teachers Seminary in that place, J. C. W. Lindemann, E. A. W. Krauss, and Theodore Brohm. Krauss was teaching at Concordia Seminary in St. Louis when the Addison school was moved to River Forest. Brohm retired at the time of the relocation. He took up residence in California, continued to teach after retirement at Concordia Lutheran College in Oakland, California, and was awarded an honorary Doctor of Philosophy degree by Concordia Seminary in St. Louis in 1921. Brohm's retirement from the faculty and presidency at Addison and the moving of the school to River Forest brought to a close the formative era in the history of teacher education in the Missouri Synod.

Suggested for Further Reading

Freitag, Alfred J. *College with a Cause.* River Forest, Illinois: Concordia Teachers College, 1964.

Gaertner, H. C. "A Brief Historical Sketch of Concordia Teachers College, River Forest, Ill." *Lutheran School Journal* 67 (May 1932): 385-412.

✛ ✛ ✛ 1865 ✛ ✛ ✛

Evangelisch-Lutherisches Schulblatt
(Evangelical Lutheran School Journal)

The establishment in 1864 of a separate institution in Addison, Illinois, for the specific purpose of training Lutheran school teachers was a major advance in the development of the Lutheran parochial school. It was only one year after that noteworthy event that another step was taken to promote the cause. In September of 1865, the first issue of the *Evangelisch-Lutherisches Schulblatt* (Evangelical Lutheran School Journal) appeared on the scene. This journal was destined to have a long life, first as a German periodical and then in English. In January of 1920, the magazine became the *Lutheran School Journal*, a name which was retained until the fall of 1947 when the publication was given the title *Lutheran Education*. Since *Lutheran Education* still exists as a professional journal, one is justified in saying that the *Schulblatt* of 1865 has had an uninterrupted existence since its inception.

The initial sponsor of the *Schulblatt* was the Teachers' Conference of the Western District of the German Evangelical Lutheran Synod of Missouri, Ohio, and Other States. The teachers in this conference came primarily from the states of Illinois and Missouri, the two major geographic areas of the Western District of the Missouri Synod at that time. The first editor of the periodical was the indefatigable J. C. W. Lindemann, director of the newly founded teachers seminary in

Addison. Lindemann had been reluctant to assume the editorial assignment, not because he was opposed to the project but because of time constraints. The Addison school was just getting off the ground and needed the kind of strong, energetic, and time-consuming leadership which new institutions often require. In his foreword to the first issue of the *Schulblatt*, Lindemann remarked that a year earlier already he had been requested to assume editorship of the proposed periodical. It had been his hope, however, that someone else with both time and ability for editorial duties could be found to accept the appointment. When that didn't happen, he was prevailed upon to assume the task.[1]

Lindemann continued as editor until August 1869. His parting words in the last issue for which he was responsible intimate that his fears about not having enough time for the work were realized, at least to some extent. Commenting on the fact that the August issue was the last which the publishers had guaranteed, Lindemann added: "If now and then individual issues (as, for example, the last two) came out late, the fault lay in part with me, in as much as I was hindered by other work from transmitting the manuscript on time."[2] The editor noted further that the future of the *Schulblatt* at the time of the conclusion of his initial editorship had not been definitely decided because the matter was to come before the Synod in its approaching convention. Before signing off as sole editor, Lindemann requested that correspondence pertaining to the periodical be delayed until subscribers received another issue

---

[1] J. C. W. Lindemann, "Vorwort" (Foreword), *Schulblatt*, September 1865, 2-3.

[2] J. C. W. Lindemann, "Schlusswort" (Concluding Comment), *Schulblatt*, August 1869, 384.

with a new editorial address.[3] That comment suggests that Lindemann was quite confident that the Missouri Synod would assume responsibility for the future publication of what had become a respectable Lutheran education journal.

His four-year term as editor of the *Schulblatt* is a tribute to the literary skill and productivity of J. C. W. Lindemann. The magazine appeared monthly, with each issue containing 32 pages. Since credit is given upon occasion to other authors and literary sources, it seems reasonable to assume that the unsigned articles, reviews, and comments were very likely written by Lindemann himself. Those contributions, it should be noted, constitute by far the bulk of the material in each issue. The articles range from serial scholarly essays like "Luther as the Reformer of the Nature of the German School" to biographies of men like the educator Johann Bernhard Basedow and the pietist theologian August Hermann Francke. The section of comments deals with miscellaneous educational phenomena or concerns in both the United States and Germany. Book reviews include critiques of texts for school use as well as books useful for the teacher as a scholar and professional. All early issues of the *Schulblatt* were written entirely in the German language. Even comments on items which the editor came across in sources written in English were made in German. Similarly, the very few English titles which are mentioned are reviewed in German. Since German printing prior to the early 1930s did not employ Roman-style letters, a book or name in English is easily spotted on a page in the *Schulblatt*. One can hardly miss, for example, the following entry in the totally German first issue of the magazine:

---

[3] Ibid.

Litterarifche Intelligenzen.

GAMES AND SPORTS FOR YOUNG BOYS. With ninety Illustrations. New York, Nr. 56 Walker St. 1859. 106 p.

Das Büchlein enthält eine Sammlung von Knabenspielen für die Stube und den Spielplatz, welche leicht zu begreifen und fast überall auszuführen sind. Manchem Unwesen unter unserer heutigen Jugend würde gesteuert werden, auch manche Thorheit würde den Knaben gar nicht kommen, wenn Eltern und Lehrer wieder anfangen wollten, den Kindern anständige Spiele zu lehren und sie bei Aufführung derselben freundlich zu beaufsichtigen. Zu dem Zwecke wird dieses Büchlein empfohlen.

A review of a book about recreational activities and written in English is a witness in itself to the variety of materials with which editor Lindemann occupied himself. He recommended the book as a resource for parents and teachers.

The 1869 convention of the Missouri Synod, meeting at Fort Wayne in September of that year, did address the issue of the publication of the *Schulblatt* and, as Lindemann seems to have expected, took over responsibility for the periodical and made it the Synod's official organ for educational matters. According to the synodical resolution, the editorship was to be delegated to the faculty of the teachers seminary in Addison. Faculty members were to have equal rights and duties in the editing of the magazine and were to be joined in their tasks by two pastors appointed by the Synod. The synodical convention then expressed its heartfelt thanks to Director Lindemann for his strenuous work as editor of the periodical.[4]

A hiatus of several months occurred after August 1869 before the *Schulblatt* resumed publication as a synodical magazine. This seems to have been intentional, for with the

---

[4] *Vierzehnter Synodal-Bericht der Allgemeinen Deutschen Evang.-Luth. Synode von Missouri, Ohio u.a. Staaten* (Report of the Fourteenth Convention of the General German Evangelical Lutheran Synod of Missouri, Ohio, and Other States), 1869, 99.

appearance of Volume 5 in January 1870 the issues were numbered to coincide with the calendar year instead of beginning with the school year. The periodical continued as a monthly publication from January to December, with Professors J. C. W. Lindemann and his colleague C. A. T. Selle serving initially as co-editors of the now synodically-sponsored journal. By 1876, however, the title page refers to the whole faculty as the editing group, and when the Addison school was moved to its new campus in River Forest, Illinois, in 1913, the periodical came under the editorship of a faculty committee. Lindemann's 32 pages continued to be the standard for the *Evangelisch-Lutherisches Schulblatt* all the way to 1920 when the name was changed to *Lutheran School Journal*.

The number of pages in each issue of the *Schulblatt* is deserving of mention because it marks the magazine as more than a short newsletter for Lutheran teachers. The periodical was substantively professional from the very start. It sought to contribute to the continuing education of Lutheran teachers by means of both theoretical and practical articles and comments. Today's historian finds the *Schulblatt* useful because of the insights it gives into what nineteenth-century Lutheran schools were like, what the educational issues of the day were, and what challenges confronted schools, teachers, and students in those days. At times, it seems, some of the things written are almost descriptive of school and society today. Some samples from the first issue are helpful to illustrate the point.

Coming out in September 7, 1865, the first number made its appearance only a few months after the close of the Civil War. The publication was produced in the Midwest where a number of German Lutheran synods had been formed and where the German language prevailed in both church and Lutheran parochial school. A steady influx of German immigrants to this part of the United States would serve to maintain the German character of the Lutheran schools. Church and school and the people using the two institutions were not living in isolation, however. Social and political conditions as well as the ongoing development of the public school and its educational practices had their effects upon Lutheran schools, with the result that the *Schulblatt* was ready regularly to address issues of the day. Articles in the initial number are evidence of that.

One concern at the time, for example, seems to have been the matter of keeping teachers in the Lutheran school teaching profession. Anxiety about this situation is suggested by a rather extensive fictitious letter included in the first issue of the periodical. The letter runs a little more than six pages and bears the title "To a friend who wants to leave the office of [Lutheran] teacher and take up a secular calling." The imaginary friend is male, since parochial school teachers at that time were ordinarily men. The writer takes up the reasons which the addressee of the letter had allegedly adduced for wanting to leave the Lutheran teaching profession, examines each argument, and then makes remaining in the Lutheran teaching profession a matter of conscience and Christian duty. The Lutheran school-teaching profession was seen as a divine calling because it involved the teaching of the Word of God. Those who occupied the position, according to the letter writer, had received a special blessing from God since as part of their work they were able to deal daily with the Word. The writer urged his friend no longer to

> take counsel . . . with flesh and blood but [to] follow the leading of the Holy Spirit and happily and joyfully [to] say: "Lord, here I am; I am determined in the future also to lead your lambs even if I gain nothing earthly by it, yes, even if I must sacrifice body and life. You are my strength, my life, and my reward."[5]

---

[5] *Schulblatt*, September 1865, 20-21.

One suspects that the letter is from editor Lindemann's pen. The appeal is deeply religious and strongly emotional. It views the Lutheran teaching profession as a high calling from God. The inclusion of a fictitious letter such as this leaves one with the impression that some Lutheran teachers might have been suffering from burnout or were looking for less demanding work with more tangible rewards. People serving in church vocations in 1865 were not immune to the pressures which have often been felt by professional church workers in the years since.

Another article in the first issue of the *Schulblatt* presented a detailed account of the arduous work required daily of a Lutheran teacher. The article is entitled "The daily work of a Christian schoolteacher." The author, very likely J. C. W. Lindemann again, explained the purpose of his essay in its first paragraph:

> As I attempt in the following to present how a workday proceeds for a conscientious Christian schoolteacher, I would like thereby not only to encourage and strengthen faithful teachers in their exhausting task and perhaps also hold a goal before the indolent; it is my desire as well to afford parents, school children, and congregation members the opportunity to become acquainted not only with the hidden joy but also with the daily work and pressure of a teacher. The latter is so little known and so easily forgotten again even where it was once known.[6]

The work of the teacher, according to the *Schulblatt* author, was considered to be much the same whether the school was in the country or city, or whether the school had many or few pupils. Part of the reason for this view was that the writer

---

[6] Ibid., 5.

emphasized how very necessary it was for a teacher to prepare his class presentations in advance, to rise early and be in mental readiness for the work of the day, to engage in personal prayer before school, and to make sure that the classroom and teaching materials were all properly arranged before the school day began. Those activities required time and effort regardless of the size or place of a school, and the teacher who did not give proper attention to preparation was thought to be remiss in his duty.

Although the author of the article ran through the entire day in detail and recommended also that the teacher engage in student games at recess, one thing becomes clear and that is that religion was not merely an addendum to secular study but at the center of the Lutheran school curriculum. Catechism lessons were to be especially well prepared and then executed with a personal demeanor which motivated the children to love the Word of God and not to hate it. Catechism lessons were not to be too long, were to be preceded by group devotion, and, if desired, closed with the singing of a hymn stanza which summarized the lesson taught. Pietistic emotionalism was to be avoided on the one hand and frivolity and indifference on the other. The teacher was counseled to speak from the heart to the heart.

It was suggested that Bible reading follow catechetical instruction. Bible reading was intended to accomplish two things. As an oral exercise it served to teach pupils how to read well and correctly, although the major point was "to comprehend the thought of what was read, to hear God in His Word."[7] By emphasizing content when employing the Bible as a reading tool, the teacher was using Holy Scripture to reinforce what was taught in Catechism instruction. The two lessons together, in the estimation of the *Schulblatt* writer,

---

[7] Ibid., 10.

would take about two hours and prompted the suggestion that the teacher at that point in the day give both himself and the students the relaxation of an outdoor recess.

The article pertaining to the daily work of a Christian schoolteacher did not include a detailed schedule for the entire school day. Such a schedule would appear in the September issue of the 1867 *Schulblatt*. The 1865 article was more concerned about teacher attitude, general classroom organization, and the extensive planning activities required for good teaching. The author was looking for a teacher who knew what he wanted to do and how he was going to do it. The *Schulblatt* was urging teachers to have a deep interest in the spiritual welfare of their pupils and to deal with them in a kindly and understanding manner. The author had no false illusions, however, about the nature of children. He recognized that wrongdoing needed correction and might result in penalties. The writer considered the teaching and practice of religion as the heart of a Lutheran school classroom and urged that faith practices be genuine and sincere. Speaking, for example, about the resuming of classes after lunch, he offered the following counsel:

> If one wishes at that time to have a prayer spoken or a song sung, then let it be short. Too much of that kind of activity is also not good, especially if the mood for it is not present. Worship exercises are easily conducted mindlessly.[8]

If, as is likely, J. C. W. Lindemann was the author of "The daily work of a Christian schoolteacher," it is easy to understand how it came about that the first Director of the Addison Teachers Seminary was held in high regard as a leader

---

[8] Ibid., 11.

in the Lutheran parochial school endeavor. His writing suggests that he was both perceptive and practical in his approach to parochial-school teaching.

An analysis of articles in the *Schulblatt* provides insights into how parochial schools were conducted in days past and what the educational issues of those days were. It is Lindemann's foreword to the first issue which furnishes a statement of purpose, however, for the periodical itself. The magazine was intended to supplement whatever formal education teachers had received in preparation for their profession. Lindemann was very severe in his criticism of teachers who were unwilling to grow professionally. He considered it a good sign that teachers had expressed a desire for an educational periodical and went on to say: "Only a person with an unsteady disposition, an individual interested primarily in serving himself, an empty fool who has no idea of his own incompetence is satisfied with himself."[9] The *Schulblatt* was intended to improve the competency of teachers by providing them with counsel and ideas for more effective classroom teaching.

The editor also planned to contend against educational positions and practices which were deemed hostile to that for which the Lutheran parochial school stood, namely, a combining of religious and general education. He perceived the spirit of the day to be antagonistic to an educational system combining church and school and under clerical supervision. One of the aims of the *Schulblatt* was to oppose such thinking and to promote schools which were designed to sustain the faith of their students. The editor's response to the question of what principles would guide his editorial activity was this:

---

[9] Ibid., 1.

To the extent that God gives me grace and that it is possible for a weak human being, every line of the [journal's] content must harmonize with the prayer of all Christendom which it learned from the Lord Himself: "Hallowed be Thy name! Thy kingdom come!" I know and believe that all human wisdom is will-o'-the-wisp, that only the infallible Word of my God can be my light and guiding star. The Word of the Father which the Son brought from heaven and which the Holy Spirit continually makes alive and, next to this, the confessional writings of our precious Lutheran Zion are to be the measure and weight according to which all my own and other contributions are measured and weighed.[10]

Whenever God's honor was at stake, there was to be "no neutrality." Such a time called for "war against everything ungodly."[11] On the other hand, "where God permitted freedom, there freedom must remain" and in matters of adiaphora both the pro and the con, it was promised, would be given a hearing.[12]

Although the main concern of the *Schulblatt* was the parochial school and things pertaining to it, editor Lindemann felt that the periodical would also be useful in the home, since parents and teachers should work together. A wide range of topics would be discussed. Articles and comments on education in a broad sense were to be included on the pages of the magazine so that not only teachers but parents and pastors would also very likely be able to profit from the periodical. In fact, since pastors often taught in parochial schools and by

---

[10] Ibid., 3-4.

[11] Ibid., 4.

[12] Ibid.

virtue of their pastoral office were supervisors of them, the clergy, too, should find the journal worthwhile.

Schulblatt was the name chosen for the educational periodical begun in 1865. It would retain that German name until two years after the close of World War I, and even after the name *Lutheran School Journal* was chosen in 1921, some articles continued to be written in German. It should be noted, however, that even prior to 1921 many items for the *Schulblatt* were also written in the English language. That being admitted, it does remain a fact, nonetheless, that many parochial schools of the Midwest continued to have more than just a little German flavor into the first two decades of the twentieth century. W. C. Kohn, president of Concordia Teachers College in River Forest, Illinois, and editor of the *Schulblatt* when its name was changed, recognized that with the general public this had often led to a misunderstanding of the Lutheran Christian day school. In his "Foreword" to the January 1921 issue of the *Lutheran School Journal* he wrote:

> That a gross ignorance prevails in our country regarding the Christian day-school was never brought to the surface more clearly than during the perturbed conditions of the World War. The slanders raised against our schools were ridiculous, and, as investigation has revealed, such defamation was not always the product of malice, but very often the fruit of ignorance. Even such absurd claims were made as that the Lutheran schools closed their daily sessions with the song, "Deutschland, Deutschland ueber

alles."[13] An abysmal ignorance reigned in the public mind regarding our schools.[14]

With its new name the decades-old journal saw another reason for its existence and that was to serve as a medium to inform a more general public about the Lutheran Christian day school and the "principles of teaching adopted in the Lutheran Church."[15] The name *Schulblatt* was replaced with *Lutheran School Journal*, but W. C. Kohn's prefatory remarks in the initial issue of the renamed periodical manifest a high regard for the contributions by the made old publication and inform the *Journal*'s readers that a change in title would not substantially alter the content of the magazine brought into existence by J. C. W. Lindemann in 1865.

---

[13] "Germany, Germany over everything." This German song from 1841, sung to the tune "Austria" by Franz Josef Haydn, became especially well-known as a rallying cry during Germany's Nazi days.

[14] *Lutheran School Journal*, January 1921, 2-3.

[15] Ibid., 3.

✤ ✤ ✤ 1872 ✤ ✤ ✤

Evangelical Lutheran Synodical Conference
of North America

The listing of the year 1872 in the present annotated calendar comes about because in that year six Lutheran church bodies formed a partnership which contributed significantly to the furthering of the Lutheran parochial school cause. The organization created in 1872 took the name Evangelical Lutheran Synodical Conference of North America. This federation of Lutherans brought what is known today as The Lutheran Church—Missouri Synod and the Wisconsin Evangelical Lutheran Synod into a fraternal relationship which lasted for 90 years. The two synods had much in common, not the least of which was a strong commitment to parish schools. As members of the Synodical Conference the two synods spoke with one voice in the endorsement of such schools. There were other groupings of Lutherans in the nineteenth century, but none promoted Lutheran schools as vigorously as did the Synodical Conference. From a general church history point of view the formation of this fraternal alliance is also evidence of the desire among nineteenth-century Lutherans to want to organize themselves into larger working groups. A few highlights from the early history of Lutheranism in America would seem to be helpful in order to understand how the Synodical Conference fit into that picture.

Lutheran immigrants began settling in what would become the United States already in colonial times. Thus, for example,

Dutch and Swedish Lutheran settlements existed in New York and along the Delaware River prior to 1700. A few Germans had also come to areas of the eastern seaboard in early colonial times but not in large numbers or in groups. At the end of the seventeenth century, however, clusters of German immigrants began to establish themselves in Pennsylvania. The early part of the eighteenth century brought German Lutherans to Georgia, the Carolinas, Maryland, and Virginia, while Pennsylvania and New York continued to attract settlers from that country. Where churches were established among these German immigrants, it was also not unusual for parish schools to be organized as well.

The political and social conditions in colonial America were quite different, of course, from those which the newly settled Lutherans had known in their European homelands. But that is not all that was different. Ecclesiastical conditions for Lutherans were also quite unlike the European experience, for in America there was no Lutheran state church such as many immigrants had known in the countries from which they were coming. This situation, moreover, was not going to change after the American colonies became an independent nation. The result was that newcomers to American soil were compelled to chart forms of church government different from those these immigrants had known in the past, and while this might have been hailed as a blessing by some settlers, the new circumstances did produce some challenges. The situation gave rise to experimentation and resulted in the gradual unfolding of various kinds of organizational structures.

The first step wherever Lutherans were living in proximity to one another was to form a congregation for worship purposes. Such congregations, however, also needed pastors, and that created problems, for without a state church or long-established system of education for the training of clergy, there was no ready source of supply in the American setting for parish pastors. The need for clergy soon kindled the desire to establish indigenous seminaries for the purpose of training pastors locally. Language, too, was a barrier for Lutherans in some places because the native languages of the various groups of immigrants were different. In this respect, Lutherans experienced problems in worship life which other religious groups did not have to confront. Roman Catholics, for example, employed Latin in worship, and even though Catholics came from varying European linguistic backgrounds and for total parish life wanted priests whose vernacular was that of the parishioners in a given parish, the native language of a priest did not affect his ability to celebrate mass in Latin. In addition, although Roman Catholics in America, like the Lutherans, were living in political and social environments different from that of their homelands, the polity of the Catholic Church made the matter of supplying priests for new-world parishes a somewhat simpler task. In the arranging of their church life, Lutheran and Reformed immigrants from continental Europe could not look back home for guidance and support in the same way that Roman Catholics could. Anglicans, Congregationalists, and Methodists were English in background and so free at least of the language problem which Lutherans in the New World had to address.

As more and more Lutheran congregations were formed during both the colonial and early national periods of United States history, Lutherans, in order to avoid isolation and to be able to engage in cooperative ventures, recognized that it would be desirable to organize individual congregations into larger working groups. Synod was the name employed for these larger groups which began to appear at the end of the eighteenth century and throughout a large part of the nineteenth. These synods were sometimes drawn up according to geographical boundaries, sometimes on the basis of language, and at other times on the foundation of common doctrinal understandings. By the year 1820, six Lutheran synods had been formed: the

Pennsylvania Ministerium (1748), the New York Ministerium (1786), the Synod of North Carolina (1803), the Synod of Ohio (1818), the Maryland-Virginia Synod (1820), and the Tennessee Synod (1820). As the nineteenth century progressed, westward expansion and constant waves of European immigrants produced synod upon synod. The story of the evolution and the early histories of Lutheran synods is often complex and convoluted. The following partial list of synods and their constituting dates will serve to illustrate, however, what was going on with respect to the forming of synods among Lutherans in the Midwest in the nineteenth century: the Evangelical Lutheran Synod of Illinois was founded in 1846, the German Evangelical Lutheran Synod of Missouri, Ohio, and Other States in 1847, the First German Evangelical Lutheran Synod of Wisconsin in 1850, the Norwegian Evangelical Lutheran Church in America in 1853, the German Evangelical Lutheran Synod of Iowa in 1854, the Evangelical Lutheran Synod of Minnesota in 1860, and the Evangelical Lutheran Synod of Michigan and Other States in 1860.

The nineteenth century witnessed not only the organizing of new synods but the forming also of federations of synods for the purpose of further joint work. Thus, for example, an organization known as the General Synod came into existence in the year 1820. The early history of that federation of synods in the eastern part of the country was a bit bumpy, but the group did hold together, increased in size, and remained a major force in American Lutheran church history until the early twentieth century when additional consolidations took place in American Lutheranism and the synods belonging to the General Synod became part of these mergers. A second grouping of Lutherans took place some 40 years after the formation of the General Synod when the General Council was organized in 1867. This federation was made up of Lutherans who, primarily for doctrinal reasons, were unwilling to remain in the General

Synod or join it. Initially, some midwestern synods, such as the Wisconsin and Minnesota Synods, held membership in the General Council. The Missouri Synod, on the other hand, although it participated in a preliminary conference prior to the formation of the General Council, did not send any representatives to the Council's constituting convention. The same was true of the Norwegian Lutheran Church in America.

A third Lutheran federation, the one of special interest in the history of the Lutheran parochial school, came into existence in the year 1872. It was a midwestern Lutheran grouping and was made up of synods popularly referred to as the Missouri, Ohio, Norwegian, Wisconsin, Illinois, and Minnesota Synods. The constituting convention was held at what was to become for a number of years the Wisconsin Synod's flagship church, St. John's Lutheran in Milwaukee, and the name chosen for the organization was Evangelisch-Lutherische Synodal Conferenz von Nord-Amerika (Evangelical Lutheran Synodical Conference of North America). Although this federation no longer exists, it did enjoy a 90-year history and during those years enthusiastically promoted the parochial school among the synods which continued their membership in the Conference.

Two of the charter members of the Synodical Conference, the Ohio and Norwegian Synods, withdrew from the federation not long after its formation, in 1881 and 1883 respectively. The Illinois Synod became part of the Missouri Synod in 1880, and the Minnesota Synod federated with Wisconsin in 1892. Several other developments, important enough in themselves but not all that noteworthy for the purpose of tracing the history of the Lutheran parochial school, occurred within the synods of the Synodical Conference during its 90-year existence. Suffice it to say that when the organization ceased to exist as a functioning federation in the 1960s, it was comprised of The Lutheran Church—Missouri Synod, by far the largest synod in the federation, the Wisconsin Evangelical Lutheran Synod, the second-largest synod, the Evangelical Lutheran Synod, a relatively small group of Lutherans of Norwegian background who trace their synodical beginnings to 1853, and the Synod of Evangelical Lutheran Churches, a small association of Lutherans of Slovak background who joined the Synodical Conference in 1908 and became part of the Missouri Synod in 1971.[1] At the time of the demise of the Conference and still today The Lutheran Church—Missouri Synod and the Wisconsin Evangelical Lutheran Synod are especially known for their flourishing systems of parochial schools, systems which include both elementary and secondary schools, have synodical offices for counsel and encouragement, and are able to look in part, at least, to synodically approved teacher-training programs for staff.

Structural or organic union was not the immediate goal of the Synodical Conference when it was organized in 1872. The constitution of that year stated that the purpose and object of the federation was to provide for

> an expression of the unity of the spirit existing among the respective synods; mutual encouragement as to faith and confession; promotion of unity as to doctrine and practice and the removal of any threatening disturbance thereof; cooperation in matters of mutual interest; an effort to establish territorial boundaries for the synods, provided that the language used does not separate them.[2]

---

[1] The Synodical Conference never formally dissolved itself. Conventions continued to be held until 1966, but the 1964 and 1966 conventions were attended by delegates from only The Lutheran Church—Missouri Synod and the Synod of Evangelical Lutheran Churches. The Wisconsin Synod and the smaller Evangelical Lutheran Synod had separated themselves from the Synodical Conference and did not attend these two conventions.

[2] *Constitution of the Evangelical Lutheran Synodical Conference* (St. Louis: Concordia Publishing House, 1924), 1.

Only at the end of the paragraph on purpose and object is "the uniting of all Lutheran synods of America into *one* orthodox American Lutheran Church" added.[3] The very next paragraph is quick to explain, however, that the "Synodical Conference is only an advisory body with respect to all things concerning which the synods constituting it have not given it authoritative power."[4]

Cooperation in matters of mutual concern and interest was the primary stated function of the Synodical Conference, and this remained the major emphasis in the organization. Such a general statement of purpose seems a bit vague, but it was envisioned perhaps that as various cooperative ventures were tried, it might eventually be possible to define joint activities more concretely. The constitution spoke succinctly of the Conference's scope of activities but did include broad areas of engagement:

> The doctrine and the practice of the Church; the relation of pastors and congregations of one synod to those of other synods in the Synodical Conference as a whole or of its individual members to church-bodies not belonging to the Synodical Conference; matters pertaining to home and foreign mission work, as also to mission-work among immigrants; hospitals and orphanages; the publishing of Lutheran literature in general and of Lutheran tracts in particular; the training of pastors and teachers; and the like.[5]

The pursuits intended for the Synodical Conference were ambitious. They encompassed theology and some ecclesiastical

---

[3] Ibid.

[4] Ibid.

[5] Ibid., 2.

organization, and, as history records, the new federation experienced difficulties in both areas almost immediately. The stated constitutional objective "to establish territorial boundaries for the synods" turned out to be one of the first issues of debate. Cooperation is an easy word to use when proposing to consolidate structures and activities of one or more organizations. Achieving the goal is not so easily accomplished. And so it was in the Synodical Conference when a proposal was made to create state synods. Granted, the names of the Conference's constituting synods give the impression that state boundaries already existed; in fact that was not the case. The Missouri Synod was strong, for example, outside of the state of Missouri. Similarly, the Ohio Synod reached beyond the boundaries of Ohio. Questions arose relative to what transition steps would have to be taken to effect the realignment of the synods, the Wisconsin and Ohio Synods especially having concerns about Missouri's presence beyond its state boundaries.[6]

It was a doctrinal issue, however, which caused an early rupture in the Synodical Conference. A controversy arose among midwestern Lutherans over the doctrine spoken of in treatises on dogmatic theology as the doctrine of election or conversion. Articles in the periodical literature of the time and conferences had been discussing the theological issues involved in this doctrine since the mid-1850s. By 1880, the matter had come to a head and resulted in the withdrawal of two synods from the Synodical Conference, the Ohio and Norwegian Synods. The Ohio Synod was generally of one mind with respect to the theological issues in the controversy. The Norwegian Synod, on the other hand, was torn within its own ranks in the dispute. In fact, the Norwegian withdrawal from the Conference was prompted in part because it was thought that the

---

[6] For a discussion of these concerns, see Edward C. Fredrich, *The Wisconsin Synod Lutherans* (Milwaukee: Northwestern, 1992), 55-58.

Norwegian Synod might be able to resolve the issues more readily by discussing them in its own linguistically homogeneous fellowship rather than in the forum of the Synodical Conference where sessions were conducted in German.[7] The hope was not realized, for a split did occur in the Norwegian Synod. That part of the Norwegian split which continued to share the doctrinal position of the Synodical Conference did not renew its membership in the Conference but did remain on friendly terms with the synods in the federation and engaged in altar and pulpit fellowship.[8] It was not until 1920, after another theological controversy, that a small group of Lutherans of Norwegian background, the group known today as the Evangelical Lutheran Synod, again affiliated with the Synodical Conference. After the election controversy of the early 1880s the Synodical Conference was for many years a strictly German Lutheran federation, Missouri and Wisconsin being the largest synods in the organization. In those two bodies and their affiliates the Lutheran parochial school was actively promoted, the Conference in its conventions also devoting time periodically to discussions of that educational enterprise.

The constitution of the Synodical Conference made no specific mention of parish schools but did include in its scope of activities "the training of pastors and teachers." The teacher-training referred to was obviously the training of teachers for serving in Lutheran parochial schools. Even as the Missouri Synod had for a time conducted a course of study for parochial school teaching together with its pre-theological curriculum at Fort Wayne, Indiana, so also pre-seminary colleges of other synods had included educational programs for the training of teachers. The Wisconsin Synod's Northwestern College at Watertown, Wisconsin, for example, continued to operate such

---

[7] See S. C. Ylvisaker, *Grace for Grace* (Mankato: Lutheran Synod Book Company, 1943), 61-62.

[8] Ibid., 62.

a course of study until 1893.[9] Similarly, the Minnesota Synod added an education department in 1887 to its Dr. Martin Luther College which had opened in New Ulm, Minnesota, only a few years before.[10] Missouri's separate teaching-training seminary, established at Addison, Illinois, seven years before the organizing of the Synodical Conference, was very likely seen as a promising place at which to consolidate Lutheran parochial school teacher-training programs for the constituting synods of the Synodical Conference.

Joint efforts for the training of teachers did not develop among the constituent synods of the Synodical Conference. Individuals from one or the other synod did, of course, make use at times of programs in an institution of a different synod, and teachers trained in one synod upon occasion took positions in another, but no formal synodical arrangements were made for joint work. The same cannot be said, however, in connection with the training of pastors. In that activity, plans were put into place immediately and continued in one way or another for a number of years during the remainder of the nineteenth century.

At the time of the founding of the Synodical Conference the Wisconsin Synod was especially receptive to joint efforts in the matter of ministerial training. In fact, Wisconsin had already closed its seminary just two years earlier, in 1870, and was sending its ministerial students to the Missouri Synod seminary in St. Louis, an arrangement which continued until Wisconsin reopened its own seminary again in 1878. The Missouri Synod, on the other hand, was favorably inclined to use the resources of Wisconsin's Northwestern College in Watertown—known at that time as Northwestern University—for the pre-seminary training of Missouri Synod students. An agreement for the

---

[9] Erwin E. Kowalke, *Centennial Story* (Milwaukee: Northwestern, 1965), 173.

[10] Morton A. Schroeder, *A Time to Remember* (New Ulm: Dr. Martin Luther College, 1984), 28.

exchange of professors had already been reached in 1869, Missouri obligating itself to send a professor to the college in Watertown and Wisconsin agreeing to provide a theological professor in St. Louis. The Missouri Synod was able to send F. W. Stellhorn to Northwestern, where he remained until 1874, but Wisconsin was unsuccessful in reciprocating at St. Louis. Although Missouri's sister synod had planned to call Adolf Hoenecke for this position, the Wisconsin Synod was unable to finance the arrangement.[11] A call for the St. Louis position was later extended to a pastor in Germany who, after he had accepted the call and had arrived in the United States, was compelled for reasons of illness to return to Germany.[12] At the Synodical Conference constituting convention in 1872, F. W. A. Notz, a professor of classics with a doctoral degree from the University of Tübingen, was selected to be Wisconsin's professor in St. Louis. By mutual agreement, however, it was decided that "both synods would be better served if he joined the faculty in Watertown,"[13] where he continued to teach until 1911 and was a leading Wisconsin Synod spokesman on issues pertaining to Lutheran schools.

One notable family in the history of Synodical Conference Lutheranism was particularly affected by the joint ministerial education efforts of the Missouri and Wisconsin Synods in the 1870s. Four brothers in this family earned their college diplomas from Northwestern in Watertown and then continued their theological training at Concordia Seminary in St. Louis.

---

[11] Hoenecke, who had been teaching at his synod's seminary department in Watertown until it closed in 1870, returned to the classroom upon the reopening of the seminary and relocating of it in Milwaukee in 1878 and then continued to teach at the institution also when it was moved to Wauwatosa. His *Dogmatik* (Dogmatics), published posthumously, was foundational in the formation of the Wisconsin Synod's approach to the discipline of doctrinal theology.

[12] Kowalke, 59-60.

[13] Ibid., 77.

The brothers were Reinhold, Franz, August, and Anton Pieper. Reinhold eventually became president of Concordia Theological Seminary in Springfield, Illinois, a Missouri Synod school. Franz was called to a professorship at Missouri's Concordia Seminary in St. Louis, served the institution as its president for many years, and was also president of the Missouri Synod from 1899 to 1911. August, after having served as a parish pastor in the Wisconsin Synod for a little over 20 years, joined the faculty of the Wisconsin Synod seminary and eventually became its president. Anton served as a parish pastor in the Wisconsin Synod and concluded his ministerial career as pastor of a congregation in the Minnesota Synod. All four brothers had been born in Germany. Their mother and her sons had immigrated to the United States in 1870 and settled in Watertown, Wisconsin, where she became housemother at Northwestern College (University). Reinhold and Franz Pieper had no seminary choice when they completed their studies at Northwestern because the Wisconsin Synod seminary had been closed. The school reopened after August Pieper had begun his studies in St. Louis and was available to both him and his younger brother Anton, but both chose to pursue their theological education in St. Louis. The case of the Pieper brothers is significant because it shows what very likely was envisioned for the training of pastors in the Synodical Conference, namely, baccalaureate education in a classical-studies college operated by one or more of the individual synods and theological training at a central seminary. Except for this very small window of experimentation in the 1870s, a joint program for the training of pastors never materialized in the Synodical Conference. As with teacher training, each synod proceeded to make its own arrangements for ministerial education.

In some other areas the Conference was able to point to more tangible results of its hope to do joint work. Mutual encouragement and the opportunity for theological discussions were always a major agenda item for the Synodical Conference, and it must be remembered that "an expression of the unity of the spirit existing among the respective synods" and the "promotion of unity as to doctrine and practice" were primary goals of the federation. Unity of spirit in doctrinal matters was an accomplished goal during many years of Synodical Conference history, even though certain types of goals in outward organization or structure were not achieved. In the area of mission endeavors, on the other hand, the Conference was successful in establishing an outreach program in Nigeria, Africa, with the founding of what today is The Lutheran Church of Nigeria. The Conference was also the agency through which the constituent synods conducted their pioneering church efforts among African Americans in the United States. Churches and schools for African Americans were originally founded under the auspices of the Synodical Conference and not by the individual Synodical Conference synods. *The Lutheran Hymnal*, sturdy Lutheran worship book for many decades, was the product not of one synod but of the Synodical Conference. In the state of Wisconsin, Synodical Conference congregations joined hands to establish a campus ministry at the University of Wisconsin in Madison and to found in Milwaukee what has become the oldest continuously operating community Lutheran high school program in the nation. The Synodical Conference held its last conventions in the 1960s and then ceased to exist, but while it functioned, it was not without a number of significant accomplishments.

Because of its size, the Missouri Synod was always the major financial contributor to the work of the Conference. Personnel for various undertakings were also drawn largely from Missouri, although the other synods made contributions in this area too. Missouri's C. F. W. Walther was the first president of the Synodical Conference but several other early presidents came from the Ohio and Norwegian Synods, and after the withdrawal of those two synods from the federation, the presidency was in the hands of Wisconsin Synod men for a continuous period of 45 years. Johannes Bading, longtime president of the Wisconsin Synod, held the position from 1882 to 1912 and C. F. Gausewitz served from 1912 to 1927. William H. Schweppe, a Wisconsin Synod pastor, was the superintendent of the Conference's Nigeria mission for 22 years, from its beginnings in 1936 until 1958. The Synodical Conference was a cooperative venture and involved members of the constituent synods in a variety of ways.

Observers from the outside noted several things about the Synodical Conference. Writing in 1934, J. L. Neve, a United Lutheran Church theologian, made the following observation about the doctrinal stance of the federation: "The Synodical Conference holds a very strict confessional position and maintains strict discipline in this respect."[14] With respect to the Conference's commitment to Lutheran parochial schools, another outside observer in a 1975 analysis of American Lutheran church history commented:

> An aspect of the educational enterprise which engaged much attention from the Synodical Conference bodies was the parochial, or congregational school. Other synods advocated and established congregational schools, but not to the same extent nor with the same commitment as those of the Synodical Conference.[15]

---

[14] J. L. Neve, *History of the Lutheran Church in America* (Burlington, Iowa: The Lutheran Literary Board, 1934), 190.

[15] Eugene L. Fevold, "Coming of Age," in *The Lutherans of North America*, ed. E. Clifford Nelson (Philadelphia: Fortress, 1975), 295.

In its 90 years of existence the Synodical Conference was known for its conservative doctrinal position and for its advocacy of the Lutheran parochial school. Doctrinal presentations and discussions were always part of convention agendas, and at several conventions in the late nineteenth and early twentieth centuries essays and time were devoted to the cause of the Lutheran parochial school. More specific reference to some of these events will be made at other points in the present volume. In addition, literature from the constituent synods promoted the institution, and congregational schools continued to be established and maintained in the synods of the federation on both the elementary and secondary levels.

The Lutheran Church—Missouri Synod and the Wisconsin Evangelical Lutheran Synod, the two church bodies in which Lutheran parochial schools on both the elementary and secondary levels are extensive and in good condition today, were charter members of the Evangelical Lutheran Synodical Conference of North America. At the time of the founding of the Conference, Lutherans of other affiliations were also operating parish schools (*Gemeindeschulen*) similar in kind to those sponsored by Missouri and Wisconsin Synod congregations. Many of the schools in all the synods were just part-time agencies, and as the curricula of elementary schools expanded, Lutheran parochial schools with limited offerings began to vanish from the educational scene, also in the Missouri and Wisconsin Synods. The Synodical Conference synods, however, were not willing to abandon the parochial school concept but continued to promote and urge the improvement of the institution. In the forum of the organization, the school issue came to the fore at several critical points in late nineteenth- and early twentieth-century Lutheran school history. The defense of full-time parish schools and the encouragement for their development were especially forceful at those times and laid the groundwork for the extensive elementary and secondary school systems existing in the Missouri and Wisconsin Synods today.

Both synods experienced fractures in their own fellowships in the second half of the twentieth century. In the case of the Wisconsin Synod this resulted in the formation in 1960 of the Church of the Lutheran Confession (CLC). The fracture in the Missouri Synod took place after a walkout of the faculty of Concordia Seminary in 1974 and resulted in the formation of the Association of Evangelical Lutheran Churches (AELC), a sizable group of congregations which eventually became part of the Evangelical Lutheran Church in America (ELCA). Included among those who withdrew from their parent synods were congregations with schools and groups of individuals committed to that type of education. The influx of former Missouri Synod churches into the Evangelical Lutheran Church in America added schools to the statistical tables of that union, whose membership consists primarily of church bodies in which K-8 Lutheran schools had all but ceased to exist, and the small Church of the Lutheran Confession, the breakaway group from the Wisconsin Synod, has schools among its congregations. The Evangelical Lutheran Synod (ELS), a small group of Lutherans with synodical headquarters, a college, and a seminary in Mankato, Minnesota, also has a number of congregations with schools. The ELS, although an independent synod and not part of the Wisconsin Synod, practices church fellowship with the latter. The Mankato-based synod traces its beginnings to the 1853 formation of the Norwegian Evangelical Lutheran Church in America and was organized as a separate synod when it chose not to enter a merger of Norwegian Lutherans in 1917. The Evangelical Lutheran Synod was organized in 1918 and became a part of the Synodical Conference in 1920.

From what has been said, it is apparent that Eugene Fevold was accurate in his assessment of the Evangelical Lutheran

Synodical Conference of North America when he said: "An aspect of the educational enterprise which engaged much attention from the Synodical Conference bodies was the parochial or congregational school."[16] Not only did the Synodical Conference address Lutheran parochial school issues in convention at various times; it also provided a friendly fraternity within which the constituent members could encourage each other in a common educational interest. Organized in 1872, the Evangelical Lutheran Synodical Conference, a 90-year alliance of Lutheran synods, performed an important support role in the development of Lutheran parochial schools as they exist today. Although not structured administratively to provide leadership for the conduct of parish schools, the Synodical Conference provided the Wisconsin and Missouri Synods a forum within which to speak together in behalf of Lutheran parochial schools.

Suggested for Further Reading

Mueller, John Theodore. *A Brief History of the Origin, Development, and Work of the Evangelical Lutheran Synodical Conference of North America.* St. Louis: Concordia Publishing House, 1948.

---

[16] Ibid.

✤✤✤ 1876 ✤✤✤

Schulzeitung
(School Periodical)

Ten and one-half years after Lutheran teachers in the Missouri Synod launched a 'professional journal with the name *Evangelisch-Lutherisches Schulblatt* (*Evangelical Lutheran School Journal*) the Teachers' Conference of the Evangelical Lutheran Wisconsin Synod undertook to publish a Lutheran school periodical for the teachers of their fellowship. The first issue of that magazine, titled simply *Schulzeitung* (School Paper or School Periodical), came out in February 1876. The name was later changed to *Lutherische Schulzeitung (*Lutheran School Periodical) and continued in existence until 1905. The publication was one of the first undertakings of Wisconsin Synod teachers who had organized themselves into a conference in the year 1872. Like the *Evangelisch-Lutherisches Schulblatt*, the *Schulzeitung* was produced in the German language and continued to appear in that tongue, since it was intended for teachers who were not only fluent in that language but used it extensively in the classrooms of Lutheran schools. Although the *Schulzeitung* was sponsored initially by the Teachers' Conference of the Wisconsin Synod, the periodical was soon adopted as the official educational journal of the Synod and was published under synodical sponsorship beginning in July of 1878.

The first editor of the magazine, a 16-page publication, was F. W. A. Notz of Northwestern University (later to be known as Northwestern College), a Wisconsin Synod institution of higher education founded at Watertown, Wisconsin, in 1865. When the Synod assumed responsibility for the publication of the periodical an editorial committee was appointed to assist Notz. The committee, in addition to Notz, consisted of three teachers from the Milwaukee area and a Northwestern colleague of the editor, August L. Graebner, a theologian trained in the Missouri Synod who eventually joined the faculty of that synod's Concordia Seminary in St. Louis.

The editorship of the magazine changed in the early 1890s when the Wisconsin Synod entered into a federation with the Minnesota and Michigan Synods. According to the constitution of the organization formed by those three synods, Dr. Martin Luther College of New Ulm, Minnesota, a school of the Minnesota Synod, became the teacher-training institution for the group. Editorial duties for the *Schulzeitung* were then handed over to the faculty of the New Ulm teachers seminary and its president, the Rev. John Schaller.

The faculty began its editorial work with the first issue of volume 19, in March 1894, and continued to edit the magazine until 1905 when publication ceased because, according to the final number, "The income from subscriptions did not cover the cost of publication."[1] Thirty years passed before the Wisconsin Synod resumed publication of a regular periodical specifically designed for Lutheran parochial school teachers. Although publication of the *Schulzeitung* came to an end in the early 1900s, during the 30 years of its existence it was an informative and well-written Lutheran educational journal. The magazine was scholarly and practical and like the Missouri Synod's *Schulblatt* was a helpful professional resource for Lutheran school teachers. The fact that both magazines had their origin in Lutheran teachers' conferences is evidence that late nineteenth-

---

[1] Morton A. Schroeder, *A Time to Remember* (New Ulm: Dr. Martin Luther College, 1984), 39.

century parochial school teachers felt the need for professional Lutheran educational periodicals. The teachers themselves requested the journals and sponsored them until the synods were willing to take over publication responsibilities. For the historian both periodicals are valuable because their articles furnish insights into the nature and operation of late nineteenth- and early twentieth-century Lutheran parish schools and give a glimpse into what was on the minds of and important to Lutheran teachers of that time.

The first editor of the *Schulzeitung*, F. W. A. Notz, remained at the task for a long time. South-German by birth, the Northwestern professor held impressive academic credentials from his native country. He was the son of a Lutheran clergyman and was born in Weinsberg, Württemberg, in 1841. He received his early education in the home of his parents and at age 10 was sent to the Latin school in Leonberg near Stuttgart. Two years later he entered the Royal Gymnasium in Stuttgart and in 1855, after having passed the necessary examinations, continued his education at a prestigious Gymnasium (secondary school)[2] in Maulbronn. He studied at this school for four years and matriculated in the University of Tübingen in 1859. At Tübingen, Notz pursued studies in theology, philosophy, and philology and was awarded the Doctor of Philosophy degree in 1863. At that time he also passed the theological examination required for entrance into the Lutheran ministerium.

Notz stayed at the University of Tübingen for an additional year after he earned the doctorate. During that year he continued to work in the area of classical philology and also pursued the

---

[2] Nineteenth-century German schools operated on a track system which required that pupils make decisions affecting their future education at a very young age. The German Gymnasium was a nine-year program. It emphasized the study of Latin and Greek and was the generally preferred route to matriculation at universities. Boys entered the Gymnasium at about age 9, after having acquired basic literacy skills at an elementary school or through private instruction.

study of pedagogy. He served a pastoral internship under the supervision of his father and then became a private tutor for a German noble family. When that family emigrated to the United States in 1866, Notz remained with the family as tutor and accompanied them to Georgia. A vacant German professorship at Pennsylvania College in Gettysburg, a school of the Pennsylvania Synod, resulted in a temporary appointment for Notz to that position for the 1868-69 school year. The vacancy was filled permanently in the following year with the appointment of Adam Martin, first president of the Wisconsin Synod's Northwestern University (College) in Watertown, to which Notz himself would be called in 1872.[3] Between 1869 and 1872, Notz held a professorship of German at Muhlenberg College in Allentown, Pennsylvania, and then moved to Watertown, Wisconsin, where for 40 years he taught Greek and Hebrew to prospective Lutheran pastors. Upon his death in 1921, the Missouri Synod's *Der Lutheraner* (The Lutheran) commented:

> In addition to his teaching activity in which Dr. F. W. A. Notz prepared most of the pastors of the Wisconsin Synod and also many who are now working in our synod [Missouri] for their later calling, he also was prominent as a writer, in particular through his translation [from Latin into German] of the so-called *Large Catechism* of Dietrich, a project which he undertook at the instigation of Dr. Walther.[4]

---

[3] On Adam Martin, see E. S. Breidenbaugh, *The Pennsylvania College Book, 1832-1882* (Philadelphia: Lutheran Publication Society, 1882), 173, and E. E. Kowalke, *Centennial Story* (Milwaukee: Northwestern, 1965), 121.

[4] *Der Lutheraner*, January 10, 1922, 7.

A classical scholar, Notz was a major force in the shaping of the pre-seminary curriculum at the Wisconsin Synod's Northwestern College. The 1872-73 college catalog included a lengthy essay written by him in Latin on what he considered to be the curricular essentials for colleges of the Lutheran church. As editor of the *Schulzeitung*, however, his audience was primarily elementary Lutheran parochial school teachers and parish pastors. When in 1889 citizens in the state of Wisconsin became embroiled in a political controversy involving parochial schools, Notz was among those selected to speak for Lutherans in the state capital.[5] After the controversy he was named school secretary for the Wisconsin Synod, a part-time assignment which he carried out from his professor's chair in Watertown. Ill health forced him to retire in 1912, although after his retirement he was appointed to the board of regents of the University of Wisconsin in Madison. In an age when academic doctorates were not as common in higher education in the United States as they are today, F. W. A. Notz with his doctorate from Tübingen possessed scholarly credentials which were somewhat out of the ordinary, especially on the American frontier. When the Teachers' Conference of the Evangelical Lutheran Wisconsin Synod chose him to edit their educational journal in 1876, they put the periodical's editorial duties into the hands of an exceptionally erudite man.[6]

In the Foreword to the first issue of the *Schulzeitung*, Notz explained why he thought that a new educational magazine was needed and what its goals should be. He admitted that in the course of recent years "the number of school periodicals . . . in Germany as well as in the United States" had "become so large

---

[5] For a detailed description of the controversy, see chapter 11 (1889) of the present volume.

[6] On Frederick W. A. Notz, see S. E. Ochsenford, *Muhlenberg College* (Allentown, PA: Muhlenberg College, 1892), 219, and E. E. Kowalke, *Centennial Story* (Milwaukee: Northwestern, 1965), 76-77, 125-26.

that an increase of the same, especially under the financially depressed conditions of the time, could be seen as unnecessary."[7] The editor maintained, however, that the number of periodicals which addressed educational and instructional matters "on the proper foundation, namely, upon the pure and unadulterated Word of God" were few.[8] To the ranks of these few journals the *Schulzeitung* was to be added. It was the intent of the editor to produce a periodical which would encourage Lutheran school teachers in their church calling and provide them with practical suggestions for their work. Lutheran teachers' conferences, of course, attempted to do the same, but, as Notz pointed out, the interval between conferences was often considerable, and at times circumstances prevented a number of teachers from attending a given conference. A regular magazine designed specifically for the Lutheran parochial school teachers in the Wisconsin Synod was deemed necessary, therefore, for the professional growth of these teachers and the advancement of their schools.

The well-being of Christian schools was to be the primary business of the *Schulzeitung*. The editor was concerned

> not only that the Word of God itself be duly studied in them but also that the skill and knowledge which are especially necessary and profitable for family living and dutiful citizenship—and for that reason always to be cultivated by the church—be diligently and thoroughly learned.[9]

Readers of the *Schulzeitung* were informed that they could expect a two-pronged approach to the discussion of educational

---

[7] *Schulzeitung*, February 1876, 1.

[8] Ibid., 3.

[9] Ibid.

matters. Drawing upon the Old Testament for an analogy, the editor wrote:

> In Nehemiah chapter 4 it is written about the Israelites who were building their city: "With one hand they did their work and with the other they held their weapons. Everyone who was building had attached his sword to his side and in that way built." Likewise we also are not only to teach what is right but are also to fight against that which is wrong.[10]

Editor Notz then elaborated on the appropriate way to address that which was seen as incompatible with Christian education. Criticism was expected to rise above mere faultfinding and negativism. The principles underlying positions or practices criticized were to be carefully examined and refuted on the basis of premises acceptable to the church. Several places were seen as the points of origin from which such unacceptable educational philosophies and practices might arise. Not the least among these sources was what the *Schulzeitung* editor called the open and secret enemies of the Christian school system. In addition to promising to defend the parochial school against such opposition, the *Schulzeitung* was determined not to be deceived by what might seem to be learning when in reality it was contrary to genuine Christian teaching. There would be warnings also against a materialism which sought to dethrone the triune God and convert parents, teachers, and pupils to heathenism and idolatry. The Foreword to the first issue of the *Schulzeitung* made it quite clear that the magazine would not hesitate to be polemical when it thought that its readers should be put on guard.

The launching in 1876 of a monthly educational journal by teachers of the Wisconsin Synod was an ambitious undertaking.

---

[10] Ibid.

The challenges of the task become apparent when one considers that the editor was a full-time college professor and that the publication's sponsoring group and audience were extremely small. The Wisconsin Synod synodical report for 1876 lists a total of only 29 teachers in the Synod, and even when one adds the 68 ordained clergy to that number, the professional group was still under 100. These pastors and teachers, according to the statistical report, were conducting 82 parochial schools (*Gemeindeschulen*). One can understand the desire for a professional journal but recognizes that the readership and the number of potential authors were very limited. This meant, as it did also in the case of the Missouri Synod's *Schulblatt* (School Journal), that much work would inevitably fall upon the shoulders of the editor.

Wisconsin's F. W. A. Notz seems to have been aware of the formidable task which he had agreed to undertake. He saw it, however, as a service in the mission of the church and subtly reflected that conviction in the way he dated his Foreword to the initial issue of the *Schulzeitung*. He noted that his introductory remarks were written on the "Second Sunday after the Day of the Epiphany of Christ." For encouragement to execute his assignment as the editor of a school paper in the church, Notz looked to a word from Holy Scripture and concluded his introductory comments by saying:

> That which gives us courage and joy to carry on the work of founding, improving, and increasing the number of orthodox elementary and high schools, that which encourages the publishers of this periodical to undertake publication, that, finally, which also moved the undersigned to assume the editorship and which, as long as such editorship remains in his hands, will be his guide is the revealed Word of our triune God who says in

Jeremiah chapter 15 . . . "If you cling to me, then I will remain faithful to you and you shall be my preacher. . . ."[11]

The conviction that the parochial school was an integral part of the work of the church, and thus an undertaking in the name of the Lord, was strong among nineteenth-century advocates of that educational enterprise. Spokesmen for the cause were not hesitant to express their belief and were strongly motivated by it. F. W. A. Notz, pioneer editor of the *Schulzeitung*, was one such person. Undertaking a difficult editorial task, he relied upon the Lord of the church for assistance and took up his assignment with this kind of enthusiasm:

> So then, since we have . . . a precious Word of God—
> "Let him who is able lay hold and go straight at it. Lazy hands will have a bad year."[12]

In addition to articles dealing with practical and theoretical matters in education, the *Schulzeitung* included a regular feature entitled "News" (*Nachrichten*). The column reported and also commented on educational issues and events in both the United States and Europe and gives evidence that the contributors to the Wisconsin Synod journal were not living in isolation. The journal brought a wide variety of items to the attention of its readers, many of whom would have been living and teaching in small Wisconsin communities and rural areas. For such readers the news column was a window to the larger world of schools and schooling.

The news column of the first issue (February 1876) supplied school statistics for four of the six synods in the Synodical Conference. The Minnesota and Illinois Synods were very likely not included because they were not maintaining schools of higher

[11] Ibid., 4.
[12] Ibid., 5.

learning. The statistical summary provides a good picture of what was going on in the area of higher education in the Lutheran synods of the Midwest in 1875 by reporting the following:

> Concerning the state of the school system within the Evangelical Lutheran Synodical Conference of North America in the 1874-75 school year we learn the following from the reports which we have in hand.
>
> The Synod of Missouri records among institutions of higher learning: 1. a theoretical theological seminary in St. Louis with 5 professors and 74 students; 2. a practical theological seminary located since the beginning of the present school year in Springfield, Ill., with 2 professors and 71 students and in conjunction with a pre-seminary which has 1 teacher and 23 pupils; 3. Concordia College in Fort Wayne, Ind., a six-class Gymnasium with 7 professors and 275 pupils; 4. the Teachers Seminary in Addison, Ill., with 5 teachers and 113 pupils; 5. the Lower Seminary in Steeden in Germany. In addition there also are: 1 secondary school in St. Louis, 3 orphan homes, and 1 deaf institute. The list of parochial school teachers contains 352 names.
>
> The Ohio synod has an institution of higher learning, Capital University, in Columbus, Ohio. The institution is a college combined with a theological seminary. The number of professors totals 6.
>
> The Wisconsin Synod owns Northwestern University in Watertown, Wis., an institution consisting of a complete Gymnasium with a seven-year course of study and a Realschule [a non-classical program of higher education]. The two divisions have a combined total of 7 professors

and 181 pupils. The number of students studying theology at St. Louis and Springfield comes to 11. The Synod recorded a total of 85 parochial schools in its last synodical report.

The Norwegian Synod operates: 1. Norwegian Lutheran College at Decorah, Iowa, a Gymnasium with 8 teachers and about 260 pupils; 2. St. Olaf's Secondary School in Northfield, Minn., with 2 teachers and 40 pupils. In addition, the Synod supports a professor of theology at each of the above-named seminaries in St. Louis and Springfield, at which it has 31 students. In its last synodical convention it was decided to erect a teachers seminary. The establishment of its own theological seminary was also given consideration at that time.[13]

As is apparent from the statistical data, only the Missouri Synod was operating a college in 1875 designed solely for the purpose of training parochial school teachers, although the Norwegian Synod had gone on record as wanting to do the same. For whatever reason, the *Schulzeitung* gave parochial school statistics for the Missouri and Wisconsin Synods only. Missouri had a teacher roster of 352, a sizable number, and Wisconsin could count 85 parochial schools. Subsequent history would show that the parochial school movement continued to grow in these two synods while losing ground in other Lutheran groups.

It is reasonable to assume that Lutheran congregations operate parochial schools because of the conviction that something takes place in them which cannot be accomplished in other educational settings. What is the purpose of the Lutheran parochial school? is a question which has been asked throughout the history of the institution. The third issue of *Schulzeitung*

---

[13] Ibid., 14-15.

(April 1876) published an article addressing that question in the context of the last part of the nineteenth century. Entitled "Why do we have parochial schools?" and written in German by A. Warnecke, a Lutheran school teacher in Milwaukee, the essay championed such schools for three reasons.

As was the case with many nineteenth-century advocates of the parochial school, the *Schulzeitung* essayist quoted from Martin Luther and contended that the Reformer was the founder of the modern Christian school movement. The essayist maintained that "the care for the education of children, the responsibility, namely, to advance them in all Christian knowledge as well as in all other fields of knowledge and learning, rests first of all upon parents (Ephesians 6:4)."[14] Parochial schools existed to assist parents in their duty and were able to do what public schools could not do because the latter "do not have the proper means for child rearing, the Word of God."[15] Since parents were not totally able to fulfill their responsibilities, parochial schools were partners with parents. In those fields of knowledge which were necessary for daily living, parochial schools were not to be in any way inferior to public schools. Congregations had the obligation to "make it their aim to develop their schools in all respects, to call only capable and competent teachers, to provide good and necessary teaching equipment, and above all to send their children to school diligently and regularly."[16]

Besides helping parents to carry out their God-given responsibilities to educate their children, parochial schools, according to the *Schulzeitung* essayist, were a means by which to preserve and extend the church. The writer argued that Lutheran congregations in the past had grown as a result of immigration from Germany but that such immigration was now

---

[14] *Schulzeitung*, April 1876, 35.

[15] Ibid., 36.

[16] Ibid.

on the decline. Parochial schools, therefore, would become an ever more necessary agency for congregational growth:

> Until now our Lutheran congregations have achieved their membership growth for the most part through immigrants, particularly here in the West, in the city as well as in the country. All of us know, however, that immigration from Germany has decreased very significantly in the last years. That will perhaps be the case even more if bad times continue here and conditions improve there. In addition, it is well-known that the government in Germany is seeking in every way to hinder emigration and make it difficult. Is it to be expected that the growth which has been experienced in our congregations until now can continue in spite of the decline in the number of immigrants? Certainly not! We will have to consider . . . attracting young members to us for our congregations and by no means merely because it is wise and practical or necessary for the self-preservation of our congregations but simply because it is our sacred duty and God's Word. God is able to build His kingdom without us, but it is His holy will to build it through us.[17]

Both Christian duty and practicality lay behind Teacher Warnecke's remarks as he made his case for the parochial school as an agency for church growth.

Lutheran schools in 1876, according to essayist Warnecke, were also expected to carry out one additional function. They were to be nurseries of German language and culture. This objective of the Lutheran elementary school was not always too readily admitted by nineteenth-century advocates of the institution, especially when the schools were under criticism. It is informative, therefore, to be able to find a clear and forthright

---

[17] Ibid., 36-37.

admission of this educational goal for parish schools. The Lutheran teacher from Milwaukee wrote:

> Our parochial schools are also to be places for the cultivation of the German language. The German school and church must help us preserve our dear mother tongue. The family is not able to do this alone, especially in view of the fact that the young offspring of German families prefer to use the English language rather than the German. In this matter we can expect nothing from the public schools since the German language is only tolerated there and can be thrown out again at any time. So then, if we want to preserve German manners and customs here in America, above all things we dare not give up our German language. To preserve this must also be a major task of our parochial schools.[18]

A little more than a decade later a major controversy would erupt in the states of Wisconsin and Illinois over the use of German as a major teaching medium in parochial schools. Contrary to what the *Schulzeitung* editorial thought might happen, immigration from Germany increased within a few years. Lutheran schools in which German was used extensively would naturally be attractive, at least initially, to newcomers, as were the churches which operated such schools and conducted worship regularly and, in many cases, solely in the German language. The continued influx of German immigrants to the United States in the late nineteenth century did not diminish but encouraged the use of German in midwestern Lutheran churches and schools and kept alive the idea that the cultivation and perpetuation of the German language and German culture was a major goal of Lutheran schools.

---

[18] Ibid., 37.

On the other hand, everything was not one-sided in connection with the use of German. Thus, for example, the author of an article in the May 1877 issue of the *Schulzeitung* (School Periodical) took issue with a position espoused in the February issue of the Missouri Synod's *Schulblatt* (School Journal). The question was whether the subject of arithmetic should be taught in Lutheran schools via English or German. The *Schulblatt* article was titled "Arithmetic—English or German?" The *Schulzeitung* response came under the title "German or English in the Instruction of Arithmetic."

The teacher who wrote the article for the Missouri Synod journal took the position that the German language should be used to teach arithmetic in the lower and middle grades. Having cited his reasons for recommending this, he invited anyone who was not convinced that this was the right approach to share his views with the *Schulblatt*. The Wisconsin Synod writer chose to voice his objection with a *Schulzeitung* article. The *Schulblatt* essayist argued the case from several points of view and then added:

> In conclusion, let us summarize once more our recommendations. Arithmetic instruction should be given in the German language in the lower and middle classes of the elementary school 1) in order to bring pupils to a correct grasp and genuine understanding of arithmetic and 2) in order to allow time for the mother tongue [German] to become the complete possession of our German-American Lutheran youth so that they may not later lose their precious treasure under the many English influences.[19]

The *Schulzeitung* essayist responded at length and was not at all opposed to developing proficiency in German among

---

[19] *Schulblatt*, February 1877, 53.

Lutheran elementary school children. He defended the use of it, for example, in the teaching of the Bible, catechism, hymnody, and even singing. He was convinced, however, that English was still the better medium for imparting a theoretical understanding of arithmetic and the practical use of it. He argued that children were using English regularly in their association with other children and at play and really had no difficulty comprehending the language. In response to the argument that teachers were not always able to communicate mathematical concepts as effectively in English as in German, the essayist considered this to be a defect which ought to be corrected as soon as possible. He also maintained that English was a much simpler language than German and for that reason also better suited to teaching arithmetical concepts and skills. With respect to the entire issue, the conclusion was: "To each his own. If we observe that and give to each language its due, then our schools, with God's help, will prosper well in spite of public schools."[20]

The little debate on the use of English or German in the teaching of arithmetic in Lutheran schools in 1877, fascinating as the discussion is in and of itself, also reflects something about the content of the two nineteenth-century Lutheran educational journals, the Missouri Synod's *Schulblatt* and the Wisconsin Synod's *Schulzeitung*. Dedicated to the cause of the Lutheran parochial school, these magazines included practical methodological materials as well as articles to inform and encourage Lutheran teachers in their calling. The periodicals were a kind of continuing education for those who read them and helped teachers to rise above their own local situations in order to see what other Lutheran teachers were doing and to keep themselves informed on what was happening elsewhere in the field of education.

---

[20] *Schulzeitung*, May 1877, 60.

✤✤✤ 1877 ✤✤✤

Sixth Convention of the Evangelical Lutheran Synodical Conference of North America

As noted under the date 1872 of the present volume, the Evangelical Lutheran Synodical Conference of North America, which was formed in that year, became known in American Lutheranism as an alliance of synods with a strong commitment to the Lutheran parochial school. The advocacy of that cause surfaced early in the organization's history since school matters came up for discussion as part of the agenda of the Conference's sixth convention in 1877.

The original constitution of the Synodical Conference had called for annual meetings of representatives of the member synods, and such meetings were held annually from the time of the constituting convention in 1872 until 1879. In that year the delegates amended the constitution so as to require biennial instead of annual meetings. Although the new schedule should have gone into effect with a convention in 1881, because of disturbances in the association over the doctrine of election, the meeting was postponed until 1882. From that time on, however, until 1966, the Conference met biennially except for two occasions. Meetings were not held in 1918 because of conditions brought on by World War I and the influenza epidemic and also in 1942 during World War II.

Much of the time at Synodical Conference conventions was devoted to theological presentations and discussions. In the year of its founding, for example, the Conference undertook to discuss 12 theses on the biblical doctrine of justification. In the following year, 1873, Wilhelm Sihler of Fort Wayne, Indiana, presented to the assembled delegates a set of 18 theses dealing with theological and ecclesiastical positions and practices of Evangelical Lutheran congregations in relationship to other Christian church bodies. These theses occupied the attention of Synodical Conference conventions until 1879, although theses 17 and 18 never did reach the convention floor.

Theses 12 and 13 came before the convention in 1877. These two theses dealt with the Lutheran parochial school and together with the convention discussion pertaining to that institution reflected the strong commitment held by many in the Synodical Conference to congregational schools (*Gemeindeschulen*) as they existed at that time. The theses read as follows:

Thesis 12

It is exceedingly inconsistent with the church's confessional position if an ecclesiastical body which calls itself Lutheran and wants to be Lutheran does not, to the extent that it is able, show earnestness and zeal to establish orthodox parochial schools where they do not exist.[1]

Thesis 13

It is a further inconsistency with the church's confessional position if a Lutheran fellowship does not insist that in its congregations only orthodox liturgical books, hymnbooks, catechisms, instruction and devotional books be used, or if it does not do its utmost to see to it that unorthodox

---

[1] *Verhandlungen der sechsten Versammlung der evangelisch-lutherischen Synodal-Conferenz von Nord-Amerika* (Proceedings of the Sixth Convention of the Evangelical Lutheran Synodical Conference of North America), 1877, 8.

books of this type be done away with where they are in use and orthodox books be introduced.[2]

The secretary of the 1877 convention was Professor August F. Ernst of the Wisconsin Synod's Northwestern College (University) in Watertown, Wisconsin. President of Northwestern from 1871 until 1919, Ernst was a German-trained theologian and scholar who came to the United States in 1863. His notes of the discussion in 1877 of Sihler's Theses 12 and 13 must have been extremely thorough, for his report of that part of the convention fills 20 pages of the total 52 in the *Proceedings* for the six-day meeting. As might be expected, the bulk of the discussion focused on Thesis 12 which presented the case for the establishment of parochial schools in parishes. On the surface, Thesis 13 seems to be more concerned with liturgical and devotional materials. The secretary's report, however, reflects a concern about the use of orthodox and appropriate reading books in Lutheran schools. Although Thesis 13 did not explain what was meant by instruction books, it should be understood that references of that kind in connection with nineteenth-century Lutheran parochial schools often included books for the teaching of reading as well as textbooks for the study of religion. The record of the convention discussion is evidence of the attention nineteenth-century Lutherans gave to the subject of reading books for Lutheran schools, especially readers for the teaching of English.

The *Proceedings* do not indicate who said what on the 1877 convention floor when the parochial school issue was under discussion. Extensive quotations from Luther and other writers suggest a formal prepared presentation of some sort, but the minutes also include a reporting of some of the floor

---

[2] Ibid., 23.

discussion, as is apparent from the secretary's comments: "Hereupon a pastor from an English district explained . . ." or in another instance, "To this the rejoinder was given."[3] Although specific speakers were not identified, a list of voting and advisory delegates is provided, so that it is known who the convention participants were.

Six synods were represented at the meeting—Missouri, Wisconsin, Ohio, Illinois, Minnesota, and the Norwegian Synod. The delegates were primarily clergy, although teacher and lay representatives were also in attendance. The convention included 106 delegates, 59 of these having voting privileges and 47 being classified as advisory members of the assembly. Some of the leading theological spokesmen of the day participated in the sessions. Representing the Missouri Synod, for example, was C. F. W. Walther, at that time president of the Missouri Synod and the first president of the Synodical Conference itself. Professor Martin Guenther of Concordia Seminary in St. Louis was another Missouri Synod delegate, as was Pastor E. A. Brauer, influential Missouri Synod pastor who had been a Concordia Seminary professor and who for many years was a prolific writer for his synod's well-known periodicals *Der Lutheraner* (The Lutheran) and *Lehre und Wehre* (Teaching and Defense). In addition, Missouri was represented by Pastor H. C. Schwan who was to serve that synod as president from 1878 to 1899.

One of the Wisconsin Synod's representatives was the Conference secretary, August F. Ernst. Joining him were Johannes Bading, Wisconsin's president, Friedrich W. A. Notz of Northwestern College, and also Professors August L. Graebner and Theodore Brohm of Northwestern. The latter two deserve special mention at this point because of their association with both the Wisconsin and Missouri Synods.

---

[3] Ibid., 21.

Graebner first taught at Wisconsin's Northwestern College and then at its seminary. In 1887, he assumed a professorship at Concordia Seminary in St. Louis. Brohm, on the other hand, served at Northwestern from 1871 to 1879 and then joined the faculty of the Missouri Synod's Teachers Seminary in Addison, Illinois, where he became director in 1906.

The Norwegian and Ohio Synods, which within a few years would withdraw from the Synodical Conference during the election controversy, also sent delegates who continued to be prominent spokesmen in their church bodies. These included Ulrik V. Koren who held a number of offices in the Norwegian Synod and eventually became its president in 1894 and Ohio's W. F. Lehmann who was elected president of the Synodical Conference in 1877, was president of the Ohio Synod's seminary for 34 years, and edited that synod's major church periodical from 1859 until his death in 1880. In short, the list of delegates to the 1877 Synodical Conference convention is a kind of who's who in nineteenth-century midwestern Lutheranism. It is that fact which makes the 1877 Synodical Conference convention an especially noteworthy event in the history of the Lutheran parochial school. The participants in the convention were leading spokesmen in their respective synods, and although parochial schools did not exist everywhere in those synods, the record in the *Proceedings* of the convention gives every indication that the general consensus was that such schools were the ideal and ought to be established whenever possible. Inconvenience or cost, moreover, should not be too quickly adduced as deterring factors to the operation of church schools.

In order to interpret fairly the 1877 Synodical Conference convention floor-discussion relative to the congregational school, it is necessary to have a clear picture of several items pertaining to elementary schooling in general at that time. Elementary schools of that era were not expected to do as many things as such schools must do today. In addition, school programs, even in the public sector, were far less regulated then than now. All of this left curriculum decisions, length of school terms, the nature of physical facilities, and the type of teaching materials to the good judgment of whoever was operating a given school. The workings of a school were far less complex in the nineteenth century than in the twentieth. In large and medium-sized Lutheran parishes a teacher or teachers had to be engaged to conduct the parochial school, but in the many smaller parishes, pastors added school teaching to their pastoral responsibilities. Such a combination of duties was possible in an age when the elementary schooling process was simpler than it is in contemporary life.

Leading the list of factors which made the operation of elementary schools simpler in the nineteenth century than today were the laws pertaining to compulsory education. In fact, until 1852, no state in the country had any compulsory school attendance law. As was the case in a number of other educational matters, the state of Massachusetts took the lead and enacted the first compulsory school law. The requirements of that 1852 law were minimal and could be easily circumvented. School attendance was required for only 12 weeks in a year, and only six of those weeks had to be consecutive. The impetus for such legislation came from a concern to curtail abusive child labor practices in a rapidly growing industrial economy, from a humanitarian desire that educational opportunities be made available to all children, and from a patriotic conviction that an educated citizenry is necessary for the well-being of a democratic society.

A number of years passed before any other state followed the lead of Massachusetts. It was in the 1870s and 1880s that state legislatures began to turn their attention to compulsory school legislation. Michigan, for example, enacted in 1871 a law similar to that of Massachusetts. Ohio waited until 1877 to do the same, with Wisconsin, Illinois, and Minnesota following suit in the years 1879, 1883, and 1885 respectively.[4] The state of Missouri enacted its first compulsory school law in 1905. The laws of the various states read much alike, the following statute from the state of Ohio being representative:

AN ACT
To secure to children the benefits
of an elementary education.

SECTION 1. *Be it enacted by the General Assembly of the State of Ohio,* That every parent, guardian, or other person in the state of Ohio, having charge or control of any child or children between the ages of eight and fourteen years, shall be required to send such child or children to a common school for at least twelve weeks in each school year, commencing on the first day of September in the year of our Lord one thousand eight hundred and seventy-seven, at least six weeks of which shall be consecutive, unless the board of local directors, or the board of education, as the case may be, having control of the school district or sub-district in which such parent or guardian shall reside, shall excuse such child from attendance on its being shown to their satisfaction that the child's bodily or mental condition is such as to prevent its attendance at school or application to study for the time required, or that its time and labor are essentially necessary for the support of an indigent parent, brother, or sister, or that such child is being otherwise furnished with the means of education for a like period of time, or has already acquired branches of learning ordinarily taught in common schools: provided, in case the common

---

[4] Edgar W. Knight and Clifton F. Hall, *Readings in American Educational History* (New York: Appleton-Century-Crofts, Inc., 1951), 366.

school of the district in which such parent or guardian resides shall be distant two miles from his residence by the nearest traveled road, he shall not be liable to the provisions of this act.[5]

The absence of compulsory school attendance laws gave to churches in the first three-fourths of the nineteenth century the freedom to operate their own schools as the congregations chose and to design those schools as best fitted local circumstances. Moreover, even after the first compulsory attendance laws were enacted, they imposed minimal requirements. No more than 12 weeks of schooling during a year, with only six being consecutive, allowed for much flexibility in the scheduling of school terms. It is to be expected, of course, that minimum standards were undoubtedly exceeded, particularly in urban areas, but it is also highly likely that in numerous places only minimal requirements were met. Limited or no legally prescribed school attendance regulations made it possible for a pastor serving more than one congregation to dovetail school terms so that he could teach at more than one place in a given year. In cities it also happened that a congregation would accommodate the children of an expanding parish by establishing a satellite school at some distance from the church and main school. Less stringent attendance requirements made such arrangements workable, and the entire situation explains parish statistical tables of that time which in some cases reported more than one parochial or congregational school (*Gemeindeschule*) under the name of a given pastor.[6]

---

[5] Ohio, *Compulsory School Act*, Statutes (1877), 57-58.

[6] An example of that kind of table can be seen in the 1887 *Proceedings* (*Verhandlungen*) of the Wisconsin Synod, 86-88.

Not only were nineteenth-century school sessions shorter than they are today, but elementary school programs of the time, both parochial and public, were also different from their contemporary counterparts in that elementary schools limited themselves to the teaching of basic skills in reading, writing, and arithmetic. To this regimen Lutheran schools, of course, added religion. Educational reformers toward the end of the century were beginning to advocate a more comprehensive curriculum. It would seem fair to assume, however, that the champions of the parochial school at the 1877 convention of the Synodical Conference were thinking more in terms of past elementary school practices rather than in what was being proposed in some quarters for the future, for church schools generally tend to be more traditional than avant-garde in matters of curricular reform. In any case, a knowledge of compulsory school attendance laws in the 1800s and an understanding of what was ordinarily the curriculum in common schools of the time are helpful when examining Theses 12 and 13 of the 1877 convention of the Synodical Conference and when interpreting the discussion of those theses. It is to the convention discussion that we now proceed.

The secretary's commentary on the presentation and discussion of the parochial school issue before the convention makes it clear that Luther's writings on the subject of schools were considered foundational to the topic at hand.[7] The Reformer was referred to and quoted extensively, although not always with a recognition that the schools he spoke about in his two educational treatises were classical language schools with a curriculum, the study of religion excepted, quite different from that of the Lutheran parochial schools of America's nineteenth century. It was stated that Luther's works had been published in America, but that they were not enjoying a wide

---

[7] A review of these documents appears in chapters 1 (1524) and 3 (1530) of the present volume.

circulation outside of the Missouri Synod. Wider distribution and use of Luther's writings, it was alleged, would aid the cause of parochial schools immensely. It was admitted that when Luther advocated the establishment of Christian schools he was addressing his remarks "To the Councilmen of All Cities in Germany," to civic officials in other words. This was taken note of on the 1877 Synodical Conference convention floor and interpreted for the American parish school setting in the following way:

> In this connection it is to be noted that "councilmen" and "council" must be rendered "congregation member" and "congregation," for at Luther's time the councilmen were Lutheran. In our country, however, we have the so-called representative system of government. For that reason the office of councilmen has been transferred to the members of the congregation.[8]

In addition to that interpretation of Luther's well-known treatise, it was maintained that children belong not only to parents but also to the church, since at their Baptism children become members of the church. For that reason, the church has an obligation to provide for the religious instruction of its baptized children.

It should not be assumed, however, that the synods of the Synodical Conference in 1877 intended their parochial schools only for congregation members. The church of that day was also interested in outreach to nonmembers and in using parish schools for that purpose, as is apparent from the following statement in the Conference's *Proceedings*:

---

[8] *Verhandlungen . . . der evangelisch-lutherischen Synodal-Conferenz von Nord-Amerika* (Proceedings . . . of the Evangelical Lutheran Synodical Conference of North America), 1877, 11-12.

An additional major reason which should spur us on to establish parochial schools is also the mission work which we are thereby able to carry on among the children of those people who do not belong to our church. Experience teaches that many such children can be won and that after confirmation they still remain faithful. . . . For that reason, a congregation must be willing to pay the price to erect schools and also not to require a higher school tax from those who are not members of the congregation. In this way we can conduct a great mission activity and through the children win the parents themselves.[9]

Because of the extensive use of the German language in Lutheran elementary schools, the outreach activity spoken of would had to have been directed to children who had basic proficiency in that language. The large numbers of German immigrants coming to the Midwest at various times in the nineteenth century and into the early twentieth provided a ready source from which to draw, although church mission work might not have been as easy as is sometimes assumed. Protestant immigrants from Germany came from a state church which embraced both Lutheran and Reformed theology. The synods of the Synodical Conference were committed to Lutheran theological positions and were not amenable to union efforts with adherents of Reformed theology. It is to be expected, therefore, that Lutheran parish schools would have taught religion from a specifically Lutheran point of view. The Lutheran parochial school was seen as an agency of the church and, as such, a place to teach the rising generation the doctrines and practices of the sponsoring congregation. Children from unchurched or non-Lutheran families were welcomed into

---

[9] Ibid., 17.

Lutheran schools, but it was the hope that through the schools both the children and their parents might be won for the Lutheran church.

The extensive discussion devoted to the topic of the parochial school at a church convention suggests that there might have been some anxiety relative to the general well-being of that type of school. Although not too many compulsory education laws had been passed by states prior to 1877, the legislation was in the air. Perceptive advocates of the Lutheran elementary school could very likely see the implication of such laws for the operation of church schools. From the present vantage point, prescribed school terms of 12 weeks, with only six of those weeks being consecutive, would hardly be seen as threatening to a private school. The fact of the matter is, however, that parish schools of the time were not always meeting those criteria, and some would perhaps not be able to meet them. Nothing is reported about this in the *Proceedings* of the 1877 Synodical Conference convention, but mention is made of the fact that the parochial school was not flourishing in the other two major Lutheran federations, the General Synod and the General Council. With respect to the former, the secretary, acknowledging first that pastors who conducted parochial schools were taking upon themselves additional burdens, commented:

> In the General Synod the pastors do not indeed put themselves to much trouble. We in the Synodical Conference, however, realize our assignment, God be praised! Because of this, our office does indeed become more difficult. . . . It is difficult, to be sure, to conduct schools, but God will give the reward if we do it for the sake of the children and the kingdom of God.[10]

---

[10] Ibid., 15.

Convention discussion relative to the obstacles standing in the way of establishing and operating parish schools seems to have been quite blunt at times. In fact, one senses that some speakers took rather strong positions and spoke perhaps a bit too uncompromisingly on the issues involved. That, at least, is what appears to lie behind the following inclusion in the convention secretary's minutes:

> To this the rejoinder was given that we Lutherans of the Synodical Conference are no legalists. One need only observe the wording of the thesis. It reads: "It is exceedingly inconsistent with the church's confessional position if an ecclesiastical body does not show earnestness and zeal, *to the extent that it is able* [emphasis in the original], to establish orthodox parochial schools." More cannot be required of a pastor than that he do as much as he is able. If, then, the actual achievement is hindered . . . the fault is not the pastor's. We do not reject synods which do not as yet have parochial schools, but earnestness and zeal must be found among them. They must not . . . take their hand from the plow.[11]

It was also recognized that "the mandate to establish parochial schools is no command specifically given in God's Word, but that the mandate is deduced through conclusions based on the divine Word."[12] It was similarly admitted that "it does not appear in direct words, of course, in the [Lutheran] Confessions that we must have parochial schools," but quickly upon that concession came the remark that "it does lie in the spirit of these Confessions, for we are to take care that God's

---

[11] Ibid., 21-22.

[12] Ibid., 20.

Word is preserved also for those who come after us."[13] And if one is looking for a really dogmatic statement, this comment should do:

> We ought to clothe the whole land with a net of Christian schools and shrink from no toil or sacrifice to achieve this noble goal. And if parents do not send their children, then one must finally exercise church discipline against them.[14]

Opinions like these were expressed with reference to what was known as the Lutheran parochial school (*Gemeindeschule*). The judgments were made, however, within the context of educational institutions and practices in the last decades of the nineteenth century when schools were different from what they are today. Elementary schools of the time were expected to deal only with the most basic tasks of functional literacy, public education was regulated only minimally, and the term parochial school (*Gemeindeschule*, i.e., congregational school) was used for confirmation-type schools which taught some reading and writing as well as for parish schools which had more extensive programs. It would be a mistake, therefore, to try to make a case for the parochial school today by citing past arguments for such a school without giving due attention to the earlier context. On the other hand, it is also not right to be overly critical of nineteenth-century Lutheran parochial school advocates who spoke so uncompromisingly at times in behalf of the institution. Their remarks reveal an intense desire to provide a thorough religious education for their children, and from such zeal, appropriately modified to meet changing circumstances and conditions, there developed the vigorous

---

[13] Ibid., 13.
[14] Ibid., 16.

parochial system for which both The Lutheran Church—Missouri Synod and the Wisconsin Evangelical Lutheran Synod are still known.

Late nineteenth-century parochial school advocates were convinced that public schools did not have the means to provide Christian children with a proper education because that could take place only "through the Word of God,"[15] which could not be employed as a teaching medium in the public school. In addition, it was argued that if inexperienced children are sent to public schools, "these children, apart from the secularization to which they fall, are bound inevitably to become religiously unionistic."[16] The Sunday school, moreover, was not considered a satisfactory complement to the education which children received in the public school. Sunday schools "are an extremely shabby substitute [for the parochial school taught by a Lutheran teacher or pastor] because never can the lambs of Christ be fed in them as the Lord has commanded."[17]

A concern was expressed in the convention that the assessment of the public school was sometimes too severe, since there were those who occasionally labeled that institution a school of the devil and a place to which it was sinful to send one's children. In that connection the comment was made that "Christians should . . . be friends of the public schools . . . because also in them a God-pleasing work is accomplished."[18] For that reason, Lutheran Christians should be willing to pay taxes for the support of public schools. For those who might possibly have had a question about the propriety of doing that, the following explanation was given:

---

[15] Ibid., 18.

[16] Ibid., 13.

[17] Ibid., 8.

[18] Ibid., 18.

> If one considers correctly the distinction between church
> and state, the answer can be easily given. The state has to
> make some arrangements which we Christians may not
> use. The state, for example, must permit divorces which
> the church forbids. . . . No Christian, however, may make
> use of this permission of the state. Even as we pay what is
> their due to public officials who assist in such divorces,
> although they are involved in proceedings which they as
> Christians may have nothing to do with themselves, so
> also we may pay our school taxes. . . .
>
> We pay our taxes for schools the same as for
> penitentiaries, although we also do not use the latter. This
> comparison addresses those who incorrectly think that
> because we pay for public schools we must also use
> them.[19]

It is apparent that the issue was not the existence of a public
school but rather the use of the parochial school as the
institution of choice for children of Lutheran parents. The
Synodical Conference was not interested in doing away with
public common schools but seeking rather to encourage pastors
and congregations to conduct parochial schools and urging
Lutheran parents to send their children to such schools.

Discussion of Thesis 12 having been completed, the
convention proceeded to Thesis 13. This thesis was not
examined as thoroughly as the preceding and on the surface
seems to deal only incidentally with school matters since
liturgical books and hymnbooks stand at the head of the list of
items for convention consideration. Attention was given
immediately, however, to reading books, indicating that the
term instruction books in the thesis was a reference to the kinds
of materials used for reading instruction. That such books

---

[19] Ibid., 22-23.

should be talked about first was quite natural since the convention had just spent much time on the topic of schooling.

The attention of the assembled delegates was directed to the content of the textbooks used in classrooms for the teaching of reading in both German and English. The question at issue was the doctrinal orthodoxy of reading books in use in Lutheran classrooms. It was lamented that no Synodical Conference synod was without a problem in this area and that difficulties arose because of the arrogance of some teachers who selected books merely because they preferred one methodology over another and were seemingly unconcerned about the religious accents in reading materials. With respect to German readers, it was admitted that an earlier book in use in the Missouri Synod did suffer from methodological deficiencies but that this had now been corrected, so that there was now no excuse for using an unorthodox book.

The situation with reading books in English was felt to be a different story. Not that English reading books were not readily available. The famed *McGuffey Eclectic Readers*, for example, had been around since 1836. This popular reading series and others did not pass Lutheran doctrinal review, for, in spite of McGuffey and other series of readers, it was still claimed that there was a dearth of orthodox materials for the teaching of English reading. To remedy the situation, both warning and appeal were expressed:

> The books for the lower grades, apart from the *Primer* which was issued by the Synodical Conference and which is good, may be used to some extent, but the books for the upper grades are exceptionally dangerous. That had already become a matter of conscience for many teachers, and for that reason they are longingly waiting for new good English textbooks. Every person in the Synodical Conference who has received the gifts from God should

help, therefore, so that this need is remedied. This situation is becoming an indictment before the church. We would be willing gladly to content ourselves with a modest book if it were only pure. Let us consider what Peter says in 1 Peter 2:2: "Like newborn babes, long for the pure spiritual milk that by it you may grow up to salvation." What mother would pour vinegar or poison into her child's milk? Woe to us if we allow the slightest poison to enter into our schoolbooks for children not of age. That would be much worse than if a liturgical book which is not pure were used somewhere; in such a case the pastor can still be selective of what he uses.[20]

That was the verdict on books for the teaching of reading in English. The literature included in school readers was expected to support and be congruent with Lutheran doctrine. The same expectation prevailed also for songbooks, for the convention was informed that

in the schools a number of religious as well as secular songs are sung which are absolutely atrocious. Pastors should exercise a watchful eye also in such matters.[21]

The Synodical Conference considered doctrinal supervision to be a matter of paramount importance in all areas of the school curriculum.

The 1877 convention was not the only meeting in which Synodical Conference delegates addressed parochial school issues. Such concerns surfaced periodically. Two examples, separated from each other by a good number of years and far removed from 1877, will suffice to illustrate the point. In 1900,

---

[20] Ibid., 24.
[21] Ibid., 25.

Johannes Schaller read an essay to a Synodical Conference convention in Bay City, Michigan. Delivered and printed in German, the essay also appeared in English under the title "The Need of Christian Education by Means of Parochial Schools." The essayist was the son of a Concordia Seminary professor in St. Louis, had served Missouri Synod parishes in Little Rock, Arkansas, and Cape Girardeau, Missouri, and in 1889 became a seminary professor in the Minnesota Synod's theological seminary at New Ulm, Minnesota. When, in a reorganization move, that seminary was designated the teachers college of the federated Wisconsin Synod, Schaller was appointed director of the institution. He was later called to a theological professorship at the Wisconsin Synod's theological seminary in Wauwatosa. It was as a member of the Minnesota Synod, however, and in his capacity as director of the teacher-training institution known as Dr. Martin Luther College in New Ulm that he presented his essay which was later reproduced in pamphlet form in both English and German and printed by the Missouri Synod's Concordia Publishing House. The separate publication in both English and German of the Schaller essay suggests that his views on the parochial school were well received at the Synodical Conference convention and shared by others. He was a leading spokesman for the cause.

In 1920, the Conference heard the first part of another essay on the subject and then continued the presentation and discussion in 1922. Entitled "Der Kampf um unser Schulwesen" ("The battle for our system of schooling"), the essay was delivered by Professor Joh. P. Meyer, a faculty member at the Wisconsin Synod's theological seminary in Wauwatosa. The presentation on this occasion came at a time when parochial schools, both Lutheran and Catholic, were contending against state legislative acts which eventually resulted in two landmark United States Supreme Court decisions. Those two cases, *Meyer v. Nebraska* and *Pierce, Governor of Oregon v. Society of Sisters*, will be reviewed separately. At the moment the point is that conventions of the Evangelical Lutheran Synodical Conference of North America devoted time periodically to parochial school issues. The report on the discussion of two theses pertaining to education at the 1877 convention reveals a deep commitment to the Lutheran parish school (*Gemeindeschule*) as it existed then. Time brought changes in schooling and certain types of parish schools closed their doors in the course of time. Where that was not necessary, however, the Synodical Conference throughout its history could be counted on to encourage the establishment and maintenance of Lutheran parochial schools.

✛ ✛ ✛ 1884 ✛ ✛ ✛

Dr. Martin Luther College
New Ulm, Minnesota

The matter of obtaining adequately trained pastors for parishes remained a problem for Lutherans regardless of where or when they established churches on American soil. Initially, of course, European sources had to be relied on for pastoral candidates, but it was uniformly recognized by all Lutheran synods that congregations in the New World would have to make provisions for the training of their own clergy. This resulted in the establishment at various times of schools for theological education. Saxon Lutheran immigrants to Missouri began an institution for that purpose even before they joined with other Lutherans to form what is today known as The Lutheran Church—Missouri Synod. Located in Perry County, Missouri, the school opened in 1839, was both college and seminary, and eventually became Concordia Seminary in St. Louis.

The Wisconsin Synod, one of the charter members with Missouri in the formation of the Synodical Conference in 1872, did not get as early a start in higher education as did the Missouri Synod. Organized in 1850 with only three pastors, the Wisconsin Synod was nevertheless ready to begin a program of theological education in 1863. In that year, the small Synod engaged a theological professor who began a seminary course of study in his home in Watertown, Wisconsin. When the Synod opened its Northwestern University in Watertown two years later, the seminary became a department of that institution and functioned in that place from 1865 to 1870. At that time the Wisconsin Synod closed its Watertown seminary program for a period of eight years and used the educational facilities of the Missouri Synod's seminary in St. Louis. When the Wisconsin Synod reopened its theological seminary in 1878, it relocated the institution to Milwaukee.

In their early history both the Wisconsin and Missouri Synods trained prospective Lutheran parochial school teachers at the pre-theological institutions of the Synods. Missouri did this at Fort Wayne; Wisconsin did it at Watertown. In both cases, the arrangement was not seen as being totally satisfactory. The teacher-education programs were not the primary focus of the institutions at which the prospective teachers were being trained and, in addition, the supply of teacher candidates was insufficient to meet the needs of the parochial schools in the respective church bodies. The Missouri Synod addressed the problem by establishing a separate teacher-training institution in Addison, Illinois, in 1864. Wisconsin had to wait until 1893 to do the same, although a history of Dr. Martin Luther College reports that the *Gemeindeblatt* (Congregational Journal), the official periodical of the Wisconsin Synod, called for an improvement in the condition of parochial schools in 1872 already and said of some of the teachers that they were "an unhappy mixture . . . from here and there who studied this and that."[1] Conditions such as that needed correction, of course, but the problem was not unique to Lutheran education. Public schools of the time were also compelled to engage teachers with varied educational backgrounds, since teacher-training and certification in the United States were still in their infant stages at the end of the nineteenth century and were regulated by very uneven standards.

---

[1] Morton A. Schroeder, *A Time to Remember* (New Ulm, MN: Dr. Martin Luther College, 1984), 37.

A turn of events in 1892 made it possible for the Wisconsin Synod to follow the pattern of its sister Missouri Synod and provide a separate teacher-training facility for itself and for two other synods with which it federated in that year. The institution was Dr. Martin Luther College at New Ulm, Minnesota. DMLC, as the school was popularly known, was founded in 1884 but did not take on its role as a synodical teacher-training school until 1893. From that time on, however, and for a full century thereafter the sole function of the college division of the institution was the training of teachers for the parish school system of what today is known as the Wisconsin Evangelical Lutheran Synod.

When Dr. Martin Luther College at the beginning of the 1893-94 school year assumed its role as an educational institution in which to prepare Lutheran school teachers, it did so as the result of a synodical development which needs to be kept in mind when considering the history of the Wisconsin Evangelical Lutheran Synod. That body is the union of several synods which had independent beginnings. These synods carried the abbreviated names of Wisconsin Synod, Minnesota Synod, Michigan Synod, and Nebraska Synod. Wisconsin, Minnesota, and Michigan formed a federation in 1892 which was called the General Evangelical Lutheran Synod of Wisconsin, Minnesota, Michigan and Other States.[2] The Michigan Synod dropped out of the federation in 1896 but then rejoined in 1910. In the meantime, the Nebraska Synod affiliated with the federation after that Synod's formation in 1904. The synods of the federation carried on a number of activities jointly but were still independent bodies and were called synods until 1917 when they merged into a single synod which then adopted the name Evangelical Lutheran Joint Synod

---

[2] Allgemeine evangelisch-lutherische Synode von Wisconsin, Minnesota, Michigan und andern Staaten.

of Wisconsin and Other States. The federated group, the merged synod, and, of course, the original Synod of Wisconsin and Other States were all often given the shorthand designation Wisconsin Synod, with the result that there is not always an awareness that the Wisconsin Evangelical Lutheran Synod of today (WELS) is in fact the product of a merger of several earlier state synods. The Synod's present name was adopted in 1959.

It was in the federation process of 1892 that Dr. Martin Luther College became a Lutheran teachers college. Each of the three synods which federated in that year owned and operated its own school for theological education. In the case of the Wisconsin Synod two schools were involved, Northwestern University (College) in Watertown and a seminary in Milwaukee. The Michigan Synod, organized in 1860, began its own worker-training program with the founding of Michigan Lutheran Seminary in 1885. After operating at a temporary site for two years, the school was permanently located in Saginaw, Michigan, where it still exists today as a preparatory high school of the WELS. The Minnesota Synod was also organized in the year 1860 and like other synods felt the need to have its own institution of higher education. Plans to establish such a school materialized in 1884 with the opening of Dr. Martin Luther College in New Ulm. That name was chosen because it was at its convention in 1883, the 400th anniversary of the birth of Martin Luther, that the Minnesota Synod voted to establish the school. The college got underway on the anniversary of Luther's birth, November 10, 1884, and had three divisions: a pre-theological course of study, a theological seminary, and an academy. The building dedicated on that day is still in use by the Wisconsin Synod's Martin Luther College.

When the Wisconsin, Minnesota, and Michigan Synods federated in 1892, it was the intent to consolidate the higher educational efforts of the three synods. The complete plan did not materialize because the Michigan Synod insisted on keeping its own theological seminary in Saginaw and operated it until 1907, for four years, in other words, while Michigan was a member of the federation and for another 11 years when it was not an affiliate. When the Michigan Synod later rejoined the federation in 1910, the Saginaw school became a preparatory high school for the purpose of providing secondary education to students who desired to matriculate in the worker-training colleges of the federated synod. Although only a high school, the Saginaw institution has continued to operate under the name Michigan Lutheran Seminary.

The Wisconsin and Minnesota Synods did realign and consolidate their institutions of higher education in 1892, even though Michigan did not close its seminary. Wisconsin moved its Milwaukee seminary to the suburb of Wauwatosa and dedicated a new building in that city in September 1893. Minnesota closed its theological seminary in New Ulm and made its Dr. Martin Luther College available as a college for the training of prospective Lutheran school teachers. Classes under the new arrangement also began in September 1893. Northwestern at Watertown discontinued its teacher education course of study and concentrated on the task of providing a baccalaureate degree program with a strong emphasis on the study of classical and biblical languages and the humanities as a preparation for entrance into the federated Synod's seminary. Attached to both schools were college-preparatory high school departments.

A change of administration also occurred at Dr. Martin Luther College when it took on its role as a teacher-training school, or normal school as colleges for teacher education were called in those days. Johannes (John) Schaller had joined the theological faculty of the Minnesota Synod's seminary department in New Ulm in 1889. He was the son of a Missouri Synod pastor, who later became a professor at Concordia

Seminary in St. Louis. From 1881 until 1889, John Schaller himself had also served as a parish pastor in the Missouri Synod. Born in the United States, he received his college education at Northwestern in Watertown and his seminary training at Concordia in St. Louis during the days when C. F. W. Walther was still active as a professor at that institution. Schaller was a staunch advocate of the Lutheran parochial school and a distinguished theologian who, although he lived only until the age of 60, left behind a legacy of several books used in the training of both pastors and teachers in the early part of the twentieth century. His introduction to the books of the Bible, originally written in German, was translated into English by him under the title *Book of Books* and with some contemporary revisions is still available from Northwestern Publishing House. His *Biblical Christology*, part of what was to have been a Christian dogmatics textbook, was written in English originally and is also available from Northwestern Publishing House. In addition, he authored a book on pastoral theology entitled *Pastorale Praxis* (Pastoral Practice). The German edition of *Book of Books* was written while he was director of Dr. Martin Luther College; the translation of that volume and his other works were written after he became president of the Wisconsin Synod's seminary at Wauwatosa.

John Schaller's literary skills and leadership abilities were also recognized by The Lutheran Church—Missouri Synod. At his funeral in 1920, the latter Synod was represented by its president, Friedrich Pfotenhauer, and by representatives from the Missouri Synod seminaries in Springfield, Illinois, and St. Louis, all of whom spoke words of condolence at the funeral. The Missouri Synod's *Lutheran Witness* included the following when it reported Schaller's death:

> By the death of this theologian the Lutheran Church loses a shining light and the Wisconsin Synod one of her ablest

and most versatile leaders. He . . . was [at the time of his unexpected death] . . . in full vigor of body and mind, intensely active as a literary worker, and at the height of his powers as a professor and preacher. Only three months ago he had published his *Christology*, a learned work treating the person and work of Jesus Christ, in which the breadth of the author's erudition and felicity of diction shines at its brightest. It was Prof. Schaller's intention to follow up this work with treatises on the other articles of the Christian faith.[3]

When Schaller assumed leadership of the New Ulm teacher-training school in 1893, the institution consisted of five classes. The three lower classes were preparatory for entrance into the teacher-education program at New Ulm and the pre-ministerial college program at Watertown. The upper two classes were designed for teacher education. In 1903, a fourth preparatory year was added for students who were planning to attend Northwestern College. Significant with respect to teacher education at Dr. Martin Luther College was the fact that women were included in the program. Permission for them to enroll took place during the Schaller presidency in the year 1896 already and was an unusually bold step for the time, since it had been customary among Lutherans of the Synodical Conference as well as in some other circles to think of teaching as a profession intended primarily for men. Thus, for example, the Missouri Synod's Concordia Teachers College at River Forest waited until the late 1930s before it became coeducational.

In 1908, John Schaller accepted a call to become professor and president of the Wisconsin Synod's theological seminary in Wauwatosa, Wisconsin. The decade following his departure

---

[3] *The Lutheran Witness,* March 2, 1920, 69.

as president of Dr. Martin Luther College is called "The Triumphant and Tragic Years" by Morton Schroeder in his centennial history of the institution. The triumph was the construction of two new buildings on campus to join the original structure of 1884 and the improvement of the municipal services to the campus. The tragedy was the abrupt resignation in 1918 of Adolph Ackermann, the school's president, a resignation triggered by the war hysteria which had gripped parts of the Midwest during World War I. The episode deserves mention because of the replay of some of its themes in the *Meyer v. Nebraska* Lutheran school case which came before the United States Supreme Court in 1923.

At the outbreak of World War I the state of Minnesota had a high percentage of residents who were foreign-born or the children of immigrant parents. Included among these were many of German descent, and no community was more German than the city of New Ulm. The pride of the community in things German was well symbolized in a monumental statue and city park dedicated to Hermann (Arminius), the German national hero who destroyed a number of Roman legions in 9 A.D. The statue and park are located across the street from Martin Luther College and were dedicated in 1897.[4] The German character of the city set it up as a ready-made target for those who were on the lookout for pro-German sentiments when the European conflict began in 1914.

At a mass meeting in New Ulm before the United States' entry into the war a number of speakers had advocated noninvolvement in the struggle in Europe. Among these speakers was DMLC's President Ackermann. He also participated in a second public meeting in New Ulm shortly after the United States had declared war on Germany. The purpose of this meeting was to explain the recently enacted

---

[4] See Morton A. Schroeder, *A Time to Remember*, 41.

draft law but apparently turned out to be something of a protest rally against the draft. Ackermann, who spoke at the meeting, said that it was his intent to vouch for the national loyalty of the citizens of New Ulm. It was not understood that way, however, particularly after he joined with some other people from the city to speak elsewhere. All of this aroused the ire of the Minnesota Commission of Public Safety which had been charged by the state legislature with the task of guiding and overseeing the war effort in the state. Pressures in the New Ulm situation continued to build and even resulted in the governor removing from office both the mayor and city attorney of New Ulm. President Ackermann did not escape either. In January of 1918, upon the recommendation of the president of the Wisconsin Synod, the school's board of control requested and received Ackermann's resignation as president of Dr. Martin Luther College. He continued in the ministerium of his church body and later served 12 years as the president of the Minnesota District of the Wisconsin Synod.[5]

In the year following the close of World War I, Dr. Martin Luther College added an additional year to its teacher-training program. Until 1919, the course of study had comprised three years in what might be termed a secondary type of school and two years in what for a number of years was called a "normal school" in American education, that is, a post-secondary college program for the preparation of teachers. The synodical convention of 1919 enlarged the New Ulm preparatory department to a full four-year high school also for students planning to become teachers, the high school department for ministerial training having been expanded already in 1903. The two-year normal department was expanded to a three-year course of study by synodical resolution in 1927.[6] It was the

---

[5] Ibid., 57-61.

[6] Dr. Martin Luther College High School and Normal, *Catalog for 1932-33* (Milwaukee: Northwestern, 1933), 10.

intent to add a fourth college year as soon as possible, a plan which did not materialize, however, until 1954 when the members of the first four-year class were graduated. The last expansion in teacher education at Dr. Martin Luther College came in 1988 when a five-year elementary/secondary education program was introduced. The object of this course of study was to prepare candidates for teaching in either elementary or secondary Lutheran schools.[7]

The purpose of the New Ulm college for a century was to train teachers for Lutheran schools. The college understood its role well in the Wisconsin Synod school system and reflected the same in a catalog issued several years before synodical action expanded the function of the institution:

> DR. MARTIN LUTHER COLLEGE EXISTS TO PREPARE QUALIFIED EDUCATORS FOR THE TEACHING MINISTRY IN THE LUTHERAN ELEMENTARY AND SECONDARY SCHOOLS OF THE WISCONSIN EVANGELICAL LUTHERAN SYNOD.[8]

For decades congregations of the Wisconsin Synod relied on their New Ulm school as the source of supply for elementary Lutheran parochial school teachers.

There were times, however, when the college, for one reason or another, was unable to meet all the demands for teachers. Teacher shortages were acute, for example, during and immediately after World War II. This resulted in the sponsoring of summer-school programs to equip high school graduates for emergency teaching assignments and having college students

---

[7] *DMLC 1991-1993 Catalog* (New Ulm: Dr. Martin Luther College), 14.

[8] Ibid., 16.

interrupt their educational programs to fill vacancies. Reporting on this situation, the synodical board of education in 1949 provided the Synod with the following information:

> Seventy-five new teachers entered our schools last fall. Twenty-one of these were June, 1948, graduates of Dr. Martin Luther College. The remainder is made up of Normal I and II students of New Ulm, former teachers in our schools, teachers from the six weeks' summer course conducted in the summer of 1948, Theological Seminary students, teachers from the Missouri Synod and public school teachers.[9]

A decade later a synodical Educational Survey Committee observed that the previous convention of the Synod had "wrestled with the urgent problem of our perennial teacher shortage,"[10] a problem highlighted a year earlier already when the synodical board of education had said in its report to the districts of the Synod:

> To point up the seriousness of the teacher shortage which confronts us, we wish to inform you that more and more public school teachers are entering our schools because New Ulm cannot supply our needs. We cannot continue indefinitely to add teachers to our schools that are trained in public institutions without seriously harming our distinctive Lutheran principles of teaching.[11]

---

[9] The Evangelical Lutheran Joint Synod of Wisconsin and Other States, *Proceedings*, 1949, 103-4.

[10] The Evangelical Lutheran Joint Synod of Wisconsin and Other States, *Proceedings*, 1959, 91.

[11] *Report to the Nine Districts of the Evangelical Lutheran Joint Synod of Wisconsin and Other States*, 1958, 37.

The teacher shortage in the Wisconsin Synod was addressed in two very concrete ways in the mid-1950s and early 1960s. Dr. Martin Luther College operated an emergency teacher-training program at the Winnebago Lutheran Academy in Fond du Lac, Wisconsin, from 1955 to 1961. The course of study consisted of two summer terms in New Ulm and an academic year at Winnebago prior to placement in an elementary school position. At the very time that that program was being operated, petitions for the establishment of a second Lutheran teachers college in the Milwaukee area were being directed to the Synod. Such a school was in fact authorized by the 1959 Synod convention and begun in the facilities of Wisconsin Lutheran High School in Milwaukee. The college was a two-year school designed with the intent that its graduates complete their baccalaureate degree at Dr. Martin Luther College or, in the case of women who chose to do so, be permitted to enter the teaching ministry upon the completion of two summer sessions as long as emergency conditions required the use of undergraduate teachers.[12] The Milwaukee institution opened in 1960 and operated until 1970, at which time the Wisconsin Evangelical Lutheran Synod chose, after much debate, to return its entire teacher-education program to its New Ulm school. By that time, Dr. Martin Luther College had discontinued its three-year curriculum and was offering only a four-year program of studies in teacher education, the arrangement having gone into effect with the 1966-67 school year.

A problem which occupied the attention of Dr. Martin Luther College and educators within the Wisconsin Synod for a period of 25 years or more was the matter of accreditation and recognition outside the Synod of the college's program. The issue came to the fore with state certification requirements for

---

[12] The Evangelical Lutheran Joint Synod of Wisconsin and Other States, *Proceedings*, 1959, 105.

Lutheran parochial teachers, particularly in the states of Michigan and Nebraska. The synodical board of education had the following to say on the matter in 1956:

> A serious problem confronts our schools and teachers in the states of Michigan, Nebraska and elsewhere as a result of stringent State legislation which governs the granting of teaching certificates to elementary and secondary school teachers. Basic to the whole problem is the fact that State Boards of Public Education are unwilling to recognize the credits of D.M.L.C. graduates inasmuch as D.M.L.C. is not an accredited school. This means that our teachers in the affected states, even after graduating from D.M.L.C. with a B.S.E. degree, must continue to study in State-accredited schools before being eligible for teaching certificates.[13]

The situation in Michigan was critical because the school code gave the state the authority to close schools which engaged uncertified teachers. In certain quarters in the Wisconsin Synod there apparently was some reluctance to the seeking of accreditation for Dr. Martin Luther College because it was felt that the validation by state agencies of teacher-education programs in church schools might possibly result in curricular decisions which would not allow the church to provide the amount of religious instruction deemed necessary for the training of parochial school teachers. Accreditation was seen as an unwholesome mixing of church and state and a potential compromise of principle. The governing board of Dr. Martin Luther College had hinted at those concerns at an earlier date when it reported how it had accommodated one

---

[13] *Report to the Nine Districts of the Evangelical Lutheran Joint Synod of Wisconsin and Other States*, 1956, 47.

concern pertaining to teacher certification in Michigan. The board said:

> In answer to a situation confronting particularly our schools and teachers in Michigan, arrangements are being made to add to our curriculum a course in Sociology in order that our teachers there may obtain the necessary certification. This step has been taken by request of the brethren in Michigan; but we suggest that it be regarded as tentative, and urge that the matter be given further study by the Synod on the basis of Scripture.[14]

In the course of time the Wisconsin Synod did authorize Dr. Martin Luther College to pursue the matter of accreditation with the appropriate agencies. The process was an extended one and reported on regularly at synodical conventions for a number of years. The first step was to seek accreditation from the University of Minnesota through its Committee on Institutional Relationships. The formal outcome in 1963 of that effort enabled the college board to report to the synodical convention of 1965 that since

> Dr. Martin Luther College has become accredited with the University of Minnesota, no insurmountable problems have arisen in connection with the certification of our teachers in the states where this is required, namely, Michigan, Ohio, Nebraska, Iowa, South Dakota, and Washington.[15]

---

[14] The Evangelical Lutheran Joint Synod of Wisconsin and Other States, *Reports and Memorials,* 1953, 49.

[15] Wisconsin Evangelical Lutheran Synod, *Proceedings*, 1965, 166.

In 1967, the University of Minnesota chose to replace the term "accreditation" in expressing its relationship with institutions of higher education in the state to "transfer recognition." Schools like Dr. Martin Luther College which had that kind of status with the University of Minnesota were then expected to seek accreditation with North Central Association of Colleges and Secondary Schools. This Dr. Martin Luther College was willing to do, providing that "the principles of an accrediting agency do not conflict with or compromise the principles of the church."[16] The procedures customary in the process of seeking accreditation from a regional accrediting agency were then engaged in, including self-study, visitation, and the granting of candidate status. Full and unqualified accreditation was granted by North Central in May of 1980, so that the Dr. Martin Luther College board could report to the Synod in 1981:

> The Commission [of North Central] commended the college for its clearly stated philosophy and purpose, . . . curriculum that meets its needs, . . . and definite progress in those areas formerly seen as weaknesses. Regional accreditation will facilitate transfer and evaluation of credits. It also carries with it a financial advantage. It simplifies the process of establishing the college as one at which students may apply for grants or loans from a unit of the government. Furthermore, a number of corporations and businesses provide qualified employees' children with grants or scholarships for use at accredited colleges. These same organizations frequently favor accredited institutions with programs of matching funds in which

---

[16] Wisconsin Evangelical Lutheran Synod, *Reports and Memorials*, 1969, 16.

they encourage and augment contributions by their employees to colleges and universities.[17]

Institutional accreditation does not carry with it teacher certification, since each state sets its own certification requirements, and it would be extremely difficult, if not impossible, to incorporate in one baccalaureate-degree program the certification requirements of the several states which mandate the certification of parochial school teachers. The certification process is assisted, however, if the college from which one has been graduated is accredited by a recognized regional accrediting association.

A few items ought still to be mentioned to complete the story of the Wisconsin Evangelical Lutheran Synod's New Ulm college. From its inception and for a period of about 80 years Dr. Martin Luther College conducted a preparatory high school department in conjunction with the college. The two divisions were separated administratively in 1962, although they continued to share the same campus until the 1979-80 school year. The high school was then moved to a separate campus in Prairie du Chien, Wisconsin. That campus was closed in 1995 when the school was merged with a similar synodically owned and operated preparatory school in Watertown, Wisconsin.

When the Wisconsin Synod in 1970 discontinued its two-year teachers college which had been operating in Milwaukee for 10 years, a new institution of higher education emerged in that city. Known as Wisconsin Lutheran College, the school is not owned and operated by the Synod as such but by an independent association of Wisconsin Synod Lutheran congregations and individuals. The college is a four-year liberal arts school designed for general education purposes and

---

[17] Wisconsin Evangelical Lutheran Synod, *Reports and Memorials*, 1981, 37.

not specifically for the training of Lutheran pastors and teachers.

The most significant change in the recent history of Dr. Martin Luther College occurred in 1993 when the Wisconsin Evangelical Lutheran Synod in convention decided to combine its pre-ministerial-training college and its teacher-education college into one institution. Northwestern College, the Synod's longtime pre-ministerial institution at Watertown, Wisconsin, and Dr. Martin Luther College, the century-old school for the training of teachers for the Synod, merged on the New Ulm campus of Dr. Martin Luther College in the 1995-96 school year. Martin Luther College was the name selected for the merged school which combined on one campus a college program for teacher education and a liberal arts college course of study for pre-ministerial students. The Synod's theological seminary is located in Mequon, Wisconsin, where it has been since 1929. The Synod maintains two college-preparatory high schools, Luther Preparatory School in Watertown, Wisconsin, and Michigan Lutheran Seminary in Saginaw, Michigan, both designed to prepare students for entrance to Martin Luther College in New Ulm, Minnesota.

Suggested for Further Reading

Schroeder, Morton A. *A Time to Remember*. New Ulm: Dr. Martin Luther College, 1984.

✤ ✤ ✤ 1889 ✤ ✤ ✤

Controversial Education Laws
in Wisconsin and Illinois

Massachusetts took the lead in 1852 and became the first state in the United States to enact a compulsory education law. Other states followed suit during the last half of the nineteenth century, Wisconsin and Illinois inviting special attention because of the controversy which their revised laws of 1889 stirred up in connection with the parochial schools in those states. Both states had enacted mandatory school attendance laws prior to 1889, Wisconsin in 1879 and Illinois in 1883. The former had also made a significant addition to its 1879 law in 1882. It was the school legislation of 1889, however, which brought state and church into open conflict over rights pertaining to elementary education. The Illinois battle remained relatively contained, but the Wisconsin situation boiled over into a political engagement which caused an incumbent governor and a sizable number of legislators to lose an election. The Wisconsin law was known as the Bennett law; the Illinois legislation the Edwards law. Both statutes were eventually repealed but only after extensive debate on the issues and a great deal of organized effort on the part of both the Lutheran church and the Roman Catholic church.

The Wisconsin story really begins with a piece of legislation enacted in 1882 and generally overlooked by the parochial school community of the time. Wisconsin's 1879 compulsory school law had required that parents or others who were responsible for children between the ages of seven and 15 send such children "to a public or private school, for at least twelve weeks in each school year . . . unless the school district board . . . shall excuse" those children from attendance.[1] In 1882, the state legislature passed a law which required that a parent whose child did not attend a public school "file with the clerk [of the public school board] a written statement showing what school . . . [his] child . . . attended, and the number of days of such attendance."[2] Although such a stipulation does not seem to be unreasonable in the eyes of present-day readers, those who conducted parochial schools in the 1880s saw the filing of such a report and the fine for noncompliance as illegal government regulation of private schools and interference with the rights of parents to decide unhindered where their children should go to school. Looking back in 1889 at the 1882 school law, a Wisconsin Synod Lutheran parochial school advocate commented, "So, for some years already, we have had a right fine kettle of fish" (*eine recht nette Bescherung*).[3]

Operators of parochial schools in the late nineteenth century regarded even the reporting of statistics to government agencies as unacceptable regulation of church-related education. This view surfaced in 1889 in connection with a bill introduced in the upper house of Wisconsin's legislature a week before the controversial Bennett legislation was introduced in the lower house. The upper house proposal was known as the Pond Bill, having being introduced by a certain Senator Levi E. Pond. The bill never moved out of the Senate and was never even acted upon there. Having been referred back to Senator Pond as a committee of one, the bill died in his pocket. Parochial school

---

[1] Wisconsin, *Laws of Wisconsin* (1879), 155.

[2] Wisconsin, *Laws of Wisconsin* (1882), 927-28.

[3] *Lutherische Schulzeitung* (Lutheran School Periodical), May 1889, 34.

operators were watching that bill, however, and voiced immediate objection to it because it required that parochial schools provide statistical information to the state superintendent's office. The statistical information envisioned included, among other things, the amount of time devoted to the teaching of English. This was judged to be inspection of parochial schools and elicited from an editor of the Wisconsin Synod's *Schulzeitung* (School Periodical) the charge that legislators were

> in reality trying to prepare for the condition which existed among the ancient Spartans, where the state took the children away from the parents and made them its own possession.[4]

The writer then added:

> The despotism of monarchy in Europe is easily laughed at; but a far more dangerous despotism is being supported here, a despotism of the masses.[5]

While all of this attention was being given to the Pond Bill, which was never even introduced into the lower house of Wisconsin's legislature and never voted upon in the upper house, a bill by Assemblyman Michael J. Bennett, a young Roman Catholic Republican, was introduced into the Assembly, passed there, as well as in the Senate, and signed into law by Republican Governor William Dempster Hoard on April 28, 1889. This law, which had not been given much coverage even in the public press during the legislative process, ignited a spark which was fanned into full flame for over a year. The law contributed to the defeat in 1890 of an incumbent Republican

---

[4] Ibid.

[5] Ibid.

mayor in the city of Milwaukee and to the ousting from office in the same year of Governor Hoard and a number of Republican legislators. The law became a political issue and the Democrats made the most of it by promising, if elected, to repeal the statute.

Citizens' committees were formed to promote political candidates who urged repeal of the Bennett law and to organize opposition against the Republican party which had enacted the legislation. The Wisconsin public press, both English and German, gave extensive coverage to the school issue and kept it before the eyes of the electorate. The church also entered the fray, some denominations supporting the law as it stood and others vehemently opposing it and calling for its repeal. Among the opponents of the law were the Wisconsin and Missouri Synod Lutherans and also the Wisconsin hierarchy of the Roman Catholic church. Even the Western District of the Evangelical Synod of North America, a Reformed church body, devoted time in its 1890 convention to the school controversy. Those who opposed the Bennett law for reasons other than political expediency were convinced either that the state had assumed power over education which it did not have or that there was a conspiracy to do away with parochial schools.

The Bennett law prescribed that every child in the state of Wisconsin was

> to attend some public or private day school in the city, town or district in which he resides, for a period not less than twelve weeks in each year, which number of weeks shall be fixed . . . by the board of education . . . of the city, town or district, and for a portion or portions thereof . . . the attendance shall be consecutive.[6]

---

[6] Wisconsin, *Laws of Wisconsin* (1889), 729-30.

As is obvious, attendance at a private day school fulfilled the requirements of the statute. Another section of the law, however, defined what was to be considered a school within the provisions of the law. According to that section

> no school shall be regarded as a school, under this act, unless there shall be taught therein, as part of the elementary education of children, reading, writing, arithmetic and United States history, in the English language.[7]

This definition of school was bound to create difficulties for smaller Lutheran parochial schools conducted by parish pastors, for the instructional language in those schools was primarily German. United States history, moreover, might not even have been a part of the curriculum in such schools since they devoted most of their time to the teaching of religion and basic reading, writing, and computational skills.

A number of things lay behind legislation like that of the Bennett law. In certain quarters in the United States there was antagonism toward immigrants who seemed to be unduly reluctant to give up their mother tongues and to Americanize. Newcomers of that mind-set were often able to function quite adequately in their adopted homeland because of the existence of sizable homogeneous immigrant communities. Those who wanted to Americanize immigrants quickly saw the parochial school in which a foreign language was the instructional medium as an agency of delay in the process. In addition, the strong Roman Catholic parochial school system in the United States was thought by some to be a major hindrance to the healthy development of public education in the nation. Both views contained the potential to generate a degree of hostility

---

[7] Ibid., 731.

toward church-related common schools and in some localities perhaps even a desire to do away with that kind of education.

Governor Hoard of Wisconsin, who signed the Bennett law and defended it, does not seem to have been antagonistic to parochial schools nor a crusader for public schools only. He was not too politic, however, when he took office in 1888, for he included in his opening message to the legislature a comment about the necessity of teaching English in elementary schools. Since public schools obviously did that, the new governor was taking a stand over against private schools which were not offering much English instruction. Whether he was yielding to pressures or was oblivious to what kind of hornet's nest he was stirring up is unimportant in the present discussion. There can be no doubt, however, that he inaugurated an unbelievable amount of political turmoil when he introduced the school issue in his initial legislative message in January of 1889. In that address Hoard said:

> The child . . . has a right to demand of the state that it be provided . . . with a reasonable amount of instruction in common English branches. Especially has it a right to demand that it will be provided with the ability to read and write the language of this country. In this connection I would recommend such legislation as would make it the duty of county and city superintendents to inspect all schools for the purpose . . . to require that reading and writing in English be daily taught therein.[8]

Although Hoard's motive was reasonable and noble, with his school comment, wittingly or unwittingly, he introduced the principle of state inspection of private and parochial schools. Since the teaching of English was not an issue in public schools,

---

[8] Robert James Ulrich, "The Bennett Law of 1889: Education and Politics in Wisconsin" (Ph.D. diss., University of Wisconsin, 1965), 154.

the inspection referred to by the governor on the part of county or city superintendents was in essence a recommendation for state inspection of the curricula and practices of nonpublic schools.

After the Bennett law was passed, Governor Hoard continued to defend the measure and tried to convince his opponents that the law was only seeking to ensure that all children have an education which made it possible for them to be good citizens and to be able to take full advantage of the opportunities available to them in a land where English was the common language. In a letter written in November 1889 and published in the public press at his request, Hoard commented:

> I have, I believe, as friendly a feeling toward our German-American population as any man in this country; and if I did not believe that the Bennett law would assist in the advancement of their youth, I certainly would oppose its continuance on the statute books. I want the little German boy and girl, the little Norwegian, the little Bohemian and the little Pole . . . to have the same chance in life as my children. Without a knowledge of the English language they cannot have this chance. . . . I plead for these children of foreign-born parents for the reason that I personally know many who were born in this country who are handicapped by ignorance of the language of the country. Should not something be done to give these bright young people an opportunity to rise according to the ability God has given them? Advancement in life for them is out of the question without a knowledge of the language of the country.[9]

---

[9] William D. Hoard to John Luchsinger, *Wisconsin State Journal*, 30 November 1889, quoted in Robert James Ulrich, "The Bennett Law of 1889: Education and Politics in Wisconsin" (Ph.D. diss., University of Wisconsin, 1965), 189.

To this defense of his position Hoard then added:

> I am confident that when the Lutheran people come to
> look at the Bennett law in its right light, and study its
> provisions, they will fail to see in it any menace to their
> rights or tenets. It seeks to interfere with no religion. It
> simply requires that for a certain number of weeks in each
> year children must attend some school where a certain
> amount of English instruction is given. It does not seek to
> abolish the parochial school, or interfere with the
> teaching of German.[10]

Neither Lutherans nor Catholics were convinced. Writing
two years after the repeal of the Bennett law, a prominent
Wisconsin Synod professor still spoke of the statute as
"oppressive school legislation."[11] Even the perspective of
history did not alter the views of Lutheran clergymen who could
personally recall the controversy, for as late as 1951 an official
history of the Wisconsin Synod commented that "the so-called
Bennett Law was quite evidently an attempt to restrict and impair
the efficiency of our day schools."[12] Similarly, a Missouri
Synod educational historian, writing in 1963, observed:

> As the Bennett law was being scrutinized, and its
> dangerous provisions became evident to the proponents

---

[10] Ibid., 190.

[11] F. W. A. Notz, "The Parochial School System of the Evangelical
Lutheran Church in the State of Wisconsin," in *Columbian History of
Education in Wisconsin*, ed. J. W. Stearns (Milwaukee: 1893), 644.

[12] M. Lehninger *et al.*, *Continuing in His Word* (Milwaukee:
Northwestern, 1951), 215.

of church schools, much protest was aroused on the part of both the Lutheran and the Catholic churches.[13]

The Bennett law was viewed with alarm in its own day and perceived even after its repeal as an unforgettable threat to parochial schools.

The involvement of the Roman Catholic Church in the controversy was considerable. Although Irish Catholic priests did not object to the law, since English was their native language, the German Catholic clergy in Wisconsin was outspoken in its opposition to the measure. Two weeks before the 1890 spring elections in Milwaukee and other Wisconsin municipalities, three clerics of the Wisconsin Roman Catholic hierarchy issued a joint statement on the Bennett law controversy. The men were Archbishop Michael Heiss of Milwaukee, Bishop Killian Flasch of La Crosse, and Bishop Frederick Katzer of Green Bay. They represented three different and strongly Catholic parts of the state, were German-born, and had this to say:

> As bishops of the Catholic church in Wisconsin, we feel called upon to make an official declaration concerning the Bennett law—in fact, to enter our protest against it. If this law were of a purely political nature, we would not have a single word to say about it; but as it touches upon questions of the greatest interest to our Catholic church and our Catholic homes, we consider ourselves in duty bound to express and explain, even at some length, our opinion concerning the same. After calm and careful study of the Bennett law we hold that it interferes with the rights of the church and parents. We, moreover,

---

[13] August C. Stellhorn, *Schools of The Lutheran Church—Missouri Synod* (St. Louis: Concordia, 1963), 237.

conscientiously believe that the real object of this law is
not so much to secure a greater amount of instruction in
and knowledge of the English language as rather to bring
our parochial and private schools under the control of the
state. And in this attempt, we cannot but apprehend the
ultimate intention—gradually to destroy the parochial
system altogether.[14]

The language was clear and the intent obvious: Roman
Catholics were being called upon to vote in local spring
elections and the later fall general election for candidates who
were opposed to the Bennett law and who would seek its
repeal. In concrete terms, that meant vote the Democratic ticket
and not the Republican.

Lest one judge the Catholic clergy to be too proactive in the
elections of 1890, it is worth noting that a Lutheran clergyman
in Milwaukee was equally blunt in his counsel to voters. The
Reverend B. P. Nommensen of St. Lucas Lutheran Church in
that city wrote a letter to the editor of the *Milwaukee Sentinel*
just prior to the Milwaukee municipal elections in April 1890.
The Reverend Mr. Nommensen argued that the state was trying
to exercise an unconstitutional guardianship over its citizens
with the Bennett law. Objecting to this, he then acknowledged
that both he and his congregation, except for a few members,
had "always voted the Republican ticket," but that "if the
Republican party holds to this guardianship," he was certain
that it would "lose at least 250 to 300 Lutheran votes . . . in the
Seventeenth Ward."[15] On the perceived rights of parents and
the church to educate children the Lutherans and Catholics
were standing together.

---

[14] Ulrich, 213-14.

[15] B. P. Nommensen to *Milwaukee Sentinel,* 26 March, 1890, quoted in
Ulrich, "The Bennett Law," 237-38.

The debate was entered into, of course, by a variety of newspapers, spokesmen, and organizations in the state. One Milwaukee German-language periodical, *Die Germania*, and its editor were especially vocal. The religious press, too, was not silent on the matter, and when it was all over in Milwaukee and other Wisconsin cities—where nothing could really be done about a state law—and at the state level in the November elections of 1890, the Bennett law turned out to be a major factor in the replacement of Republican incumbents with Democrats. In 1888, the Republicans held 95 seats in the Wisconsin legislature and the Democrats 35. In 1890, the Republicans numbered 47 and the Democrats 85. Republican Governor Hoard and other Republican office holders also yielded their seats to Democrats. The victory for the latter was impressive, especially in view of the fact that not all incumbents had to face reelection in that year. The year 1890 was also a national election year which brought issues other than the Bennett law, of course, to the electorate in Wisconsin. The school issue, however, received prime time throughout the campaigns of 1890 and contributed mightily to the election results in Wisconsin.

The Democrats in the Wisconsin legislature remained true to their campaign promises. Milwaukee's Democrat Mayor George W. Peck was inaugurated as governor of Wisconsin on January 5, 1891. He delivered his first message to a joint session of the legislature on January 15. In that message he said that he considered the Bennett law "unwise and unnecessary" and an "arbitrary and unjustifiable interference with parents' rights, individual freedom and the liberty of conscience."[16] The Bennett law was repealed on February 5, 1891, and a new school law passed on April 6 of the same year. The new law read as follows in the areas which had been under debate:

---

[16] George W. Peck, quoted in Ulrich, "The Bennett Law," 487.

Every parent or other person having under his control any child between the ages of seven and thirteen years, shall cause such child to attend, for at least twelve weeks in each and every school year, some public or private school; provided, however that this act shall not apply to any child that has been or is being otherwise instructed, for a like period of time in the elementary branches of learning, or that has acquired such knowledge.[17]

This section of the law differed from the repealed Bennett law in three respects. First, a child was not required to attend a school in the city, town, or district in which he lived, a stipulation required by Bennett. Second, no mention was made of who was to determine school terms. The 1889 Bennett law gave that power to local public school boards. Third, nothing was said about consecutive attendance. According to Bennett, the local public school board determined how many days or weeks of the total 12-week period had to be consecutive. In short, the new law in this paragraph and in one or two other places took away from local school boards any supervisory powers over private or denominational schools. In this respect the 1891 law also modified the statute of 1882, according to which application for exemption from attending public school had to be filed with a public school clerk.

The most obvious alteration of the Bennett legislation, however, was the complete omission in the 1891 statute of a definition of what constituted a school. The Bennett law had stated that "no school shall be regarded as a school . . . unless there be taught therein . . . reading, writing, arithmetic and United States history, in the English language.[18] The new measure included no such paragraph, thus permitting the use of

---

[17] Wisconsin, *Laws of Wisconsin* (1891), 217-18.

[18] Wisconsin, *Laws of Wisconsin* (1889), 731.

a foreign language as the instructional medium where that was preferred. This was a clear accommodation to the large German-speaking church element which was still employing a good measure of that language in its parish schools.

The Edwards law in the state of Illinois did not end in the same kind of political upheaval that took place with Bennett in Wisconsin, although the issues were the same and the objections to the statute identical. Taking note of the fact that the compulsory education law of Illinois did not become quite the political issue that its counterpart in Wisconsin did, one writer has observed that "in Illinois . . . the Republicans saw the handwriting on the wall, retreated, and saved their political skins."[19] The Illinois act read very similarly to the Wisconsin law and prescribed for an educational milieu not unlike that of Wisconsin, for in Illinois, too, there were many parochial schools. Missouri Synod Lutherans, for example, operated parochial schools in Illinois as well as in Wisconsin and conducted them in much the same way and for the same purposes. Use of the German language in these schools was not uncommon, and it was partially to that circumstance that the Illinois Edwards law addressed itself when it required that

> every person having under his control a child between the ages of seven and fourteen years, shall annually cause such child to attend for at least sixteen weeks, at least eight weeks of which attendance shall be consecutive, some . . . school. . . . But no school shall be regarded as a school . . . unless there shall be taught therein in the English language, reading, writing, arithmetic, history of the United States, and geography.[20]

---

[19] Ulrich, 470.

[20] Illinois, *Laws of the State of Illinois* (1889), 237.

The striking similarity between the wording of the Bennett law and the Edwards law suggests that a pattern for phrasing was readily available to legislatures desiring to enact this type of school statute.

The Illinois law differed from its Wisconsin counterpart in that the former required attendance at school for 16 weeks instead of 12 and prescribed that eight of those weeks be consecutive. A parent was permitted to send his child to a private school provided that the school selected was "approved by the board of education or directors of the city, town or district in which such child lives."[21] Local boards of education had the duty to appoint truant officers to monitor school attendance, arrest children who were not attending school, and place truants in a public school. Parents were to be fined for noncompliance and the monies used for local public school purposes.

The Missouri Synod's educational periodical *Schulblatt* (School Journal) in its June 1889 issue reported that the law had been signed by Governor Fifer on May 24. The *Schulblatt* editor promised a detailed discussion of the law in one of the next issues and, after having announced in German the passage of the bill, provided the complete text of the law in English. In response to the request of a reader, the *Schulblatt* gave the complete text of Wisconsin's Bennett law in the November-December issue of the magazine. The eyes of the Lutheran parochial school community were focused on both laws.

The two laws triggered intense opposition because of specific provisions in the laws and because of what was thought to be behind the passage of them. Since parochial schools taught religion, the congregations operating those schools considered them to be an integral part of church life. Interference with the operation of these schools by the government was seen as an infringement on freedom of religion as guaranteed in the

---

[21] Ibid.

Constitution. It was also maintained that parents had the right to determine in what institutions their children should be educated. The churches argued, furthermore, that there was no general evidence to suggest that the products of parochial schools were turning out to be bad citizens. Advocates of church-operated schools were becoming suspicious, therefore, that the laws were an initial attempt on the part of an overzealous American nativism to do away with parochial schools because they were thought to be a threat to the development of public schools in some communities.

Several specifics in the laws were also a matter of concern. Local public school boards were empowered by the statutes to determine school terms for all schools in a city, town, or district. This touched off the fear that local authorities not friendly to the parochial school might set schedules which prevented children from celebrating religious holidays. Both laws, moreover, required attendance at schools in the city, town, or district in which the school-age children lived. This provision was objected to because parochial school children sometimes went to schools outside their community of residence. The Illinois law also assigned the task of approving schools to local public school boards, a stipulation not included in Wisconsin's Bennett law. The Lutheran position here was that public school board members who were not conversant in a Lutheran philosophy of education or who did not share it were unqualified to make a judgment on the quality of a Lutheran school. In addition, there was the uneasiness that local relationships of one kind or another might too easily result in unfair evaluations and judgments.

Ever present, of course, was the complex foreign language issue. Although more than one foreign language was in the picture, the focus was primarily on the use of German in Lutheran schools. German immigrants were often proud of their culture and language and were able to perpetuate both rather easily in the Midwest because of large German settlements there and because of a continuing influx of German immigrants to that part of the country. In fact, the number of German immigrants in the 1880s was considerable. Lutheran churches and schools in which German was spoken were attractive to these newcomers, and the presence of large numbers of new immigrants tended to retard whatever transitions to English might have been taking place. In order to minister effectively to their constituents, midwestern Lutheran churches and schools could not avoid a regular use of the German language. Services were often conducted in that language only, German was the official tongue at synodical conventions, and the majority of church publications were produced only in German. Some pastors and teachers did not always speak English particularly well, and those who were fully bilingual often preferred and were by necessity compelled to express themselves in the language of their ancestors. With respect to the school laws, both the church professionals and the laity were also not quite convinced that children learned arithmetic better by saying that two plus two equals four rather than by asserting that *zwei und zwei machen vier*.

Many supporters of the Edwards and Bennett laws were convinced that the arguments of the opponents of the laws were nothing more than a screen to cover up a stubborn determination on the part of German-speaking Americans to preserve a lively use of that language in the United States. The opponents of the laws, however, did have legitimate fears about the ultimate intent of legislation like Bennett and Edwards, for in some quarters there was, in fact, intense opposition to parochial schools and an apparent desire to remove them from the scene. In his annual report to the 1889 convention of the Wisconsin Synod, synodical President John Bading remarked:

The parochial schools are an institution which seems to give the native American a headache. The school superintendent of Manitowoc County [Wisconsin] expresses himself very openly and frankly: "The parochial schools are a constant danger to the public schools," and he predicts that in a short time the public schools will be supplanted by the parochial schools and English instruction will be replaced by the German. Similar and at times even worse assertions are expressed in the statements of legislators, journalists, and advocates of this cause.[22]

The statement of the public school superintendent must have been public knowledge, for a United States senatorial candidate from Wisconsin also referred to it when in the 1890 election campaign he observed that "one of the county superintendents of schools had reported to the state superintendent: 'The denominational school is a perpetual menace to the public school and is gradually undermining favorable sentiment.' "[23] In 1890, the Missouri Synod's English periodical *The Lutheran Witness* chose to print a letter by United States Senator H. W. Blair which also reflected a certain antagonism to denominational schooling. The letter, reprinted from a nonchurch periodical, stated:

Only a homogenous people can be great. No nation can exist with more than one language, more than one religion, more than one general form of education for the masses of the people. . . .

---

[22] *Verhandlungen der Evangelischen Lutherischen Synode von Wisconsin* (Proceedings of the Evangelical Lutheran Synod of Wisconsin), 1889, 13.

[23] Ulrich, 450.

> The people will not rest . . . in the regulation of the educational forces of the land, until they have compelled all citizens to be the masters of the English tongue—until they have secured the eradication of all religious teaching which enslaves the soul of the child to any other master than its Supreme Father, or which clothes a mere man with powers which partake of the prerogatives of God.[24]

Public statements of this kind were alarming to churches operating parochial schools and explain why suspicions arose with respect to what might possibly lie behind legislation like that of Bennett and Edwards.

The Bennett law in Wisconsin was not on the books long enough to get a good reading of how it was implemented. Passed in April of 1889, a political issue already in the municipal elections of early 1890, and the undoing of a number of politicians in the state elections later in that year, the act was repealed by February 1891, having existed for less than two years, and a sensitive issue during that entire time. Although not long-lived either, the Edwards law did remain in force for almost four years, from July 1889 until February 1893. Local officials had the obligation to enforce the law and proceeded to do so. Concerns relative to the implementation of the law arose as early, however, as September 1889. In that month, for example, the Missouri Synod's *Der Lutheraner* (The Lutheran) informed its readership of a case of enforcement in Cook County, Illinois.[25] According to the periodical, a pastor in Cook County reported to the local public school superintendent that reading, writing, arithmetic, United States history, and geography were being taught in the English language in this pastor's parish school. The local school board was not content

---

[24] *The Lutheran Witness*, May 21, 1890, 189.

[25] *Der Lutheraner* (The Lutheran), September 24, 1889, 153.

to leave the matter at that but informed the pastor of the board's decision that private schools must also use the same textbooks which the public schools used in the subjects specified in the compulsory education act. In addition, the parochial school was told that it was expected to be open for visitation by local public school officials at any time as well as for monthly inspections, as was the case with the public schools.

The editor of the Lutheran periodical took issue with the action of the school board in Cook County and pointed out to his readers that while the law required certain subjects to be taught in English, it said nothing about the textbooks to be used in those subjects. It was noted further that the law also did not in any way instruct local school boards to visit approved private schools or arrange for monthly inspections of them. This very early action in an Illinois school district could do nothing but fuel the flames of distrust with regard to local enforcement of the state statute.

A few months later, in February of 1890, *Der Lutheraner* (The Lutheran) reported again on the effects of the Edwards law in a number of other school districts. The intent of the report was to demonstrate that under the compulsory school law parochial schools were now at the mercy of local school boards. In one case the local school board served notice through its truant officer to two sets of parents that their children were in violation of the law by attending a Lutheran school not approved by the board. When state counsel was unwilling to pursue the case, allegedly because the school was fulfilling legal requirements, the board chose to get a ruling from a justice of the peace. That officer ruled in favor of the board and fined one of the parents. The editor of *Der Lutheraner* then added the note that the parish was planning to appeal the decision in Circuit Court.

In another instance a parochial school teacher was being told that he would have to take a state examination. A resident of the district informed one of the public school directors that if he continued to harass the parochial school in this way, he would soon be out of office. The threat was successful, for the directors backed off, apparently because they perceived that the threat was not an empty one and that it could be carried out by the citizens of the community. And, in another case, a parent who was sending his children to a parochial school outside of the district in which the family lived was served notice that his children were to attend the public school of the district, the board allegedly being unwilling to recognize attendance at a parochial school outside of the district as fulfilling the legal requirements of the Edwards law.[26]

All of this suggests that parochial school advocates and users did have legitimate reasons for objecting to the Bennett and Edwards laws. In an unusual move, therefore, Lutheran churches in the Midwest entered into public politics. The Missouri Synod, for example, meeting in Milwaukee in the summer of 1890, declared:

> We must, as Lutheran Christians, grant our cordial approval to the fact that our brethren in the states of Wisconsin and Illinois have, whether in courts of law or at the ballot-box, taken up and hitherto carried on the contest forced upon them against such [school] laws . . . [27]

Having said that, the convention went on to recommend that contributions be solicited in order to be able

---

[26] *Der Lutheraner*, February 25, 1890, 43.

[27] *The Lutheran Witness*, July 21, 1890, 29.

to lend pecuniary aid to such district synods as are unable to defray the costs incurred in opposing [adverse] . . . compulsory school laws.[28]

The convention also encouraged districts of the synod to appoint committees whose task it would be

to obtain correct information about all measures and resolutions respecting the school question, . . . to attend to lawsuits that may arise, to procure the funds required, in times of election to find out what position the candidates have taken in respect to the school question, and eventually to endeavor to secure the nomination of such candidates as we may support.[29]

The Republican party in the state of Wisconsin chose not to give in on the Bennett law. The Republican party which had been responsible for the Edwards law in Illinois followed a different course of action. Meeting in convention in June of 1890, Illinois Republicans issued the following statement:

We recognize the American public-school system as the chief agency in securing intelligent citizenship . . . and we declare in favor of a compulsory education law. . . . But we are at the same time opposed to any arbitrary interference with the rights of parents . . . to educate their children at private schools, no matter where located, and we favor the amendment of the existing compulsory education law . . . and also the repeal of so much of said law as provides for public supervision over private schools.[30]

---

[28] Ibid.

[29] Ibid.

[30] Ibid., 31.

Republican candidates for public office in Illinois ran on this platform on the school issue and did not suffer at the polls the way Wisconsin Republicans did.

No action was taken on the compulsory school law in the 1891 Illinois legislative sessions and the legislature did not convene in 1892. In February of 1893, however, the Edwards law of 1889 was repealed and replaced with a new compulsory education act. The new law required attendance at "some public or private day school" for a period of "at least sixteen weeks, twelve weeks of which . . . shall be consecutive." Nothing was said about what subjects were to be taught in elementary schools nor about teaching in English. There was likewise no reference to having a private school approved by either a state or local agency. Churches were now free to operate their schools as they chose and to use English or a foreign language as the medium of instruction. Schools had to be in session for 16 weeks and 12 of those had to be consecutive, but beyond that the law imposed no further requirements.[31]

Churches operating parochial schools were jubilant over the turn of events in both Wisconsin and Illinois. Others, however, were not only disappointed in the outcome but also angry with the involvement and organized efforts of Lutherans and Catholics in the controversy. The Missouri Synod's *Lutheran Witness* included in its December 7, 1890, issue a column entitled "Venomous Comments Of The Bennett Press Of Wisconsin On The Recent Election." A small-town Wisconsin newspaper lamented the outcome of the November 1890 state elections in the following way:

> Wisconsin is in deep disgrace today. Laggard Bennett men who did not vote are responsible for it. Most disgraceful

---

[31] Illinois, *The Revised Statutes of the State of Illinois* (1893), 1336.

of all is the defeat of Wm. D. Hoard. The state of Wisconsin is in deep disgrace today—humiliated, branded un-American and unpatriotic before the nation.[32]

More vitriolic, however, was the *Milwaukee Journal*'s quotation from *America*, a periodical of the New Know-Nothing Society called the Sons of America:

At every polling place Lutheran clergyman and Polish priest worked hand in glove for the defeat of a benificent (*sic*) law, the sole scope and intent of which is to lift the cloud of illiteracy from the unfortunate people who happen to be members of their churches. The spectacle will not be lost upon the American voters. They will interpret it as meaning that the Lutherans and Roman Catholics of Wisconsin prefer ignorance rather than knowledge, because their ways are dark and their intentions disloyal.[33]

The Missouri Synod's active role in the school issue in Illinois also drew a sharp comment from a religious periodical called *Church Messenger*. The October 1892 issue of that magazine commented:

With regret we chronicle the report that Lutheran pastors of the Missouri Synod in the State of Illinois have entered into the current political campaign. The occasion for this step is the school law recently enacted by the Republicans, certain provisions of which menace the prosperity and even existence of parochial schools.

---

[32] *The Lutheran Witness*, December 7, 1890, 101.

[33] Ibid., 101-2.

We can sympathize with these brethren in their anxiety to preserve the schools which they have built up with much cost and labor for the religious education of their children. But, it is not pleasant to read that the official organ of the Synod is calling for money for campaign purposes, that leading pastors have been in consultation with the Democratic National Committee in New York, and that the *New York World* (published by a Jew) has contributed $10,000 for the cause. We would rather hear that pastors confine themselves to preaching the Word and calling on the Lord of hosts for help; then hoping in Him join the laity in fighting the enemy with the only lawful ammunition the paper bullet (the ballot).[34]

The *Witness* editor offered a lengthy rebuttal to the *Church Messenger*'s comment and closed with the remark:

In conclusion we would express our sincere regrets that the *Church Messenger* should print so mean and contemptible (or egregiously foolish) an article. We had much respect for the *Church Messenger*, but now it is sorely taxed.[35]

It is apparent from statements in the public press, both religious and secular, that the controversy stirred up by the Bennett and Edwards compulsory school laws was anything but tame. Emotions ran high. Politicians, journalists, educators, clergy, and church members all became involved.

The Wisconsin Bennett law was repealed in February 1891; the Illinois Edwards law in February 1893. The latter remained on the books longer partially because the Illinois legislature did not convene in 1892. Since the Illinois Republicans who had been instrumental in enacting the statute were promising repeal

---

[34] *The Lutheran Witness*, October 21, 1892, 76.

[35] Ibid., 77.

of the law in the political campaigns of 1890 already, support for a rigid enforcement of the legislation might well have diminished long before the official act of repeal in 1893.

Although the churches which were operating parochial schools were successful in getting two laws repealed, the skirmish was not without a wholesome influence on the Lutheran system of schools. The controversy prompted Lutherans to ask critical questions about the nature and purpose of their parish school programs. In fact, it could be said that the controversial legislation of 1889 was a kind of watershed event in the history of the Lutheran parochial school. The two laws, so vigorously opposed by Lutheran synods in the Midwest, created an awareness in church circles that confirmation-type schools which taught religion, German, some English reading and writing, and arithmetic—and that for only limited periods of time—were inadequate to meet the educational needs of children who would have to function as adult Americans in the twentieth century. All parochial schools, of course, were not substandard, but it was recognized that those that were would have to be brought up to grade. Almost immediate steps were taken by Lutherans, therefore, to provide better advisory services at the synodical level to assist parishes in the operation of their schools. Even as public schools were reshaping themselves at the end of the nineteenth century, so also Lutheran parochial schools would have to redesign their curricula. The Bennett and Edwards laws of 1889, although quickly removed from the statute books, were effective agents in this process.

Suggested for Further Reading

Ulrich, Robert James. "The Bennett Law of 1889: Education and Politics in Wisconsin." Ph.D. diss., University of Wisconsin, 1965.

✢ ✢ ✢ 1894 ✢ ✢ ✢

Concordia Teachers College
Seward, Nebraska

When the German Evangelical Lutheran Synod of Missouri, Ohio, and Other States met in convention in 1893, it received and acted on reports from its five educational institutions. These schools included the two theological seminaries at St. Louis, Missouri, and Springfield, Illinois, the Lutheran Teachers Seminary at Addison, Illinois, and the two Progymnasia or pre-theological schools at Fort Wayne and Milwaukee. In addition to the reports of these educational institutions, the Synod also had before it proposals to establish two new schools. One was for a pre-theological school in the state of Minnesota and the other for a teachers college in Nebraska. The Minnesota school was to be like those in Fort Wayne and Milwaukee; the Nebraska school like the teachers seminary in Addison.

The memorials urging the establishment of the two schools included one common reason for expanding the higher educational system of the Synod. The Minnesota request put it this way: "There is a crying need for pastors and teachers in spite of the existing synodical training schools and the fact that they are filled."[1] The overture for a Nebraska college argued the teacher shortage case in a bit more detail:

---

[1] *Synodal-Bericht der allgemeinen deutschen ev.-luth. Synode von Missouri, Ohio und andern Staaten* (Synodical Report of the General German Evangelical Lutheran Synod of Missouri, Ohio and Other States) (St. Louis: Concordia, 1893), 76.

> For a number of years the long-existing shortage of
> teaching personnel for our parochial schools has become
> increasingly greater and felt more and more. In the last two
> years, in our opinion, the shortage has grown even more
> significantly. . . . This lack of teachers, we are firmly
> convinced, can be remedied only through the immediate
> establishment of a new teachers seminary. . . . The
> teachers seminary in Addison is filled with pupils and even
> if it would be overfilled, it could still not supply enough
> teachers for the field. We know from experience with our
> Gymnasia in Ft. Wayne and Milwaukee that the founding
> of a new institution in another geographic area of our
> Synod draws many a student to it who would otherwise
> not enroll in a school. The new institution, moreover,
> does not harm the older one in any significant way.[2]

The comparison between the schools in Milwaukee and Fort
Wayne was to counteract any argument that a second teachers
college might cause a decline in enrollment at the Synod's
Addison school, for Milwaukee's Concordia College had been
founded in 1881 and served the same purpose as Concordia in
Fort Wayne, which came under synodical control in 1847. Both
institutions were able to prosper after the founding of the
Milwaukee school even though the educational programs of the
two were the same. A teachers seminary in Nebraska was not
to be seen, therefore, as a competitor to the well-established
school in Addison.

The faculty and board of the latter institution had also
deemed it advisable to expand the synodical system of higher
education in some way. In its report to the synodical convention
of 1893 the Addison board of control stated that it considered
the founding of additional preparatory schools a matter of great

---

[2] Ibid., 74.

importance and referred the Synod to a faculty-prepared memorial dealing with the issue. The board endorsed the faculty report and clarified its position in the following manner:

> We would only add that we are not of the opinion that the Synod itself should immediately erect preparatory schools in several places but that the Synod might want to encourage individual districts, where it is practicable and feasible, to start such a project. If time should prove that a given institution in this or that place has become viable, then the Synod can take over the school. The Honorable Synod should resolve, however, that the individual preparatory schools to be erected must arrange their curricula to correspond with that of our Teachers Seminary.[3]

Like the people in Nebraska, the faculty and board at Addison were also aware of a parochial school teacher shortage in the Missouri Synod. A recommended solution to the problem was the creation of more preparatory schools (proseminaries, as they were called) with curricula like that of the preparatory department at the Addison Teachers Seminary. Such schools would be able to attract a larger number of boys, provide them with three years of high school education, and then transfer them to Addison for the final two years of teacher training.

The 1893 synodical convention acted favorably on the requests for new schools in Nebraska and Minnesota. The Synod resolved that a ministerial preparatory school (*Gymnasium*) be established in the St. Paul-Minneapolis area, thus bringing Concordia-St. Paul into existence. The petition for a Minnesota school from the joint pastoral conference and a number of congregations of the Minnesota-Dakota District also included a

---

[3] Ibid., 60-61.

proposal for an academy for general educational purposes. The Synod declined that proposal with the following resolution:

> Resolved, that to this institution [the *Gymnasium*] an academy be joined in which young people be instructed who do not intend to enter professional church service but wish to receive further education be declined.[4]

The Synod did agree, however, that it was desirable for boys in their teens who lived at a distance from Addison to begin their teacher training closer to home. The major difference between the curricula for future pastors and future teachers in the first two preparatory years in synodical schools had to do with language and music study. Prospective pastors received instruction in Latin while future teachers were expected to acquire piano keyboard skills. Recognizing that those were the only differences in the first two preparatory years of study, the Synod sanctioned the combining of a preparatory teacher-training program with the lower classes of the Minnesota pre-ministerial college. The ministerial track required Latin study; the teacher track music. Students in the teacher program would then transfer to Addison when they were several years older in order to complete their education.

The overture to establish a teachers college in Nebraska also fared well at the hands of the 1893 convention of the Missouri Synod. Originally, the Nebraska District had been interested in a preparatory school similar to the one approved of for Minnesota. Organized as a district in 1882, Nebraska spent time at its sixth convention already, in 1889, discussing the possibility of establishing a pre-ministerial college within the district. Residents from Blue Hill, Seward, and Lincoln had even offered land, money, or both if such a school would be

---

[4] Ibid., 78.

established in their communities.[5] Considerable time was given over to the subject again at the district convention in 1892, offers of assistance having come in at that time also from individuals and groups in Norfolk. The memorial to the Synod in 1893, however, proposed not a pre-ministerial college (*Gymnasium*) but a teachers college (*Lehrerseminar*) for Nebraska. Persuaded of the usefulness of such an institution, the Synod resolved "that a second teachers seminary be established and that it be located in the state of Nebraska."[6]

With a school approved for the state of Nebraska, the next issue to be resolved was that of specific location within the state. The overture to the Synod had included the remark that "the proposed teachers seminary should be located in a larger city for reasons which are indeed clear and apparent to everyone and confirmed also by experience."[7] Additional resolutions by the 1893 convention make it clear that the larger city being thought of was Lincoln. The synodical board of trustees was authorized, for example, to visit that city and to investigate the proposed location for the school and the offer of land which had come from there. If the trustees and the synodically appointed board of control for the new school were convinced that it was in the best interest of the Synod to establish the new teachers college in Nebraska's state capital, they had the authority to proceed to locate the institution in that city.

Although Lincoln was mentioned more than once in both the proposal for a Nebraska teachers seminary and in the synodical resolutions pertaining to it, the convention delegates were aware that other locations were also under consideration. That becomes apparent from the fact that the convention gave the Synod's

---

[5] *Synodal-Bericht des Nebraska-Districts* (Synodical Report of the Nebraska District), 1889, 63.

[6] *Synodal-Bericht der . . . Synode von Missouri . . .* (Synodical Report of the . . . Synod of Missouri . . .), 1893, 75.

[7] Ibid., 74.

trustees and the synodically elected board of control authority to proceed with the construction of a building, "be it in Lincoln or in another place," and if in Lincoln, only after the committee "has examined still other offers."[8] It was also resolved that "in the event that the new teachers seminary is not erected in Lincoln but in another place in Nebraska, the Nebraska District be empowered to appoint the board of control for the institution."[9] The Nebraska District was also given permission to solicit funds within the entire Synod for both the building of the school and, until the next synodical convention, also for the support of a professor.

Things moved rather fast. The Synod was apprised at its next convention in 1896 that the men entrusted in the spring of 1893 with the task of studying and acting on the Nebraska school matter had come "to the conclusion that the offer made by . . . brethren . . . in Seward, Nebraska, was the most suitable and advantageous for the Honorable Synod."[10] The Seward offer promised "to give the Synod of Missouri, Ohio, and Other States 20 acres of land . . . together with $8,000 in cash under the condition that the Synod erect suitable facilities within three years."[11] The deed for the land in Seward was transmitted to the Synod on April 2, 1894. Construction was begun immediately, a professor was called in October, and the first school year was under way in November with an enrollment of 12. The first building was dedicated on November 18, 1894, at which time George Weller was also installed as professor at the new school. Within a year and a half after the Missouri Synod in convention had approved the establishment of a second teachers seminary to be located in Nebraska, a campus site was selected and

---

8 Ibid., 75.

9 Ibid.

10 *Synodal-Bericht* (Synodical Report), 1896, 56.

11 Ibid., 56-57.

Concordia Teachers College—as the school was to be known for many years—began its service to the church.

Although the choice of Seward rather than Lincoln for the location of a second teachers college does not seem to have received any large-scale synodical criticism, in its 1896 report to the Synod the school's board of control described Seward in almost idyllic terms and provided information obviously intended to affirm the wisdom of the decision to locate the institution in that city. In a report under the heading "Second Teachers Seminary in Seward, Nebraska," the board said:

> It would seem to be appropriate at this point to say something . . . about the place and site of the second teachers seminary.
>
> Seward, which is located 25 miles . . . from Lincoln, the capital of the state, is a lovely little city of about 2,000 inhabitants. Our congregation there has 53 voting members and a flourishing parochial school. . . . In the vicinity of Seward there is a circle of seven Missouri Synod congregations and two belonging to the Honorable Synod of Wisconsin. The neighborhood, therefore, is a good one. That our congregations have the necessary interest in the seminary is evident, among other things, from the fact that they contributed foodstuffs in such generous measure that the school was supplied with flour, potatoes, and the like for an entire year. In keeping with an old and good custom in our Synod, also the women in the congregation at Seward did the laundry for the pupils at the school without remuneration.
>
> Our second teachers seminary is also easily reached from all directions. By means of its three railroads . . . Seward has the best possible connection with the outside world,

which is not an unimportant matter to parents who want to have their sons study there. . . . Because Seward has such convenient railroad connections, congregations of our Synod which are situated farther away can supply the school with provisions just as easily as congregations which are located closer.

With respect to the nature of the 20-acre piece of property surrounding our building, special attention should be called to this that the land is located at the edge of the city in the most beautiful part of it. In spite of the high location of the property our wells there are not deep and have supplied excellent and healthful water during the most arid time of the year without drying up.[12]

The board of control of the Seward school seems not to have been disappointed with the selection of that city for the Synod's second teachers seminary. Martin P. Simon in *College on the Cornfield,* a doctoral-dissertation history of Concordia Teachers College in Seward, addresses the question of why Lincoln was passed by and Seward chosen for the college. From an interview in 1952 with a relative of an advocate of the Seward location, Simon learned that the property offered in Lincoln might have been bottom land and for that reason undesirable. The glowing commentary on the land features of the Seward campus in the 1896 report of the school's board of control lends credence to that theory. Simon suggests, however, that another factor might also have been involved in the selection of Seward over metropolitan Lincoln and that is

the fear of the temptation of the big city, the feeling that a quiet little town like Seward would be a better place to bring up students. . . . According to some, the city of

_____

[12] Ibid., 57.

Lincoln at that time had a questionable reputation as being a rough, wide-open town.[13]

It is not difficult to accept the possibility of this objection to a large city location since students began their teacher-training education in their early teens. Monitoring the off-campus life of teenage boys in a boarding school would very likely have had fewer challenges in a small town than in a large city. It is also worth noting perhaps that not only Lutheran but also other church-related colleges established in the nineteenth century were located in smaller cities. In that respect, then, the Seward choice was not an unusual phenomenon.

The decade in which the Missouri Synod founded its second teachers seminary turned out to be a period plagued with numerous economic difficulties in the United States. The year 1893 is known as a panic year in United States history. Hundreds of banks and thousands of commercial institutions failed at that time. A number of railroads went into receivership and unemployment soared. In Nebraska the situation was exacerbated by drought in the western part of the state. In 1891, for example, the Nebraska District commission on relief reported that

> the total receipts in money for those suffering need in the western part of our state amounted to $8,073.46. . . . 13 carfuls of grain, such as corn, oats, wheat, as well as foodstuffs were gathered and delivered. . . . In addition, many boxfuls of used and new clothing and a number of boxes of new shoes were contributed.[14]

---

[13] Martin P. Simon. "College on the Cornfield" (Ed.D. diss., University of Oregon, 1953), 21.

[14] *Synodal-Bericht des Nebraska Districts der Synode von Missouri* (Synodical Report of the Nebraska District of the Missouri Synod), 1891, 48.

The need for assistance did not end quickly, as becomes evident from the report made to the Nebraska District as late as 1895:

> In the past year 868 families with 4,555 members were helped. $11,960.68 were distributed to these people together with foodstuffs and grain delivered in 52 railroad cars.[15]

The severity of the economic situation in western Nebraska becomes apparent also from an appeal in the November 6, 1894, issue of the Missouri Synod's official periodical *Der Lutheraner* (The Lutheran). That issue carried a relatively short notice announcing the November 18 dedication of the new building in Seward and a longer appeal for help for those who were suffering because of the drought in Nebraska. The appeal read:

> The western part of Nebraska has been struck again by a drought. The need is great, since the harvest is a total failure and nothing remains from last year. Many are lacking the most necessary things for life. If these people are not helped from the outside, they and their families will have to starve and freeze. Among those in need are about 150 families from our congregations. As far as can be determined, about six carfuls of wheat and corn for flour and feed as well as a number of boxes of clothes and shoes, the latter especially for children, would be necessary to help these people through the winter. Cash would also be very welcome.[16]

---

[15] *Synodal-Bericht des Nebraska Districts der Synode von Missouri* (Synodical Report of the Nebraska District of the Missouri Synod), 1895, 81.

[16] *Der Lutheraner*, November 6, 1894, 191.

The effects of the general harsh times were felt not only in Nebraska, of course. The author of a short journal article on the history of Concordia Teachers College in Seward made the following observation in the 1930s with respect to the general financial condition in the Synod in the 1890s:

> Many treasuries contended with deficits. In 1896 the Treasurer of the Missouri Synod complained that he had never before been in such a serious plight. President E. A. W. Krauss of the Addison Teachers Seminary in those years regularly announced the opening of the schoolyear with the warning that only money-orders, no checks, would be accepted.[17]

An example of such an announcement by President Krauss appeared among the school-opening notices in the August 15, 1893, issue of *Der Lutheraner*. The Addison president's announcement was the longest of all the institutional notices, was very specific with respect to school fees and when they were due, and concluded by saying: "Do not send checks at this time but solely and only money orders, payable here in Addison."[18] To that was added the warning: "Many a father who has sent cash in a letter has had to lament the loss of the same."[19]

The economic conditions of the time had a far-reaching effect on the development of the Seward Teachers Seminary. Limited financial resources would quite naturally affect plans for both building projects and staffing. More important perhaps than

---

[17] H. O. A. Keinath, "Historical Sketch of Concordia Teachers College, Seward, Nebr.," *Concordia Historical Institute Quarterly*, October 1935, 93. This article also appeared in the *Lutheran School Journal* of December 1934.

[18] *Der Lutheraner*, August 15, 1893, 134.

[19] Ibid.

that, however, was a sudden decrease in the demand for teachers. Even if parishes wanted and needed more teachers, hard-pressed congregational treasuries required churches to make do with the staff they could afford. While it was agreed when the 1893 Missouri Synod convention resolved to open a second teachers college that there was a critical need for more parochial school teachers, by 1897 the need had diminished. Reporting on the placement of teacher candidates for that year and for 1898, the Addison Teachers Seminary informed the Synod at its 1899 convention:

> In the year 1897, 42 candidates entered the teaching office. At the time of placement 14 of these were left without calls; they did, however, receive calls within three months. In the year 1898, 45 students completed their examinations; all received calls except for two who were offered only a provisional call.[20]

From this it becomes apparent that if Addison was just barely placing its teacher candidates, a second full-sized teachers college was not needed.

The diminished need for teacher candidates and the financial stringencies of the times hindered Seward from becoming a five-year teacher training school in the 1890s. The plan had been to develop the full program one year at a time. Thus, the first class began in the 1894-95 school year, the second class was added in 1895, and the third class came into existence with the 1896-97 school year. The expansion ended at that point, requiring that students who had completed their preparatory education then transfer to Addison for their last two professional years of teacher training. Seward continued as that

---

[20] *Synodal-Bericht der . . . Synode von Missouri . . .* (Synodical Report of the . . . Synod of Missouri . . .), 1899, 45.

213

kind of preparatory school until the Missouri Synod in its 1905 convention approved the expansion of the school's program to a five-year teachers seminary to begin with the 1906-7 school year. The specific requests that Seward be granted that status had come from both the board of control of the institution and the Nebraska District. In its overture to the Synod, the Nebraska District called attention to the teacher shortage which had arisen again in the Synod. The District also noted, however, that transfer to Addison by students who had taken their first three years at Seward had not been too successful:

> Experience has shown that a sizable number of pupils withdraw [from teacher training] and take up another calling because they are unable to complete their studies at Seward in order to prepare themselves for the teaching office but must still go to Addison.[21]

The Seward board of control in its report to the Synod pointed out that enrollment at the school had been increasing steadily, to such an extent, in fact, that an additional building was needed. The board noted further that "from the beginning, it was the intention of the Synod to expand this school in the course of time in such a way so that its pupils would be able to complete their study for the teaching profession there."[22] In view of the need for Lutheran school teachers and on the basis of encouragement from several other synodical districts, the Seward board argued that the time to expand the institution had arrived. To do that, a new classroom building would be needed, for which the board had ready cost figures and other details.

---

[21] *Synodal-Bericht der . . . Synode von Missouri . . .* (Synodical Report of the . . . Synod of Missouri . . .), 1905, 41.

[22] Ibid., 40.

The 1905 convention of the Missouri Synod was convinced. It resolved that "the second Teachers Seminary in Seward, Nebr., be expanded to a full teachers seminary."[23] To implement the decision the convention delegates voted funding for the erection of two new buildings on the Seward campus, gave the institution's board of control authority to call professors as needed, and empowered the board to procure housing for the new faculty. The school which had opened its doors to an initial class of teacher-training students in 1894 and had continued for 12 years as a three-year high school department for prospective Lutheran school teachers inaugurated its full five-year teacher-education program in 1906. This put Seward on an equal basis with Addison in the synodical system of higher education. At its next convention, in 1908, the Missouri Synod approved six-year normal school programs, four high school years plus two college years—the regular term in those days for teacher education— for both institutions.

Leadership in the pioneering days of Concordia-Seward was in the hands of George Weller. A graduate of Concordia College in Fort Wayne and Concordia Seminary in St. Louis, Weller was pastor of a Lutheran congregation located in Seward County when he was called to the Missouri Synod's second teachers seminary. He had served in that parish for 12 years and had been on the building committee for the new Seward school before he was called to be the first professor at the institution. Although he was the acting director of the school from the beginning, his permanent appointment to that position came at the 1899 convention of the Missouri Synod. When he undertook his duties in Seward, he taught all subjects except music, a local Lutheran school teacher having taken on that assignment. Weller's work was arduous, but it must be remembered that the school was really no more than a ninth-grade class. The

---

[23] Ibid., 41.

curriculum taught by him included the following subjects: catechism, Bible history, German, English, geography, arithmetic, history, and penmanship.

The 12 students in the first class and the Weller family lived in the same building during the first year of the school's existence. Mrs. Weller, with the aid of one helper, did the cooking and was housemother for the boarding-school boys. Professor and Mrs. Weller owned and kept cows and chickens on campus for their own large family and also for needs in the school kitchen. The Seward enterprise was a pioneer venture in more ways than one, prompting the writer of an obituary for Weller, when he died in 1924, to say of the early years of the school:

> Everything at the institution was in the state of becoming, and much was very primitive. Like all pioneer labor, the work of the deceased involved a great deal of unselfishness on the part of both him and his wife.[24]

George Weller took on the Seward assignment at age 34 and remained active at the school for 30 years. He stepped down from the directorship of the institution after 20 years but continued to teach until three weeks before he died. According to one author who sketched the history of Concordia Teachers College in Seward, "Professor Weller possessed many qualities necessary for steering a fragile little ship through the storms of adverse conditions."[25] Of the pioneering president's presentations, a colleague who wrote the *Der Lutheraner* obituary for Weller said: "The content of his speeches,

---

[24] *Der Lutheraner*, January 20, 1925, 29.

[25] H. O. A. Keinath, "Historical Sketch of Concordia Teachers College," *Lutheran School Journal*, December 1934, 147. This historical sketch also appeared in the *Concordia Historical Institute Quarterly* in October 1935.

catecheses, and sermons was always first-rate and clear, the language lofty and polished, the delivery impressive."[26] Others who knew the man gave him the same high marks, and when the 30th anniversary of his tenure at the school arrived, former students arranged a service in his honor. Weller was unable to attend, however, having become ill the night before the event. The illness turned out to be fatal and brought Weller's life to an end with, according to his obituarist, the words of the hymn "Jesus, your blood and righteousness my beauty are, my glorious dress" on his lips.

Weller relinquished his presidential chair in 1914, 10 years before his death. An additional professorship was established in Seward at that time and Weller was called to it. Friedrich W. C. Jesse was chosen to succeed Weller as the school's administrative head and was installed into office in 1914 on Martin Luther's birthday, November 10. A native of Texas, Jesse had received his education at St. Paul's College in Concordia, Missouri, at Concordia in Milwaukee, and at Concordia Seminary in St. Louis. Since 1908 he had been president of a Lutheran college operated by the Norwegian Synod in Clifton, Texas. The Norwegian Lutherans in the United States had been separated into several synodical affiliations because of doctrinal differences since the late nineteenth century. Reunification was in the making, however, in the second decade of the twentieth century and effected finally in 1917. The major issues in both the initial dividing of the Norwegians and in their efforts to reunite were the biblical doctrines of conversion and election. Differences on that doctrine had prompted the Norwegian Synod to withdraw from the Synodical Conference in the 1880s. Cordial relationships continued to exist, however, between members of the Synodical Conference, of which the Missouri Synod was the largest

---

[26] Paul Reuter, *Der Lutheraner*, January 20, 1925, 29.

affiliate, and one of the Norwegian Lutheran groups, a circumstance which explains Friedrich Jesse's position as president of a Norwegian Lutheran college. Synodical Conference theologians were convinced that the Norwegian Lutherans as they were approaching merger had really not resolved their doctrinal differences. F. W. C. Jesse shared that view, tendered his resignation as president of the Clifton school, and accepted the call to become president of the Missouri Synod's teacher-training college at Seward.

It is usually not difficult to identify significant changes and developments which occur during any president's tenure at an institution of higher education. That is particularly true of Concordia at Seward in its first 60 years because each of the presidential incumbents stayed at his post long enough for a number of important things to happen. The fact of the matter is that the school had only four presidents during the first 60 years of its history. The shortest tenure was that of Jesse, who after serving as president from 1914 until 1923, accepted a call to become pastor of a congregation in Atchison, Kansas, where he remained active until 1940. Several things took place during Jesse's presidency, however, which are especially worthy of note.

Jesse took over the helm at Seward in the very year that World War I began in Europe. The *Lusitania* was sunk by the Germans in May of 1915, with a number of Americans on the casualty list. War fever and anti-German sentiment began to escalate in the United States. The Lutheran Teachers Seminary in Seward, which in the course of some of its early history had also been known as the German College, became suspect in the eyes of certain American patriots. German was taught at the school and spoken regularly by faculty members. Graduates of the institution were expected to be able to function as teachers in the congregational schools of German-speaking parishes. The teachers college at Seward and its faculty were in a position similar to that of the Wisconsin Synod's Dr. Martin Luther College at New Ulm, Minnesota. Both had been given the assignment to prepare teachers for Lutheran parish schools in which a certain amount of German was used, notably in classes in religion. As a result, the two colleges, together with other educational institutions in which the German language was used extensively, were sometimes viewed with a degree of suspicion and thought to be unpatriotic.

Jesse was the Seward president during these war years and didn't hesitate to take steps to place the school of which he was head, as well as the church to which he belonged, in a favorable light. At the initiation of the United States Secretary of War, the state of Nebraska organized the Nebraska State Council of Defense in April 1917. It was the task of this council to promote the national war effort in a variety of ways. In *College on the Cornfield*, Martin P. Simon reports that Jesse became a member of this council and also offered his services as a speaker at public meetings called to support and explain the war effort.[27] A symbolic act took place on campus in May of 1917 when the college replaced a flagpole which had been destroyed in a tornado. The new flagpole was reportedly the highest in Seward County.

Antagonism toward things German in the United Sates was extremely strong in Nebraska during the war and remained so even after it, as the *Meyer v. Nebraska* Supreme Court case of 1923 later showed.[28] In an attempt to clear up misunderstandings about Lutheran parochial schools, former President Weller and another Seward faculty member conducted a survey of Missouri Synod Lutheran schools in the

---

[27] See Martin P. Simon, "College on the Cornfield" (Ed.D. diss., University of Oregon, 1953), 112.

[28] See chapter 15 (1923) of the present volume.

state of Nebraska and transmitted their findings to the State Council of Defense. Among other things the men reported:

> 4. Of the 134 pastors and teachers from whom we received answers to date, 110 are American citizens by birth, 20 by adoption, 3 have their first papers, and one has failed to take out his first papers.
> 5. All the schools fly the American flag. . . .
>
> 9. All the secular branches, such as arithmetic, geography, physiology, United States History, drawing, penmanship, etc., are taught in English. . . .
>
> 11. The German National Hymn is not sung in a single one of our schools.
> 12. The American National Hymn and other American patriotic songs are sung in all our schools.
> 13. As to German text-books used, see samples presented. All are published by the Concordia Publishing House, St. Louis, Mo. They contain nothing that could be used in any way to make propaganda for the cause of the enemy of our country. . . .[29]

It becomes apparent from the above report what some of the public perceptions of the Lutheran school were. That the German language was spoken and taught in Lutheran churches and schools in Nebraska cannot be denied. That there was a pride among German-speaking Americans in German culture and language was also a fact. That German-speaking communities in World War I were anti-American breeding places and subversive propaganda pockets for the German Kaiser was more

---

[29] *Synodal-Bericht des Nebraska Distrikts* (Synodical Report of the Nebraska District), 1918, 92.

myth, however, than reality. Very interesting in the entire situation, however, is the fact that a subtle language shift took place on the Seward campus immediately upon Director Jesse's installation as head of the school. His wife did not speak German, and that meant that faculty, faculty wives, and students had to converse in English in her presence. That turn of events was perhaps not at all harmful for the college after the United States entered the war.

Friedrich Jesse did more during his tenure, of course, than steer the Synod's teachers college without serious incident through some unfriendly waters stirred up in Nebraska by World War I. One highly significant step was the admission to the school in 1919 of women who desired to become Lutheran school teachers. The number of women teachers in the elementary schools of the Missouri Synod was increasing, but there was no synodically sponsored training program available for prospective women teachers, since the student body at River Forest (formerly Addison) at the time was also all male. The Seward report to the Synod at its convention in 1920 was very brief on the matter, saying merely:

> Finally, we do not want to leave unmentioned that in the past year we had several girls as pupils at our institution; there were five of them, all of whom entered with the intent to serve at a later date in a parochial school.[30]

This was a new move in the institutions of higher education in the Missouri Synod and resulted in a specific action on the part of the Synod two conventions later, in 1926. At that time the Synod addressed the issue of coeducation at Seward and adopted a committee report which recommended that

---

[30] *Synodalbericht der . . . Synode von Missouri . . .* (Synodical Report of the . . . Synod of Missouri . . .), 1920, 53.

Synod approve the work which is now carried on, and the continuation thereof, under the restrictions now obtaining and . . . that the present arrangement for the education of woman teachers existing at Seward . . . be for the present retained without change, which means that the attendance of female pupils will not exceed 20 per cent of the total enrollment.[31]

With Jesse's departure from the Seward faculty in 1924, the school's pioneer days had come to an end. Much of the physical plant had been developed under Director Weller. Internal changes had taken place during Jesse's years and additional buildings planned, the construction of which was just beginning at the time of his departure. His successor was the president of the Nebraska District and chairman of the Seward board of control, the Rev. C. F. Brommer. Brommer was pastor of Zion Lutheran Church near Hampton in Hamilton County, Nebraska, a parish which had come before the public eye one year earlier when the case of *Meyer v. Nebraska* was decided in the United States Supreme Court. The Meyer of that case was the teacher of the Lutheran school operated by Brommer's parish.[32]

The Brommer presidency turned out to be a long one. Begun in 1924, it did not come to an end until 1941 when the incumbent tendered his resignation at age 71. Those years were eventful in a number of ways. Buildings were erected, enrollments grew, and the Great Depression of the 1930s brought its litany of woes. Among the various things which happened at Seward during the Brommer years, several are especially worthy of note because of their relationship to the history of the Lutheran parochial school movement generally.

---

[31] *Proceedings of the Thirty-third Regular Convention* (1926), 77.

[32] See chapter 15 (1923) of the present volume.

The first of these items is the name of the school itself. In its early years, it was referred to in a variety of ways. One can understand, of course, that when the school was being planned and in its early years it was spoken of in synodical discussion simply as the "Second School Teachers Seminary." Local newspapers sometimes called it "The German College." A class ring of 1916 had the initials LNS (Lutheran Normal School). The diplomas of 1925 bore the name "The Lutheran Seminary." The cornerstone for the new administration building in 1924, however, was inscribed with the name "Concordia Teachers College." That was the name by which the school continued to be known until the last decade of the twentieth century, when the shorter and, in terms of what the school had become, more accurate title "Concordia College" was adopted, a name which was altered to Concordia University in 1998. Legally, however, it was not until 1941 that the institution's 1918 articles of incorporation were amended to change the name "The Lutheran Seminary" to "Concordia Teachers College."[33]

The 1930s were both good times and bad times for the Teachers College. The Great Depression during the first part of that decade resulted in supplying more teachers than could be absorbed by financially hard-pressed Lutheran congregations. This brought about a decline in enrollments at the college. At the same time that these things were happening, however, there was a national trend to expand teacher-training programs beyond the two-year normal school pattern which still existed in many places. The Missouri Synod's colleges at Seward and River Forest were two church-related schools in that category but were expanded in the very decade that the Depression had hit hard. At its 1935 convention, the Synod approved a three-

---

[33] See Martin P. Simon, "College on the Cornfield" (Ed.D. diss., University of Oregon, 1953), 159-61.

year teacher training program for Seward. Beginning the program in the 1936-37 school year, the faculty made the following comment in a supplement to Concordia's catalog for that year:

> Pursuant to a resolution of Synod . . . in June, 1935, Concordia Teachers College is adding one year to the college department. This addition involves a fundamental reorganization of the curriculum. In the same meeting the synodical body authorized the appointment of a curriculum committee which was charged with the task of studying and building a curriculum suited to the needs of the field and consonant with the best educational practices of today.

> The final report of the synodical curriculum committee is not as yet available. Concordia Teachers College therefore finds itself in a transition period. The major lines of future development have been established.[34]

The major lines of development mentioned in the *Catalog* supplement referred to the desire within the Synod to have a full four-year college for teacher education. Proposals for such a program of studies had been discussed in the 1920s already. By 1938, the national Depression having run much of its course, the Synod was ready to approve a fourth year of teacher education. The fourth year of study was optional and reported on in the following way in the 1939-40 Seward *Catalog*:

> The fourth college year, authorized by Synodical resolution in 1938, is optional for those who desire to qualify for a bachelor's degree and a lifetime teaching

---

[34] *Catalog of Concordia Teachers College*, 1936-37, Supplement.

certificate according to the new Nebraska certification requirements.[35]

Accreditation of its educational programs by outside agencies was a gradual process at Concordia Teachers College. The first step occurred in 1919 when the school was granted permission by the state of Nebraska to issue teaching certificates. In that same year, the University of Nebraska recognized the Seward school as an approved junior college. The board of control made the following comment about the actions in its 1920 report to the Synod:

> We wish to inform the Synod that our institution was accredited in the past year. The advantages arising from this, especially under the existing circumstances, are not insignificant. Our institution is now entitled to issue to all its graduates certificates recognized by the State. In addition, the school gained approval so that teachers also in other states, provided that they have studied at our institution, are recognized. Thus, for example, all teachers in Kansas . . . have received their certificates.[36]

In 1939, the high school department received accreditation from the North Central Association of Colleges and Secondary Schools. The three-year college program was accredited by the University of Nebraska and the state within two years after the inception of that course of study, with various other components of the total college program receiving accreditation from regional agencies at later times in the history

---

[35]*Catalog*, 1939-40, 6.

[36] *Synodalbericht der . . . Synode von Missouri . . .* (Synodical Report of the . . . Synod of Missouri . . .), 1920, 52-53.

of the school.[37] Outside recognition of its teacher education programs was especially advantageous for Concordia at Seward in the middle of the twentieth century when Nebraska began to press for state certification of private school teachers.

Concordia College was established at Seward initially in order to equip young men to become Lutheran parochial school teachers. This remained the sole purpose of the school for 25 years. At that juncture women were permitted to matriculate to prepare themselves for the same profession. The college discontinued its high school department in 1972 but had been expanding its college offerings along the way. This included developing the institution into a college for general education. Thus, for example, the college *Catalog* as early as 1939-40 stated that the school's

> development has been progressively carried on by the Board of Control and the Faculty under the auspices and with the support of the Missouri Synod, so that the institution today has come to include three major divisions: the HIGH SCHOOL, with a four-year program; the LUTHERAN TEACHERS COLLEGE, with a three or four year program; the SENIOR COLLEGE, with a four-year program of general education.[38]

Although the college's offerings have expanded considerably, the school continues to carry out its original assignment of preparing candidates for the Lutheran school teaching profession.

---

[37] See C. T. C. Brandhorst, *A Short Story of Concordia Teachers College* (n.d., n.p.), 16.

[38] *Catalog*, Concordia Teachers College, 1939-40, 6.

Suggested for Further Reading

Schmidt, Allan Hermann. "A College on a Mission: Leadership of Concordia College, Seward, Nebraska, 1941-1991." Ed.D. diss., University of Nebraska, 1992.

Simon, Martin P. "College on the Cornfield." Ed.D. diss., University of Oregon, 1953.

✢ ✢ ✢ 1913 ✢ ✢ ✢

Concordia Teachers College
River Forest, Illinois

At the end of the first decade of the twentieth century, teacher education for the synods of the Evangelical Lutheran Synodical Conference of North America was taking place in three locations: Addison, Illinois, New Ulm, Minnesota, and Seward, Nebraska. The school at Addison was the oldest of these three teachers colleges—or normal schools as they were called then. A decision of the delegates to the Missouri Synod convention of 1911 brought about a change for the Addison school. By a narrow margin the convention decided to relocate the institution to River Forest, Illinois. With the move, effected in 1913, the oldest of the three teachers colleges continued its history on a new campus and made River Forest—or RF as it is popularly referred to—a household word in the chronicle of Lutheran teacher education.

Proposals to relocate synodical schools often stir up strong feelings. The Addison-River Forest move was no exception. For a number of years the Addison campus had begun to show its age and the school's requests for updating were not always readily granted at synodical conventions. Electricity, for example, was a luxury never enjoyed at Addison. Steam heat was installed in 1896, but it took a second synodical convention before that bit of modernization was approved. The Addison board of control in its 1896 report to the Synod made its request for steam heating by quoting from its 1893 convention report. The board said:

> We would like to make . . . the following request of the Honorable Synod, namely, to be permitted to install steam heat in the seminary buildings. This matter was presented to the last Honorable Synod already in the following words:
>
> "For many years already we have felt that it was a very bad situation that our seminary buildings were not equipped with steam heat. Stoves for each of the many rooms is very costly. We have 58 stoves in use. . . . Many of the stoves are decrepit. Students have to buy about 275-300 tons of coal annually. . . .
>
> "In addition, in one building the danger of an outbreak of fire is always present with the stoves. To avoid this . . . it has been necessary till now to have the students alternate in keeping night watches through the entire winter. But even with all this caution, it has often happened that fire has broken out. If a fire should ever move so quickly and so extensively that the existing fire-fighting equipment is inadequate, then . . . the entire property of the Synod would be destroyed. . . . Finally, the stoves in one building—apart from the extensive soot which they produce and the damage which they cause to the pianos and especially to the organs—are in no way conducive to the health of the students. . . . Since the students themselves have to regulate the stoves, the temperature of a room frequently alternates . . . between African heat and Siberian cold."[1]

---

[1] *Synodal-Bericht der allgemeinen deutschen ev. luth. Synode von Missouri, Ohio und andern Staaten* (Synodical Report of the Evangelical Lutheran Synod of Missouri, Ohio, and Other States), 1896, 55-56.

The Synod approved the request for steam heating and was able to fund the installation of it by the end of 1896. The steam system was not less expensive to operate than the many stoves, but it did heat more rooms and provided more even heat.

Modernization of the heating system at the Addison school took place 15 years before the Synod decided to move the institution to River Forest and several years before relocation talk gained momentum. After the turn of the century, however, more and more people seem to have been giving consideration to the advisability of relocating the teacher-training facility. The conversation included the desirability of separating the preparatory department from the professional college program and, after Seward added college years to its curriculum, the possibility of combining the normal school programs of Addison and Seward on one campus. Talk of this kind made it difficult for Addison to persuade the delegates at synodical conventions to invest much in the physical plant of the school, although the absolutely pressing need for a new septic tank was such that the 1908 convention of the Synod approved funding for the modernizing of the plumbing and toilet facilities on the campus.

The 1908 convention of the Missouri Synod also had to address a new building request from the Addison board of control. It was that request which seems to have brought the relocation issue fully into the open. The board introduced its request for a new building by saying: "It is far from our minds to recommend improvements or expansion of our facilities because we want to imitate other institutions which have been provided for in a better way."[2] The board then proceeded to point out that not only were the living and sleeping quarters at the school inadequate but that classrooms, library space, and piano rooms were also desperately needed. The board's request

---

[2] *Synodal-Bericht der . . . Synode von Missouri . . .* (Synodical Report of the . . . Synod of Missouri . . .), 1908, 56.

was for a $29,000.00 appropriation for a new building for academic purposes.

The convention committee assigned to make a recommendation on the Addison request proposed that " 'a commission be appointed with the assignment to make recommendations to the next synodical convention relative to the feasibility of relocating this institution.' "[3] The committee then added that " 'the request of the [Addison] board of control for $29,000.00 to erect a new building be declined. . . .' "[4] The convention's response to the committee's recommendation was reported on as follows:

> Hereupon a lively debate followed, which was concluded with a decision to refer the matter for the present to a special committee session for further deliberation. This was carried out immediately and the result of the same reported to the assembled Synod the next morning as follows: "We are unanimous in the opinion that the $29,000.00 requested by the [Addison] board of control for a new building be approved, with the stipulation, however, that the sum of $30,000.00 may not be exceeded."[5]

The convention approved the committee recommendation.

The story did not end there, however. When the Synod met three years later, the Addison board of control reported:

> A resolution of the . . . Synod . . . to erect a new building in Addison, sad to say, could not be carried out. We are able to assure the brethren, however, that the fault lay not

---

[3] Ibid., 57.

[4] Ibid.

[5] Ibid.

in this that the board lacked the determination to proceed nor in this that the need in Addison was removed. No, that building did not take place in Addison was attributable to the fact that the necessary money for construction was not collected.[6]

It is not unusual, of course, that funds for projects approved by synodical conventions are not always available, resulting, therefore, in a failure to carry out this or that project. In the case of the 1908 Missouri Synod decision to erect a new building at Addison, however, one suspects that the necessary funding was not available because of a lack of enthusiasm for the project, especially in the Chicago area where proponents of relocation had become very active after 1908.[7]

On the other hand, opponents of relocation were also expressing themselves. A case in point would be the action of the Northern Illinois District at its 1910 convention. Aware that the synodically approved building project had not materialized, the District recommended an alternate plan for improvements in the physical plant at the Addison school and submitted its proposals in an overture to the 1911 convention of the Missouri Synod. The Northern Illinois District convention recommended that the Synod not proceed with the construction of the $30,000.00 building approved in 1908 but erect instead a new dormitory and then remodel the existing buildings to accommodate the various existing academic needs of the school. This would be a far more expensive project than what had been envisioned in 1908. To show its commitment to this alternate proposal for Addison, the District promised to gather

---

[6] *Synodal-Bericht der . . . Synode von Missouri . . .* (Synodical Report of the . . . Synod of Missouri . . .), 1911, 48.

[7] See Alfred J. Freitag, *College with a Cause* (River Forest: Concordia Teachers College, 1964), 80-81.

$30,000.00 from its own membership and give it to the Synod
for the substitute building project, so that "the . . . Synod might
see that we [the Northern Illinois District] are serious"[8] about
what we have proposed.

The Northern Illinois District memorial was presented to
the crucial 1911 convention of the Missouri Synod. The
assembled delegates were in possession, however, of another
overture from several groups in the Chicago area. That overture
addressed the situation somewhat differently:

> With great joy we observe with what interest in all parts
> of the Synod attention is turned to Addison and . . . the
> conviction emerges: For this our oldest Teachers
> Seminary something quite out of the ordinary must finally
> happen once and for all with respect to suitable, modern
> buildings. No one who is acquainted with the state of
> affairs at Addison can shut his eyes to this conclusion.
>
> We would like, however, to go one step farther. We are
> of the opinion that the time has come for the seminary to
> be separated from the preparatory school and be relocated
> in a larger city.[9]

Two proposals were thus clearly before the Synod: (1) expand
and modernize the facilities at Addison or (2) relocate at least the
college department to a larger city. The Addison board of control
was in favor of the first proposal, that of the Northern Illinois
District, and requested that the Synod "approve the round
figure of $75,000.00 for new construction, remodeling, heating,

---

[8] *Synodal-Bericht des Nord-Illinois-Distrikts der . . . Synode von
Missouri . . .* (Synodical Report of the Northern Illinois District of the . . .
Synod of Missouri . . .), 1910, 74.

[9] *Synodal-Bericht der . . . Synode von Missouri . . .* (Synodical Report
of the . . . Synod of Missouri . . .), 1911, 52.

electric lighting, and the improvement of the nine professorages."[10]

The convention was in session from May 10 to 20, with debate on the issue extending over several days. When the vote on relocation was taken, it was passed, according to the synodical *Report*, by a "narrow majority."[11] Citing a postcard communication, Alfred Freitag in *College with a Cause* reports that the vote was 216 to 206.[12] The close vote was a matter of concern and was very likely the reason for an interpretative comment in the official report of the convention. At the point in the record of the proceedings where the resolution to appropriate money for a new campus in the Chicago area was reported, the following parenthetical note was included:

(Remark from the minutes taken by the assistant secretary for the afternoon of May 18 which were read aloud and accepted the next morning: "If from the discussions of various convention delegates there was evidence already how also those who on the previous day had voted against relocation of the institution to Chicago were resolved to work together shoulder to shoulder with their brethren for the carrying out of the decision which had been made, then this intention became especially clear now at the voting on the approval of funding, since that resolution was unanimously accepted and adopted.")[13]

In addition to allocating funds for the relocation project, the convention also requested that the Northern Illinois District donate the $30,000.00 it had already gathered for building at

---

[10] Ibid., 49.

[11] Ibid., 52.

[12] Freitag, *College with a Cause*, 82.

[13] *Synodal-Bericht* (Synodical Report), 1911, 53.

Addison toward the planned construction on the new campus. The Lutheran Education Society of Chicago, which had been formed in early 1911 and had been a strong proponent for relocation, affirmed its offer to provide a suitable piece of property. The Society and the Northern Illinois District were both thanked in advance for their demonstrated love for the Synod's Teachers Seminary, and the relocation project was to have precedence over all other approved distributions from the Synod's building fund. The Addison era was coming to an end; the name River Forest was about to enter the vocabulary of The Lutheran Church—Missouri Synod.

The campus at River Forest was ready for occupancy in the fall of 1913. A picture of the dedication ceremonies shows a huge crowd in attendance, estimated by some to have been between 30,000-45,000.[14] Things in Addison had come to an end with graduation ceremonies in the previous June. That occasion marked the close of the presidency of Theodore Brohm, who entered retirement at that time. After the distribution of diplomas to the last Addison graduates, William C. Kohn was installed as fourth president of the school which was moving to River Forest.

Kohn had been president of the Northern Illinois District and had been in favor of the move from Addison to the Chicago area. Born in Germany in 1865, he came to the United States with his parents when he was only three months old and grew up in the city of Chicago. He attended a Lutheran parochial school in that city and then entered Concordia College in Fort Wayne, Indiana. He was graduated from Concordia Seminary in St. Louis in 1887, the year in which the life and ministry of C. F. W. Walther had come to an end at the St. Louis school. Upon graduation, Kohn returned to Chicago to serve first as an assistant pastor in a Chicago church and then as the first pastor

---

[14] See Alfred J. Freitag, *College with a Cause*, "Pictures."

of the new St. Andrew's congregation on the city's south side. At his death in 1943, Kohn's obituarist said of him in the Synod's *Der Lutheraner* (The Lutheran): "He was an impressive and persuasive preacher who subscribed to the principle expressed in Article 24 of the Apology of the Augsburg Confession: 'There is nothing which keeps people with the church more readily than good preaching.' "[15] The same writer said of Kohn in the Synod's English periodical:

> His views and policies made for a happy combination of conservatism and progressiveness—a conservatism determined upon "holding fast the faithful word" as he had been taught from Holy Scripture, and a readiness to perceive in a new enterprise its possibilities for the advancement of Christ's kingdom. . . . The manner of his administration was characterized by a firmness and insistence in matters regulated by the Word of God or dictated by the welfare of the school or Church at large. . . . As an instructor—he taught classes in religion and pedagogy—he was clear, definite, and emphatic in his presentation and eminently practical in applying the principles of teaching to schoolroom situations.[16]

Kohn's presidency at River Forest extended from 1913 until 1939. He retired in the latter year but continued to teach some classes for two years after that. Kohn had a new campus of five buildings when he began his tenure at River Forest. The complex included a striking administration-classroom building, two dormitories, a dining hall and kitchen, and a music building. By the time classes began in 1913, the school had also acquired a new name. The institution at Addison had always

---

[15] T. C. Appelt in *Der Lutheraner*, April 6, 1943, 102.

[16] T. C. Appelt in *The Lutheran Witness*, April 13, 1943, 125-26.

been known simply as the Teachers Seminary at Addison. Just before the move to River Forest, the faculty had proposed naming the school "Lutheran Normal College of the German Evangelical Lutheran Church," an appellation which would surely have been changed quickly after the outbreak of World War I in 1914. The name finally chosen, however, was Concordia Teachers College. That name appeared on the title page of the school's 1913-14 *Catalogue* and became the legal designation of the institution in 1915.[17] An easily identifiable era in the history of teacher education in The Lutheran Church—Missouri Synod began in 1913 when the old Addison school was moved to another community and continued its mission on a new campus, under a new name, and with a new president, who would serve in that capacity for 26 years.

The celebration which accompanied the occupancy of new and modern facilities came to a screeching halt in River Forest in less than five months after the campus was dedicated. In the evening of February 28, 1914, a severe fire broke out in the administration-classroom building. Although it was thought initially that the structure was a total loss, it was later found that some structural elements had not been damaged. Nonetheless, the interior of the building had been gutted by the fire, resulting in the loss of records, furnishings, the library, and educational materials. The sad irony of the situation, of course, was the fact that the buildings at Addison had long been considered a fire hazard, a condition which contributed to the arguments that the school should be moved to another location with buildings less vulnerable to fire. It was only materials, however, which had been lost in the disaster at River Forest. There were no injuries or loss of life and even though wind conditions were unfavorable, the adjacent dormitories were not damaged.

---

[17] See Alfred J. Freitag, *College with a Cause*, 85.

The Lutheran Witness and *Der Lutheraner* notified the synodical membership officially of the loss in March issues of those periodicals. The president of the Northern Illinois District used the official church papers to report the details of the fire, while Synod President Friedrich Pfotenhauer informed the constituency about his action with respect to the restoration of the damaged building. In his assessment of the damage immediately after the fire, President Pfotenhauer had this to say:

> As regards our loss, I might add the following. The cost of the destroyed Administration Building was $68,000. Mr. Walker, member of the General Board of Supervision . . . estimates the damage at $50,000. To this must be added $10,000, loss of furnishings, museum, and library. As generally known, our Synod does not carry insurance on its property. The local board, however, in order to protect those that participated in the construction, secured a policy, the life of which was to terminate on March 31. The fire insurance companies will pay us the sum of $18,500.[18]

The question which had to be addressed was how to provide classroom facilities for the college. Obviously, makeshift arrangements in the undamaged buildings had to be made for the remainder of the academic year. Since the fire insurance would not be adequate to cover the losses, synodical action was required for any additional expenditures. The Synod was scheduled to meet later in 1914 and could speak to the matter then, but that would result in a serious construction delay and prolong temporary measures into the next academic year. Encouraged by others, both orally and in writing,

---

[18] *The Lutheran Witness*, March 26, 1914, 53.

President Pfotenhauer spoke to the rebuilding situation in the following way:

> What, then, would be the correct answer to the query, What shall we do? Shall we begin at once on the rebuilding of our Administration Building, or wait until the convening of our Delegate Synod? The Board of Control together with many of our brethren are of the opinion that expediency demands that we rebuild without delay. . . . In order to be rightly advised in the present situation, and as far as possible to ascertain the opinion of Synod, I have addressed a circular letter to all officials of Synod and to all district presidents enquiring whether in their opinion building operations ought to begin at once or not. To these 29 letters I have received . . . 25 replies; only four district presidents, living far distant from here, have not replied. All have expressed themselves most explicitly and positively in favor of rebuilding at once. This, they opined, would be the correct procedure and meet with the full approbation of our congregations.
>
> We shall therefore begin at once with the rebuilding of our Administration Building with the firm conviction that this action will not only be heartily approved by our congregations, but also that everywhere within the extensive domain of our Synod liberal and general collections will be made.[19]

With the approval of the synod president, construction began immediately, resulting in a rebuilt administration-classroom building which was dedicated in October 1914, not quite eight

---

[19] Ibid., 52.

months after the fire and in the same month in which the new campus had been dedicated a year earlier.

The curriculum for the six-year teacher education program at the time of the move to River Forest was comprised of the general areas of religion, pedagogy, German, English, mathematics, history, civics, geography, science, music, and penmanship. With the exception of civics, each of the areas was divided into subcategories, so that in a field like religion, for example, there were courses in catechism, symbolics, Bible history, sacred history (Old and New Testament), isagogics, and catechctics. Since four of the six years of study were in reality a high school, the offerings in some of the departments were what one would expect to find in an American secondary school of the day. Common high school offerings such as English language and composition, American literature, United States history, and physics were all included in the first four years of study. From the catalog descriptions of a few of the courses it is apparent, however, that some elementary school skills also had to be taught in the lower classes at River Forest. In the mathematics department, for example, attention was given in the first class to fundamentals of arithmetic. Geometry, on the other hand, was not taken up until the fifth year, the first ycar of the college course, in other words. Although entrance requirements and academic standards had been raised considerably since the early days of Lutheran teacher education at Addison, the apparent lack of uniformity in elementary school programs in 1913 still required that some attention be given in the first year of study at River Forest to a few grammar school basics.

It was the German department, however, which was able to assume a relatively high level of proficiency on the part of entering students at River Forest at the time of the move to that community. The study of that language was required of all students, but evcn the lowest level courses began beyond the basics. Students regularly entered with a knowledge of German. In fact, without a knowledge of German it was not possible to take classes in religion, for even the 1917-18 college *Catalogue* still contained the comment:

> Religious instruction is conducted largely in the German language. The textbook used during the first three years is Dr. Luther's Small Catechism with a Short Exposition by Dr. H. Schwan. The German and the English texts of the Small Catechism, all German proof-texts and about 60 English ones, a number of hymns and Bible chapters are memorized.[20]

The popularity of the German language declined steadily among American citizens of German heritage after World War I, not only because of the antipathy toward that language engendered by the war but because of the natural tendency for people to replace even a cherished foreign tongue with the language of the country in which they live. This is especially the case among the young, so that an institution like Concordia at River Forest eventually admitted fewer and fewer students who were fluent in German at the time of matriculation. The German character of the River Forest school did not seem to have stirred up quite as much local controversy during World War I as surfaced in connection with the two Lutheran teachers colleges at New Ulm, Minnesota, and Seward, Nebraska,[21] although "federal authorities," according to Alfred Freitag (*College with a Cause*), " 'spoke to' President Kohn in 1919 because he made a German speech at graduation."[22] That a graduation assembly

---

[20] *Catalogue of the Concordia Teachers College* (River Forest), 1917-18, 17.

[21] See chapters 10 (1884) and 12 (1894) of the present volume.

[22] Freitag, 120. Freitag's source for this information is the Faculty Minutes of December 10, 1919.

at River Forest should have been addressed in German at that time is quite understandable both because of the role of that language in the curriculum of the school and because of the many German-speaking guests who would very likely have attended the graduation event. Time, however, would soon remove both arguments.

The reason for the use of German in the religion curriculum at River Forest during the second decade of the twentieth century lay not only in the fact that students were functional in that language but also in the very purpose of the parochial school as an institution. It was an agency intended to carry out the mission of the church. A River Forest professor writing in 1930 was careful to note that fact even when speaking about the academic and professional training of prospective teachers:

> In all the learning through the mind which God has given man to use, the student is trained not to overvalue human learning, and never to forget that he is preparing to be a servant of the Savior in a special sense. He is led to appreciate that the main objective in Lutheran education must always be faith in Jesus, and that nothing must stand in the way of securing this objective in all of his teaching activities.[23]

If the religious objective is primary in the parochial school and if such a school is an agency of the church, then it is incumbent upon the teachers in those schools to prepare their pupils for the worship life of a parish. In most parts of The Lutheran Church—Missouri Synod in the first two decades of the twentieth century, public worship was conducted extensively in the German language. This necessitated the use of that

---

[23] Alfred F. Schmieding, "The Teacher Training Department at Work," *Northern Illinois Messenger VI* (April 1930): 5-6, quoted in Alfred Freitag, *College with a Cause*, 127-28.

language in at least the religious instruction of congregational elementary schools and warranted the emphasis upon German in synodical teachers colleges.

Another congregational need which Lutheran teachers were expected to be able to fill was that of parish musician. Singing had long been a part of the Lutheran elementary-school curriculum, the singing of both hymns and secular songs. Since one- and two-room schools were the kind frequently operated by local parishes, such a thing as departmentalization was not on the scene. Each teacher had to conduct his or her own singing class. This was the general practice, moreover, in schools with several teachers. For that reason, music was an integral part of the curriculum of a Lutheran teachers college. That is well-reflected in the following comment of River Forest's 1913-14 *Catalogue*:

> As the study of music (vocal and instrumental) is obligatory for all students, ample provision is made for this department by a specially designed and constructed building, known as Music Hall. . . . At present 16 pianos and 6 pipe organs (these all motor-driven) are placed at the service of the students for practice purposes.[24]

The music program for prospective Lutheran teachers when the Missouri Synod moved its Addison campus to River Forest included required music courses in each of the six years of study. The *Catalogue* of the time stipulated that "the study of piano playing is obligatory for five years."[25] In addition, there was a three-year course in organ instruction. Voice training, harmony, and music history rounded out the college preparation of Lutheran elementary parochial school teachers in 1913.

---

[24] *Catalogue of the Concordia Teachers College* (1913-14), 12.
[25] Ibid., 21.

Things had not changed by 1921, the *Catalogue* of that year explaining why such extensive music offerings were necessary:

> This [the music] department offers courses in organ, violin, harmony, and singing. The aim and object is to enable all students to teach singing in school, to lead church choirs, to fulfill the duties of church organists, and to give them a general knowledge of music, its history, and construction.[26]

Lutheran school teachers were expected to serve their parishes as church musicians. Such responsibilities required that a fair amount of music instruction be given not only at River Forest but also at the Missouri Synod's teachers college in Seward, Nebraska, and at the Wisconsin Synod's Dr. Martin Luther College in New Ulm, Minnesota. As the years went by, Concordia at River Forest became especially well-known, not only in Lutheran circles but elsewhere as well, for its emphasis on church music, and toward the end of the century the institution offered a Master of Church Music degree in the school's division of graduate studies.

Graduate education was hardly in the picture, of course, when the Missouri Synod's teachers college moved to River Forest. The school's six-year course of study at that time was comprised of a four-year high school and a two-year normal school. By 1926, however, the Synod was beginning to consider the expansion of the normal department into a full four-year college. It would take more than a decade for that plan to materialize, but a step toward a four-year program was taken in 1933 when an experimental third year was made available to students who had not received a teaching assignment in the spring of that year, depression conditions

---

[26] *Catalogue* (1921-22), 20.

having caused a scarcity of teaching positions. The 1935 convention of the Missouri Synod discussed the entire matter and at that time resolved the following:

1. That a third year be added to the normal course at River Forest;
2. That a third year be added to the normal course at Seward;
3. That Synod take no action at this time on the request of the River Forest Teachers' Seminary Board of Control to "add an elective fourth year."[27]

When the Synod met in convention three years later, it approved the addition of a fourth year to the River Forest curriculum. The synodical resolution was implemented beginning with the 1939-40 academic year.

The addition of college years to the course of study at River Forest always brought the high school department of the school under scrutiny. The desirability of keeping the normal school and high school combined on the same campus was discussed already at the time of the move from Addison to River Forest. When the Synod's Committee on Higher Education recommended to the Synod in 1935 that a third and eventually a fourth college year be added at River Forest, the group also remarked: "Your Committee believes . . . that the high school and college departments should not be permanently conjoined, but that the problem of separating them must be solved in the light of future developments."[28] Although certain kinds of separations were effected along the way, the high school department continued on the River Forest campus until 1950. Several factors contributed to the discontinuance of the

---

[27]*Proceedings of the Thirty-sixth Regular Convention of the Ev. Lutheran Synod of Missouri, Ohio, and Other States*, 1935, 40.

[28] Ibid., 39.

preparatory department at that time. There was an urgent need for more Lutheran parochial school teachers immediately after World War II. The demand for more teachers resulted in an increase of enrollment in the River Forest college department, with a concomitant overburdening of the physical facilities of the campus. In addition, the area or community Lutheran high school movement was beginning to gain momentum. Such schools, it was felt, would be able to furnish an adequate high school education for students who wanted to enroll in the teacher-education program at River Forest. The college's preparatory department was thus thought to be dispensable.

Twelve years before the discontinuation of the high school department of Concordia Teachers College, another major change had occurred at the school. By action of the Synod in 1938, the River Forest institution was permitted to become coeducational. Its sister Missouri Synod teachers college in Seward, Nebraska, and the Wisconsin Synod's Dr. Martin Luther College in New Ulm, Minnesota, had been accepting women students in their teacher-education programs for quite some time before that. The call for women teachers had grown considerably in the early part of the twentieth century, with the depression years of the 1930s increasing the demand, since women teachers could be engaged for salaries lower than those paid to men. A study committee had recommended to the 1938 synodical convention an experimental coeducational program for River Forest, and the school's board of control had requested such an experiment. At the same time that the study committee was considering the coeducation issue, the committee was also giving attention to the feasibility of using synodical colleges for general education purposes rather than just for the training of future pastors and teachers. River Forest was among the schools being thought of as campuses which might be permitted to enroll general higher education students.

The Synod postponed action in 1938 on the general education issue for River Forest but granted the request of the College's board of control to permit the school "to enroll women and girls for teacher training up to thirty per cent of its male enrollment."[29] The resolution was put into effect in the fall term of 1938. By 1941, the 30 per cent quota-figure was modified because "the demand for synodically trained women teachers had become so insistent that Synod acceded to the request of the board and faculty of Concordia Teachers College and turned over to the College of Presidents the responsibility of periodically adjusting the quotas of women students at River Forest and Seward, according to the needs of the field.[30] So it was that coeducation came to River Forest because, according to the school's 1944 request for a women's dormitory,

> congregations want women who are thoroughly grounded in Bible history and Christian doctrine. Some of them need women who are able to assist in the musical program of the congregation in school and church. All desire women who are trained to meet the educational standards of the States and communities in which they are called upon to teach.[31]

By the time Concordia Teachers College in River Forest became coeducational in 1938, women were teaching in many parochial school classrooms of both the Wisconsin and Missouri Synods. There had been some debate at various times, however, on whether or not women should be permitted to hold that kind of teaching office in the church and under what conditions they might occupy it. The Missouri Synod had addressed the issue at

---

[29] *Proceedings of the Thirty-seventh Regular Convention of the Ev. Lutheran Synod of Missouri, Ohio, and Other States*, 1938, 61.

[30] *Proceedings*, 1944, 61.

[31] Ibid., 60.

its 1926 convention. At that time the Southeastern Conference of the English District of the Synod had submitted an overture petitioning the synodical convention

1) To make it Synod's policy to educate girls with a view to their becoming teachers in its Christian day-schools;
2) To go on record as favoring the general Christian education of girls in educational institutions maintained by Synod.[32]

The Joint School Board of the Northern and Southern Nebraska Districts had also memorialized the Synod in that year to "approve the education of woman teachers for our Christian day-schools at one of our synodical institutions and permit it to continue to do so in the future."[33]

The 1926 convention floor committee assigned to deal with the issue recommended approval of coeducation at the teachers colleges and did so in the words of the overture from the Southeastern Conference of the English District mentioned above. The Synod adopted the recommendations of the convention floor committee, thus granting official approval to the coeducational practice already in operation at Seward. It might be noted in this connection that the Wisconsin Synod, Missouri's partner in the Synodical Conference, had been accepting women at the former's teacher training school in New Ulm, Minnesota, for a number of years prior to the Missouri Synod action of 1926. The 1919-20 catalog of Wisconsin's Dr. Martin Luther College stated "that the 'institution is open to young ladies,' "[34] a practice which had been in effect already since the first decade of the century. Even though River Forest

---

[32] *Proceedings*, 1926, English edition, 76; German, 130.

[33] Ibid., English edition, 76; German, 129.

[34] Morton A. Schroeder, *A Time to Remember* (New Ulm: Dr. Martin Luther College, 1984), 72.

did not begin to educate women for the profession of Lutheran school teaching until 1938, two other teachers colleges within the Synodical Conference had begun doing that much earlier.

In 1929, three years after the Missouri Synod had expressed itself officially on the doctrinal acceptability of engaging women as Lutheran parochial school teachers and providing for their college training, the Synod addressed the issue once more. In this case synodical action came in response to a letter written by a teacher who objected to the employment of women teachers in Christian day schools. The convention of 1929 responded to the objection by adopting a committee report which, while expressing a preference for the calling of male teachers, also approved the engaging of women teachers and recommended that such teachers obtain their college education at a synodical school. The Synod said:

> We hold that the calling of regular male graduates of our synodical normal [teacher education] institutions as teachers to our parish schools must by all means remain the rule and order in our Synod. All congregations are therefore urged to call male teachers in preference to employing women teachers and to strive that woman teachers are replaced by regularly called male teachers as soon as local conditions will permit.

> At the same time we are of the opinion that the employment of woman teachers in our parish schools cannot be avoided altogether, nor should it be discountenanced under all circumstances. We hold that woman teachers often are especially adapted to fill positions successfully in the lower grades of our schools. However, congregations in engaging woman teachers should exercise great care that only such women are appointed as teachers in our parish schools as have been

thoroughly trained also in the teaching of religion and in every way have received a full training, preferably in our own institutions, that will fit them for Christian parish-school work.[35]

Although coeducation came to Concordia Teachers College in River Forest at a rather late date, when the school finally did open its doors to women desiring to become Lutheran parochial school teachers the question of whether women should be permitted to teach in Lutheran elementary schools had already been answered.

The 1938 synodical convention which approved coeducation at River Forest also granted approval to the adding of a fourth year to the teacher-education program of the school. The addition to the curriculum of that year of study opened the door for the seeking of accreditation from a regional accrediting agency for the school's college department. In its 1938 report to the Synod, the River Forest board of control had noted that its high school department was accredited not only by the Department of Public Instruction of the State of Illinois and the University of Illinois but also by the North Central Association of Colleges and Secondary Schools. With respect to the college department, however, the board had this to say:

> The college department is accredited by the Department of Public Instruction of the State of Illinois; the University of Illinois allows credit for the junior-college work and in cases of students with a superior record also for the third year of work. Northwestern University and Chicago University allow a similar credit. The college department lacks accreditation by the North Central Association of

---

[35] *Proceedings*, 1929, 73-74.

Colleges and Secondary Schools. Only if a fourth year is added, can complete accreditation be attained.

Since public authorities more and more generally are requiring that any one who teaches in an elementary school, either public or private, must have gotten his training at an accredited school, the accreditation of our Concordia at River Forest is of vital importance to our teachers and the continuance of our parochial schools.

Our Board of Control can testify that the accrediting agencies have not in a single case recommended anything that might have been to the detriment of our institution or required the elimination of any courses; on the contrary, the efforts toward accreditation have been entirely of benefit to our Concordia.

We want to call attention, however, to the need of full accreditation of the college department by the North Central Association. . . .[36]

As previously noted, the request to add a fourth year of study was granted by the Synod and was inaugurated as an option for students in September 1939, the same year in which W. C. Kohn, who had been president of the institution since 1913, retired.

With the fourth year in place, the desire for accreditation could be pursued under the administration of Arthur W. Klinck, successor to Kohn. In its report to the Synod in 1938, the River Forest board had emphasized that in their experience accrediting agencies had not "in a single case recommended anything that might have been to the detriment of our

---

[36] *Proceedings*, 1938, 59-60.

institution or required the elimination of any courses,"[37] a statement intended very likely to allay any fears within the Synod that accreditation might interfere with the courses in religion at the school. The accreditation process itself would take time, of course, especially so after the entry of the United States into World War II and the disruption which the war caused in the normal routine of American life. By 1950, however, the task was done, and President Klinck was able to announce that the college department of Concordia Teachers College had been granted accreditation by the North Central Association of Colleges and Secondary Schools.

The year in which Concordia received accreditation from North Central might be termed a turning-point year in the history of the school, for it was in that year, 1950, that the high school department of the institution was terminated. The closing of the high school and the endorsement of the college program by a regional accrediting association marked the beginning of efforts to broaden the mission of the school. A graduate program was begun in 1957, together with a course of study to prepare teachers for secondary school teaching. Accreditation for these programs was sought and obtained in 1964 from the National Council for the Accreditation of Teacher Education (NCATE). The addition of nonteaching programs of study resulted in a change of the school's name from Concordia Teachers College to Concordia College and finally Concordia University. Owned and operated by The Lutheran Church—Missouri Synod, the institution is part of that church's Concordia University system.

Teacher education in The Lutheran Church—Missouri Synod on a separate campus began with a private venture in Milwaukee in 1855. The program operated for only two years, at which time the Missouri Synod established a teachers seminary in conjunction with its theological seminary at Fort Wayne and

---

[37] Ibid., 60.

called one of the Milwaukee faculty members to head the teacher-education department at the Indiana location. In 1864, the Missouri Synod transferred its Lutheran teacher-education program to a separate campus in Addison, Illinois. Forty-nine years later, in 1913, the Synod moved its Addison school to River Forest, continued teacher education in that place, and in the course of time expanded the offerings of the school to include programs of study other than teacher education. Addison and River Forest definitely stand in a direct line with one another, since the school in the latter location was not a new institution but merely a relocation of the former. From that point of view, River Forest celebrated its centennial in 1964, although some of the school's academic catalogs have counted the years from 1855. In either case, however, Concordia University at River Forest has the longest history of a continuous Lutheran teacher-education program in both the Missouri and Wisconsin Synods.

Suggested for Further Reading

Freitag, Alfred J. *College with a Cause*. River Forest, Illinois: Concordia Teachers College, 1964.

✦ ✦ ✦ 1920 ✦ ✦ ✦

Full-time Synodical
Parochial School Officers

Meeting in convention in June of 1920, the Evangelical Lutheran Synod of Missouri, Ohio, and Other States[1] had before it a number of overtures requesting the creation of a full-time executive position at the synodical level in order to provide guidance and counsel for the parochial schools within the Synod. Two years prior to that, three synodical districts had established the office of district superintendent of schools, and in 1919 three other districts did the same. The call now was for an executive officer who would have the time to give attention to parish school matters on a synodwide basis. The authors of the overtures were not in any way suggesting that the district offices of superintendent be abolished. It was in fact admitted that those offices had been effective and beneficial in their jurisdictions. It was felt, however, that an overall administrator would be in a position to have a more comprehensive view of the total school situation and be able to provide professional resources which would be useful for parish schools in all districts. The convention floor committee was persuaded by the arguments and recommended to the Synod that the synodical "School Commission be empowered to appoint a secretary who is to devote all his time and energy to the work spoken of and

---

[1] The word German had been removed from the Missouri Synod's name in 1917.

be responsible to the Commission."[2] The 1920 convention accepted the recommendation, which resulted in the calling in 1921 of August C. Stellhorn as the first secretary of schools for The Lutheran Church—Missouri Synod, a position he continued to hold until his retirement 40 years later.

The Wisconsin Synod had established the office of full-time school administrator at the synodical level a year earlier. The Synod itself had been reorganized in 1917 when it moved from a federated synod with the Minnesota, Michigan, and Nebraska Synods to a merged synod of the four bodies and took the name Evangelical Lutheran Joint Synod of Wisconsin and Other States.[3] The name chosen in 1919 for the educational executive was school visitor. Claus Gieschen, principal and teacher at Friedens Lutheran School in Kenosha, Wisconsin, a school with eight grades, six teachers, and 271 pupils, was installed into that office in January of 1920, the same year in which the Missouri Synod later resolved to establish its office of synodical school secretary. The Wisconsin Synod did not have district superintendents as did the Missouri Synod, so that Wisconsin's school visitor was expected to do some tasks which a district superintendent would have been doing in the Missouri Synod. The Wisconsin Synod was not as far-flung as its sister synod but did have eight districts at the time, three of which were in the state of Wisconsin. Both synods avoided the use of the term used in Germany for a school executive, namely, school inspector, although the Wisconsin Synod nomenclature makes it clear that visitation, if not inspection, was a definite part of the work of its synodical school officer. Since the executive positions in both synods were new, the duties

---

[2] *Synodalbericht der . . . Synode von Missouri, Ohio und Andern Staaten* (Synodical Report of the . . . Synod of Missouri, Ohio and Other States), 1920, 236.

[3] The name in German was Die allgemeine evangelisch-lutherische Synode von Wisconsin und anderen Staaten.

and responsibilities of the offices were a bit vague. The 1920 beginnings of these synodical administrative posts make that year a notable one in the history of Lutheran parochial schools.

The Missouri Synod parochial school executive office has continued under one title or another uninterruptedly since its inception in 1920. August Stellhorn in his book *Schools of The Lutheran Church—Missouri Synod* reports that there was a slight attempt in 1923 to have the Synod consider abolishing the office but that this move was not widely supported. The position did not fare quite so well in the Wisconsin Synod. When that group met in 1929, it responded to the report of its school commission in the following way:

> Although we do find definite good results of the work of the Superintendent of Schools, yet in view of the lack of funds we nevertheless recommend that the School Committee be asked to take steps to bring about a reasonable arrangement for the future employment of the superintendent and that the office of School Visitor be then temporarily vacated and that the School Committee be asked to continue as much of this work as possible.[4]

The dissolution in 1929 of the office of school visitor was attributed to a lack of funds. Since that was an ill-fated year in United States economic history, it might be concluded that the educational office was done away with as a result of the October stock market crash. The Wisconsin Synod action occurred in August, however, and although there had been warnings about a possible eclipse of the prosperity of the 1920s, other

---

[4] *Synodal-Bericht: Verhandlungen der . . . Synode von Wisconsin und anderen Staaten* (Synodical Report: Proceedings of the . . . Synod of Wisconsin and Other States), 1929, 40. It is rather interesting to note that this action is reported in the English language in the otherwise German *Proceedings*.

circumstances explain the belt-tightening better. The Synod had been accumulating a sizable debt for general operational expenditures. In addition, two major building projects had just been completed. Dr. Martin Luther College, the Synod's Teachers College in New Ulm, Minnesota, had erected a new classroom-administration building on its campus in 1928. The Synod had also relocated its seminary with a set of new buildings to Thiensville (present-day Mequon), Wisconsin, and dedicated the new campus during the 1929 synodical convention. In the midst of all this spending, the position of school visitor, for whom a very modest salary increase had been proposed by the school commission, was temporarily suspended. The suspension was only temporary, however, for by 1933 a new plan for school visitation was approved and put into practice. The plan called for an executive secretary, but the convention did not permit the engaging of a person for that position at that time. At the Synod's next convention, in 1935, the school commission emphasized that the position needed to be filled, saying:

> The new plan of school visitation . . . is not only in full operation, but has also proved very satisfactory. The plan, however, is very incomplete without the executive secretary. . . . Your committee feels very keenly the necessity of an executive secretary and *urgently requests that an executive secretary be granted* (italics in the original).[5]

The request was granted, resulting in the installation of F. W. Meyer into the office in 1936. Thus, after a hiatus of only a few years, the Wisconsin Synod's school administrative position, filled for the first time in 1920, had its second incumbent.

---

[5] *Proceedings of the . . . Evangelical Lutheran Joint Synod of Wisconsin and Other States*, 1935, 84.

Several factors were fueling the desire around 1920 to have a synodical school administrator in both the Wisconsin and Missouri Synods. Some general kind of coordinating and supervisory office was seen as absolutely necessary if, in the opinion of a number of spokesmen, Lutheran parochial schools were going to be able to continue to exist. Thus, for example, Theodore Graebner, professor of theology at Concordia Seminary in St. Louis, wrote a strongly worded two-part article for his synod's homiletical magazine. The article was entitled "The Crisis in Our School Affairs." Graebner opened the article with the words:

> More and more, the signs are pointing to this that our parochial schools have arrived at the chapter "To be or not to be." We are not standing in <u>a</u> crisis but in <u>the</u> crisis.[6]

The Wisconsin Synod's school commission said something similar when it reported to that synod's 1921 convention:

> Our schools, attacked on all sides, are now struggling for their very existence. That which can be done for their promotion must be done now. If we do not put forth all efforts at this time to preserve with God's help this well of blessing of our church, then we must be prepared for what follows, namely, to lose that fountain in a short time.[7]

It is obvious that advocates of the Lutheran parochial school around 1920 were of the conviction that the institution was in

---

[6] Theodore Graebner, "Die Krisis in unserer Schulsache," *Magazin für ev.-luth. Homiletik* (Magazine for Evangelical Lutheran Homiletics or Homiletic Magazine), February 1920, 69.

[7] *Synodal-Bericht, Verhandlungen . . . der . . . Synode von Wisconsin u. a. Staaten* (Synodical Report, Proceedings . . . of the . . . Synod of Wisconsin and Other States) 1921, 79.

jeopardy. Their fears were not without foundation, as becomes clear from the United States Supreme Court decisions in the cases of *Meyer v. Nebraska* and *Pierce v. the Society of Sisters*, treated in the present volume under the dates 1923 and 1925 respectively. Although parochial schools are congregational ventures in both the Missouri and Wisconsin Synods, the creation in 1920 of full-time synodical offices for school matters is evidence that broader administrative services are sometimes necessary if a system of parish schools is to thrive.

In the Missouri Synod, Theodore Graebner's 1920 school article in *Homiletic Magazine* was definitely an influence on what came to be asked for in the school overtures to the Synod's convention of that year. One printed overture specifically named Graebner; others, while not mentioning him by name, reflected his analysis of the current situation and his recommendations for a central office and its duties. Graebner's essay together with the whereases in the memorials to the 1920 Missouri Synod convention provide helpful insights into what was going on in that period of Lutheran school history.

The historically best-remembered activities of the time were the political maneuvers in various states to place restraints upon parochial school curricula or to do away with private elementary schools altogether. The curriculum problem had come to the fore already in 1890 with the Bennett and Edwards laws in the states of Wisconsin and Illinois.[8] The issue for Lutherans at that time was the use of German in Lutheran elementary schools. Although that usage had diminished considerably by the time of the United States' entry into World War I, the German language was still being used in Lutheran parochial schools both during and after the war. State councils of defense had often focused on that aspect of the Lutheran school and in so doing had contributed to a spirit of animosity against the

---

[8] See chapter 11 (1889) of the present volume for a discussion of these laws and church involvement with them.

institution itself. The Missouri Synod's school commission took note of that when it remarked in its 1920 report to the Synod:

> In many a district our brothers had to wage difficult battles against councils of defense and legislative bills which were damaging to the continuance of our schools, yes, placed their very continuation into question.[9]

That the Lutheran parochial school was instrumental in keeping the German language alive among midwestern Americans even during World War I cannot be denied. Even members of Lutheran churches, it seems, might have been of the opinion that once parochial schools were not needed to teach German and provide religious instruction in that language, the schools themselves would be dispensable. Graebner in his "The Crisis in Our School Affairs" essay acknowledged the close connection between the German language and the parochial school of his day, but then went on to add that German was not the major reason for Lutheran churches to maintain parish schools. Drawing upon both *Der Lutheraner* (The Lutheran) and the 1919 *Proceedings* of the Minnesota District of the Synod, he wrote:

> "Wherever the language in the homes and families of a congregation is predominately or exclusively English, there the school quite naturally follows the same practice, for the school is not there for the sake of the language" (Lutheraner 1912, page 120) . . . . "Catechism and Bible history must be taught in the best and most thorough way and, to be sure, in the language which serves the child best. Local circumstances will have to determine the language medium" (Minnesota District 1919, page 70). If local conditions may decide about the language,

---

[9] *Synodalbericht der . . . Synode von Missouri . . .* (Synodical Report of the . . . Synod of Missouri . . .), 1920, 226.

therefore, the principle must be: The school is there for the sake of religion.[10]

The point that Graebner was making was that congregations should not get lost in a language discussion relating to the schools when the prime purpose for their existence was not the teaching of German but religion. He had emphasized that earlier in his essay when he had commented that "religion was a principal subject" in Lutheran elementary schools, "yes the chief object of them."[11] An understanding of that purpose, he maintained, was the appropriate motivating factor for the support of Lutheran schools. The language issue was to be regarded as incidental to the situation.

Another side issue which Graebner felt was diverting attention away from the crisis facing Lutheran parochial schools was the discussion in synodical circles relative to the Sunday school. Midwestern German Lutherans were latecomers to that institution, but it was well on its way by 1920, and the pros and cons of its usefulness for Lutheran parishes were under debate. Some saw the Sunday school as an adequate substitute for the Christian day school. Others viewed the Sunday school as a threat to full-time parish schools and, for that reason, an agency whose spread should be opposed. Another position was that the Sunday school was an excellent means by which to do mission work. And, finally, some argued that the Sunday school was a stepping-stone to the establishment of a Christian day school. Graebner was fearful that too much time and energy were being consumed with Sunday school philosophy while the critical educational issue of the day—the threat to the parochial school from within and without—was being overlooked. Indifference to the Christian day school in Lutheran congregations, he felt,

---

[10] *Magazin für ev.-luth. Homiletik* (Magazine for Evangelical Lutheran Homiletics), March 1920, 139.

[11] Ibid., February 1920, 70.

should be overcome by positive motivation, by pointing out "that the weekday school is the only adequate means by which to educate our youth."[12]

Graebner did not lay what he spoke of as the crisis in parochial school matters at the door of external forces only. He spoke also of the spirit of pride among Lutherans who in some places were embarrassed with their parochial schools and for that reason disinclined to use them. "Consider," he said,

> the spirit of pride which our people's improvement in earthly circumstances has brought about. People are ashamed of their school. Yonder stands the huge public school building, so amply equipped with all sorts of educational tools; over here in the outskirts, our school, so small and modest. One teacher, perhaps two, or even only the pastor! And such a small band of students: thirty, twenty, perhaps only ten! For pride, that is pure vinegar. Get rid of the institution, be up to date, be in the swim, be modern, be American![13]

The Lutheran parochial school of 1920 was feeling pressures not only from the outside with state laws but in some quarters also from within. There seems to have been a concern among some Lutheran parishioners about the adequacy of the educational facilities and resources available in some Lutheran schools. Graebner attributed this to pride, but one suspects that the very establishment of a synodical office to give counsel and guidance to congregations with schools suggests that there might have been at least some justification for the concern.

In any case, Graebner concluded his essay with a number of specific suggestions with respect to the crisis he had described.

---

[12] Ibid., March 1920, 138.

[13] Ibid., February 1920, 74. The phrases "up to date" and "in the swim" are in English in the otherwise German article.

Among them was a recommendation that a central synodical bureau be established for congregational school matters. Reports were to be sent to this office from all districts in order to keep it informed about all activities aimed against Lutheran schools. The central office was then to compile the information and disseminate it to all synodical districts, so that even those districts in which there were no immediate legal dangers might not become complacent. This central bureau of education was to provide leadership for the improvement of schools as well as for the warding off of any dangers. A central office would have as part of its duties the preparation of tracts, periodical articles, speeches, lectures, and other materials in behalf of Lutheran schools. For this work, salaried personnel would be necessary.

Of the various overtures which came before the Missouri Synod's 1920 convention floor committee, the one from the Pastor-Teacher Conference of the Texas District made specific reference to Graebner's *Homiletic Magazine* essay and in brief form reflected his arguments. The memorial read in part:

> WHEREAS, besides the increasing secularization and indifference of our congregations over against [Lutheran] schools, many dangers are threatening our schools from without. . . . [and]
> WHEREAS, in our opinion it is absolutely necessary, if we want to be successful, that we lead the way with a plan and unity in order to counteract these dangers and that this work be directed by a central office;
> THEREFORE, we recommend . . . that the . . . Synod . . . appoint a salaried director expressly for this purpose . . . and establish a central [school] office . . .[14]

---

[14] *Synodalbericht der . . . Synode von Missouri, Ohio und andern Staaten* (Synodical Report of the . . . Synod of Missouri, Ohio and Other States), 1920, 234-35.

The floor committee, having taken note of the school commission's report, of the various overtures, and of the fact that 500 schools had been lost in recent years, recommended that the Synod approve the establishment of such an office and the calling of an executive for it. The committee also recommended that one of the members of the Synod's school commission be an attorney, thus recognizing the importance of that kind of expertise when it was necessary to examine legislative proposals pertaining to schools and to be ready for possible litigation. In addition, the school commission was to introduce a press service (eventually called *News Service*) for the purpose of disseminating school information to the synodical membership. The 1920 Missouri Synod convention accepted its floor committee's recommendations and so established its first central education executive position.

The Wisconsin Synod, as already mentioned, had created a similar post a year earlier, although there did not exist in that much smaller synod a counterpart to the office of district superintendent which some districts in the Missouri Synod had created prior to either synod's approval of a central education office. The members of both church bodies were always wary of moves which might lead to a restriction of congregational autonomy and the centralization of authority in synodical offices. One detects a concern about that in the Wisconsin Synod from a February article which appeared in both the English and German church papers of that church body. The article, written over the signature of the school committee, informed pastors, teachers, and church members that the newly appointed school visitor had begun his work and would be arranging his travel schedule. Congregations were encouraged to welcome him and not have any misconceptions about his authority. "Mr. Gieschen [the appointed school visitor] comes," the report stated, as a visitor in the real sense of the word, as a man charged with paying a friendly visit in the interests of Christian elementary schools. He does not claim the title of superintendent, nor is he clothed with the authority which would be implied by that title. He is not a superior officer, authorized to give orders how school work must be carried on in our congregations, but he will be ready at all times to give advice to the best of his ability. Some day we may be ready to do the reasonable and desirable thing by systematizing all our church schools under one direction, and then we shall have to appoint one or more superintendents to carry the system through; but that day is still far away.[15]

Having tried to assure congregations that there was nothing to fear with a visitation of their schools, the school committee then explained that the primary purpose of Mr. Gieschen's first visits was to gather statistical information:

We need much more than the meagre and incomplete school returns furnished by our ministers in their annual parochial reports. The Visitor is required to note . . . the number of teachers working in each school, and the number of children enrolled . . . and he is to find out how the enrollment of pupils compares with the number of children of school age in the congregation. . . . Where the minister is the only school teacher in his congregation, it is important to know whether his school is a school according to the laws of the state, or merely a school of catechetical instruction. . . . Where he finds a congregation which is doing nothing whatever for the

<hr>

[15] *The Northwestern Lutheran*, February 22, 1920, 55. The same article appeared in German in the February 29 issue of the *Evangelisch-Lutherisches Gemeindeblatt* (Evangelical Lutheran Congregational Journal).

Christian schooling of their children, he is to inquire as to the reason for this deplorable state of affairs. . . .

This is obviously the only way for Synod to determine the actual extent and the real value of our parochial school work. . . . At the same time, we shall discover where our efforts are deficient. . . . We are aware . . . that the violent and sometimes malicious attacks against our parochial schools owe their origin not at all to the alleged insufficiency of these institutions, but to the universal hatred of the world against the Gospel which is taught there. Nevertheless, if we succeed in removing the shortcomings which actually do lessen the value of our school work, we shall have shorn their attacks of the pretense, showing them up in their true colors as a form of religious persecution. Moreover, we should ourselves feel the need of making our Christian school work fully efficient, to insure for our children a thorough training in all necessary knowledge. . . .[16]

To gather statistics and to determine the status of the parochial school system within the Synod was to be the first task of the Wisconsin Synod school visitor. Such statistical information would be useful, it was hoped, to combat an antiparochial school spirit evident in various parts of the country at the time, especially in states like Michigan and Nebraska, and to provide facts helpful for analysis and self-study by individual schools and churches.

Visitor Gieschen's first synodical convention report demonstrates that he did what he was asked to do in the matter of gathering statistics. His report, presented to the Wisconsin Synod in 1921, is brief, but includes a variety of statistics. Although his statistical data are only a small sample of what

---

[16] *The Northwestern Lutheran*, February 22, 1920, 55-56.

was going on in parochial schools, it seems reasonable to assume that the particulars upon which he focused were very likely those which had come under scrutiny both within and outside of the churches operating Christian day schools. The statistics are deserving of a closer look.

In a period of 15 months, the Wisconsin Synod school visitor visited 126 pastors. Seventeen of those pastors conducted schools entirely by themselves, schools being classified as such only if they offered instruction in all the ordinary elementary school subjects. The teaching staff in the 73 schools visited was comprised of 17 pastors, 55 male teachers, and 46 women teachers. Forty-six of the schools were one-room schools, 19 were two-room, 1 was three-room, 6 were four-room, and 1 was six-room. The language for instruction in religion was tabulated for 60 schools: 33 of these conducted religious instruction in two languages, 18 in German only, and 9 in English only. The visitor's report gave special attention to how instructional time was divided in 31 one-room schools. The usual school week for that kind of school was 27 hours and 30 minutes, 5 1/2 hours per day. No information was provided on how many of those schools had eight and how many had fewer grades. Anyone having had any experience with a one-room school is keenly aware of how little time is available for each subject in that type of classroom and how precise the teacher has to be in his scheduling and use of time. When religious instruction and possibly also a small amount of German teaching were inserted into the schedules of Lutheran one-room schools, time had to be taken away from the teaching of other subjects, which already had only small time blocks. Gieschen's report indicates that teachers seem to have balanced their time differently, some concentrating a bit more on one subject, others on another. Reading, arithmetic, and religion regularly received the largest allotment of time, with United States history, geography, spelling, and language arts getting a smaller portion of the week's schedule. Although a few one-room schools found time for the teaching of German reading and writing, formal instruction in that language seems to have been minimal, if done at all outside of the use of it in religion classes.

The analysis in the Wisconsin Synod school visitor's first report of how time was divided among the subjects taught in one-room schools hints at what was perhaps the focus of attention relative to Lutheran elementary schools around 1920. There still was a sizable number of one-room schools in Lutheran circles at that time. The question was whether such schools had enough time available to make quality teaching and learning possible. Granted, the forces of Americanization had become very active as a result of World War I, and antipathy toward Lutheran schools had arisen in some places. On the other hand, the church also seems to have been aware that some parish schools were in need of improvement and that a central church office might be of assistance in that process. The matter of pastors teaching school and also carrying out their other pastoral functions was a concern as well. A 1969 anniversary booklet of a Milwaukee church, for example, reports that the congregation closed its school in 1919 because "enrollment was seriously affected by public school expansion" and "the pastor was no longer able to teach and serve the needs of the growing congregation."[17] The school commission of the Missouri Synod had begun to run into another problem in connection with pastors teaching school. Some states had teacher certification requirements which pastors did not meet. In its 1920 report, the commission felt compelled, therefore, to recommend the following to the Synod:

> Since in some states pastors are prohibited from conducting school because they have not received

---

[17] Siloah Lutheran Church (Milwaukee, WI), *Continuing in His Grace* (Seventy-fifth Anniversary), 4.

> training in pedagogy, the Synod should advise the
> theological seminaries to introduce into their curricula
> such branches of study as deal with pedagogy.[18]

Operators of Lutheran parochial schools were confronted with
a number of critical issues at the time of World War I and the
years immediately following it. At that time, both the
Wisconsin and the Missouri Synods deemed it advisable to
appoint an executive school officer to assist in addressing the
challenges of the day.

In an effort to keep the leadership of both synods informed
about the dangers from without which were threatening
Lutheran schools, two conferences were held in River Forest,
Illinois, to discuss the situation, one in February of 1921 and
the other in the same month of 1922. Representatives from
various parts of the country took part in the discussions.
Missouri Synod President Friedrich Pfotenhauer opened the
first conference and was present at the second. District school
superintendents or representatives not only from the Midwest
but from places like New York, Texas, California, and Oregon
were present at one or both of the meetings. Both teachers
colleges of the Missouri Synod as well as its St. Louis
seminary were represented. A faculty member from the
Wisconsin Synod seminary together with the presidents of its
two colleges and three or four additional representatives were
also on hand. The delegate roster included top-level
educational and synodical leaders in the Missouri and
Wisconsin Synods, so that the very definite impression is left
that Lutherans were keenly aware that they had to be alert to
what was going on and take very seriously possible

---

[18] *Synodalbericht der . . . Synode von Missouri . . .* (Synodical Report
of the . . . Synod of Missouri . . .), 1920, 227.

governmental actions which would make it difficult or even impossible to continue to operate Lutheran parochial schools.[19]

Within a few days after the River Forest conference, August C. Stellhorn was called to be the first executive secretary of the Missouri Synod's General School Board, a position created by synodical action in 1920. He accepted the call and remained the Synod's chief executive school officer for the next 40 years. His long tenure at that post, plus his previous service as a Lutheran school teacher and district school superintendent, mark him as Mr. Lutheran Education in the Missouri Synod during the first part of the twentieth century.

Stellhorn was born in 1887 in Red Bud, Illinois, a small community not far from the city of St. Louis. His teacher training was obtained at the Missouri Synod's Teachers Seminary in Addison, Illinois, and he did not pursue any formal academic education beyond that point. He was graduated from the Addison school in 1908 and began his teaching career in that year at St. John's Lutheran School in Red Bud. From 1911 to 1918, he taught at St. Paul's Lutheran School in Indianapolis, Indiana, and was then appointed school superintendent for the Synod's Central District, an area comprising Indiana and Ohio. He conducted his district office from Indianapolis and did the same in his first years as the synodical school executive.

Stellhorn began his work as the Missouri Synod's education executive without a detailed description of what he was to do. Several of the districts already had school superintendents to function as school visitors, to gather statistics, and to provide counsel in educational matters within their districts. Some of the things which an education executive might have been expected to do were already being taken care of by district administrators, and one would not be surprised to discover that a voice was heard here or there in criticism of what was perceived of as

---

[19] Reports on both conferences appeared in the *Lutheran School Journal*, June 1921 and April 1922. The reports are in German.

incipient bureaucracy. The duties of the synodical school secretary were, admittedly, somewhat vague. He was to devote his time to the carrying out of the assignments which the Synod had given to its school commission. These assignments, too, were, for the most part, general and broad, but did include the publication of promotional materials in the interest of Lutheran schools and serving as the agency which would keep the Synod informed about external movements and actions potentially harmful to the continued existence and well-being of Lutheran parochial schools. What these generalities meant was that the specific responsibilities of the office of school secretary would be shaped to a large extent by the person holding the position.

During his 40-year tenure as chief synodical school administrator, August Stellhorn did use his pen extensively. For a period of 25 years he edited *News Service*, a monthly Missouri Synod educational publication. An early brief, but unanticipated task which he assumed was the editorship of the Concordia Edition of the *Bobbs-Merrill Readers*, a project to be discussed under the year 1926 in the present volume. He also wrote several articles dealing with the history of education in The Lutheran Church—Missouri Synod and left as his final legacy a 500-page volume entitled *Schools of The Lutheran Church—Missouri Synod*. This book, although out of print, remains an invaluable source of information for the study of Lutheran school history.

Stellhorn has been criticized as a historian of education because of his sometimes anecdotal approach to the subject of Lutheran school history and his interpretation of it. In a critique of the man as an educational historian, a contributor to *Lutheran Education* remarked with respect to Stellhorn's final work:

> Evident in *Schools of The Lutheran Church—Missouri Synod* was a parochial celebrationism similar to that of

Cubberley and Monroe's interpretation of American
public education. . . . Stellhorn's role as a Lutheran
school promoter caused him to use Synodical educational
history for its inspirational value. As he sold the concept
of Lutheran parochial education, Stellhorn's history
revealed a parochial celebrationism that occasionally
slanted his interpretation of the growth of his historic
ideal: the Lutheran parish school.[20]

Such a comment about Stellhorn's approach to Lutheran
educational history brings to mind the late Lawrence A.
Cremin's intriguing title for his essay on historiography in
American education. He titled his work *The Wonderful World
of Ellwood Patterson Cubberley*. An evangelistic zeal lay
behind Cubberley's descriptions of American public school
history; the same can be said of Stellhorn.

Stellhorn's way of writing Lutheran school history is not
difficult to explain. The position's description for his
administrative post in 1920 might have been lacking in
specifics, but one thing was very clear: He was expected to be
an energetic promoter of Lutheran parochial schools. Personal
conviction and professional engagement kept him in that mode
even when he wrote history. From a number of points of view,
however, his *Schools of The Lutheran Church—Missouri
Synod* remains a most valuable source book. It contains an
exceptional amount of detail not conveniently found in any
other single place. The author's long period of service in
Lutheran education enabled him to provide a firsthand report of
certain events, a recording which might need interpretation but
which is, nonetheless, valuable to have. In addition, Stellhorn
was fluent in the German language and could function with

---

[20] William C. Rietschel, "August C. Stellhorn's Conception of
Lutheran Educational History," *Lutheran Education*, November/December
1984, 80-81.

ease in the synodical documents written in that language, which was used regularly in much official synodical business until into the 1930s. His translations of German materials are invaluable for those not proficient in that language, and his careful references to the German sources which he used are most helpful for those who can use the language. In short, *Schools of The Lutheran Church—Missouri Synod*, the last work from the pen of August Stellhorn, has uncovered for the historical inquirer a vast amount of factual material pertaining to the history of Lutheran schools prior to 1960 and made that information easily accessible.

Lutheran schools in the states of Illinois and Wisconsin were confronted in 1890 with legislation which interfered to some extent with the free operation and curricula of those schools. The laws were repealed, and adjustments in curricula were made from school to school and time to time in order to accommodate changing needs and demands. One of the issues had been the degree to which the German language was being used in Lutheran schools. The employment of German in both church and school at the time of World War I brought Lutheran schools under scrutiny a second time, and in this case in more than two states. America's entry into World War I had brought a new dimension into the German language issue in the United States, with the result that strongly vocal forces of Americanization had been successful in arousing a spirit of antagonism against Lutheran schools in a number of states. In fact, the animosity went beyond the question of language and began to be directed against private schools in general. Heedful of the attacks from the outside and aware of a growing lukewarmness toward the Lutheran parochial school within the church itself, the Evangelical Lutheran Synod of Missouri, Ohio and Other States and the Evangelical Lutheran Joint Synod of Wisconsin and Other States considered it advisable to have a synodical education executive to assist with the promotion and improvement of Lutheran schools. The Missouri Synod established such an administrative post at its convention in June of 1920; the Wisconsin Synod had installed a person into the same kind of office in January of that year. With the exception of an interval of six years in the Wisconsin Synod in the early 1930s, the positions have continued, with additions of personnel and duties, to the present time.

Suggested for Further Reading

August C. Stellhorn. *History of the Superintendents Conference*. St. Louis: Concordia, 1956.

——— . *Schools of The Lutheran Church—Missouri Synod.* St. Louis: Concordia, 1963, 282-300, 377-89.

✤✤✤ 1923 ✤✤✤

The United States Supreme Court:
Meyer v. Nebraska

World War I brought with it a degree of conflict between certain extreme forces of Americanism in the United States and some citizens in the land who were of German-American ancestry or German-born. One of the most significant aspects of any culture, of course, is its language, and it was that component which came to the fore when the United States Supreme Court, on June 4, 1923, decided the case of *Meyer v. Nebraska*. At issue was a Nebraska law which forbade the use or teaching of a modern foreign language in elementary schools. Although the Nebraska statute which the United States Supreme Court declared unconstitutional and under which a Missouri Synod Lutheran parochial school teacher had been fined was not enacted until after the armistice of November 1918, language strife sparked by the war was what lay behind the *Meyer* case. Both Lutherans and Catholics in Nebraska had been employing languages other than English in their parochial schools. German was the principal foreign language used in Lutheran schools, but other modern foreign languages were also being spoken in parish schools. A case in point was a Roman Catholic school in Omaha. When the Nebraska school-language law was first contested at the state level, it was reported to the supreme court of Nebraska that St. Francis Catholic Church of South Omaha operated a parochial school in which Polish was used and that St. Francis School

> regularly enrolled . . . more than six hundred (600) pupils, all of the Roman Catholic faith and with few exceptions, when first enrolled, unable to understand the English language in consequence of which it is impossible to instruct such children . . . on any subject by means of the English language alone, or to impart to them a knowledge of English except by the use of the language of their parents. . . .[1]

The Nebraska school-language law forbade the use of all modern foreign languages in elementary schools in the state, but conversation in German by American citizens was resented most by those who were promoting a restriction in Nebraska and in other states on the use of a foreign language in elementary schools.

It cannot be denied that Americans of German background had been rather aggressive at the turn of the century in the promotion and perpetuation of German culture in the United States. Various communities had German societies of one sort or another, and in 1901 an organization known as the German-American Alliance (Der Deutsch-Amerikanische Nationalbund) was formed. That organization together with the strong German-language press in the United States, as might be expected, advocated that the United States remain neutral when World War I erupted in 1914. In the election of 1916, German-Americans and others who supported noninvolvement in the European war which was raging backed Charles Evans Hughes for president of the United States rather than Woodrow Wilson. Irish-Americans, interested in an Ireland independent of England, formed a kind of coalition with the German-Americans during the election, supported Hughes, and, according

---

[1] Nebraska, *Brief of Appellants in the Supreme Court of Nebraska*, General Number 21153, 6.

to one writer, prompted incumbent President Wilson "to reject as unpatriotic those Americans who needed hyphens in their names."[2] Cartoonists even pictured candidate Hughes "wearing a German spike helmet and as a mercenary trudging in the shadow of the Kaiser."[3] The pro-German opposition notwithstanding, President Wilson was reelected, and the United States entered the war several months after his election, in April 1917. The strong antiwar stance of German-Americans in the 1916 presidential campaign caused a number of people and groups in the United States to question the national loyalty of individuals, organizations, churches, and schools which in any way employed the German language, and the resentment against that language did not subside even after the war was over.

Once the United States entered the European conflict, a certain amount of war hysteria set in among those who resented the use of German by American citizens. The very speaking of the language, formally or informally, cast suspicion on the users of the foreign tongue. Hostility and suspicion turned into harassment and a determination to get, if possible, the force of government behind efforts to eradicate the use of German by Americans. The Council of National Defense, created by Congress in 1916, urged the states to establish state councils to assist with the war effort once the United States had entered the conflict. In Nebraska, there were also county defense councils. They, together with the national and state agencies, served the country by promoting Liberty Loan drives, the work of the Red Cross, and other activities helpful to a nation at war and for the well-being of its armed forces. At the local level, however, the fervor of some American citizens occasionally turned into zealotry. This was especially the case in Nebraska where

---

[2] Rippley, La Vern J. *The German-Americans* (Lanham, MD: University Press of America, 1984), 182.

[3] Ibid., 183.

Americans of Russian-German background were apparently more reluctant than other German-American groups to relinquish the language and customs of their forefathers. Little by little, all of this contributed to school language laws which were put to the test in *Meyer v. Nebraska*.

Hostility toward German-Americans during the war sometimes produced extravagant actions and activities which, in retrospect, bordered on the absurd. The railroad-terminal sign in Bismarck, North Dakota, had painted on it the words "To hell with this stupid Hun. What did he ever do for us?" Otto von Bismarck, architect of Prussia's nineteenth-century rise to power, was an obvious embarrassment to some citizens of the United States city named after him. German books were burned in Baraboo, Wisconsin, as were German-language newspapers in Columbus, Ohio.[4] A Lutheran school in Lincoln was burned to the ground in 1918; a Lutheran pastor was beaten by a mob in Papillion, Nebraska, and another Lutheran pastor in Nebraska was hanged in effigy and ordered to leave town.[5] Names of people, places, and things were changed to remove or hide their German associations. Germantown, Nebraska, became Garland; Berlin, Iowa, became Lincoln; Hamburg Avenue in Brooklyn, New York, was changed to Wilson Avenue, while hamburger and sauerkraut were referred to in some circles as salisbury steak and liberty cabbage respectively.[6] How many Americans might have changed their German names because of war fever is not known, for that phenomenon was taking place already long before open conflict with Germany, so that even behind the family name of American General John J. Pershing of World War I fame there lurked the German name Pfoerschin.

---

[4] Ibid., 186.

[5] Williams G. Ross, "A Judicial Janus: *Meyer v. Nebraska* in Historical Perspective." *University of Cincinnati Law Review* 57 (1988), 138-39.

[6] Rippley, 186.

Lutheran churches of German heritage in the Midwest were keenly aware of the difficult situation they were in. Among these churches were the Missouri Synod with parishes in various places throughout the country, the Wisconsin Synod, the Iowa Synod, and also the Ohio Synod. Many lay members of these synods and their leaders, too, had harbored pro-German sympathies before the United States entered the war. Although the confessional position of these synods required a loyalty to the government under which they lived, the regular use of German in the public worship of parishes in these synods, in official synodical conventions, and also in parochial schools made these church bodies easy targets for accusations of anti-Americanism. The continuing presence of the German language in midwestern Lutheran church life was sufficient to drown out in the ears of critics a repetition of Lutheranism's stance on church and state as articulated in the denomination's Augsburg Confession:

> Ecclesiastical and civil power are not to be confused. The power of the church has its own commission to preach the Gospel and administer the sacraments. Let it not invade the other's function . . . nor abrogate the laws of civil rulers, nor abolish lawful obedience, nor interfere with judgments concerning any civil ordinances.[7]

Although the language of worship could not be changed quickly, the Missouri Synod did take a very early step to remove some criticism of its German character. The official name of the Synod at the outbreak of the war still included the word German, namely, the German Evangelical Lutheran Synod of Missouri, Ohio, and Other States. At its convention in

---

[7] The Augsburg Confession in *The Book of Concord*, trans. and ed. Theodore G. Tappert (Philadelphia: Fortress, 1959), Article XXVIII, sections 12-13, 83.

June 1917, two and one-half months after the entry of the United States into the war, the Synod removed the word German from its official name. By 1918, the Synod's Concordia Publishing House had in print a pamphlet entitled *Testimony and Proof Bearing on the Relation of the American Lutheran Church to the German Emperor*. The editor of the tract argued that a review of Missouri Synod history was sufficient to contradict any charge that the Synod was promoting an allegiance to the German government, for, it was pointed out, a large contingent among the founders of the Synod had emigrated from Germany in order to be free of government interference in matters of religion. With such argumentation, by purchasing war bonds, and by supporting other aspects of the war effort, many German-American Lutherans were trying to demonstrate their loyalty to the United States and its cause in Europe.

The use of the German language, however, persisted in Lutheran congregational life both during the war and after. The use of English, of course, was on the rise, but that would have happened even without the war. That was the case in both the Missouri and Wisconsin Synods and in their parochial schools. In connection with the *Meyer v. Nebraska* Supreme Court case in 1923, it is significant to note that the official convention-language in both synods at the time was still German. An English version of the Missouri Synod's convention proceedings of that year reported the following with respect to an overture to the Synod to make English the official language of the church body:

> In a memorial the request was made that English be made the official language of Synod. Synod's reply was that the time for such action had not yet come. For the present our congregations should be satisfied if all Districts, like the

General Body, grant the right to use both languages on the floor of synod.[8]

Three years later a similar request was presented to the Missouri Synod at its convention. The overture came from the 1925 New Orleans meeting of the Southern District of the Synod. The memorial included the following reasons for requesting a change to English:

1. The language of our country is English, and this is the language most generally spoken by the members of our Synod.
2. Whereas Home Mission work in our country is chiefly carried on in the English language, the adoption of English as the official language will greatly promote the expansion of our beloved Church among our English-speaking countrymen and will not prejudice its work among the foreign-tongued.
3. As long as Synod carries on its deliberations in the German language, it is difficult, and it is becoming increasingly difficult, to obtain delegates for our triennial conventions.[9]

The floor committee of the convention was not persuaded, nor was the convention itself. In its recommendation to the general convention, the floor committee said:

The conditions of Synod have not changed materially in the last three years. Our Church is still bilingual in the

---

[8] *Proceedings of the Thirty-Second Regular Meeting of the Ev. Luth. Synod of Missouri, Ohio, and Other States*, 1923, 45.

[9] *Proceedings of the Thirty-Third Regular Convention of the Ev. Luth. Synod of Missouri, Ohio, and Other States*, 1926, 150.

true sense of the word. We, therefore, recommend that both languages be used at synodical conventions. This includes: —

1. That we have a German-English service at the opening of synod;
2. That a summary of the President's report be given also in the English language;
3. That all motions and committee reports be presented to Synod in both languages.[10]

The *Proceedings* then simply reported that the recommendations of the committee were adopted.

The transition from German to English was a slow and arduous process, but in spite of whatever efforts might have been made at any level to deter the movement, the change was bound to take place. By 1930, it was clear that it was only a matter of time for the transition to be completed. In parishes in which bilingual ministries were conducted, German was the language of choice only for a rapidly declining number of older members. Assessing the situation in the Wisconsin Synod, Edward C. Fredrich remarks that it is impossible to specify a particular year in which that synod became an English synod. If he had to choose a date, however, he was willing to select the years 1929-30.[11] Anglicization in the Wisconsin Synod required a few more steps officially, but they came in the synodical conventions of the 1930s. The convention report of 1931 appeared in both German and English, with the note, however, that the German document was to be considered the official report. In 1935, the official proceedings were published in English with an appended narrative report in German.

---

[10] Ibid., 150-51.

[11] Edward C. Fredrich, *The Wisconsin Synod Lutherans* (Milwaukee: Northwestern, 1992), 139.

Geographically, the Missouri Synod served many more parts of the United States in 1930 than did the Wisconsin Synod, the smaller partner in the Synodical Conference. The German-English language transition in the two church bodies followed a similar pattern, however. The Missouri Synod convention of 1926, as noted above, had responded to a request to make English that synod's official convention-language by saying that the Synod was "still bilingual in the true sense of the word." By 1932, however, the convention delegates were ready to adopt the following procedures for their sessions:

1. Short daily minutes are to be read in English and German to keep the delegates in touch with the business transacted.
2. The synodical proceedings are to be printed in English, since a separate German edition is evidently not required, only about thirty German *Synodalberichte* [Synodical Reports] having been sold in 1929. If, however, the official committee report on the floor of the convention and therefore also the synodical resolution was drawn up in German, the German version besides the English will be given in the *Proceedings*.
3. For our German readers the report in the *Lutheraner* [The Lutheran] will take the place of a separate German edition of the *Proceedings*, although unofficially.[12]

In 1935, John W. Behnken replaced German-born Friedrich Pfotenhauer as president of the Missouri Synod. Behnken delivered his opening address at the Synod's next convention, in 1938, in both English and German. The *Proceedings* for the

---

[12] *Proceedings of the Thirty-Fifth Regular Convention of the Ev. Luth. Synod of Missouri, Ohio, and Other States*, 1932, 254.

convention included the English text of the address and then
added the comment:

> President Behnken delivered the above address also in
> German. However, in the first session of Synod it was
> *resolved* to omit the presentation of the President's
> address in German in the future.[13]

At the synodical level this brought the transition process to an
end in the Missouri Synod. The change from German to English
in segments of American Lutheran church life had taken a long
time in the United States, coming as it did in the 1930s when
the world was almost on the brink of World War II.

A review of the language story in Lutheran synods especially
strong in the Midwest helps to explain the tenacity of those who
contested a school-language law and pursued their case all the
way from a rural parish school in Hamilton County, Nebraska,
to the United States Supreme Court. Simple compliance with a
Nebraska state statute would seem to have been a much easier
course to follow, but Lutherans and others did not see it that way.
Robert T. Meyer, a Lutheran parochial school teacher, was
arrested, tried, and fined in 1920 for violating a Nebraska law
by teaching religion via the German language to elementary
school children. Lutheran churches were still using that
language for public worship, in printed materials, and in in-house
church business and continued to do so for some time beyond
the court case of 1923. The United States Supreme Court decided
the case on the basis of the Fourteenth Amendment. Although
the case was not decided on the basis of the First Amendment,
the church was convinced that the Nebraska law was an
infringement of that amendment's free-exercise-of-religion

---

[13] *Proceedings of the Thirty-Seventh Regular Convention of the Ev.
Luth. Synod of Missouri, Ohio, and Other States*, 1938, 9.

clause. Prohibiting the teaching or use of German among elementary Lutheran school children was seen as unjustifiable interference with the life and religious practices of the church. An analysis of the long transition from German to English in Lutheran synods headquartered in the Midwest suggests that the argument was not without validity, since German was still being used so extensively in worship and church business.

The law at issue in *Meyer v. Nebraska* was known as the Siman Act. It was introduced into the Nebraska legislature in early 1919, after the cessation, in other words, of armed hostilities in World War I. The law was not the first school legislation presented to Nebraska lawmakers. One bill had proposed that all children attend public schools, while another sought to have all private and parochial schools placed under the jurisdiction of the state. The Siman Act, signed into law by Governor Samuel R. McKelvie on April 9, 1919, was more temperate. It read as follows:

Section 1. **Instruction in foreign languages prohibited.** No person, individually or as a teacher, shall, in any private, denominational, parochial or public school, teach any subject to any person in any language other than the English language.

Sec. 2. **Same, exception.** Languages, other than the English language, may be taught as languages only after a pupil shall have attained and successfully passed the eighth grade as evidenced by a certificate of graduation issued by the county superintendent of the county in which the child resides.

Sec. 3. **Violation, penalty.** Any person who violates any of the provisions of this act shall be deemed guilty of a misdemeanor and, upon conviction, shall be subject to a fine of not less than Twenty-five ($25), nor more than One Hundred ($100) Dollars or be confined to the county jail for any period not exceeding thirty days for each offense.[14]

Nebraska was not the only state to enact legislation of this kind in 1919. Iowa and Ohio had done the same. The Iowa statute, entitled "AN ACT requiring the use of the English language as the medium of instruction in all secular subjects in all schools within the state of Iowa," was brief and general.[15] The Ohio law, on the other hand, singled out German specifically and required

> that all subjects and branches taught in the elementary schools of the state of Ohio below the eighth grade shall be taught in the English language only. The board of education . . . shall cause to be taught in the elementary schools all the branches named in . . . the General Code. Provided, that the German language shall not be taught below the eighth grade in any of the elementary schools of the state.

> All private and parochial schools . . . within this state which instruct pupils who have not completed a course of study equivalent to that prescribed for the first seven grades of the elementary schools of this state shall be taught in the English language only, and the person or persons . . . in control shall cause to be taught . . . such branches of learning as prescribed in . . . the General Code . . . ; provided that the German language shall not be taught below the eighth grade in any such schools within this state.[16]

---

[14] Nebraska, *Laws, Resolutions and Memorials* (1919), 1019.

[15] Iowa, *Acts and Joint Resolutions* (1919), 219.

[16] Ohio, *Legislative Acts* (1919), 614-15.

Ohio lawmakers joined the Nebraska and Iowa legislatures in prohibiting the use of a foreign language as a teaching medium in private as well as public schools. The Ohio statute, however, did not forbid the teaching of all modern foreign languages in elementary schools, only the teaching of German.

Everyone was not really convinced that foreign languages were the ultimate object of the various laws. Arthur F. Mullen, a liberal Democrat and the attorney who took up the case for both Lutherans and Catholics in Nebraska, was one doubter. In his autobiography, *Western Democrat*, he analyzed the situation in the following manner:

> The real purpose of the Nebraska legislation was to destroy parochial schools, both Catholic and Lutheran. . . . The method of attack was, eventually, by forbidding the teaching of or in any foreign language in any grade below the ninth.

> Out of this circumstance the cases which went through the Nebraska courts and up to the Supreme Court of the United States were popularly known as the Foreign Language Cases. As a matter of fact, this was a misnomer. They should have been called the Private School Cases or the Freedom of Education Cases: for upon them rested the right of every private school in the United States to operate and the right of every American citizen to direct the education of his child, provided only that such education is consonant with public morality. If these cases had been lost . . . the determination of the form of education of American children would be today the prerogative of the state and not of the parent.

> This was the real struggle, the fight for the principle of freedom of education against the doctrine of state control.

The fact that the laws enacted dealt with the question of teaching foreign languages was purely adventitious. . . . The Nebraska legislative directors had passed the law against this language teaching only after they had failed in their more direct method.[17]

The Missouri Synod's Franz Pieper was in agreement. In his *Christian Dogmatics* (Christliche Dogmatik), completed in 1924, when writing about evil angels, Pieper spoke about "persecution and oppression of the Church by the State and organizations within the State." To that comment he added the footnote: "Among other things we are thinking of the bills in various legislatures aimed at our Christian schools" (*Gemeindeschulen*). The German edition of Pieper's work then specifies with a parenthetical remark, "presently again in Oregon and Iowa."[18] The Supreme Court had ruled on the Nebraska case when Pieper wrote. Iowa, however, had not been resolved, while *Pierce, Governor of Oregon v. the Society of Sisters* would become another landmark Supreme Court school case in 1925. Supporters of parochial schools at the time of the school language-laws disputes felt that more was at stake than language study; they were convinced that the right to operate parochial schools was in jeopardy.

In a sense, the challenge to the constitutionality of Nebraska's Siman law began with the Catholics and ended with the Lutherans. The fight got under way not with Robert T. Meyer and Zion Lutheran Church and School in Hamilton County but with St. Francis Roman Catholic Church and School of South Omaha in Douglas County. The Catholics and

---

[17] Arthur F. Mullen, *Western Democrat* (New York: Wilfred Funk, Inc., 1940), 208-9.

[18] Francis (Franz) Pieper, *Christian Dogmatics* (St. Louis: Concordia, 1950) vol. 1, 510. *Christliche Dogmatik* (St. Louis: Concordia, 1924), vol. 1, 616.

Lutherans joined hands from the beginning to contest the law. The legal counsel of the Nebraska District of the Missouri Synod entered into the Omaha case with Arthur C. Mullen, who represented a parent of children at St. Francis School. The first strategy was to obtain from the district court of Douglas County a temporary injunction to restrain the enforcement of the language law at St. Francis School where Polish was used. A temporary injunction was granted, but only during the time that a ruling was pending on a general demurrer interposed by the state authorities who held the responsibility to enforce the law. The demurrer was sustained, which meant that the law and its penalties would be enforced. The Nebraska District of the Missouri Synod and others then appealed the case to the Nebraska State Supreme Court.

Things did not go well for the parochial school advocates before that body. The Lutheran appellants argued their case to a large extent on the "free-exercise" clause of the First Amendment, contending that the school-language law was

> in contravention of the constitution of the United States . . . because it denies . . . to patrons and pupils of parochial schools . . . the free exercise of their religion.[19]

Arthur Mullen was careful, however, to include the "due-process" clause of the Fourteenth Amendment in his presentation before the Nebraska courts. That clause forbids deprivation of "life, liberty, or property, without due process of law." It was argued that St. Francis School had considerable property assets and that both the usefulness and value of the holders' property would be impaired and diminished if the teachers in the school were not permitted to do some teaching through the medium of the Polish language. Although this

---

[19] Nebraska, *Brief of Appellants*, General Number 21153, 8.

argumentation might not seem as compelling today as the "free-exercise" reasoning, it should be noted that the United States Supreme Court, when it finally ruled that the language provision of the Nebraska law was unconstitutional, made its decision on the basis of the deprivation of liberty and property without due process of law and not on the basis of the free exercise of religion.

The Nebraska Supreme Court handed down its decision at the end of December in 1919. Although one judge dissented, the court was satisfied that the Siman Act was constitutional and could be enforced. In explaining itself, however, the court opened the door to the possibility of imparting foreign language instruction in schools outside of regular school hours. "There is nothing in the act," commented the court, "to prevent parents, teachers or pastors from conveying religious . . . instruction in the language of the parents, or any other language . . . provided that such instruction is given at such time that it will not interfere with the required studies."[20] This comment did not escape the notice of the administrators of Zion Lutheran School in Hamilton County where the action shifted for a second challenge to the Siman law.

In January of 1920, Zion Lutheran changed its daily school schedule. Instead of conducting classes from 9:00 a.m. until 12:00 noon and from 1:00 p.m. until 4:00 p.m., as had been the case from September to December, the noon recess was extended by one-half hour. The pupils continued to assemble, however, at 1:00 o'clock and under the guidance of their teacher, Robert T. Meyer, read biblical materials in the German language. All other instruction during the day was conducted via the English. Technically, under this arrangement, the religious instruction via the German language was being given during the school's noon recess and so did not interfere with the day's required studies.

---

[20] *Nebraska Reports* (1919), 100.

County officials seem to have known what was going on, for the county superintendent of schools made an inspection of Zion School between 12:00 and 1:45 p.m. on May 17, 1920. He observed that Meyer and his class of about 50 pupils were reading religious materials in German and warned the teacher that he was violating Nebraska law, although, as already mentioned, the reading was taking place outside of the announced daily schedule. A little over a week later, on a warm spring day, the county attorney appeared in the school doorway between 1:00 and 1:30. Mcyer was teaching a narrative from the Old Testament in the German language and did not stop doing so. Arthur F. Mullen, who would eventually represent Meyer and others before the United States Supreme Court, later recalled his personal conversation with Meyer on the event:

> "I had my choice," he [Meyer] told me afterward in that quiet voice which was more impressive than any shouting. "I knew that, if I changed into the English language, he [the county attorney] would say nothing. If I went on in German, he would come in and arrest me. I told myself that I must not flinch. And I did not flinch. I went on in German."
>
> "Why?" I asked him.
>
> He widened his gaze a little. "It was my duty," he said simply. "I am no pastor in my church. I am a teacher, but I have the same duty to uphold my religion. Teaching the religion of their fathers in the language of their fathers is part of that religion."[21]

The freedom to teach a foreign language outside of official school hours hinted at in the Nebraska Supreme Court decision

---

[21] Arthur F. Mullen, *Western Democrat*, 218.

did not deter the Hamilton County district court. Meyer was arrested, tried, and fined $25.

It has been speculated that when the district attorney appeared in the doorway of Zion Lutheran School in May 1920, he had hoped with his presence to persuade Meyer to make a quick change into English. Teacher Meyer seems to have been determined, however, to see this case through. He was not intimidated and apparently also refused the offers of community members to pay his fine for him. He was encouraged in his action also by his pastor, the Rev. C. F. Brommer, an experienced Lutheran clergyman and president of the Nebraska District of the Missouri Synod. Shortly after the United States Court decision in the case, Brommer began to serve a term of 17 years as president of the Synod's Concordia Teachers College in Seward, Nebraska. The conviction of Meyer in district court moved the language law issue to the Nebraska Supreme Court a second time. A Roman Catholic school and Polish were the particular circumstance in the first encounter; a Lutheran school and German in the second.

The outcome of the challenge was the same the second time; the constitutionality of the state's school-language legislation was upheld. In presenting its case before the court, the state of Nebraska reacted to the Zion Lutheran schedule change by saying that Meyer never "attempted to comply with the spirit of the language law, but like a moth with a candle flitted as near as he thought he could without being burned."[22] While all of this was going on, the Nebraska legislature stepped into the picture, repealed the Siman law, and replaced it with the so-called Norval Act. The new law, approved April 14, 1921, removed the possibility of the interpretation which the Nebraska Supreme Court had put upon the Siman Act when that court had previously commented that the teaching of foreign languages in

---

[22] Quoted in William G. Ross, "A Judicial Janus: *Meyer v. Nebraska*," *Cincinnati Law Review* (1988), 147, n. 116.

elementary schools was possible if all other required elementary branches were adequately handled. That was not what the lawmakers had in mind, and they made that clear in 1921 when in the Norval Act they forbade the teaching of foreign languages in elementary schools except on weekends. The law stated:

> Section 1. . . . The English language is hereby declared to be the official language of the state, and all official proceedings, records and publications shall be in such language, and the common school branches shall be taught in said language in public, private, denominational and parochial schools.

> Sec. 2. . . . No person, individually or as a teacher, shall, in any private, denominational, or parochial or public school, teach any subject to any person in any language other than the English language.

> Sec. 3. . . . Languages other than the English language may be taught as languages only, after a pupil shall have attained and successfully passed the eighth grade as evidenced by a certificate of graduation issued by the county superintendent of the county or the city superintendent of the city in which the child resides. Provided, that the provisions of this act shall not apply to schools held on Sunday or on some other day of the week which those having the care and custody of the pupils attending same conscientiously observe as the Sabbath, where the object and purpose of such schools is the giving of religious instruction, but shall apply to all other schools and to schools held at other times. Provided that nothing in this act shall prohibit any person from teaching his own children in his own home any foreign language.[23]

---

[23] Nebraska, *Session Laws* (1921), 244-45.

The supreme court did not alter its earlier stance. In the state court's opinion, the school-language law was constitutional, although one judge and the chief justice dissented from the majority opinion. In their dissent, these two judges commented:

> It is patent, obvious, and a matter of common knowledge that this restriction [on the teaching of a foreign language in elementary schools] was the result of crowd psychology; that it is a product of the passions engendered by the World War, which had not had time to cool.[24]

By this time some parochial school advocates were undoubtedly growing weary of the entire affair and ready to throw in the towel. Robert Meyer and his pastor, C. F. Brommer, were not inclined to do so, and were encouraged to carry the case to the United States Supreme Court by Attorney Arthur F. Mullen, who then represented the Lutherans before the highest tribunal in the land. Mullen was Roman Catholic but was always careful to keep his Catholicism in the background as he argued his case in behalf of the Lutheran church. He was convinced that the Nebraska courts had erred and went on to win a Supreme Court decision favorable to his clients. Mullen's assessment of the Nebraska Supreme Court decisions was confirmed by the United States Supreme Court. That body ruled that the Nebraska courts had erred, and history has not argued with the ruling. Looking back upon the 1922 decision of the Nebraska State Supreme Court, a law professor in 1988 said:

> The court's utter lack of concern over the presumed short-term abridgement of the religious freedom of children

---

[24] *Nebraska Reports* (1922), 669.

whose parents had not yet mastered the English language is startling.[25]

Arthur F. Mullen had both a formidable and delicate task before him when he argued *Meyer v. Nebraska* before the United States Supreme Court. The obvious difficulty in the case was the fact that the constitutionality of the Nebraska school-language legislation had been challenged in several lower courts and had been upheld. It is possible, of course, that local pressures might have affected decision making at the district and state levels, but the basic constitutional issues had been presented and addressed from the very beginning, and more than one court had been persuaded that the legislation in question was not unconstitutional. In addition, *Meyer v. Nebraska* was a pioneer education case before the United States Supreme Court. As such, it could not rely on precedent but was itself a precedent-setting case.

Mullen also had to handle his case with care because of his own convictions. He was a supporter of Roman Catholic schools at a time when Catholicism was a sensitive issue in politics, as the presidential election of 1928 later showed. By his own admission, Mullen tried to keep personal elements in the background and proceeded to argue on the basis of principles of freedom to which he was committed and which he felt were at stake. He admitted that state legislatures had the right to regulate all common school curricula but did not have the power to require parents to send their children to public schools. Supreme Court Justice McReynolds asked Mullen pointedly whether he believed that states had the right to require all parents to send their children to public schools. To that the attorney replied:

---

[25]Ross, *Cincinnati Law Review* (1988), 154.

I deny that a state can, by a majority of the legislature, require me to send my children to public schools. I deny that any such legislative power exists in constitutional government. That question is here at the very base of this case. It is a blow to education. It is a striking down of the principle that a parent has control over the education of his child.[26]

Mullen maintained that a requirement that all children attend public schools lay outside a reasonable exercise of the state's police power.

Mullen, as well as his clients, would like to have debated the case on the basis of the First Amendment to the United States Constitution. It was unlikely, however, that the case could have been won on those grounds in 1923. The First Amendment prohibits "Congress" from making a "law respecting an establishment of religion, or prohibiting the free exercise thereof." According to this amendment, it is the United States Congress only which may not interfere with the free exercise of religion. Nothing is said about the states being able to do that. The Fourteenth Amendment, adopted several years after the Civil War, made some of the provisions of the Bill of Rights (the first Ten Amendments to the Constitution) applicable to the states. The Fourteenth prohibits states from depriving "any person of life, liberty, or property without due process of law," but does not specifically mention anything about the curtailment of religious practices. It was not until 1940, more than 15 years after *Meyer*, that the United States Supreme Court ruled in *Cantwell v. Connecticut* that

the First Amendment declares that Congress shall make no law respecting the establishment of religion or

---

[26] Mullen, *Western Democrat*, 224.

prohibiting the free exercise thereof. The Fourteenth Amendment has rendered the legislatures of the states as incompetent as Congress to enact such laws.[27]

Mullen bombarded the Supreme Court with a number of fundamental principles of freedom, but in 1923 he had to be careful, if he wanted to win his case, to argue also on the basis of how the United States Constitution had been interpreted up to that time. That included showing how individuals and institutions were deprived of property and certain liberties by the Nebraska school-language law. The "free exercise" of religion did not enter the picture then as it would today.

The United States Supreme Court saw its task in the context of the judicial precedent of its day. In reversing the decision of the Nebraska Supreme Court, the majority of the United States Supreme Court justices said:

> The problem for our determination is whether the statute [the Nebraska school language law] as construed and applied unreasonably infringes the liberty guaranteed to the plaintiff in error by the Fourteenth Amendment. "No state shall . . . deprive any person of life, liberty, or property without due process of law."

> While this Court has not attempted to define with exactness the liberty thus guaranteed, the term has received much consideration and some of the included things have been definitely stated. Without doubt, it denotes not merely freedom from bodily restraint but also the right of the individual to contract, to engage in any of the common occupations of life, to acquire useful

---

[27] Quoted in Thayer S. Warshaw, *Religion, Education, and the Supreme Court* (Nashville: Abingdon, 1979), 24.

knowledge, to marry, establish a home, and bring up children, to worship God according to the dictates of his own conscience, and generally to enjoy those privileges long recognized at common law as essential to the orderly pursuit of happiness by free men.[28]

To this the Court also added the following comment:

Mere knowledge of the German language cannot reasonably be regarded as harmful. Heretofore it has been commonly looked upon as helpful and desirable. Plaintiff in error taught this language as part of his occupation. His right thus to teach and the right of parents to engage him so to instruct their children, we think, are within the liberty of the Amendment.[29]

The Court continued:

The challenged statute forbids the teaching in school of any subject except in English. . . . The Supreme Court of the State had held that "the so-called ancient or dead languages" are not "within the spirit or purpose of the act.". . . Evidently the legislature has attempted materially to interfere with the calling of modern language teachers. . . .[30]

Two United States Supreme Court justices dissented from the majority opinion. The dissent was mild and focused on the

---

[28] Herbert M. Kliebard, *Religion and Education in America: A Documentary History* (Scranton, PA: International Textbook Company, 1969), 117.

[29] Ibid.

[30] Ibid., 118-19.

reasonableness of the purpose of the Nebraska legislation. Writing the minority report, Justice Oliver Wendell Holmes said:

> It is with hesitation and unwillingness that I differ with my brethren with regard to a law like this. . . . I am not prepared to say that it is unreasonable to provide that in his early years [a child] shall hear and speak only English at school. But if it is reasonable it is not an undue restriction of the liberty either of teacher or scholar. . . . I think I appreciate the objection to the law but it appears to me to present a question upon which men reasonably might differ and therefore I am unable to say that the Constitution of the United States prevents the experiment being tried. . . .[31]

Although Justice Holmes dissented in the Nebraska case, when the Ohio law which prohibited the teaching only of German was reviewed, he considered that law unconstitutional because it discriminated against one modern foreign language. In *Meyer v. Nebraska*, he dissented from the majority opinion of his colleagues because he thought that the law was within reason and an educational experiment which could justifiably be tried without being seen as a restriction of constitutional liberty.

The Nebraska case was finally over. It had begun with a state law enacted April 9, 1919; it concluded with a United States Supreme Court decision on June 4, 1923. The Nebraska Supreme Court was considered to be in error in its rulings that the challenged law was constitutional. All actions and proceedings relative to the Nebraska school-language law were required to be consistent with the United States Supreme Court ruling.

---

[31] Ibid., 121.

The teaching and use of a foreign language was the subject of dispute in *Meyer v. Nebraska*. It would be a mistake, however, to think that once that issue was resolved or had disappeared, the United States Supreme Court decision in the case would be of no consequence. The fact of the matter is that the Court would continue to draw upon its *Meyer* opinion in subsequent cases related to private schools and schooling. Because of the Court's ruling, legislatures would also have to be careful about the kinds of regulations they might wish to impose on private schools. Lutherans and Catholics were pleased to have had the highest court of the land acknowledge that parents of children in private schools had the freedom to make certain curricular decisions for those institutions. On the other hand, the Court emphasized that the right of the state "to compel attendance at some school and to make reasonable regulations for all schools, including a requirement that they shall give instruction in English, is not questioned."[32] In *Meyer v. Nebraska* certain individual liberties in educational matters were guaranteed without sacrificing any legitimate concerns or interests of the commonwealth.

Suggested for Further Reading

Duker, Sam. *The Public Schools and Religion: The Legal Context*. New York: Harper and Row, 1966: 31-40.

Kliebard, Herbert M. *Religion and Education in America: A Documentary History*. Scranton, PA: International Textbook Company, 1969: 115-21.

---

[32] Ibid., 120.

Krug, Edward. *Salient Dates in American Education: 1635-1964*. New York: Harper and Row, 1966: 127-30.

Ross, William G. "A Judicial Janus: Meyer v. Nebraska in Historical Perspective." *Cincinnati Law Review* (University of Cincinnati) 57, no. 1 (1988): 125-204.

Schmidt, Wayne E. "The Religious Dimension in the *Meyer v. Nebraska* School Case." *Concordia Journal* (Concordia Seminary) 17 (July 1991): 307-22.

✛✛✛ 1925 ✛✛✛

The United States Supreme Court:
Pierce, Governor of Oregon, et al. v. Society of Sisters

When in November 1922 the state of Oregon enacted a school law which was to go into effect in September 1926, the number of Lutheran parochial schools in that part of the country was not large. In his 1922 address to the convention of the Oregon and Washington District of the Missouri Synod, the district president reported that there were 53 pastors in the district, a region which included Idaho as well as Washington and Oregon. The district had a total of 24 parochial schools staffed by 9 male teachers, 1 female teacher, 15 pastors, and several students. The schools had an enrollment of some 800 pupils.[1] Since some of the schools in the district were in the state of Washington, the number of schools which would be affected by the Oregon law was small. Lutherans, Catholics, and other operators of private schools of various kinds throughout the country had a deep interest, however, in what was taking place in Oregon. The focus was on Oregon because it was quite likely that the school law of that state would become a United States Supreme Court test case. That did happen in 1925 when the Court in *Pierce, Governor of Oregon, et al. v. the Society of the Sisters*

---

[1] *Synodal-Bericht des Oregon- und Washington-Distrikts der Ev.-Lutherischen Synode von Missouri, Ohio, und andern Staaten* (Synodical Report of the Oregon and Washington District of the Ev. Lutheran Synod of Missouri, Ohio, and Other States), 1922, 4.

of the Holy Names of Jesus and Mary and Hill Military Academy affirmed a lower federal court decision which had declared the Oregon school law unconstitutional.

The law in question required that all normal children between the ages of eight and 16 attend the public schools of the state. There were to be few exceptions to the rule, and fines were to be imposed for violations of the act. In essence, private and denominational elementary schools were being put out of business. The United States District Court said the same when in its ruling it commented:

> The act could not be more effective for utterly destroying the business and occupation of complainants' schools, except perhaps the college and higher preparatory grades, if it had been entitled "An Act to prevent parochial and private schools from teaching the grammar grades."[2]

Lutherans and Catholics were really not caught off guard with legislation of the type passed in Oregon. Two years earlier, in Michigan, an amendment to that state's constitution was proposed which would also have resulted in the demise of parochial and private schools in the state. The amendment stipulated:

> Section 16: All children of the State of Michigan between the ages of five years and sixteen years, shall attend the public school in their respective districts until they have graduated from the eighth grade; Provided, that in districts where the grades do not reach the eighth, then all persons herein described in such districts shall complete the course taught therein.

---

[2] A. B. Cain, *The Oregon School Fight* (Portland, OR: A. B. Cain, n.d.), 141. This book is a documentary history containing the texts of campaign materials and the court proceedings in the Oregon school case.

Section 17: The legislature shall enact all necessary legislation to render Section sixteen effective.[3]

Several factors lay behind these intense efforts to make public schooling mandatory for all children of elementary school age. The *Portland Journal* of April 2, 1924, observed, for example, that more than 8.5 million people over 10 in America could not read or write the English language and that 24.6 percent of men subject to the draft in World War I had to be classified as illiterate.[4] Compulsory attendance at public schools in which English would be used exclusively was expected to rectify this situation. The War had also raised questions about the loyalty of Americans who before the entry of the United States into the conflict had urged neutrality or had been sympathetic to the cause of the Central Powers. It was thought that the parochial schools were possible seedbeds of anti-Americanism. In addition, there were strong anti-Catholic sentiments among many in the United States. A dynamic Roman Catholic school system was seen by some as a threat to the healthy development of public schools in the country. There were those also who even considered spiritual allegiance to the pope a variety of loyalty to a foreign monarch such as the German Kaiser. An overzealous patriotism engendered by the War concluded that attendance at public elementary schools by all children was necessary in order to instill American ideals in the young during their formative years. A public document in favor of the Oregon school law when it was under consideration was even bold enough to say, "A divided school can no more

---

[3] John Frederick Stach, "A History of the Lutheran Schools of the Missouri Synod in Michigan" (Ph.D. diss., University of Michigan, 1942), 147.

[4] Cain, *The Oregon School Fight*, 145.

succeed than a divided nation."[5] Although the statement was made in connection with more than one kind of possible division in schools, such as social status, for example, creed was also included in the list.

In Michigan, where there were more Lutheran schools than in Oregon, congregations of the Michigan District of the Missouri Synod took energetic steps to organize a campaign to defeat the proposed constitutional amendment which would have abolished parochial schools in that state. The amendment question was to be presented to voters in November 1920. Michigan Lutherans took action and began their campaign against the proposed amendment by forming an Executive Campaign Committee. The Rev. John C. Baur of Fort Wayne, Indiana, was engaged as campaign manager. Each county had a campaign chairman who was to appoint a committee for his area, and individual congregations were asked to take up the issue in their communities. Money was raised for the campaign and mass meetings were held. Campaign literature, newspaper advertisements, and a tract written by a professor at Concordia Seminary in St. Louis were produced and distributed. Lutherans were not in the battle alone, of course, but were joined by Roman Catholics, the Christian Reformed Church, and others who were convinced that the proposed amendment was undemocratic and unconstitutional. The result was that the proposal was defeated by a vote of 610,699 to 353,817, and when the amendment was placed before the voters a second time, in 1924, it was again defeated, thus bringing to an end the attempt to do away with parochial and private elementary schools in Michigan.[6]

The controversy in Oregon also involved a referendum at the polls. The people of the state were not being asked to amend

---

[5] Ibid., 7.

[6] Stach, 145-55.

their state constitution, as had been the case in Michigan, but rather to enact a law to require attendance at public elementary schools. An initiative petition to that effect was filed with the secretary of state in July of 1922 and submitted to the voters at the general election in November. After listing the initiators, the bill took the following form on the ballot:

> **COMPULSORY EDUCATION BILL**—Purpose: Requiring any parent, guardian or other person having control, charge or custody of a child over eight and under sixteen years of age, from and after September 1, 1926, to send such child to a public school during the entire school year, excepting: (a) children physically unable; (b) children who have completed the eighth grade; (c) children between the ages of eight and ten living more than one and one-half miles, and children over ten years of age living more than three miles from a public school, except when transportation is furnished; (d) children taught by parent or private teacher.[7]

The ballot, as printed, might not have been as clear as it could have been. The measure was entitled Compulsory Education Bill, which might have left some voters with the impression that Oregon did not already have a compulsory education law. Such a law did exist, and it is highly likely that the extensive publicity in connection with the proposed law removed any misunderstanding for most voters.

The complete text of the bill followed the referendum question on the ballot and provided voters with the specific wording of the act. The exceptions to mandatory attendance at public schools included an exemption for children who were

---

[7] Cain, *The Oregon School Fight*, 5.

instructed by parents or private teachers. The law excused from attending at public school

> any child who is being taught for a like period of time by the parent or private teacher such subjects as are usually taught in the first eight years in the public school; but before such child can be taught by a parent or private teacher, such parent or private teacher must receive written permission from the county superintendent, and such permission shall not extend longer than the end of the current school year. Such child must report to the county superintendent or some person designated by him at least once every three months and take an examination in the work covered. If, after such examination, the county superintendent shall determine that such child is not being properly taught, then the county superintendent shall order the parent, guardian or other person, to send such child to the public school the remainder of the school year.[8]

The exception granted by the above paragraph allowed for private tutoring but not group instruction in a private school. After the 1922 measure was declared unconstitutional, Oregon did amend its school code but was careful to include a paragraph on private and parochial schools in its revised legislation. Among those not required to attend public schools according to the revised code were:

> *Children Being Taught in Private School.* Any child, or children, who is, or are, being taught for a like period of time in a private or parochial school such branches as are

---

[8] Oregon, *General Laws* (1923), 9-10.

usually taught in the first eight years in the public schools
. . . shall not be required to attend public schools.[9]

In spite of predictions that the initiative bill of 1922 would very
likely be declared unconstitutional, the voters of Oregon, as
recorded in the 1922 *General Laws* of the state, approved the act
on November 7 of that year by a vote of 115,506 to 103,685.

The demographics of Oregon in the 1920s do not seem to
make it a likely place for the enactment of such a controversial
school law. The foreign-born population was small, so that the
language issues so prominent in the Midwest did not play that
much of a role in Oregon. A group of citizens from Portland
noted in their opposition to the proposed bill that 85.1 percent of
the population of the state was native white and only 13 percent
foreign born. Of these foreign born, three-fourths were
naturalized.[10] An attorney for the Hill Military Academy in his
appeal before the United States District Court observed that 95
percent of the students in the state were in public schools and
that attendance in public schools had increased 60.8 percent in
the preceding seven years, while attendance in private schools
had grown by only 4.1 percent.[11] According to one report,
Catholics made up about only 8 percent of the population.[12] The
statistics would suggest that private schools were really not
much of a threat to public schools in Oregon and that alleged
pro-German sympathies were very likely not that prevalent
there during the war. On the other hand, the Oregon situation

---

[9] Oregon, *General Laws* (1929), 44.

[10] Cain, *The Oregon School Fight*, 11.

[11] Ibid., 93.

[12] David Tyack, "The Perils of Pluralism: Oregon's Compulsory
School Bill of 1922," 2. Tyack notes in a mimeographed essay in the
possession of the author that the Lutheran Schools Committee kept an
extensive file of materials pertaining to the Oregon case and that this file is
deposited with the Oregon Historical Society in Portland.

had sparked national interest, for groups in other states were promoting legislation similar to that in Oregon.

A major force in securing the passage of the so-called compulsory school bill in Oregon was the Ku Klux Klan. World War I had brought about a resurgence of that organization whose antiforeign and anti-Catholic biases found some ready listeners. The Klan was especially active in Oregon, so active, in fact, that Governor Ben Olcott felt compelled to issue an executive proclamation denouncing the activities of the group. Issued in May of 1922, the proclamation read:

> Dangerous forces are insidiously gaining a foothold in Oregon. . . . parading under the name of the Ku Klux Klan, whose forces . . . are stirring up fanaticism, race hatred, religious prejudice and all of those evil influences which tend toward factional strife and civil terror. . . .
>
> In a sister state this same organization is under judicial inquiry as a result of felonious assaults and unspeakable outrages committed under the veil of darkness.
>
> Oregon needs no masked night riders, no invisible empire to control her affairs. . . . Danger lurks when masked men parade the streets on missions of a character known to none but themselves. . . .
>
> The true spirit of Americanism resents bigotry, abhors secret machinations and terrorism and demands that those who speak for and in her cause speak openly, with their faces to the sun.[13]

Governor Olcott did not endear himself to the Ku Klux Klan with that kind of proclamation. In addition, he indicated that he

---

[13] Cain, *The Oregon School Fight*, 21-22.

was opposed to the proposed school bill which the Klan favored. Walter Pierce, Olcott's opponent in the 1922 gubernatorial race, spoke in favor of the bill requiring all elementary school children to attend public schools. That made Pierce, the man whose name became associated with the United States Supreme Court case, the Klan's candidate for governor. He was elected, as were a number of other candidates endorsed by the Ku Klux Klan, the mayor of Portland being among them.[14] The Klan was an organization to be reckoned with in the 1922 Oregon elections and school referendum.

The clash between the Ku Klux Klan and religious groups operating schools was quite in the open. A certain Geo. Estes, for example, produced a pamphlet in which he tried to persuade his readers that denominational schools would eventually spell the undoing of public schools. Entitled *The Old Cedar School*, the pamphlet was a fictional account of a father who had attended Cedar School and his children who had also gone to that school. The children, however, chose spouses who belonged to religious denominations which operated various kinds of church-related schools. One married an Episcopalian, another a Seventh Day Adventist, a third a Methodist, and a fourth a Roman Catholic. These sons and daughters sent their children to the schools of their denominations rather than to the public Cedar School, causing the latter to be in want of pupils. The implication was that parochial schools were destroying America's public school system. The pamphlet closed with two cartoons, one showing an Episcopalian bishop, a Seventh Day Adventist minister, and a Methodist presiding elder knocking out the foundation posts of the wooden school. A Catholic priest in clerical garb was on his way with a lighted torch to set fire to the old cedar building. The second cartoon shows the structure collapsing and going up in flames.

---

[14] Tyack, "The Perils of Pluralism," 3.

The King Kleagle for the Pacific Domain of the Knights of the Ku Klux Klan wrote a short introduction to the Estes pamphlet after the November election. He lamented the bitterness of the campaign but blamed it on the churches because, as he saw it, they had injected the issue of religious persecution into what he contended was a beneficial school law. He maintained that attendance at public elementary schools by all children was vital for the good health of the nation. He concluded his preface with the following paragraph:

> There is a fundamental principle involved here which means the ultimate perpetuation or destruction of free institutions, based upon the perpetuation or destruction of the public schools. To defend them from encroachments either open or secret, is the settled policy of the Ku Klux Klan and with its white-robed sentinels keeping eternal watch, it shall for all time, with its blazing torches as signal fires, stand guard on the outer walls of the Temple of Liberty, cry out the warning when danger appears and take its place in the front ranks of defenders of the public schools.[15]

To inform citizens on the school issue a *Voter's Pamphlet* was prepared and sent to all registered voters in the state. This pamphlet included an argument, prepared on the initiative of Scottish Rite Masons, in favor of the referendum and seven briefs in opposition to it. The latter included submissions from the Oregon and Washington District of the Evangelical Lutheran Synod of Missouri, from a group of Portland citizens, from the office of the Seventh Day Adventists of Oregon, from a group of Presbyterian ministers in the state, from the Catholic Civic

---

[15] Geo. Estes, *The Old Cedar School*, with a Foreword, "The Ku Klux Klan and the Public Schools," by Luther I. Powell (Portland, OR: Luther I. Powell, 1922), 9.

Rights Association of Oregon, from the Board of Trustees of St. Helen's Hall, and a joint presentation from the principals of four private schools, Hill Military Academy being one of them.[16]

Those in favor of mandating attendance at public elementary schools argued that a primary goal of public schools was the teaching of principles of American government and citizenship. Since nonpublic schools were apart from the mainstream, the environment which they created, it was held, was in itself unfriendly to American principles of democracy. The foreign-born were to be mixed with the native-born and the rich with the poor. What was seemingly overlooked in the latter argument, as opponents were quick to point out, was that in metropolitan areas neighborhood schools did not always mix the rich and poor together too well, since the cities themselves were often somewhat segregated into affluent and less wealthy or poor districts. The melting-pot idea and the conviction that only the public school could produce "a true American" formed the foundation of the argument of the proponents of the Oregon compulsory school law:

> The permanency of this nation rests in the education of its youth in our public schools, where they will be correctly instructed in the history of our country and the aims of our government, and in those fundamental principles of freedom and democracy, reverence and righteousness, where all shall stand upon one common level.[17]

The seven groups which submitted arguments to the *Voter's Pamphlet* in opposition to the school referendum presented a variety of objections. Some arguments were held in

---

[16] The complete text of the arguments of these groups can be found in Cain, *The Oregon School Fight*, 7-20.

[17] H. Baldwin et al., "Argument (Affirmative)," included in documents compiled by A. B. Cain, *The Oregon School Fight*, 7.

common, of course, but each group had a concern specific to its own circumstances. The board of trustees of St. Helen's Hall, a school sponsored by the Episcopal Church, submitted the following succinct argument against the Compulsory Education Bill:

> We are opposed to proposed bill because the enactment of it will constitute an unwarranted and unjustified invasion of the civil and religious liberty of the citizens of this state. No invidious fact or condition affecting public interest has been called to our attention that would furnish in the slightest degree an excuse for the proposed legislation.
>
> We ask all citizens to register their vote against this bill.[18]

The Missouri Synod's Oregon and Washington District emphasized the duties and rights of parents to provide for their children:

> The state has a right to compel you to educate your child, just as it has a right to compel you to feed and clothe your child. But the state has no more right to choose the teacher for your child and the school it shall attend than it has to tell you what style of clothing it must wear. . . .
>
> Under the constitution of the United States and of the state of Oregon you enjoy religious liberty, that is, the liberty to worship God according to the dictates of your conscience. . . . If you see fit to send your child to a school in which the religion of your choice is taught, not one day in the week, but every day and the whole training

---

[18] Walter Taylor Sumner, Bishop of Oregon, et al., "Argument (Negative)," included in documents compiled by A. B. Cain, *The Oregon School Fight*, 12.

of the child is permeated by such religion, the state, under the constitution, must not prohibit you from doing so.[19]

Two emphases are worth noting in the Lutheran statement. First, it becomes apparent that Lutherans see their parochial schools as agencies which do something in addition to offering formal instruction in religion: "The whole training of the child is permeated by . . . religion." That means that various school subjects are taught from the perspective of Lutheran theology. In addition, the total environment and discipline of the school are shaped by the religious principles to which the Lutheran church is committed. This expression of the purpose and aims of Lutheran schools, not new in 1922, was consistent with a philosophy of education long held by advocates of Lutheran parochial schools. Second, the Oregon and Washington District statement is making its case against the law somewhat on the basis of the "free-exercise" clause of the First Amendment and not just on the general liberty provision of the Fourteenth. Before the United States Supreme Court, however, the Fourteenth Amendment would be the basis for ruling on the constitutionality of the Oregon law. Lutherans wanted to go a little beyond that and include the issues of the infringement of religious liberty and the free exercise of religion. To their argument they also added a quotation from President Harding which suggests that the Lutherans perceived that they were the victims of religious intolerance. The following was included in the Lutheran brief:

President Harding Warns

"In my experience of a year in the White House there has come to me no other such unwelcome impression as the manifest religious intolerance which exists among many

---

[19] J. A. Rimbach, "Argument (Negative)," included in documents compiled by A. B. Cain, *The Oregon School Fight*, 9.

of our citizens. I hold it to be a menace to the very liberties we boast and cherish."[20]

The Seventh Day Adventists in their *Voter's Pamphlet* brief affirmed their commitment to compulsory education laws and acknowledged the right of the state even to inspect private schools. This church group was not willing to grant, however, that citizens educated in private schools were less well educated or less patriotic than men and women who had attended public schools. It was observed, moreover, that many anarchists and criminals had attended public schools, making it futile to argue that public schools were an "infallible road to good citizenship." Of special concern to Seventh Day Adventists, however, was their practice of wanting to begin the training of world missionaries for their denomination with elementary school children. Holding that the proposed Oregon law was a trampling upon the constitutional rights of parents, the Seventh Day Adventists concluded:

> The government that turns its citizens into subjects and makes them mere cogs in a wheel, without any rights of their own, is a government that is transforming itself into a tyranny. . . . The measure is "paternalism" on the part of the state. . . . It should be defeated.[21]

A group of Oregon ministers from the Presbyterian church also expressed their opposition to the proposed law and recorded the same in the pamphlet sent to the registered voters of the state. One of their concerns was that much of the propaganda in favor of this bill had been conducted in the

---

[20] Ibid.

[21] H. G. Thurston, "Argument (Negative)," included in documents compiled by A. B. Cain, *The Oregon School Fight*, 16-17.

name of Protestantism. These Protestant clergymen felt that the proposed legislation was inimical to human welfare because

> it is based on the philosophy of autocracy that the child belongs primarily to the state; it is an unjustifiable invasion of family authority and threatens ultimately the guarantees of our American liberty.

> The proposed legislation, promotion and execution violates what we conceive to be the spirit of fraternity and brotherly love taught by our Master.[22]

Several citizens of Portland, Oregon, expressed the fear that a law of this kind, if passed, could open the door to attempts to establish a Puritan Sunday, a code of blue laws, and requirements that all citizens receive medical treatment from state physicians. After insisting that parents had the right to choose what type of school their children should attend, these residents of Portland drew upon the international scene to argue against mandatory public school attendance. Of the proposed law they said:

> This measure imitates the method of public education which brought Prussia to her deserved destruction— giving the state dictatorial powers over the training of children and destroying independence of character and freedom of thought.

> In the present day Russia the Bolshevist government treats the child as the ward of the state. This measure proposes to adopt this method and to substitute state control for the

---

[22] W. H. Boddy et al., "Argument (Negative)," included in documents compiled by A. B. Cain, *The Oregon School Fight*, 18.

authority and guidance of the parents and is destructive of American independence.[23]

The authors of the above also warned that requiring all children to attend public elementary schools would create a strain on public school facilities and result in a substantial increase in taxes. In that way the men from Portland added an economic dimension to their arguments of principle, and one can only wonder what lay behind their reference to blue laws during the time when the Prohibition Amendment was in force.

After the referendum was passed, the Sisters of the Holy Names of Jesus and Mary and the Hill Military Academy challenged the constitutionality of the act in the federal district court and before the United States Supreme Court. Both organizations presented their positions in the *Voter's Pamphlet* before the election but did so together with others. Hill Military Academy joined three other nonsectarian schools in urging a negative vote on the issue. The Roman Catholics formed a separate organization, the Catholic Civic Rights Association of Oregon, to explain their position. Hill Military Academy and its partners defended the rights of parents to choose where they wanted their children to be educated but then pointed out how the act would deprive the four independent schools of their property. The principals of these schools objected to the proposed bill because

> 1. It will destroy the capital invested in our schools. . . . The buildings and equipment are of little value except for private schools and the use of the endowment funds is limited to private educational purposes. . . .

---

[23] W. M. Ladd et al., "Argument (Negative)," in Cain, *The Oregon School Fight*, 11.

2. It will deprive us and our teachers of the right to earn a living in a lawful occupation.[24]

The principals of the four private schools in Portland did not hesitate to brand the proposed legislation anti-American and tyrannical, but they were careful to assert that the Fourteenth Amendment, which forbade deprivation of property without due process of law, was applicable to states as well as to the federal government. The four independent administrators apprised Oregon voters of this fact before the 1922 November election.

Among the signers of the Catholic Civic Rights Association argument against the school law were three attorneys who would later represent the Society of the Sisters of the Holy Names of Jesus and Mary before the United States District Court in Oregon. The Association's statement emphasized that existing circumstances in Oregon argued against any need for an educational law such as was being proposed. The group maintained that illiteracy was no major problem in the state, that Oregon had been free of racial and religious strife for a long time, that private schools were giving instruction via the medium of the English language, that the vast majority of children of foreign-born parents were already attending public schools, and that there was "not the slightest antagonism to the public schools from any source."[25] The Association lent its support to those who were stressing the rights of parents in school matters by saying:

The right of the parent to select the mental and moral training of the child is fundamental and inalienable. It is the most primary right recognized by enlightened

---

[24] Joseph A. Hill et al., "Argument (Negative)," in Cain, *The Oregon School Fight*, 13-14.

[25] J. P. Kavanaugh et al., "Argument (Negative)" in Cain, *The Oregon School Fight*, 20.

countries. That right cannot be invaded without violating the constitutional guarantees.[26]

The Catholic Association contended that the title of the proposed legislation, Compulsory Education Bill, was intended to mislead because it gave the impression that Oregon did not have a compulsory education law. The bill was branded "freak legislation" proposed by persons desirous of arousing racial or religious prejudices.

The *Voter's Pamphlet* had a clear majority of statements opposing the education bill proposed by the referendum. Of the eight brief commentaries, only one favored the proposed law; seven groups stated their opposition. Several newspapers expected the bill to be defeated, and it seems to have been anticipated that the law would not pass muster if contested in the courts. But when the voters went to the polls the story was different. The proposed school measure became law by a margin of 11,821 votes, 115,506 in favor and 103,685 against. In addition, Walter Pierce, who had favored the bill, defeated incumbent Governor Ben Olcott, who had spoken against it. Pierce was a Democrat and Olcott a Republican in a normally Republican state, although the two parties themselves were split on the school issue.[27]

The education act became law with the vote of November 7, 1922, but was not to go into effect until September 1, 1926. Not a great deal of time was lost, however, in contesting the constitutionality of the act. Bills of complaint were filed in the federal district court by the Society of Sisters of the Holy Names of Jesus and Mary and Hill Military Academy against Governor Pierce and others responsible for enforcing the statute. The Missouri Synod Lutherans who had been active in the campaign against the law and who had joined with others to

---

[26] Ibid., 19.

[27] Tyack, 13.

mail the *Voter's Pamphlet* to Oregon voters were also interested in pursuing the case in court but were hindered from doing so because of a lack of funds. The school board of the Oregon and Washington District of the Synod reported on the matter to the 1924 convention of the district, at which, in light of the school controversies of the time, it is interesting to note that the convention doctrinal essay was still delivered in German. The school board said:

> During the past two years the work of the District school board was almost exclusively limited to the work of the Oregon Schools Committee appointed by Synod at Salem, Oreg., to fight the Compulsory Education Bill which was enacted by the voters of Oregon in 1922. . . .
>
> Soon after the bill had been passed, a meeting was held with the officials of Synod to discuss the matter. The board of directors of Synod encouraged us to keep up the fight and promised to assist us morally and financially. Hereupon we consulted prominent attorneys of Portland. They were willing to fight our case for $20,000. The board of directors was opposed to spending so large a sum. . . . In the meantime others had begun litigation. . . . The decision which was handed down by the court proved favorable to our cause. Parental rights, for which we had contended, had also been vouchsafed in the decisions. An appeal is now to be made to the Federal Supreme Court, and the question is whether we should now enter or not. It seems very doubtful . . . whether anything substantial could be gained thereby. . . .[28]

---

[28] *Synodal Bericht* (Synodical Report), Oregon and Washington District (1924), 40.

The complaint of the Society of Sisters and Hill Military Academy was heard in the District Court of the United States for the District of Oregon on January 15, 1924. The state's interest in the case did not seem to be too high when one considers the attorneys chosen to represent Governor Pierce and his associates. Oregon's Attorney General did not argue the case before the court. The task was delegated to the Assistant Attorney General. The chief spokesman, moreover, in defense of the recently enacted school law was an attorney who, in his own words, appeared "primarily as the representative and at the instance of the Scottish Rite Masonic bodies."[29] The attorney for the Masons then proceeded to explain that he had also been asked by Governor Pierce to represent him. It seems unusual, to say the least, that an attorney for a secret society should have been asked to represent government officials. A major argument for the state was that it was premature to contest the law over two years before it was to go into effect, because it was possible to repeal the statute before its effective date.

The three judges handed down their decision on March 31, 1924. By that time they had access to the 1923 United States Supreme Court decision in *Meyer v. Nebraska* and did cite that ruling in their own unanimous decision. Recalling the Nebraska case, the District Court said:

> It can scarcely be contended that complainants' right to carry on their school, whether parochial or private, is not a property right, and the right of parents and guardians to send their children and wards to such schools as they may desire, if not in conflict with lawful requirements, is a privilege they inherently are entitled to enjoy.[30]

---

[29] "Transcript of Discussions" in Cain, *The Oregon School Fight*, 45.

[30] "Text of School Act Decision" in Cain, *The Oregon School Fight*, 136.

In conclusion the federal district court then ruled:

> In our opinion, the state acting in its legislative capacity has . . . exceeded the limitations of its powers—its purpose being to take utterly away from complainants their constitutional right and privilege to teach in the grammar grades—and has and will deprive them of their property without due process of law.[31]

The case was decided on the basis of the Fourteenth Amendment and not on the free-exercise-of-religion clause of the First.

Operators of parochial and private schools were pleased, of course, with the district court decision. The *Catholic Sentinel* had commented after the passage of the law that the electorate of Oregon had temporarily abandoned American principles. Now that the state was restrained from enforcing the law, the *Sentinel* felt that its confidence in constitutional government had been vindicated.[32] The *Portland Journal* reflected a bit on the unpleasantness of the campaign and paid tribute to the American system of government when it said:

> The decision in the compulsory school case is not a surprise. It is what a great many people expected.
>
> Looking backward, the wonder is that there should have been so much bitterness in the campaign when the bill was pending. People became very much wrought up, and there were harsh words. . . .
>
> Yet beyond the election and beyond the controversy were the courts. If, as was vehemently argued in the campaign,

---

[31] Ibid., 143.

[32] *Catholic Sentinel* (April 3, 1924) in Cain, 150.

the bill was unconstitutional, the courts would discover it and declare it. That has been done. This is a country in which there is always a legal remedy. It is the great redeeming factor in the American system.[33]

The Ku Klux Klan, however, was not ready to let the case rest. *The Western American*, a Klan paper, reported that "the decision which was handed down . . . while rather sweeping in its intended effect is by no means final, as appeal will be perfected and the whole matter pertaining to the constitutionality of the law will be placed before the supreme court of the United States. . . ."[34] The *Oregonian*, on April 1, 1924, printed the following news item from Seattle which also shows the determination of the Ku Klux Klan to continue its school agenda in the state of Washington:

> The decision of the federal court that the Oregon compulsory school law is unconstitutional has no bearing whatever on the fight for the enactment of a similar law in the state of Washington, according to the opinion expressed here today by John A. Jeffrey, grand dragon of the Ku Klux Klan for this realm. . . .
>
> "The Oregon decision will make no great difference in the fight we have started in Washington," said Jeffrey today. . . .
>
> "Knowing that the court decision was about to be rendered, the executive committee [of the Washington Good Government League] met in Seattle Sunday night

[33] *Portland Journal* (April 2, 1924), in Cain, 145.

[34] *The Western American*, in Cain, 147.

and resolved to go right ahead no matter what the decision might be."[35]

The Ku Klux Klan was able to exert a fair amount of influence in a number of places in the United States after World War I. Oregon and its 1922 compulsory school law was one such place and situation.

The United States Supreme Court heard the case of *Pierce v. Society of Sisters* and *Pierce v. Hill Military Academy* on March 16 and 17, 1925. The Court in deciding the case on June 1, 1925, unanimously affirmed the decision of the Oregon district federal court. The Oregon school law was declared unconstitutional.

In explaining its decision, the United States Supreme Court emphasized that property rights were being violated by the Oregon law. The Court noted, for example, that the Society of Sisters was a legally organized Oregon corporation which owned valuable buildings and operated a remunerative business. The Society had argued that its business and property would suffer irreparable harm unless the enforcement of the Oregon law was enjoined. Hill Military Academy had argued the same way with respect to its property rights. In its appeal the Academy pointed out that it had considerable personal and real property and that it had to negotiate long-term contracts for teachers, equipment, and supplies. Even though the law was not yet in effect, their school business, according to the appellees, was already suffering harm. The Supreme Court agreed when it said:

> The inevitable practical result of enforcing the Act under consideration would be destruction of appellees' primary schools, and perhaps all other private primary schools for normal children within the State of Oregon. . . .

---

[35] *Oregonian* (April 1, 1924), in Cain, 151-52.

Appellees . . . have business and property for which they claim protection. These are threatened with destruction through the unwarranted compulsion which appellants are exercising over present and prospective patrons of their schools. . . .

Generally it is entirely true . . . that no person in any business has such an interest in possible customers as to enable him to restrain exercise of proper power of the State upon the ground that he will be deprived of patronage. But the injunctions here sought are not against the exercise of any *proper* power. Plaintiffs asked protection against arbitrary, unreasonable and unlawful interference with their patrons and the consequent destruction of their business and property.[36]

This said, the United States Supreme Court affirmed the decrees of the federal district court of Oregon.

As was the case in *Meyer v. Nebraska*, astute observers were aware at the time of *Pierce v. the Society of Sisters and Hill Military Academy* that legal precedent in the United States and previous constitutional interpretation made a claim to property rights a stronger argument in 1925 than an appeal to the free exercise of religion. Hill Military Academy, of course, was unable to argue on the basis of religion, but the Sisters of the Holy Names of Jesus and Mary were and did so in part, as is apparent from the Supreme Court's summary of their plea. After having detailed briefly the situation with respect to the property holdings of the Catholic order, the Court added that the Society also alleged that the enactment of the Oregon school law conflicted with the rights of parents to choose

---

[36] Herbert M. Kliebard, *Religion and Education in America: A Documentary History* (Scranton, PA: International Textbook Company, 1969), 125-26.

schools which they deemed appropriate not only for mental but also for religious training. The Court responded to that concern, drew in part upon the doctrine articulated in *Meyer v. Nebraska* two years earlier, and penned the following memorable lines on parental rights:

> The child is not the mere creature of the State; those who nurture him and direct his destiny have the right, coupled with the high duty, to recognize and prepare him for additional obligations.[37]

This classic pronouncement of the highest court in the land, made in 1925 in connection with private and parochial schools, would not be forgotten decades later in the Amish case of *Wisconsin v. Yoder* (1972) and also again when home schooling became a controversial issue and practice more widely engaged in.

Writing in 1963, a Roman Catholic constitutional scholar commented that the United States Supreme Court's decision in *Pierce v. Society of Sisters and Hill Military Academy* has always been favorably received. Looking back at the case, he said:

> *The New York Times* applauded the decision and described the Oregon law as inspired by the most partisan and vicious motives ever recorded in American history. The ruling of the Supreme Court elicited comment in 496 newspapers in 44 states, all overwhelmingly favorable to the decision.[38]

---

[37] Ibid., 125.

[38] Robert F. Drinan, *Religion, the Courts, and Public Policy* (New York: McGraw-Hill, 1963), 123.

The same writer also observed that Felix Frankfurter, a contributing editor to the *New Republic,* commended the decision in the June 17, 1925, issue of that periodical. Frankfurter would himself one day become a United States Supreme Court justice. Writing in 1925, the future justice called the *Pierce* decision a "service to liberalism" because the ruling brought to an end "the effort to regiment the mental life of Americans through public school instruction." The Court, Frankfurter said, "stifled the recrudescence of intolerance."[39] Lutherans who operate parochial schools are just as ready to applaud that 1925 decision of the Supreme Court, for the decision upheld the right of parents to send their children to church-related elementary schools.

Suggested for Further Reading

Cain, A. B. *The Oregon School Fight.* Portland: A. B. Cain, 1924.

Drinan, Robert F. *Religion, the Courts, and Public Policy.* New York: McGraw-Hill, 1963: 122-27.

Duker, Sam. *The Public Schools and Religion: The Legal Context.* New York: Harper and Row, 1966: 40-49.

Kliebard, Herbert M. *Religion and Education in America: A Documentary History.* Scranton, PA: International Textbook Company, 1969: 121-26.

---

[39] Ibid.

✦ ✦ ✦ 1926 ✦ ✦ ✦

Bobbs-Merrill Readers - Concordia Edition

Writing in the December 1926 issue of the *Lutheran School Journal*, a book reviewer commented:

> The series of revised Bobbs-Merrill Readers is now complete. All teachers who are interested in teaching good reading . . . will hail the new Readers with delight. Not only do the new Readers rank among the first when measured by the highest requirements of modern education, but by elimination of objectionable and unsuitable lessons and insertion of Christian and specifically Lutheran material they have been made good Lutheran books. They contain more positively Christian— and indeed Lutheran—reading-matter than any series of Readers which has ever been used in our schools.[1]

The *Lutheran School Journal* review was an assessment of the Missouri Synod's Concordia Edition of a series of elementary school Readers published in 1923 and 1924 by the Bobbs-Merrill Company of Indianapolis. The Concordia Edition was a revision and adaptation of the Indianapolis firm's books and was published by Concordia Publishing House in St. Louis. The revision and adaptation of the original Readers, authored by Clara B. and Edna D. Baker of National Elementary College

---

[1] *Lutheran School Journal*, December 1926, 476.

in Chicago, was the work of August C. Stellhorn, Executive Secretary for the General School Board of the Evangelical Lutheran Missouri Synod.

The Concordia Edition of the *Bobbs-Merrill Readers* is significant in the history of Lutheran education for a number of reasons. First, according to the reviser, "within a short period of time, 80 percent of the Missouri Synod schools had introduced these readers."[2] In addition, the books continued to be used in Lutheran elementary schools for nearly 20 years. More important than either of these two circumstances, however, was the fact that with this publishing effort Lutherans committed to Lutheran parochial schools brought to a close a long chapter in the history of producing Readers designed specifically for the teaching of elementary reading skills in Lutheran schools. An analysis of the Concordia Edition of the *Bobbs-Merrill Readers* provides a view of what late nineteenth-century and early twentieth-century Lutheran educators saw as desirable or objectionable in elementary school Readers for Lutheran schools.

Synodical concern for orthodox school reading books found expression already in the constitution of the German Evangelical Lutheran Synod of Missouri, Ohio, and Other States with the constitutional statement that only "doctrinally pure" Readers should be used in congregations affiliated with the Synod.[3] The dearth of Readers deemed appropriate for Lutheran schools was periodically lamented in the nineteenth century. Thus, for example, the 1868 convention *Proceedings* of the Western District of the Missouri Synod made the following comment relative to a convention overture dealing with school books:

---

[2] August C. Stellhorn, *Schools of The Lutheran Church—Missouri Synod* (St. Louis: Concordia Publishing House, 1963), 409.

[3] See chapter 4 (1847) of the present volume for further comment on this membership condition.

A major obstacle under which our schools suffer consists in this that the most diverse kinds of textbooks are being introduced into the schools. Experience shows that even unorthodox books have come into congregations. Under such circumstances, it would seem to be most necessary and the right time for the Synod to attend to the matter of having orthodox books brought into the schools, as is also required by our synodical constitution.[4]

Among the books recommended for publication for Lutheran schools was a new German first reading book (*Fibel*), a Reader for middle classes, and a series of English reading books. According to a writer in the *Evangelisch-Lutherisches Schulblatt* (Evangelical Lutheran School Journal), the overture presented to the Missouri Synod's Western District had noted that books from rationalistic and Roman Catholic sources were even being used.[5] Midwestern German-speaking Lutherans of the late nineteenth and early twentieth centuries were much concerned about what was contained in elementary Readers used in Lutheran schools and, for that reason, committed themselves to the production of their own materials for the teaching of reading. The Concordia Edition of the *Bobbs-Merrill Readers* in 1926 was the last comprehensive reading series produced under synodical auspices.

The publication of a synodical edition of a set of Readers produced outside of Lutheran circles was a departure from earlier practices. Previously, reading books in the Missouri Synod had been compiled and edited by individuals or committees within the Synod. At its 1923 convention, however, the Ev. Lutheran Synod of Missouri, Ohio, and Other States resolved "that the General School Board select a suitable series of readers now on the

---

[4] *Verhandlungen . . . des Westlichen Districts* (Proceedings . . . of the Western District), 1868, 48.

[5] *Evang.-Luth. Schulblatt*, August 1868, 371.

market and have it so amended, revised, and edited that it will meet our peculiar requirements."[6] The series initially selected by the General School Board for revision was a Scott, Foresman Company publication known as the Elson Readers. The number of revisions and alterations requested by the board did not meet with the approval of the Scott, Foresman Company, so that the latter refused to grant permission for a Lutheran edition of its reading series. After examining several other series, the recently published *Bobbs-Merrill Readers* were chosen for revision. Permission for the revision was sought and obtained, making possible, therefore, a Lutheran edition of a series of reading books not originally designed for use specifically in Lutheran schools.

In order to understand the concerns which nineteenth- and early twentieth-century Lutherans had about the reading selections in elementary school Readers of the time, it is necessary to recall that several popular early American Readers were arranged not only to teach reading skills but to inculcate values as well. One of these reading books was the well-known *New England Primer*, which made its appearance in America just before 1700 and continued to be printed in various editions for another 150 years.[7] Another popular book for the teaching of reading was Noah Webster's *The American Spelling Book*, a little volume which appeared first in 1783 and in its various editions sold millions of copies throughout the nineteenth century.[8] Better known perhaps than either of these books and of greater importance in a discussion of Readers for Lutheran

---

[6] *Proceedings . . . of the Ev. Luth. Synod of Missouri . . .* , 1923, 55.

[7] For a brief history of the *New England Primer* and a reproduction of the earliest extant copy of it, see Paul Leicester Ford, *The New England Primer*, in *Classics in Education*, ed. Lawrence Cremin (New York: Teachers College, Columbia University, 1962).

[8] For a brief commentary on this book and a reproduction of an 1831 edition, see *Noah Webster's American Spelling Book*, in *Classics in Education*, ed. Lawrence Cremin (New York: Teachers College, Columbia University, 1962).

schools are the celebrated *McGuffey Eclectic Readers*. The first edition came out in 1836 and although the books have been revised numerous times, they have continued to be available in various editions. Thus, a May/June 1998 catalog of Christian Book Distributors (Peabody, MA) advertised a new edition under the title *The Christian Eclectic First Reader Collection* with the comment: *"McGuffey's Readers* have been popular with homeschoolers for years—now they're even better. These new editions update old spelling and punctuation . . . but all of McGuffey's original poetry and literature selections are here!"

Since the *McGuffey Readers* were so popular and readily available in the last half of the nineteenth century, they would seem to have been the natural choice for nineteenth-century Lutheran immigrants to the Midwest and to other parts of the country for the teaching of English reading in their congregational schools. It is at this point, however, that one must remember that the selections in nineteenth-century elementary reading books were often strongly moralistic in tone. McGuffey was an ordained Presbyterian minister whose reading books promoted many values to which Lutherans would also have subscribed, but the motivation in the *McGuffey Readers* for the living of the Christian life was different from that of Lutheran theology. Lutherans begin their walk of faith at the cross of Christ, where atonement for the sin of the world was made. Lutherans teach that good works are the fruit of faith in a crucified and risen Lord who sent His Holy Spirit to create that very faith and to empower God's people to pursue virtues such as kindness, honesty, goodness, and the like. When religious materials were to be included in reading books, Lutherans wanted such selections to present a loving God in Christ Jesus. From that God and not from threats of punishment, Lutheran theology maintained, came the effective power to lead a God-pleasing life.

The *McGuffey Readers* did not overlook religion in its selections. Respect for God was taught and excerpts from the Bible were included in the reading selections. The truth of the Bible was not questioned and its message was highly regarded. In assessing the approach to morality advocated by the Readers, historian Henry Steele Commager perhaps caught what Lutherans objected to in at least the early editions of *McGuffey*:

> Yet for all its preoccupation with religion, the morality of the Readers was materialistic and worldly. It taught a simple system of rewards and punishments. Virtue was rarely its own reward: the kind old lady found out that the vagabond she had befriended was really a rich nephew returned from the goldfields; the honest farmer was given five hundred dollars by his rich neighbor as a reward for his honesty; the poor boy who helped the old man across the street was promptly provided with a job; the little chimney sweep who resisted the temptation to steal a gold watch was adopted by its enraptured owner. Wickedness, too, was invariably detected and punished, and once again the punishments were material and physical. The disobedient boy drowned; the greedy boy found himself in want; the rude boy, the meddlesome boy, the inquisitive boy, failed to get the job, or forfeited the rewards that went to his exemplary companions.[9]

The *McGuffey Readers* incorporated along with the teaching of reading skills a heavy dose of moralistic didacticism in their reading selections. When casting about for English reading books for Lutheran schools, the Lutheran church bodies which comprised the conservative Evangelical Lutheran Synodical

---

[9] Henry Steele Commager, Foreword to *McGuffey's Fifth Eclectic Reader* (New York: The New American Library of World Literature, Inc., Signet Classics, 1962), vii-viii.

Conference of North America were unwilling to recommend the use of what has perhaps turned out to be the single most-celebrated series of reading books in American history.[10]

The Synodical Conference, formed in 1872, took up the matter of English reading books for Lutheran schools at its convention in 1875. A committee reported that a manuscript for a beginning Reader in English was ready. The book was published by the Evangelical Lutheran Synodical Conference under the title *A Pictorial Primer or First Reader for Parochial Schools*. A picture accompanied each letter of the alphabet, thus following a pattern set already by the *New England Primer* of colonial times. The Lutheran Synodical Conference book, however, did not introduce its alphabet with biblical references or pictures. Instead of something like the *New England Primer's* "The Judgment made *Felix* afraid" for the letter *f*, the Lutheran book pictured a fox. In place of "Young Samuel dear, / The Lord did fear," the letter *s* used the word sun and showed a picture of it. The title page, however, did have a large picture of mothers bringing their children to Jesus for His blessing. The picture, incidentally, also included two men standing in the background apparently discouraging the mothers from bothering the Master. Although no text accompanied the frontispiece, the illustration was a quiet reminder of Lutheranism's starting point when seeking to shape character while teaching children how to read. Baptized children were to be presented with an inviting Gospel call to Christian living rather than with the Law or fear motivation so evident especially in the early *McGuffey Readers*. The specifically religious materials in the Lutheran book were adaptations of Bible narratives from both the Old and New Testaments. The language was that of the King James

---

[10] An excellent compilation of selections from the *McGuffey Readers* is contained in *The Annotated McGuffey* by Stanley W. Lindberg (New York: Van Nostrand Reinhold, 1976). There is also a McGuffey Museum in Oxford, Ohio.

Version, and each narrative was accompanied with a picture to portray the account.

Although the *Pictorial Primer*, which was completed in manuscript form at the time of the 1875 Synodical Conference convention, did come into print, it is apparent from the convention *Proceedings* that additional reading books in the English language were wanted as soon as possible. This became evident at the conclusion of the committee report on English school books when a directive to the Missouri Synod delegates to the convention was read to the assembly. The Missouri Synod had instructed its representatives to make it clear that an English Reader following upon the *Primer* was needed immediately and that

> if nothing materialized on the part of the Synodical Conference, then the Missouri Synod would see itself as compelled to take up the publication of English reading books on its own and that this should not be interpreted then as separatistic action.[11]

Arrangements for the producing of a second reading book were approved by the convention. The materials already partially prepared by Professor Selle of the Addison Teachers Seminary were to be the starting point. The Missouri Synod's St. Louis Seminary faculty was to serve as the theological reviewer of the manuscript and the Wisconsin Synod's Northwestern College faculty the pedagogical reviewer. It was reported in 1877 that the Northwestern faculty was unwilling to approve the initial materials, and although efforts continued to be made to have a committee author a Synodical Conference English Reader to follow upon the *Primer*, the book never came into existence.

---

[11] *Verhandlungen . . . der . . . Synodal-Conferenz (*Proceedings . . . of . . . the Synodical Conference), 1875, 32.

The publication plans of the Synodical Conference to produce English reading books not having materialized, the Missouri Synod proceeded to embark on the course which it announced in 1875 that it would take if the Conference did not publish additional English Readers. By 1886, Concordia Publishing House, the publishing arm of the Missouri Synod established by it in 1869, had completed a set of four English Readers for Lutheran schools.[12] A synodical reviewer of the First and Second Reader was not too pleased that those two books had included so very little specifically religious material. In his review he commented: "Apart from a biblical quotation at the very end, the little book contains nothing specifically Christian, even as the Second Reader, sad to say, deals very little with such material."[13]

One of the very striking features of this reading series, however, was the way in which it reflected the bilingual nature of late nineteenth-century Lutheran parochial schools. At the head of each lesson was a list of the more difficult words in the reading selection of the lesson. In addition to English definitions, German equivalents were also given. Recognizing perhaps the somewhat unusual nature of this arrangement, the editors commented on it in their preface to the *Second Reader*: "This we deemed the more practical way of defining the

---

[12] It should be understood that nineteenth-century reading books were not graded as books are today. Thus, a Third Reader was not intended for use in the third grade as we might think but was to be used whenever the material of the First and Second Readers had been completed. Such completion could occur at any time in a child's school career. This was especially the case in one-room schools where children of the same age might be at very different reading levels because of the amount of time they had been in school. Home responsibilities, particularly in farm communities, resulted in sporadic school attendance for some children. The books were also intended as literature books for use in the home.

[13] *Evang.-Luth. Schulblatt* (Evangelical Lutheran School Journal), Second Quarter 1885, 91.

English words to young German readers."[14] The following poem by William Woodsworth taken from the *Fourth Reader* illustrates the point:

VII.—MARCH.

re-treat′, *to withdraw;* ſich zurückziehen.
whoop, *to hollow;* ſchreien.
a-non′, *again;* wieber.
pre-vail′, *to gain the superiority;* bie Oberhanb haben ober bekommen.

1. The cock is crowing,
   The stream is flowing,
   The small birds twitter,
   The lake doth glitter,

   The green field sleeps in the sun;
   The oldest and the youngest
   ·Are at work with the strongest;
   The cattle are grazing,
   Their heads never raising;
   There are forty feeding like one!

2. Like an army defeated,
   The snow hath retreated,
   And now doth fare ill
   On the top of the bare hill;
   The ploughboy is whooping anon, anon.
   There's joy in the mountains;
   There's life in the fountains;
   Small clouds are sailing,
   Blue sky prevailing;
   The rain is over and. gone!

   William Wordsworth. 15

Having no more prestigious a title than *First Reader, Second Reader,* and the like, these four books were replaced in the first decade of the twentieth century by Concordia Publishing House's *Standard American Series* of Readers. Authorized by

----

[14] *The Second Reader* (St. Louis: Concordia, 1882), v.

[15] *The Fourth Reader* (St. Louis: Concordia, 1895), 14-15. The English definition of whoop, the German *schreien*, is obviously a typographical error. The English should be "holler" and not "hollow."

the 1896 convention of the Missouri Synod, this series of Readers was the immediate predecessor of the Concordia Edition of the *Bobbs-Merrill Readers*. The *Standard American Series* was the work of a synodical committee and drew its selections from a variety of sources. Biblical materials were included but not in large amounts, very likely because Lutheran schools had available to them Bible history books in both German and English. Those books, used in religion classes, provided ample biblical reading materials. A prayer or religious poem occasionally found its way into the Readers, but here, too, there was no special need for such literature in reading books because the synodically produced songbooks for Lutheran schools included hymns and sacred songs, primarily in German, but to some extent also in English. It is also interesting to note that several selections had even been taken from *McGuffey Readers*, and not to be overlooked is the absence in word lists of German definitions for difficult English words.

When the *Standard American Series* was in preparation, the Milwaukee, Wisconsin, Teachers' Conference adopted a set of principles which it felt should govern the compilation of the new reading series. The principles were printed in an 1899 issue of the *Schulblatt* (Lutheran School Journal) with the request that synodical teachers react to those principles. Of the 23 items, numbers V and XI are especially significant with reference to the religious flavor which the Milwaukee teachers wanted the books to have:

V

The main object of these readers is to teach reading. At the same time other features will not be overlooked. Space will be given to lessons that cultivate the child's powers of observation and reasoning, his sense for the beautiful, his appreciation of God's foresight and wisdom as seen in nature, his love of his home and his country, his sense of duty.

XI

. . . Anything not in strict accord with our Lutheran faith
can find no place in our Readers.[16]

The stipulation that the *Standard American Series* of Readers
be in "strict accord" with the Lutheran faith was not new in the
discussion of reading books for Lutheran schools. When the
Synodical Conference was addressing the issue of English
Readers, a directive from the Missouri Synod to its delegates
observed that "the customary American Readers cannot be
tolerated in our parochial schools any longer because of the false
doctrine contained in those books."[17] A major concern about the
Readers called for at that time was that their "content be entirely
free of false doctrine and their language correct."[18] The report
on the *Primer* manuscript reviewed in 1875 was that its content
"throughout was consistently in harmony with the Word of
God."[19] When August Ernst, president of the Wisconsin
Synod's Northwestern College, wrote about the German Reader
which he had compiled for Lutheran schools, he said that a
Reader for such schools "must have an unequivocally Lutheran
stamp upon it."[20] In fact, it can be said that the German Readers
produced by both the Wisconsin and Missouri Synods in the late
nineteenth century had a more conspicuous religious imprint than
did the later *Standard American Series*. The editors of the latter
seem to have been concerned more with the teaching of basic
reading skills than with the additional goal of compiling

---

[16] "Principles Governing the Compilation and Issue of Our New Series
of Readers," *Evang.-Luth. Schulblatt*, July 1899, 219-20.

[17] *Verhandlungen der . . . Synodal-Conferenz* (Proceedings of . . . the
Synodical Conference), 1875, 32.

[18] Ibid., 33.

[19] Ibid., 32.

[20] *Schulzeitung* (School Periodical), April 1883, 27.

something of an anthology of inspirational literature for home reading.

Reviews of two of the Readers in the *Standard American Series* are informative with respect to the reading methodology advocated by Lutheran school educators at the time and their view of the purpose of the parochial school in relation to high school and college education. The first of these reviews appeared in 1902 at the time of the appearance of the *First Reader* in the series. Of this first book of 66 pages, the *Schulblatt* reviewer said:

> This neat little book reminded us of the time when, as a boy, we were "put through" the old McGuffey. Comparing the makeup of this *our* Reader with those of that antiquated school-book, we find that it is up to date in every detail and respect. . . .
>
> . . . In 55 lessons the child is taught to read by the *phonic method*. Besides reading lessons, a *phonic exercise*, or word drill, follows the introduction of each vowel sound, a feature we have been looking for all along. . . . Beginning with the very first lesson the *script* alphabet is introduced, which enables the teacher to freely use the blackboard in connection with each lesson from the book. . . .
>
> *Thirty-two* . . . illustrations, . . . of which *ten* are . . . *in colors*, will not only delight the children, but also furnish to the teacher matter for oral exercises on the lesson to which they belong.[21]

McGuffey didn't fare too well with this *Schulblatt* reviewer, but his reference to that Reader is evidence that the book had been

---

[21] *Evang.-Luth. Schulblatt* (Evangelical Lutheran School Journal), January 1903, 28.

in use among Lutherans. The *First Reader* of the *Standard American Series* employed the phonetic method for the teaching of reading and included illustrations which the reviewer expected teachers would use as a guide when engaging children in oral exercises on the reading selections.

A little over six years later, the *Schulblatt* printed a review of the *Fifth Reader*, the last book in the *Standard American Series* published by Concordia Publishing House. Of the final book in the series the reviewer said:

> This Reader completes the *Standard American Series* and is intended for the sixth and seventh school years. It is not illustrated, partly, to reduce the expenses of publication, and partly, because pictorial representations of events are often of doubtful value in the upper grades. This *Fifth Reader* comprises lessons on natural history, physiology, natural phenomena, inventions, discoveries, commodities, geography, general history, the history of the United States, Indians, civil government, the races of mankind, and ecclesiastical history; it presents biographies, selections from the Bible, legends, patriotic, poetic, and humorous selections, proverbs, stories, and miscellaneous topics. This shows that the lessons cover a wide range of subjects, but only a few classical selections were found available, as these were written for mature minds, not for the pupils of elementary schools. Our *Fifth Reader* is intended to assist in educating our pupils for practical life, and in this respect it is superior to other books of the same class. In American Fifth Readers we usually find a large number of selections from the classics, for the average grammar school does not prepare the children for practical life, but for the high school, its efficiency being judged solely by the percentage of its pupils that pass the required examination for the high school. The high school prepares for the college, and the college for the university. This

state of affairs is deeply deplored by all pedagogues who are convinced that the elementary schools should prepare their pupils for practical life and not for entrance into a higher institution of learning. As this is the correct view, the *Standard Fifth Reader* should be heartily welcomed, not only within our synod, but also, like its second cousin, the *Standard Arithmetic*, by public schools.[22]

Informative as the above assessment is with regard to the content of the *Fifth Reader* in the *Standard American Series*, not to be overlooked is the reviewer's somewhat incidental comment about the relationship between the grammar school and high school. It is apparent that he held the position that the upper grades of grammar school should be taught primarily from the point of view that they were terminal in the education of most youth. That many students at that time did conclude their formal schooling after the grammar grades cannot be disputed, particularly in the case of rural and small-town areas where many Lutheran parochial schools in the Midwest were located. Any view which taught that education would stay that way was more of a look backward than forward, however, for the American high school had been on an emerging path since about 1880, and by 1920 the high school would begin to take on many of the characteristics we have come to associate with secondary schooling today. As far as Lutherans were concerned, they, too, were beginning to think about community-based Lutheran high schools. In fact, Missouri and Wisconsin Synod congregations in Milwaukee established a Lutheran high school in that city in 1903. Missouri Synod congregations in Chicago founded the

---

[22] *Evang.-Luth. Schulblatt* (Evangelical Lutheran School Journal), October 1909, 317. This review, as well as the one on the *First Reader* in 1903 and the previously mentioned "Principles Governing the Compilation and Issue of Our New Series of Readers" (1899), was written in English, although the majority of the articles in the *Schulblatt* at that time were still in German.

same kind of institution in 1909, the very year in which the *Schulblatt* reviewer commended the *Standard American Fifth Reader* for its selection of reading materials which he was convinced prepared for "practical life" rather than for high school. Just how far apart the two goals are is not the issue. The point is that some Lutheran educators in the first decade of the twentieth century saw Lutheran elementary schools as terminal institutions and did not seem to feel a strong responsibility for educating with the high school in mind. With time, as a high school education became the norm on the American educational scene, that view would change, of course.

Looking back at the dates of the synodical authorization of the *Standard American Series* of Readers and the date of the publication of the final volume, one is struck with how long it took to produce the books. The Missouri Synod commissioned the project in 1896; the last of the five books came out in 1909. A long time for the production of a set of elementary school Readers! The extensive time span required to complete the series is readily understood, however, when one recognizes that the editorship was in the hands of a committee of individuals who held full-time callings in the church. The difficulty of trying to produce and edit reading books under such circumstances became apparent in the Synodical Conference in 1879 already when a certain Pastor Lange of Chicago asked to be relieved of his duties as chairman of an editorial committee for English Readers "because of a lack of help on the part of committee members who had been appointed to assist him with the preparation of those books."[23] It takes both a vast amount of time and expertise to design, edit, and publish a respectable set of elementary school reading books. It was a recognition of that fact perhaps which lay behind the 1923 Missouri Synod convention resolution to revise an existing set of Readers for

---

[23] *Verhandlungen der . . . Synodal-Conferenz* (Proceedings of . . . the Synodical Conference), 1879, 43.

use in Lutheran schools rather than produce such a series entirely with synodical resources.

Once permission was obtained to adapt the 1923-24 reading series of the Bobbs-Merrill Company, the revision process moved along quickly. An action of the Missouri Synod in its 1920 convention was extremely helpful to make that possible. It was at that time that the Synod established the full-time position of Executive Secretary of the General School Board. August C. Stellhorn was called to the position in 1921 and assumed the role of editor after the decision was made in early 1925 to revise the *Bobbs-Merrill Readers*. From his full-time executive position and with the assistance of two professors from River Forest, Stellhorn was able to direct his time and energies to the project. The result was that the *Third* and *Fourth Readers* were ready by September of 1925, with the remainder of the series becoming available for the 1926-27 school year. Compared with the 13-year interval between synodical resolution and completion of the *Standard American Series*, the *Bobbs-Merrill* project was on the fast track indeed.

The rationale expressed by conservative Lutherans in the nineteenth century when the matter of Readers specifically designed for Lutheran schools was at issue was still strongly supported when the *Bobbs-Merrill* books received their Lutheran cover in the mid-1920s. The Lutheran school was seen as an institution whose primary purpose was the teaching of the Christian faith and the shaping of Christian character and judgment from the perspective of Lutheran theology. This position was vigorously affirmed in an essay review of the *Third* and *Fourth Readers* of the *Bobbs-Merrill* Concordia Edition. Writing for the *Lutheran School Journal* in 1925, Arthur Diesing of the River Forest faculty remarked:

> *Christian training* is the main purpose of our schools. In order that this main purpose may be carried out effectively,

all the subjects taught in our schools must be permeated with the principles laid down by God in His holy Word and summarized in the confessional writings of the Lutheran Church. Present-day conditions, the increased demands upon the schools, the introduction of text-books not written from a Christian point of view, the increasing tendency to follow state, county, or city courses of study . . . all of these conditions are exerting a strong influence to sidetrack the main purpose of our schools. . . .

The desirable features of modern reading-texts . . . have proved so enticing to many of our teachers that our own series [*Standard American*] has extensively been replaced by other texts. This change has been in some cases even suggested and advocated officially. These changes have, no doubt, in most cases been beneficial from a pedagogical point of view. But there has been a corresponding loss in giving up distinctively Lutheran material. . . .

The readers used in our schools . . . must reflect the ideals and the sentiments that *we* consider essential and desirable in the training of *our* children. Any other Reader is out of place in a Lutheran school. . . .

The main value of the adaptation [of the *Bobbs-Merrill Readers*] . . . must be sought in its ability to provide for Christian training. . . .[24]

August C. Stellhorn, the *Bobbs-Merrill* Concordia Edition reviser, was also committed to that position. When the revision was completed, he commented that reading classes in Lutheran elementary schools should assist children to

---

[24] *Lutheran School Journal*, December 1925, 452-55.

develop proper Christian judgment and discretion in the selection of their reading materials and in what they read! The highest and, at the same time, the most immediate goal in reading is for the Christian child to read the Word of God effectively. His reading course should be so designed that he will read himself into the Church and the Bible, not out of them; and the *Concordia Edition of the Bobbs-Merrill Readers* aims for just this objective.[25]

Stellhorn did not overlook, however, that other purposes were also served by the new reading series, for the books sought to train pupils "to read for definite facts, for information . . . for enjoying the beauty of language," as well as "for edification and spiritual strength."[26]

The Concordia Edition editor rehearsed the entire revision process rather extensively in a series of articles in the March to August issues of the *Lutheran School Journal*. The articles assessed the merits of the unrevised *Bobbs-Merrill Readers*, gave a detailed account of the revision process, and also addressed the subject of methods for the teaching of reading. The books themselves gained almost instant popularity in Lutheran schools, for the reviser, when asking teachers to report mistakes and shortcomings, announced that a second edition of the Concordia revision would soon be printed. This was in June of 1927, just one year after the set had been completed.

When Stellhorn and his committee, Professors F. H. Schmitt and Alfred F. Schmieding of River Forest, began their revision process, they looked at the original books done by Clara and Edna Baker and asked the following three questions: "1) what *must* be changed, 2) what *should* be changed, and 3) what *might* be changed."[27] Decisions were not always made on

---

[25] Ibid., August 1927, 290.

[26] Ibid., 288.

[27] Ibid., June 1927, 208-9.

the basis of doctrine or a desire to include specifically Lutheran materials, although that was a frequent consideration and the manuscript would eventually, as Stellhorn put it, be "submitted both to the [whole] Committee and to Concordia Publishing House's censor, a member of the St. Louis [Seminary] faculty, for final ratification."[28] The following table is helpful to gain something of a view of how extensive the revision of the original *Bobbs-Merrill Readers* was:

	Total No. Pages Reading- Material	Pages Substi- tuted	Per Cent	Pages Christian Material*	Per Cent
Primer	149	2	1.34	3	2.01
Book I	165	9	5.45	9	5.45
Book II	215	28	13.02	21	9.81
Book III	269	68	25.28	67	24.90
Book IV	374	72	19.24	43	11.49
Book V	443	124	27.99	73	16.02
Book VI	447	135	30.20	128	28.63
Book VII	510	165	32.35	114	22.35
Book VIII	520	126	24.23	109	20.96

* Including Christian material already in the books.[29]

The above table includes only complete pages of substituted material and does not reflect word, title, or illustration changes in the original. Considering the substituted pages and the other changes, some of which were in mechanical matters such as punctuation, the reviser called the revision a "thorough cleansing." And why was it done?

> Briefly: 1. Because of the undesirability or dangerous character of selections, expressions, directions, or

---

[28] Ibid., 209.

[29] Ibid., May 1927, 168.

teachings, from a Christian point of view. 2. Because of the desire for books with a distinctively Luthero-Christian motive and aim. 3. Because of the necessity of making Christian pupils appreciate and read Christian material. 4. Because of the need of making or keeping the books as correct as possible as to mechanical details.[30]

There is no doubt that the Concordia Edition of the *Bobbs-Merrill Readers* followed in the nineteenth-century tradition of producing for Lutheran Christian day schools reading books with a distinctively Lutheran stamp.

The table presented above reveals that the Concordia Edition of the *Bobbs-Merrill Readers* removed a sizable amount of material from the original series compiled by its authors for use in public schools. A smaller percentage of pages was substituted in the lower-level texts than in the books for the upper grades. From Book III onward, however, the substitutions were extensive. In Book VII, for example, the number of substituted pages was 165, 32 percent of the total number of pages in other words. In his *Lutheran School Journal* review of the revision process, A. C. Stellhorn adds that numerous alterations other than the page substitutions had to be made. In some instances, these were minor alterations such as punctuation changes, while in other cases the revisions were more substantive. New materials required new study notes, for example, as well as additions or deletions from the glossaries. The pagination in the two editions remained very similar, the selection or number of selections removed being replaced by inclusions of the same length, a kind of matching which must have been quite a challenge for the editors.

Contemporary educators, even Lutheran ones, might question some of the judgments of the Concordia Edition revisers. It would be a mistake, however, to think that the

---

[30] Ibid., 169.

revised books had become inferior or a provincial set of Readers designed to give Lutheran school children a generous dose of religion at the expense of literary artistry. The fact is that selections common to many Readers of the 1920s and pieces of literature considered classics, but also understandable to children in grades eight and below, were retained in the Concordia Edition. Standard selections of that era for seventh and eighth graders, such as Henry Wadsworth Longfellow's *The Courtship of Miles Standish* and *Evangeline*, were in the Concordia *Bobbs-Merrill* as well as in the original. John Greenleaf Whittier's *Snowbound* and Washington Irving's *Rip Van Winkle* were among the eighth-grade selections. Robert Browning's *The Pied Piper of Hamelin* was in the *Fifth Reader* as was Jonathan Swift's *Gulliver's Travels* and Daniel Defoe's *Robinson Crusoe*. Choice lyrics such as William Cullen Bryant's "To a Waterfowl" and Sidney Lanier's "Song of the Chattahoochee" were also brought to the attention of pupils using the Concordia or regular edition of the *Bobbs-Merrill Readers*. The list could go on with the naming of other authors and various types of literature. The *Bobbs-Merrill Readers* themselves and the Concordia Edition were not lacking in quality literary pieces suitable for elementary school children.

The original books by Clara and Edna Baker included religious as well as secular selections. Since the books were designed for public schools, however, the religious material was not extensive and was drawn for the most part from the Bible, especially from the Old Testament. Thus Psalms 23, 91, 121, and 147 found their way into the editions published by Bobbs-Merrill. The *Second Reader* gave the title "The Baby in the Basket" to the biblical narrative of the infant Moses and identified the selection as a Hebrew Tale. The Concordia Edition retained the title of the narrative but indicated that the selection was taken from the Bible. "The Boy Champion" of the *Third Reader*, also called a Hebrew Tale, took the more familiar title

"David and Goliath" in the Concordia Edition, which again noted that the source of the narrative was the Bible. A somewhat unusual inclusion relating to a biblical event and retained, very likely without much hesitancy on the part of the Concordia revisers, in the *Sixth Reader* was George Gordon Lord Byron's vividly descriptive poem entitled *The Destruction of Sennacherib*. 2 Kings 19:35-36 was the inspiration for Byron's well-crafted anapestic creation which concluded with the couplet:

> And the might of the Gentile, unsmote by the sword,
> Hath melted like snow in the glance of the Lord.

The market for the original *Bobbs-Merrill Readers* required, of course, that any religious materials in the books remain general in character. It is in that connection that the Concordia Edition supplemented to include very specific Christian references. The *Primer* would be a case in point. In the Baker and Baker original, the little volume concluded with the following Christmas carol:

> All the bells on earth shall ring
> > On Christmas day,
> > On Christmas day;
> All the bells on earth shall ring
> > On Christmas day in the morning.

> All the men on earth shall sing
> > On Christmas day,
> > On Christmas day;
> All the men on earth shall sing
> > On Christmas day in the morning.[31]

---

[31] Clara B. Baker and Edna D. Baker, *Bobbs-Merrill Readers Primer* (Indianapolis: The Bobbs-Merrill Company, 1923), 152.

To this carol the Concordia Edition added a third stanza:

> Jesus did salvation bring
> On Christmas day,
> On Christmas day;
> Jesus did salvation bring
> On Christmas day in the morning.[32]

The Concordia Edition closed its Primer with the following Christmas prayer:

> Dearest Jesus, Holy Child,
> Born in Bethlehem,
> Bring me to Thy Father mild,
> Let me be with Him!
> Make me like the angels clean,
> Wash all sin away;
> Make me on Thy arm to lean
> On my heavenly way![33]

With an addition of that kind in its beginning reading book already the Concordia revision sought to emphasize that Jesus Christ is the focal point of the Christian religion. He is the Son of God and the Savior and Redeemer from sin. Children were taught to confess their sin and to rely on Christ for forgiveness. The biblical message of sin and grace, Law and Gospel, were brought together in the classic Lutheran way. Concordia's *First Reader*, which followed upon the Primer, did the same thing in a closing prayer entitled "At Night." The second stanza of the poem reads as follows:

---

[32] Concordia Edition *Bobbs-Merrill Readers, The Primer* (St. Louis: Concordia Publishing House, 1926), 153.

[33] Ibid.

Forgive the wrong this day I've done,
For Jesus' sake, Thine own dear Son;
And may His blood, once shed for me,
From all that's sinful make me free.[34]

The Concordia Edition of the *Bobbs-Merrill Readers* had its
religious focus upon Him who said of Himself that the
Scriptures are "they which testify of Me" (John 5:39).
Concordia's *Primer* and *First Reader* further emphasized the
importance of Jesus Christ in the life of Christian children with
the frontispiece opposite the title page of each volume. The
Primer had a picture of Jesus blessing little children; the *First
Reader* an illustration of the 12-year-old Jesus in the temple.

The *Second Reader* added its voice to the message of
forgiveness of sins in Christ Jesus with a story which placed
the certainty of that forgiveness into the foreground. The story
is a bit sentimental and contrived but makes its theological
point clearly. Little Mary, according to the narrative, went on a
long trip to visit her aunt. While at her aunt's house, Mary
became sick and died. Recognizing that she would die before
her parents could get to her bedside, Mary wrote a farewell
letter to her parents. In that letter she said: "I know that my
dear Savior has forgiven me all my sins and I shall surely be
saved and go to heaven." The aunt commended the little girl
for the letter which she had written, but then said: "I believe
you have made a mistake. You should not say, 'I know that my
dear Savior has forgiven me all my sins.' That is not quite
right. Nobody can know that for sure. . . . I shall, therefore,
write that you have prayed much, and hoped that God would
forgive you." Mary responded: "No . . . leave the letter as I
have it. One can know it, and I do know it." The story then

---

[34] Concordia Edition *Bobbs-Merrill Readers, The First Reader* (St.
Louis: Concordia, 1926), 169.

concludes by saying that Mary died in that faith and adds the lines:

> Never be afraid to die in Jesus,
> He, the Life, the Truth, the Way,
> Gently in His arms will bear you
> To the place where angels stay.[35]

Although contemporary educators would undoubtedly consider the story of "Little Mary" too morbid to be included in an elementary reading book, it must be remembered that the Lutheran edition of the *Bobbs-Merrill Readers* was produced at a time when childhood diseases were not as well understood nor as effectively treated as they are today. In addition, the books were published within the shadow of the 1918 influenza epidemic and the rather sudden nature of flu attacks. In any case, the theological point emphasized by Lutherans was made: the forgiveness of sin won by Christ's atoning sacrifice on the cross is an accomplished fact and awaits only the hand of faith to grasp the blessing. Little Mary did not have to hope for salvation; she could be certain of it.

Even as the beginning books in the Concordia series included christological religious materials, so did the Readers for the upper grades. One such selection appears in the *Seventh Reader*, another in the *Eighth*. Both of them are poems. One is entitled "Sinai and Calvary"; the other is a Christmas song. The Law/Gospel relationship is reflected already in the title of the *Seventh Reader's* "Sinai and Calvary," and after the Study Notes accompanying the selection, a stanza from a well-known Lutheran hymn filled out the page. The hymn, inadvertently attributed to Martin Luther by the editors, was in fact from the

---

[35] Concordia Edition *Bobbs-Merrill Readers, The Second Reader* (St. Louis: Concordia, 1924), 182-184.

pen of Paul Speratus, a contemporary of Luther. The stanza quoted was the sixth in Speratus' 14-stanza hymn "Salvation unto Us Has Come":

> Since Christ hath full atonement made,
> And brought to us salvation,
> Each Christian therefore may be glad,
> And build on this foundation:
> Thy grace alone, dear Lord, I plead,
> Thy death my life now is indeed
> For Thou has (*sic*) paid my ransom.[36]

The *Eighth Reader*'s Christmas song carries the title "Sing, Christmas Bells," speaks of Christ as "Him who died upon the tree," and hails Him as the Savior-King. The benefits of that death for the sinful human race are announced in these words:

> Sing, sons of earth!
> O ransomed seed of Adam, sing!
> God liveth, and we have a king!
> The curse is gone, the bond are free –
> By Bethlehem's star that brightly beamed,
> By all the heavenly signs that be,
> We know that Israel is redeemed;
> That on this morn
> The Christ is born,
> That saveth you and saveth me![37]

---

[36] Concordia Edition *Bobbs-Merrill Readers, The Seventh Reader* (St. Louis: Concordia, 1926), 472.

[37] Concordia Edition *Bobbs-Merrill Readers, The Eighth Reader* (St. Louis: Concordia, 1926), 515-16.

Lest these samples leave the impression that the Concordia Edition of the *Bobbs-Merrill Readers* was a collection of various types of Lutheran sermonic treatises, it should be remembered that the kinds of material just cited did not appear with a great deal of frequency. The two examples just given came from books more than 500 pages long and appeared among writings by Robert Browning, Nathaniel Hawthorne, James Fenimore Cooper, Henry David Thoreau, Abraham Lincoln, Walt Whitman, Percy Bysshe Shelley, Alfred Lord Tennyson, and a host of other well-known writers. Granted, some of the books for the middle and upper grades contained, according to the reviser's tabulation, anywhere from 11 percent to 28 percent of pages of Christian material. The first three books had less than 10 percent of selections of that kind, however, and the materials classified as Christian in the other books would have encompassed a wide range of literary types, some of which would have been in the original series. On the other hand, it is a fact that the Concordia Edition revisers very consciously added a fair amount of selections with Lutheran theological emphases.

When the Concordia Edition was completed and in use, editor August C. Stellhorn explained that

> the revision was necessitated not so much because of the amount of material we sought to include as on account of the need of clearing the books of undesirable content. Quite generally the removal of undesirable selections made room enough for the Christian material we wished to insert. In fact, sometimes we failed to fill the gaps with such material and were obliged to insert clean selections of a non-religious nature.[38]

---

[38] A. C. Stellhorn, "The Bobbs-Merrill Readers, Concordia Edition," *Lutheran School Journal*, May 1927, 169.

Materials in the original Baker and Baker version of the *Bobbs-Merrill Readers* which were replaced often dealt with the spirit world. Elves, fairies, goblins, and references to them were items regularly excluded in the Concordia Edition. Thus, for example, the two-stanza poem entitled "The Elf Man" in the original version of the *Second Reader* became "The Little Man" in the Concordia Edition. Four selections, 30 pages of material, at the end of the *Third Reader* were replaced. The items removed carried the titles "The Elf and the Dormouse," "Brownie's Ride," "The Fairies," and "The Fairy Shoes." Fable itself was not objected to, for the Concordia Edition included legends and selections from Aesop and the Grimm Brothers. Part of the reason for some of the exclusions might have been a concern that small children would not be able to distinguish clearly between the unreal world of sprites and the factual existence of God's holy angels. Whatever the reason, a comparison between the original *Bobbs-Merrill* series and the Concordia version reveals a consistent elimination of fairy-lore from the latter.

The Concordia Edition revisers were also especially careful with literature relating to the celebration of Christmas. It is not surprising, therefore, that the revisers did not retain "The Visit from St. Nicholas" in their edition of the *Third Reader*. The piece is so familiar so that only a few couplets need be quoted to bring it to mind:

> 'Twas the night before Christmas,
>   when all through the house,
> Not a creature was stirring, not even a mouse.
>
> The stockings were hung by the chimney with care,
> In hopes that St. Nicholas soon would be there.

A poem with Dancer and Prancer and St. Nicholas, too, was deemed unsuitable for a Reader designed specifically for Lutheran parish schools. In the 1920s, as today, there was a concern about the secularization or misinterpretation of Christmas. Three selections replaced the story of the man who "had a broad face and a little round belly / That shook, when he laughed, like a bowl full of jelly." One substitution was a two-page compilation from Holy Scripture of the accounts of the circumcision and naming of Jesus, His presentation in the Temple in the presence of Simeon, the visit of the Wise Men, the flight of the holy family into Egypt, the slaughter of the infants at Bethlehem, and the return of Mary, Joseph, and Jesus to Nazareth. Another replacement for Jolly Old St. Nick was a poem which attributed to Jesus the bringing of "toys and other pretty things" as tokens

> That God now loves the world indeed,
> Since we from sin and death are freed.[39]

The third substitution was a five-stanza poem by editor Stellhorn himself. Entitled "Beginning Christmas Joys," the poem spoke of the shepherds' joy at the birth of Christ and then concluded with the stanza:

> What we want more than gifts and toys
> Is to return today
> To those beginning Christmas joys
> On Christmas holiday.[40]

A sizable amount of mythological material was removed from the opening part of the *Sixth Reader*. The first section of the Baker and Baker edition of that book had the caption "Heroes of Long Ago" and comprised about 130 pages. There

---

[39] Concordia Edition *Bobbs-Merrill Readers, The Third Reader* (St. Louis: Concordia, 1926), 81-82.

[40] Ibid., 83.

were three groups of heroes: Norse, Greek, and Hebrew. Selections which were eliminated included an excerpt from Homer's *Odyssey* and four pieces dealing with Norse heroes. Among the latter pieces was Henry Wadsworth Longfellow's "The Challenge of Thor," the first stanza of which reads:

I am the God Thor,
I am the War God,
I am the Thunderer!
Here in my Northland,
My fastness and fortress,
Reign I forever![41]

The revisers chose to subdivide their sixth book into categories different from those of the original *Bobbs-Merrill*. One of Concordia's classifications was "Religious and Historical." Obviously, Longfellow's "The Challenge of Thor" would have been inappropriate in that category, but its replacement was the same poet's familiar "The Village Blacksmith," which didn't fit the category either and for that reason was inserted in the Concordia Edition under the heading "Character."

One type of revision which the Concordia editors ordinarily did not engage in was to try to give a Christian cast to a fable by superimposing upon it a tint of pious coloring. In one case, however, this was done. The *First Reader* of the unrevised *Bobbs-Merrill* included the Grimm tale about a poor shoemaker and his wife. Destitute and with enough leather to make only one more pair of shoes, the shoemaker cut out the leather for them and left it on the table. In the morning, he found a quality pair of shoes on the table. He sold them for a good price, bought more leather, cut out more shoes, left the materials on the table before he went to bed each night, and found handsome

---

[41] *Bobbs-Merrill Readers, The Sixth Reader* (Indianapolis: Bobbs-Merrill, 1924), 37.

and excellent shoes on his table the next morning. The products were the work of two wee little men, elves if you will, who with their labors lifted the poor shoemaker and his wife out of poverty. The Concordia version of "The Poor Shoemaker" removed these nighttime mythological visitors and alleviated the poverty of the shoemaker and his wife by having them pray for God's help and receiving in answer to their prayer unexpected help from a wealthy benefactor. The table of contents of Concordia's *Sixth Reader* also no longer attributed the story to the Brothers Grimm.

The original *Bobbs-Merrill Fifth Reader* devoted a page to a discussion of what to look for when reading fanciful tales. Introducing a section of the Reader entitled "Magic and Wonder," the authors commented:

> In ancient times the people told wonderful tales and believed them. The world for them was inhabited by strange and wonderful creatures. There were nymphs in the waters and dryads in the trees; there were gnomes in the valleys and giants in the hills. . . .
>
> In America we do not believe all the old wonderful tales, but we love to read them. . . . for we know that in every great story, behind the magic and the wonder, there is some real and wonderful truth.
>
> The stories that you are now going to read . . . are wonderful, and all of them are true, if only you know how to find their truth.[42]

The table of contents of the Concordia *Fifth Reader* did not divide that Reader into sections and replaced the above brief essay on "Magic and Wonder" with a piece entitled "My Rock

---

[42] *Bobbs-Merrill Readers, The Fifth Reader* (Indianapolis: Bobbs-Merrill, 1924), 1.

and My Fortress." The latter quoted from 2 Samuel 22:1-3 which included the words of King David: "The Lord is my rock and my. . . . shield and the horn of my salvation; my high tower and my refuge,—my Savior." These words were followed by the first half of stanza 1 of Luther's hymn "A Mighty Fortress Is Our God." Two verses of Psalm 91, which begins with the words "He that dwelleth in the secret place of the Most High shall abide under the shadow of the Almighty" completed the page. Beginning a Lutheran Reader with a religious selection was not unusual. Both German and English Readers in the Lutheran tradition in the nineteenth and early twentieth centuries did that regularly. A number of the revised *Bobbs-Merrill* books continued the pattern.

Concordia's *Bobbs-Merrill Fifth Reader* did not list any of its reading selections in a category entitled "Magic and Wonder." Four pieces of literature from this section of the original *Bobbs-Merrill* were included, however, in the Concordia Reader. One of these was John Ruskin's "The King of the Golden River." Some very minor but not unexpected editing was done to make this tale and its Study Notes acceptable to Lutheran editors. Since the use of holy water was part of the story, the discussion guide at the end of the selection in the original *Bobbs-Merrill* asked the question, "What caused the holy water that Hans carried to become unholy?" The Concordia Edition put the question this way: "Is there such a thing as holy water?" Several exclamations in the Ruskin story were also altered. "Amen" in ordinary conversation became simply "Yes." "Bless my soul!" was rendered with "Well! Well!" "Off, and be hanged!" was reduced to "Off with you!" "Pray Heaven it may be!" was turned into, "Yes, let us hope so!" And "Confound the king and his gold, too," was changed to "What of the king and all his gold!" The revised expressions were considered more appropriate for reading books in Lutheran fifth-grade classrooms.

A rather consistent word-alteration in the Concordia Edition involved the word dance. Dancing as a social activity was frowned upon at that time by many conservative Lutheran clergy. Clear evidence of the position can be seen in a booklet written by Theodore Graebner, a professor at Concordia Seminary in St. Louis, and issued in a number of printings and editions by Concordia Publishing House. Entitled *The Borderland of Right and Wrong*, the book deals with matters spoken of as adiaphora in the church, that is, practices and activities neither commanded nor forbidden by Holy Scripture. The last chapter of the book includes an extensive treatment of social dancing. That chapter of the Graebner book carries the heading: "No Longer on the Borderland, but Inherently Sinful."[43] Dancing in its many forms was considered sinful, prompting the Concordia *Bobbs-Merrill* editors to remove any references to dancing in the reading books designed specifically for Lutheran schools. From the *Second Reader* there was removed, therefore, the song "London Bridge Is Broken Down" with its refrain "Dance over, my Lady Lee." In a small group of fables from Aesop in the *Third Reader* a line in "The Milkmaid and Her Pail" was altered slightly. The milkmaid, expecting to sell the milk in her pail and then invest the money in the raising of chickens, was looking forward to being able to buy a new dress. With that in mind, she said to herself, "In this dress I shall go to the fair, where all the boys will want to dance with me." The Concordia Edition concluded the line with "where all the boys will think me a pretty maid." The alteration in the line eliminated the possibility of the question of dancing coming up on the basis of a text in a third-grade Reader. To avoid any misconception, it should be noted that alterations of the kind just mentioned did not have to be made frequently in the materials retained in the Lutheran *Bobbs-Merrill*.

It is to be expected that a Reader compiled for use in a denominational parochial school will also include reading

---

[43] Theodore Graebner, *The Borderland of Right and Wrong* (St. Louis: Concordia, 1941), 114.

selections apropos to the denomination. One is not surprised in a Catholic book, for example, to find titles like the following from the *Misericordia Reader* produced in 1934 by the Sisters of Mercy in Baltimore, Maryland: "The Altar Boy," "The Names of Our Lady," "St. Francis Xavier."[44] Similarly, in the Concordia Edition of the *Bobbs-Merrill Readers* there were a number of items one would expect to find only in a Lutheran textbook. Three such selections were included in the *Eighth Reader*. One of these was an excerpt from the Fourth Commandment of Martin Luther's Large Catechism. Children in parochial schools would have memorized in religion classes Luther's Small Catechism explanation of the Fourth Commandment, "Thou shalt honor thy father and thy mother." The *Eighth Reader* introduced these children to Luther's more comprehensive treatment of that commandment. That same Reader had an excerpt entitled "The Witness before Caesar" from William Stearns Davis' historical novel *The Friar of Wittenberg*. "At the Home of a Great Man" in the *Sixth Reader* was a story about Martin Luther written by Concordia editor A. C. Stellhorn. A story about C. F. W. Walther, distinguished nineteenth-century theologian of The Lutheran Church—Missouri Synod, appeared in the *Fifth Reader* under the title "A God-Chosen Leader," while the *Seventh Reader* introduced children to Friedrich Wyneken, pioneer Lutheran missionary and second president of the Missouri Synod. The home reading suggestions in the *Eighth Reader* also included numerous articles written by various Missouri Synod authors.

The *Eighth Reader* added two rather unusual pieces, one dealing with Luther and the other with the American Revolutionary War commander Baron Frederick von Steuben. The Luther selection is Henry Wadsworth Longfellow's poem "Martin Luther." The four-part poem takes its structure from

---

[44] *Misericordia Readers Eighth Reader* (New York: Rand McNally, 1934), xxv, xxvii, xxviii.

Luther's four-stanza hymn "A Mighty Fortress Is Our God." Polemical lines, such as the one which speaks of the pope of Rome "with all his diabolic crew . . . that sorely infest and afflict the earth," were enough to keep this work out of general anthologies of American literature. The von Steuben article is part of an address delivered by a congressman from Missouri upon the occasion of the unveiling on December 7, 1910, of a statue in Washington, D.C., in memory and honor of the German officer who assisted the American colonies in the Revolutionary War. A tribute to the Missouri Synod's German heritage rather than to Lutheran history seems to lie behind the inclusion of that speech in the Concordia Edition of the Readers.

The Concordia books were off the press and ready for use in time for the 1926-27 school year. In a brief review of the completed work, a *Lutheran School Journal* writer remarked:

> The series of revised Bobbs-Merrill Readers is now complete. All teachers who are interested in teaching good reading . . . will hail the new Readers with delight. . . . Great credit is due the committee, which has worked so faithfully and well to revise the series.[45]

Considering what was involved in the revision, one cannot argue that the task was a formidable one. It must be granted that the *Primer* and *First Reader* received only minimal alterations, but from that point on the amount of revision and substituted selections and pages were considerable. The task of revision was not as large, of course, as trying to produce within-house resources a totally new set of Readers for Lutheran schools. That was much more readily done in the late nineteenth century when less was required of elementary schools than was the case in the 1920s. Reflecting on the synodical decision to revise an existing set of Readers rather

---

[45] *Lutheran School Journal*, December 1926, 476.

than produce a completely new series, a River Forest professor observed:

> Synod decided that a series of Readers already on the market be revised and adapted to our needs. The reasons for this decision are sound. An adaptation is not as good as a series of Readers entirely our own, viewed from the standpoint of material. But such an adaptation is far better from a pedagogical point of view than a series we could develop, lacking, as we do, the time and money needed for a thorough scientific development of a reading system with all the problems this entails.[46]

Published in 1925 and 1926, the Concordia Edition of the *Bobbs-Merrill Readers* remained in print for 20 years.

In the early part of the decade following the initial publication of the Concordia *Bobbs-Merrill*, another significant book for Lutheran schools came on the market. Entitled *Music Reader for Lutheran Schools*, the book was not a revision of another publication but the student textbook for singing and music courses ordinarily required in Lutheran elementary schools of the time. The book of 241 pages contained secular and sacred songs for both unison and part-singing. The authors, Missouri Synod elementary school teachers, held that "since one of the chief aims of the Lutheran school is to prepare children for Lutheran Church-membership . . . in . . . which the character of music learned in childhood plays a very important part, it is the part of wisdom to utilize our own unsurpassed *chorales* and other classics both as practise material and as a body of songs to be worked over into the repertory of the individual as a lasting treasure."[47] The purpose of singing classes in Lutheran

---

[46] *Lutheran School Journal*, December 1925, 457.

[47] J. Grundmann and B. Schumacher, *Music Reader for Lutheran Schools* (St. Louis: Concordia, 1933), iv.

schools was not just to teach children music fundamentals such as note values and time signatures but to acquaint them with hymns and music suitable for use in church. Obviously, with such a goal in mind, a textbook specifically designed for Lutheran schools was necessary.

The emphasis upon church music in the *Music Reader for Lutheran Schools* became apparent from the fact that two-thirds of the selections in the book were sacred songs. The cover of the book, too, with its church window design, sought to impress upon the users of the book that singing classes in Lutheran schools serve a church purpose. The two men who put together the course of study and compiled the *Manual for the Music Reader* to accompany the course urged Lutheran school teachers "to arouse and develop an appreciation of good church music" in their pupils, since this was "one of the major aims in Lutheran school music."[48] They expressed the fear that if this would not be done, "we may some day awaken to discover that our treasure in church music has been buried under a great heap of inferior hymns."[49]

A primary interest of the *Music Reader* editors was the development of an appreciation for the Lutheran chorale. It was recommended not only that these hymns be sung and their texts studied but also that biographical information about the authors and composers of Lutheran chorales be given, or stories of interest relating to their origins be told. To demonstrate the effectiveness of providing such background information, the *Music Reader* authors told about an incident in a sixth-grade class which had read a story in its *Bobbs-Merrill Sixth Reader* about Georg Neumark, author and composer of the chorale "If You but Trust in God to Guide You":

---

[48] J. Grundmann and B. Schumacher, *Manual for the Music Reader for Lutheran Schools* (St. Louis: Concordia, 1933), 30.

[49] Ibid.

> Three-fourths of the members of a sixth grade selected
> *Wer nur den lieben Gott laesst walten* [If you but trust in
> God to guide you] as their favorite hymn. The teacher
> inquired of the class what had prompted them to make
> this selection and was informed that the story about the
> origin of this hymn had taught them to appreciate it.
> (*Bobbs-Merrill Sixth Reader.*)[50]

The point of citing this comment from the *Manual for Music
Reader for Lutheran Schools* is not necessarily to argue for the
position held by the *Music Reader* editors but rather to show
what the authors of books designed specifically for Lutheran
schools sought to accomplish. The *Bobbs-Merrill Readers*
were intended to teach reading skills and an appreciation of
literature. Incorporated in the Concordia Edition of those
Readers were some materials which dealt with topics of special
interest to Lutherans or were written by Lutheran authors. The
Music Reader for Lutheran Schools was compiled for the
purpose of teaching basic singing skills and an appreciation of
music to children in Lutheran schools. To do this, the book
relied heavily on the use of hymns and sacred songs
appropriate for use in Lutheran worship. This made the *Music
Reader* a distinctively Lutheran book, a collection of songs
quite different from general music education texts.

At about the same time that the *Music Reader* became
available, a small book for a quite different area of study was
published for Lutheran school teachers in Minnesota. Written
and published by Herbert A. Sitz, a Wisconsin Synod teacher
in New Ulm, Minnesota, the book was intended as a text for
use in citizenship classes in Lutheran schools. Of the author's
approach to the subject, a Missouri Synod reviewer observed:

---

[50] Ibid., 31. The story about the hymn was in the Concordia Edition
Sixth Reader.

He shows how the teacher can instil into the minds and hearts of the children their duties as Christians toward the government in city, county, State, and nation. Special chapters treat of the Christian home, the Christian day-school, the Church, and their places in the State. After every chapter there are "Things to Do" for the pupil, and also here the author shows opportunities for teaching the Christian attitude toward the government.[51]

The book reviewed was a Minnesota edition of Sitz' *Elementary Citizenship for Lutheran Schools*. A state of Wisconsin edition came into existence later and the book itself was enlarged so that what was 61 pages in 1934 eventually became some 130 pages. The aim of the author was not just to teach facts about government but to impress upon Lutheran elementary school children that responsible citizenship is part of the Christian way of life. In the words of the author: "Whatever makes us better Christians makes us better citizens of our country, of the world, and of the world to come."[52]

According to the founding constitution of The Lutheran Church—Missouri Synod, one of the reasons for forming a synod was to make possible the promotion of special church projects. Listed among those projects was the production of schoolbooks. According to the same constitution, congregations in the Synod obligated themselves to use doctrinally pure schoolbooks—Readers, in particular, having been mentioned. The dearth of materials in English was especially lamented throughout the last part of the nineteenth century. This was the case not only in the Missouri Synod but also in the Wisconsin Synod, for the teachers of that body complained already at a conference in 1877 that "American readers fitted to the needs

---

[51] *Lutheran School Journal*, November 1934, 144.

[52] Herbert A. Sitz, *Elementary Citizenship for Lutheran Schools* (n.p., n.d.).

of an evangelical Lutheran school were not as yet available."[53] Although requests for Lutheran-oriented textbooks in areas such as geography and United States history were periodically expressed and outlines even produced, with the exception of books for religious education, the production of Readers in both the English and German languages was the most successfully implemented publication activity engaged in by Lutherans. The Concordia Edition of the *Bobbs-Merrill Readers* was the last major undertaking in the history of publishing reading books for Lutheran schools.[54†] To those who might be critical of the use of denominationally designed Readers for Lutheran elementary schools, defenders of the

---

[53] *Souvenir of the Seventy-fifth Anniversary of the Founding of the Wisconsin State Teachers' Conference* (n.p., 1946), 12.

[54] In 1999, Concordia Publishing House put out its own edition of a series of science textbooks published by Silver Burdett Ginn, Inc. Prepared for grades 1 to 6, the Concordia Edition of *Science Discovery Works* includes the following comment: "Silver Burdett Ginn Inc. does not express any view or opinion as to the religious content and views included in this edition. The religious views and beliefs presented are those authored and authorized by Concordia Publishing House." This end-of-the-century science series by Concordia follows the precedent set by the Missouri Synod's publishing company in 1926 when it issued its own edition of the *Bobbs-Merrill Readers*.

[†] *Editor's Note:* In 1942 and 1943 Concordia Publishing House published a Concordia edition of the *Reading for Interest* series originally published by D. C. Heath and Company. The adaptation for Lutheran schools of these Readers for grades one through six was done for CPH by Alfred Schmieding, William W. Bloom and William A. Kramer. This series was not as extensively revised, nor, apparently, as long-lived as the Concordia Edition *Bobbs-Merrill Readers*. To this series was added in 1949 *Treasury of Christian Literature*, a Reader for the seventh and eighth grades compiled and edited for CPH by William A. Kramer and Alfred Schmieding. See *Lutheran School Journal*, June 1943, 446-47; *Lutheran School Journal*, March 1944, 305-7; and August C. Stellhorn, *Schools of the Lutheran Church—Missouri Synod* (St. Louis: Concordia Publishing House, 1963), 417.

practice in 1926 might well have responded: "Train up a child in the way he should go, and when he is old, he will not depart from it" (Proverbs 22:6).

Suggested for Further Reading

Stellhorn, August C. *Schools of The Lutheran Church—Missouri Synod*. St. Louis: Concordia, 1963: 112-27, 198-206, 323-33, 407-22.

_____. "The Bobbs-Merrill Readers, Concordia Edition." *Lutheran School Journal* 62 (March, April, May, June, July, August 1927): 91-96, 127-32, 168-72, 205-11, 249-52, 287-90.

Grundmann, J. and B. Schumacher. *Manual for the Music Reader for Lutheran Schools*. St. Louis: Concordia, 1933. In the collection of Concordia Historical Institute, St. Louis, MO.

Sitz, Herbert A. *Elementary Citizenship for Lutheran Schools*. Milwaukee: Northwestern, 1943. In the collection of Wisconsin Lutheran Seminary, Mequon, WI.

Baker, Clara B. and Edna D. *Bobbs-Merrill Readers*. Edited by George Herbert Betts. Indianapolis: Bobbs-Merrill, 1923-24. The *Primer* through the *Sixth Reader* are in the collection of Harvard University, Gutman Library, Graduate School of Education (microfilm). *Bobbs-Merrill Readers,* Concordia Edition. Revised and adapted by A. C. Stellhorn. St. Louis: Concordia, 1925-26. The *Primer* through the *Eighth Reader* are in the collection of Concordia Historical Institute, St. Louis, MO.

✤ ✤ ✤ 1930 ✤ ✤ ✤

A Christian Pedagogy
Edward W. A. Koehler

A common curricular offering in schools or departments of education is a required course for prospective teachers to introduce them to teaching as a profession. The name for such a course will vary from institution to institution, but the purpose is generally the same, namely, to provide a general orientation to the nature, scope, and aims of schooling and teaching in American society. Some courses of this type will include a generous dose of educational history; others will lean more toward philosophy. Some instructors will focus on relationships in the educational enterprise, how teachers are to relate to students, parents, colleagues, and administrators, in other words, while other professors of education might choose to concentrate more on the learning process itself. In any case, educators by and large have felt that some sort of familiarization with teaching as a profession is useful in the academic preparation of would-be elementary and secondary school teachers.

Edward W. A. Koehler's *A Christian Pedagogy* was written to acquaint future Lutheran teachers with some biblical principles which are foundational for approaching the task of education in Christian schools. The book was published in 1930 by a man who at the time was teaching a required course entitled Christian Pedagogy at Concordia Teachers College in River Forest, Illinois. Thus, the book is a window from which to get a view of the kind of orientation to Lutheran school teaching which was given to college students at River Forest at that time. In fact, the course description of Koehler's course in the 1929-30 college catalog corresponds exactly to the major headings of *A Christian Pedagogy*.[1] What is equally or perhaps even more important about the book, however, is its link with the past. In the year 1879, the year in which J. C. W. Lindemann, the first director of the Missouri Synod's Teachers Seminary at Addison, Illinois, died, a book written by him on teaching in Lutheran schools was published. The book was in German and carried the title *Amerikanisch-Lutherische Schul-Praxis* (American Lutheran School Practice). Lindemann's book became the standard textbook for Missouri Synod college students who were preparing themselves for the Lutheran teaching profession. The book is listed, for example, in the 1913-14 Concordia Teachers College general catalog as the textbook for a course entitled Principles of Education and taught by the president of the school. Koehler also confirms that Lindemann's *Schul-Praxis* was the regularly used textbook for introducing students to Lutheran educational principles when he says that since he could find

> . . . no suitable text for his classes in Christian Pedagogy, he was compelled to write his own. The German text, Lindemann's *Schulpraxis*, which formerly served as a basis of instruction at our Lutheran normal schools, is out of print. Moreover, it was deemed advisable to have an English text for our students. Thus the author was requested to prepare his manuscript for print.[2]

---

[1] *Catalog* (1929-30), Concordia Teachers College, River Forest, Illinois, 23.

[2] Edward W. A. Koehler, *A Christian Pedagogy* (St. Louis: Concordia, 1930), VII.

Koehler then adds that much of the subject matter for his own book "was taken from J. C. W. Lindemann's . . . chapters on *Schulerziehung*" (School Nurturing).[3] Thus, Koehler's *A Christian Pedagogy* reflects a Christian philosophy of education commended to students for more than 50 years at a teachers college of The Lutheran Church—Missouri Synod.

Lindemann's book addressed more school topics than did Koehler's. The earlier book, for example, discussed matters pertaining to school discipline, classroom planning and scheduling, and teaching methods for specific subjects. Koehler, on the other hand, limited himself to what Lindemann dealt with in the last part of his book, namely, the spiritual formation both men wanted teachers to try to effect in children attending Lutheran Christian schools.

The parochial school of Lindemann's day was far less comprehensive and more diverse from locality to locality than is the case with that institution today. He was unable to see, of course, what the parochial school would eventually evolve into, but he was unequivocal in stating his position on the fundamental objective of a church-related school. The institution existed to carry out God-ordained purposes. He argued that the parochial school was built upon the parental and preaching offices established by God in the Garden of Eden. Relating these two offices to the parochial school, he said in the opening paragraph of his *Schulpraxis*:

> The Triune God Himself, at the beginning of the world already, laid the foundations upon which the Christian school has built itself since ancient times and especially upon which the Evangelical Lutheran parochial school has built itself since the time of the Reformation. It is upon these very foundations that the Christian school must continue to build itself, namely, the parental office

---

[3] Ibid.

and the preaching office. The former belongs to the kingdom of nature, the latter to the kingdom of grace.[4]

Lindemann did not insist that the parochial school was the only means by which the responsibilities of the parental and preaching offices with respect to children could be carried out, but he did consider it the superior means.

The director of the Addison Teachers Seminary assigned responsibilities for the education of children in America to parents and church only. That is understandable, for he was writing in the 1870s when state compulsory education laws were only beginning to be enacted. He had not been compelled to grapple with the impact of these laws on the operation of parochial schools. Local church autonomy in directing and managing the parish school was firmly upheld by Lindemann, as is apparent from the following comment in his book:

> The congregation itself (not the state, not the synod) is at all times the owner and governess of the school. As the congregation has the duty to maintain a school and, when possible, always to improve it, so it also has the right to organize the school as it pleases, provided that this takes place to the honor of God, for the true benefit of the church and civic communities, and in keeping with the church's confession. Thus, the congregation also has the sacred duty earnestly to watch that the school is conducted in keeping with its purpose. The congregation stipulates the regulations for the school; it determines the curriculum; and the course of study is also put into operation only through the congregation's approval.[5]

---

[4] J. C. W. Lindemann, *Amerikanisch-Lutherische Schul-Praxis* (St. Louis: Concordia, 1879), 1.

[5] Ibid., 4.

Lindemann recognized that the parochial school was to serve a civic purpose but did not yield to the state any authority to regulate a church-operated school. Similarly, the synod had no governing authority over a congregation's school, although Lindemann agreed that when a congregation held "membership in an evangelical Lutheran synod, then the synodical officers have the right and the duty to visit the school, since all congregations have united themselves into a synod also for the very purpose of establishing, maintaining, and promoting schools in the best possible way; therefore visitation is in order."[6] In keeping with Missouri Synod polity, the Synod provided counsel and guidance in school matters but had no authority to control or regulate the parish schools of synodical congregations.

Local supervision of a parochial school, according to Lindemann, resided in the pastor, who had the duty to see to it that everything was functioning in keeping with the Word of God. In addition, the pastor was to encourage the teacher in his work and, when the opportunity presented itself, to mention the school and its importance in sermons. The pastor's responsibility toward the school dealt primarily with the supervision of the religious teaching and life in the school, although if the congregation wished it and consented to it, he could also be assigned supervision of the secular aspects of the school program. To the extent to which circumstances made it possible, pastors were also expected to teach children in the parish school.

Teachers in parish schools were to be called to their office by the entire congregation and were to understand that their call came from the Holy Spirit through the mediation of the congregation. The latter issued a diploma of vocation and assumed responsibility for the physical well-being of the teacher. Lindemann considered the office of teacher to be a

---

[6] Ibid.

twofold one, a public church office and a private civic office. With respect to the teacher's calling he reasoned:

> This office is first and foremost a public church office, for since the Lutheran teacher carries out a part of the public office of preaching (the office of pastor)[7] by teaching Law and Gospel . . . to school-age children and . . . helps bring it about that true faith is alive in the congregation and a sanctified life led, and thus carries on that which belongs to the pastor's office, to that extent he is the pastor's co-worker and a servant of the Word.—At the same time, as a parental assistant, he also steps into the place of parents by bringing up their children in the nurture and admonition of the Lord (Ephesians 6:4).

> In this case the office of a Lutheran teacher is a private civil office. It is a civil (secular) office in as much as the teacher, as the substitute and helper of the parents who have entrusted their children to him, imparts to those children such knowledge and skills as belong to the secular life and productive living.[8]

It is clear from Lindemann's remarks that when he spoke about the office of the Lutheran school teacher he was always referring to a teacher who had as part of his tasks the formal teaching of religion in a classroom. The teacher shared in the preaching office because he taught God's Word to children.

In some cases where the parish pastor was the only teacher in what was called a parochial school (*Gemeindeschule*, parish school) in Lindemann's day, not much more than religion was

---

[7] Lindemann used the word *Predigtamt* (Office of Preaching) and *Pfarramt* (Office of Pastor) to designate the same thing, as is apparent from his use of a parenthesis at this point.

[8] Lindemann, *Schulpraxis*, 7-8.

taught in the congregation's school. But even when the curriculum was more comprehensive, the teaching of Holy Scripture and Christian doctrine was considered the primary purpose of the school. Members of a Lutheran parish established their parish school, according to Lindemann, in order to have their children

> thoroughly instructed by a teacher first of all and chiefly in the saving doctrine of God's Word as this is set forth in the Lutheran confession of faith and to advance the children in piety. After that [the parochial school exists] also to give children instruction and knowledge, to the extent possible, in the learning and skills needed for their life as citizens.[9]

Even learning how to read was seen as serving the primary purpose "of equipping children to be able to read the Bible throughout their lives."[10] *Amerikanisch-Lutherische Schul-Praxis* (American Lutheran School Practice), the basic philosophy of Lutheran education textbook used for two decades both before and after the turn of the twentieth century at the Missouri Synod's teacher-training college in Addison and River Forest, Illinois, emphasized beyond a doubt that Lutheran parochial schools had as a primary reason for existence the teaching of religion and godly living.

E. W. A. Koehler's *A Christian Pedagogy* was not a translation into English of the time-honored Lindemann book nor was it as exhaustive. As mentioned before, only the third part of Lindemann's German *Schulpraxis* (School Practice) was used by Koehler for his work. The 1930 author said the same in his Foreword to *A Christian Pedagogy* when he wrote: "The general groundwork of the present volume and much of

---

[9] Ibid., 3.
[10] Ibid., 23.

the subject matter was taken from J. C. W. Lindemann's excellent chapters on *Schulerziehung*"[11]–a word which might be rendered school education, school training, or school nurturing in English but which needed as much definition and explanation in German as does the word education in English. Koehler chose the word pedagogy for the German *Schulerziehung* and then added Christian as a modifier because, as he said,

> It is the Biblical principle of education the author has endeavored to set forth in the chapters of this volume. The reader will therefore understand the frequent references to the Scriptures. Psychological problems were touched on only to the extent that it was necessary to make clear the fundamental functions of soul-life.[12]

Lindemann, when he was speaking in his book about education or the training of Christian children, put it this way:

> Christian education includes everything which God would have parents do for their children to familiarize them from small on with a God-pleasing way of life and to preserve and further them in the same, so that they are able to live as the children of God.[13]

Foundational to a correct understanding of Lutheran educational principles is the realization that Christian education is more than an encyclopedic transmittal of facts, religious or secular, but is a spiritual formation which acknowledges Jesus Christ as God and Lord and seeks to live life in conformity with Christ's saving Gospel.

---

[11] E. W. A. Koehler, *A Christian Pedagogy*, VII.

[12] Ibid., VI.

[13] J. C. W. Lindemann, *Schulpraxis*, 217.

Koehler's *A Christian Pedagogy* was intended to introduce college students in education to biblical principles which were fundamental to an understanding of the calling of a Lutheran school teacher and instructive for the performance of the tasks of that Christian calling. The course from which *A Christian Pedagogy* evolved and for which it served as a textbook had the following catalog description:

> *Christian Pedagogy.*—This course considers the principles for the Christian training of children. I. Definition of Education and Educational Agencies. II. The Educator: his duty, his qualifications. III. The Child. IV. The Aim of Christian Education. V. The Means of Christian Education. VI. The Method of Education.[14]

Although Koehler was a strong promoter of the Lutheran parochial school and considered it, next to the Christian home, "the most effective agency for the Christian training of children,"[15] he also commented on the Sunday school as an agency for Christian education and on instruction given in public schools. He felt that parents ought to send their children to a parochial school whenever there was the possibility of doing so. On the other hand, he warned against an indefensible criticism of public education when he remarked:

> We ought to be very careful in our criticism of the public schools. We must not imagine that, because they lack Christian instruction and training, they are also of no account in every other respect. Let us study their courses and their methods, their requirements and their

---

[14] *Catalog* (1929-30), Concordia Teachers College, River Forest, Illinois, 23.

[15] *A Christian Pedagogy*, 31.

achievements, and make use of whatever is sane, good and profitable. . . .

We must not create the impression as though we expect the state schools to make suitable provision for the Christian instruction and training of children. We oppose every attempt on the part of the state to do so. It is in the interest of the state to provide facilities for the education of its citizens. But it is no fault nor neglect of the civil authorities if they do not provide a religious education. On the contrary, they would transgress the limit of their power and trespass upon the most personal rights of individuals if they would teach and enforce upon all under their jurisdiction a certain type of religious education.[16]

This view, not new with Koehler and expressed from time to time by Lutheran educators since his day, recognizes the necessity of public schools for the well-being of the country and the wisdom of keeping that kind of school as neutral as possible in matters of religion. In that position, however, there resides the conviction that a combining of the teaching of the common branches of schooling with the Word of God is a superior approach to education and one that can be carried out only in a school sponsored by the church.

In assessing the Sunday school as an agency for the teaching of religion and Christian doctrine, Koehler's verdict was that such a part-time agency was not the most efficient institution for Christian education. He lamented especially the meager amount of time available for the teaching task and the irregularity of pupil attendance. He observed that the Sunday school was originally not intended for children who were part of a Christian congregation but rather for youngsters whose secular and Christian education had been neglected.

[16] Ibid., 28-29.

Nonetheless, he saw the Sunday school as a mission agency and means by which to gain members for the church and for the parochial school. He conceded that Sunday schools were also necessary where it was honestly or temporarily impossible to provide better and more effective ways for the teaching of religion to the rising generation. Setting the parochial and the Sunday school side by side, Koehler came to the conclusion:

> It stands to reason that a child occupying himself . . . intensely with the study of God's Word and being subject to Christian influence five days a week will receive more lasting impressions and a more thorough Christian training than a child that attends Sunday-school but once a week for a brief hour. While half a loaf is better than none and a good Christian Sunday-school is better than no Christian school at all, a true evaluation of the Christian parochial school will show that both in instruction and training it is far superior to the best Sunday-school.[17]

In order to have quality teaching in Sunday schools, it was Koehler's contention that the teachers in the parochial school should take charge of the Sunday school. "Being commissioned to teach and train the children," he said, "our teachers should not hesitate to do so, whether this be during the week or on Sunday."[18] A publication issued by the Missouri Synod's General Sunday-School Board in 1922 said something similar when it spoke about the administration of the Sunday school:

> The *pastor* is supervisor, or superintendent, of the Sunday-school by virtue of his office. In most cases he will be present in person, taking charge of one of the Bible classes. The *day-school teachers* should be intensely

---

[17] Ibid., 34.
[18] Ibid., 30.

interested in the Sunday-school, not only as members of the congregation . . . but as trained educators who will be able to serve as leaders in the work. . . . Their logical place is that of department superintendents and teachers in the teachers' training-school, which is usually established in some form, even if no more is done than to prepare the teachers for the next lesson. The *superintendent* is elected. . . . to supervise the school, especially on its mechanical side.[19]

From these comments it is apparent that parochial school teachers around 1930 were being urged to participate actively in the Sunday school programs of congregations operating Christian day schools. This was done because those teachers by virtue of their professional training and experience were thought to be the best equipped for teaching religion to children.

Although parochial school teachers were being encouraged to participate actively either as teachers or leaders in parish Sunday schools, the institution itself was considered to be an outreach agency in congregations where a parochial school was in existence. Koehler saw it that way, and so did the synodical Sunday-School Board, as is apparent from its comment in 1922: "Remember that a Sunday-school is chiefly a mission school."[20] Congregation members were expected, if at all possible, to send their children to the Christian day school. In fact, there was debate at the time about whether children in the Christian day school should attend Sunday school. The Synod's Sunday-School Board acknowledged the debate when it said: "The question is often discussed whether the children attending the Christian day-school ought to attend the Sunday-school or

---

[19] General Sunday-School Board of the Ev. Luth. Synod of Missouri, *The Lutheran Sunday School* (St. Louis: Concordia, 1922), 15-16.

[20] Ibid., 14.

not, those opposed to their attending insisting that the work done during the week is sufficient."[21] The Sunday-School Board was in favor of having parochial school children attend Sunday school, although the board recognized the potential problem inherent in repeating on Sunday morning for parochial school children things which had been presented and discussed more thoroughly during the week. The board even suggested that it might be necessary to have separate classes on Sunday morning for day-school pupils in the senior department, although it was admitted that such an arrangement was fraught with difficulties, too. The point is that the parochial school was seen as a five-day-a-week Sunday school in which Bible, catechism, and hymnbook were used daily and combined into a well-integrated and thorough program of religious studies.

Since the teaching of religion is an essential part of the curriculum of a parochial school, Lutheran teachers ought to be knowledgeable, therefore, in Holy Scripture and have a good understanding of biblical doctrine. Knowledge of the subject matter is only one qualification of a good teacher in any field, of course, but it is a necessary one. E. W. A. Koehler was aware of this, and a large part of his career was dedicated to equipping prospective Lutheran teachers with that knowledge of biblical doctrine which would contribute to their effectiveness as teachers of the Word. With respect to knowing Scripture, he observed:

> As the Word of God is the chief means of Christian training, it is evident that a Christian pedagog must acquire an exact knowledge of its teachings and of their use. . . . In order . . . to teach plainly and to train effectively, the educator must himself have a thorough knowledge of the Christian doctrine. . . . Vague and hazy

---

[21] Ibid., 26.

knowledge is often the cause of indefinite and ineffective teaching.[22]

In addition to knowing Scripture, it is also important to recognize its chief purpose, namely, to make people "wise unto salvation through faith which is in Christ Jesus," as the apostle Paul said to Timothy (2 Timothy 3:15). Koehler, who stressed the importance of imparting knowledge in the teaching of religion, spoke of that aspect of religious education as a preliminary objective and was then quick to add that "an intellectual knowledge of Bible-truths is by no means the ultimate aim of Christian education."[23] Faith in Christ as the Son of God and Savior from sin is the ultimate aim of all Christian education and from that primary objective there also flows a secondary aim, namely, guidance and encouragement to live a God-pleasing life. Koehler was careful to keep intellectual and faith goals in a proper relationship when he discussed the aims of Christian education in *A Christian Pedagogy*. Factual knowledge of Holy Scripture and its doctrines was not an end in and of itself but rather a medium by which to effect and inform Christian faith.

In *A Christian Pedagogy* E. W. A. Koehler set forth principles of Christian education to guide Lutheran teachers in their work of shaping the spiritual life of children in Lutheran parochial schools. It was in a second book, however, that Koehler sought to provide college students and teachers with a systematic presentation of the doctrines of Holy Scripture. Entitled *A Summary of Christian Doctrine*, the book came off the press nine years after *A Christian Pedagogy* and was destined to have a far longer life. Like many books in the field of education, *A Christian Pedagogy*, too, was subject in some of its aspects to that kind of dating which comes as educational

---

[22] Koehler, *A Christian Pedagogy*, 62.

[23] Ibid., 114.

patterns and professional terminology undergo change. Koehler's *A Summary of Christian Doctrine*, on the other hand, was still to be found in the 2000-2002 catalog of Concordia Publishing House. The initial use of the book was as a text for courses in Christian doctrine at Concordia Teachers College in River Forest, Illinois. The book was also used at junior colleges of The Lutheran Church—Missouri Synod as well as at the Wisconsin Synod's Dr. Martin Luther College in New Ulm, Minnesota, where *A Summary* was introduced as a textbook in the 1947-48 school year in the teacher-training curriculum of that institution.

Koehler's purpose with *A Summary of Christian Doctrine* was to make available a book on Christian doctrine which would stand between the synodically prepared expositions of Luther's Small Catechism used in basic catechetical classes and the more comprehensive works on Christian dogmatics used in theological seminaries. Although a Wisconsin Synod reviewer took sharp issue with Koehler's brief comment on a topic on which the Wisconsin and Missouri Synods had long expressed themselves differently, i.e., on the nature of synod and local congregation in church polity, the reviewer was, nonetheless, extremely positive about the work of his Synodical Conference colleague:

> A book of this kind, where the doctrines are so clearly yet concisely stated with the Scripture proofs and citations from the Lutheran confessions and verbatim quotations from some dogmaticians, should prove of great value to any diligent student and seeker after the truth of salvation. . . . On paging through this volume we find every doctrine, necessary for the Christian to know, fully and adequately presented. There is no quibbling here on such important topics as verbal inspiration, on the time of

creation . . . on the intuitu fidei . . . and unionism. . . . We heartily recommend this Summary.[24]

Students at River Forest who were enrolled in the college courses using Koehler's *A Summary of Christian Doctrine* were expected to have had a high school course in biblical doctrine equivalent to what was offered in the high school preparatory department at River Forest. Those who had not taken such a course were required to take an introductory doctrine course, described as follows in the Concordia catalog:

> **A-20. Introductory Course in Doctrine** — This course gives an extended review of the principal teachings of the Bible, as presented in the Catechism. It is a prerequisite for the regular college courses in Doctrine for all those who have not taken the high school courses in Doctrine or their equivalents. Text: *The Annotated Catechism*. This course carries no formal credit toward the number of hours required for graduation.[25]

The Annotated Catechism text used for this prerequisite course had also come from the pen of Koehler. When the Missouri Synod issued its 1943 *A Short Explanation of Dr. Martin Luther's Small Catechism*, Koehler updated his previously authored Annotations to correlate with the revised synodical expository catechism and published it in 1946. Like *A Summary of Christian Doctrine*, the River Forest professor's annotated *Small Catechism* was still listed among the catechetical materials in the 2000-2002 catalog of Concordia Publishing House. The intent of the book was to provide a

---

[24] *Theologische Quartalschrift* (Theological Quarterly), July 1939, 221-22.

[25] *Catalog* (1943-44), Concordia Teachers College, River Forest, Illinois, 17.

resource for teachers in their preparation of lessons on the Catechism. In the Foreword to his 1946 catechism volume Koehler expressed himself once more on the importance of knowing Scripture well by repeating an admonition from the first edition of his *Annotated Catechism*:

> Ignorance begets indifference. It is largely due to a general lack of accurate knowledge of the Scripture doctrines that the spirit of indifference and unionism was able to gain so many adherents. Let us diligently study the Catechism; let us faithfully teach our children; let us indoctrinate our young people, so that, firmly rooted and grounded in the knowledge of God's Word, they may stand unshaken in the tide of indifferentism that in these days is sweeping over the Church.[26]

Koehler's *A Christian Pedagogy* is a book quite different in content and purpose from his *Summary of Christian Doctrine* and *Annotated Catechism*. The commonality among the three, however, was the fact that the author intended them to be used as textbooks in the training of Lutheran teachers or as resource books for such teachers. The two doctrinal books sought to equip the Lutheran teacher with those essentials of biblical theology which are necessary if one is to be a competent teacher of religion to children. The pedagogical treatise employed Holy Scripture as its foundation, too, but was far more limited in scope, relating specific Scripture teachings and passages to the art and practice of Christian education. Koehler thought it important for a teacher to understand the implications for teaching of what the Bible has to say not only about the nature of the child as a fallen creature of God but also as an individual

---

[26] Koehler, *A Short Explanation of . . . Luther's Small Catechism . . . with Additional Notes* (River Forest: Koehler Publishing Co., 1946), iii-iv.

reborn through the power of the Holy Spirit. A Lutheran parish school teacher dare never lose sight also of the ultimate aim of Christian education, namely, the eternal salvation of souls in Christ Jesus. It is essential for a Christian teacher to recognize the difference between Law and Gospel as revealed in the Bible and the appropriate use of each in the teaching and disciplining of children. Holy Scripture is also not silent on the spiritual and natural qualifications of a Christian teacher as well as on those general Christian characteristics such as kindness, patience, and self-control, all of which are much to be desired in a classroom. It was these various things which Koehler brought together in *A Christian Pedagogy* in order to give the beginning Lutheran parochial school teacher an introduction to that calling and a biblical perspective on it.

Lutheran contemporaries of Koehler who were engaged in the shaping of attitudes among Wisconsin Synod educators showed a similar interest in looking at teaching and learning from a biblical point of view. Thus, for example, E. R. Bliefernicht, longtime professor at Wisconsin's Dr. Martin Luther College, prepared, in 1939, a short introductory psychology text for education students at that school. Entitled *An Elementary Christian Psychology*, the book began with a brief review of what Scripture has to say about the human being as a creature of God. Another professor at the same institution, H. R. Klatt, produced a 16-page pamphlet with the title *History: An Outline from the Christian Point of View*, while the Synod's school board did a seven-page tract entitled *An Appraisal of Educational Principles in the Light of Scriptures*. With respect to that little pamphlet, the school board reported to the Synod at its 1945 convention:

> The pamphlet . . . , made available to our congregations for free distribution, has been favorably received. Just recently a third edition of 5,000 copies had to be printed.

We . . . recommend this pamphlet to our pastors and teachers for discussion in the various agencies of their congregations. We also suggest that it be studied at the delegate conferences throughout the Synod so that our members might be thoroughly grounded in the correct principles of Christian education.[27]

These materials from within the Wisconsin Synod were not as comprehensive as Koehler's *A Christian Pedagogy*, but they attempted to do the same thing, i.e., to give meaning to the term Christian education by explaining that it is an all-embracing term and incorporates very specific biblical concepts. It consists of a worldview from a perspective of faith in Jesus Christ who has been revealed to the human race by God in the Holy Scriptures. This perspective produces an approach to education which at times is markedly different from a teaching and learning situation in which pupil and teacher are not directed by biblical precepts and instruction. Drawing upon J. C. W. Lindemann's nineteenth-century *Schulpraxis*, an exposition of Lutheran educational principles written in German, E. W. A. Koehler made some of the content and biblical argument of that book available to English readers in *A Christian Pedagogy*. When the book appeared in 1930, a Wisconsin Synod professor of theology was unqualified in his endorsement of the River Forest professor's work. Of the book Joh. P. Meyer wrote:

For lack of time the reviewer was unable to read the entire book, but sample pages selected at random suffice to fill a Christian educator's heart with joy. We heartily welcome Prof. Koehler's volume and recommend it to our readers. The author, a man of deep Christian convictions, outlines the work of one who would be a professional educator

---

[27] *Proceedings of the . . . Evangelical Lutheran Joint Synod of Wisconsin and Other States*, 1945, 65.

from a sound Christian standpoint and gives all aims and
means and methods of education, no matter by whom
suggested or recommended, a . . . sanely Christian
evaluation.[28]

A Missouri Synod professor of theology chose a somewhat
unusual format for his comments on Koehler's book. Theodore
Laetsch, professor of Exegetical and Practical Theology at
Concordia Seminary in St. Louis, combined into one article a
review of a report on a conference held at Northwestern
University in Evanston, Illinois, a critique of a book entitled
Child Life and Religion, and comments on Koehler's *A
Christian Pedagogy*. Laetsch began by saying:

Alas, most modern books on pedagogy are written in an
unchristian, too frequently an antichristian spirit. Reading
these books, one is astonished on the one hand by the
mass of learning displayed on every page, and the
astonishment grows as one sees that in spite of this mass
of learning these recognized leaders in the field of
education . . . are in a state of hopeless confusion as to the
aim, the means, the method, yea, the very meaning of
religious education.[29]

Laetsch then cites the following statement on prayer from the
book *Child Life and Religion*: "No matter what one's
interpretation of the 'psychology of prayer' may be, the only
belief in its efficacy which can survive self-conscious
intellectual development and the criticism of modern
psychology is that which looks upon it as a collection of inner

---

[28] *Theologische Quartalschrift* (Theological Quarterly), April 1931,
76.

[29] Theodore Laetsch, *Concordia Theological Monthly*, December
1930, 958.

resources, a calling up of strength to will and to do."[30] Laetsch's response to that statement came in two succinct sentences: "Try that definition in the hour of death. Pity the poor children of preschool age who are thus taught to pray."[31]

One is not surprised, of course, that Laetsch was favorable in his evaluation of Koehler's work. With respect to it the Missouri Synod seminary professor commented:

> It is refreshing to turn . . . to a book of the nature of Koehler's *Pedagogy*. Here we breathe an altogether different atmosphere, that of absolute submission to the Word of God. . . . Koehler's pedagogy is that of the Bible. Based on the infallible Word of God it is sure of its grounds, its purpose, its means, its scope, its final end. We have here not a rudderless ship drifting on an uncharted ocean; rather do we gain the impression that the author knows whereof he speaks, knows that he is in possession of the truth. Such positiveness, if it is, as it is here, the fruit of humble submission to the Scriptures, begets confidence and like assurance that one is on the right track in this important duty of training one's children to be good citizens of Church and State.[32]

The reviews of *A Christian Pedagogy* in the theological journals of two seminaries within the Synodical Conference are evidence that leaders within that body in the 1930s were committed to the position that Lutheran school teachers needed the foundation of Holy Scripture in order to know how to go about their work and understand their calling. The Lutheran school was more than just a place where formal classes in

---

[30] Ibid., 959.

[31] Ibid.

[32] Ibid., 959-60.

religion were conducted. It was also a place in which the Word of God was to be the guide and where Christian faith was to be practiced and lived. E. W. A. Koehler's *A Christian Pedagogy* was a reaffirmation of that view articulated by J. C. W. Lindemann in a book written in 1879 and endorsed in the Lutheran school teacher-training programs of the late nineteenth and early twentieth centuries.

Koehler's association with Concordia Teachers College in River Forest went back to the days when that institution was located in Addison, Illinois. He began his work there in 1909, filling a faculty vacancy created by the unexpected death of Friedrich Lindemann, son of the first director of the Addison school. Koehler taught in the areas of German, Christian doctrine, and education. He was born in Germany in 1875 and came to this country with his parents in 1886. He received his college education at Concordia College in Fort Wayne and his seminary education in St. Louis. Prior to going to Addison he had served as a parish pastor and continued to assist in parishes in the Chicago area until a year before his death.

Koehler retired as a full-time Concordia faculty member in 1946 but continued to teach on a part-time basis after that. Concordia Seminary in St. Louis conferred the Doctor of Divinity degree, *honoris causa*, on him in 1941. At his death in 1951, an obituary in *Der Lutheraner*, official German periodical of the Missouri Synod, stated: "With the passing of Dr. Koehler one of the most distinguished theologians of our Synod has again departed this life."[33] It was the editors of *Lutheran Education*, however, who paid an exceptionally fine tribute to the man when they wrote:

> The death of Prof. Edward W. A. Koehler . . . marks the passing of a teacher who by the grace of God was

---

[33] *Der Lutheraner*, June 19, 1951, 209.

permitted to exert a far-reaching influence in our Church. . . . During the past five years, from the time he had reached the retirement age until a few weeks before his death, he continued to teach at his own request. He seemed not to be comfortable and content unless he was in the classroom proclaiming and explaining the Word of God. His magnetic influence filled one with a burning desire, an inner zeal to be of service. He spoke with conviction and clarity. His students, past and present, remember him with sincere respect and deep affection.[34]

E. W. A. Koehler's tenure as a faculty member at a Lutheran school teacher-training college of The Lutheran Church— Missouri Synod spanned a period of more than 40 years. His books and his classroom teaching made a not inconsequential contribution to the college preparation of many Lutheran parochial school teachers.

Suggested for Further Reading

Koehler, E. W. A. *A Christian Pedagogy*. St. Louis: Concordia, 1930.

_____. *A Summary of Christian Doctrine*. 1939, 1952; distributed by Concordia Publishing House, St. Louis, MO.

---

[34] *Lutheran Education*, June 1951, 509-10.

✦✦✦ 1942 ✦✦✦

Lutheran Education Association
(LEA)

When the General Teachers' Conference of The Lutheran Church—Missouri Synod met from July 7-9 in 1942, the group was ready to dissolve its organization and form a new one. Plans to do this had been in the making since the Conference's convention of the preceding year when a report was accepted which recommended the formation of a National Lutheran Teachers' Association. To implement that proposal, the approximately 125 teachers who had gathered in 1941 elected "an organization committee to draft a constitution and formulate the aims, objectives, and the necessary machinery for this organization to function."[1] The appointed committee attended to its assignment and presented a constitution for a new organization to the meeting of the General Teachers' Conference at River Forest, Illinois, in July 1942. The proposed constitution was adopted and brought into existence the Lutheran Education Association (LEA), the name chosen by the committee which had drafted the constituting document. With that action the General Teachers' Conference went out of existence and the Lutheran Education Association proceeded to conduct its first annual meeting.

---

[1] From the General Teachers' Conference resolution given in full in the *Lutheran School Journal*, December 1941, 180.

Two hundred forty-four people from 14 states had registered for the 1942 founding meeting of the Lutheran Education Association. World conditions had changed considerably between the time of the proposal for a national Lutheran education association and the actual formation of LEA. War had been raging in Europe since 1939, but the United States was not drawn into the conflict until the attack on Pearl Harbor in December 1941, about halfway between the meeting at which Lutheran teachers recommended the establishing of a new organization and the time of the founding of it. Alfred F. Fricke, the first president of the Lutheran Education Association, acknowledged the turmoil of the times when he opened the 1942 business meeting of the organization with the words:

> It would be difficult to find a period of world's history to compare with that of our times. This is truly a period of devastating destruction. . . . Nations have risen against nation until the whole world is engaged in a titanic struggle.[2]

At that time no one could predict how long the war would last or what its outcome would be. What had become apparent to LEA's first president in the few months in which the United States was at war was that the nation had found it necessary to coordinate its efforts and pool its various resources if it hoped to achieve its goal of victory. Fricke felt that Christian educators should likewise combine their efforts in behalf of Christian schools through an organization such as the Lutheran Education Association. Sentiments of that kind had been expressed before by those who were pressing for an organization such as LEA. The writer of a letter to the editor of the *Lutheran School*

---

[2] Lutheran Education Association, "First Annual Convention Proceedings," Concordia Historical Institute Collection, St. Louis, 2, mimeographed.

Journal, for example, over a year before LEA was founded commented:

> We need to be better organized. What a pooling of resources and formulation of programs of national and international scope can achieve has, I think, been amply demonstrated by the Walther League and the Lutheran Laymen's League as well as many organizations outside the church. United we stand; divided we fall.[3]

The Lutheran Education Association was expected to bring together into an organization individuals who shared a common commitment to Lutheran schools and who would with a united voice promote the cause of Lutheran Christian education.

The constitution adopted by LEA in 1942 was intended to serve the organization temporarily until its meeting in 1943. The initial document opened membership not only to Missouri Synod Lutherans but to "all members of the Synodical Conference (pastors, teachers, laymen, and laywomen)."[4] The constitution made it clear that the Lutheran Education Association, although having emerged from the Missouri Synod's General Teachers' Conference, was seeking to involve more than teachers and Missouri Synod members in the organization. LEA was soliciting a broader membership, a goal not too successfully achieved, since members of the Wisconsin Synod, the Missouri Synod's major partner in the Synodical Conference and in the Lutheran parochial school movement, did not have a great deal of interest in the new association. Pastors and lay members in the Missouri Synod, moreover, also never joined in large numbers. The Association membership was primarily Missouri Synod teachers.

---

[3] Walter H. Voth, *Lutheran School Journal*, May 1941, 428-29.

[4] Lutheran Education Association, *Bulletin 1*, October 1942, 13.

At the same time that LEA in its first convention approved an interim constitution, it also adopted for temporary use the following objectives for the organization:

1. To assist the church in the promotion of Christian education.
2. To stimulate the latent power of the church's teaching personnel.
3. To coordinate and fuse educational thinking.
4. To preserve the precious heritage of the purity of doctrine through emphasis on Christian education as carried on in the various educational agencies of the Church.
5. To promote the expansion of the Christian day school system.
6. To foster greater interest in the establishment and support of secondary schools and higher educational agencies.
7. To engage in educational research.
8. To disseminate the results of research.
9. To promote and support educational publications.[5]

The objectives were ambitious, wide-ranging, and for the most part, general. For dues-paying members the most tangible benefit to which they could look forward was the promise that the Lutheran Education Association intended to serve its membership "thru publications and bulletins designed to promote the expansion of our educational agencies."[6] LEA was quick to implement that goal and published its first monograph

---

[5] *Lutheran School Journal*, September 1942, 38. These objectives also appeared on the inside of the front cover of LEA's *Bulletin 1*, October 1942.

[6] Lutheran Education Association, *Bulletin 1*, October 1942, inside of the back cover.

in October of 1942. The publication of short treatises of that type, occasional papers, and, for many years, also yearbooks continued to be a major activity of the organization.

The first convention of LEA in 1942 was planned to be more than just a constituting meeting. The three-day conference had a full program of professional presentations. Among these was an essay by Paul W. Lange entitled "The Association, the Profession, and the Church." The essayist was a 1927 graduate of Concordia in River Forest and the recipient of the Ph.D. degree from the University of Chicago in 1940. His essay, chosen to be the first in the long line of monographs published by the Lutheran Education Association, was sent in the convention year to every teacher in the Synodical Conference. Lange minced no words as he spoke about the value and purpose of Lutheran Christian day schools in the mission of the church. A primary function of such schools was, in his opinion, to provide thorough and comprehensive instruction in the doctrines of Holy Scripture. The word used by Lange when speaking of such instruction was indoctrinate. He used that term, however, in a more neutral sense than it is perhaps used today. He was not advocating a classroom methodology which stifled student thinking or critical analysis. He was convinced, however, that the Bible was the Word of God and that the parochial school had the mandate to communicate the teachings of that Word in a thorough and comprehensive way. By indoctrinate Lange meant, then, teaching to the young the content and message of Holy Scripture.

The author called for "a rededication to the fundamentals of Christian education" and then added, "Stripped of its glowing generalities and confusing vagaries, the issue facing us as members of the Lutheran church is simply this: Indoctrinate or Disintegrate."[7] He then continued:

---

[7] Lutheran Education Association, *Bulletin 1*, October 1942, 3.

By indoctrination I do not mean superficial, indefinite, or spasmodic instruction, but I do mean a systematic, vigorous, and consistent type of instruction and guidance that is specifically designed to influence, direct, and mold the thoughts, attitudes, and actions of the individual into clearly defined channels so that the end-product of such instruction and training will result in the development of an individual who thinks and acts in conformity with the teachings of Christ. . . . Like the state, the Lutheran church is also interested in education. Like the state, we also have a priceless heritage to preserve, defend and pass on to future generations. Like the state, we too are faced with the choice of indoctrinating or disintegrating. Upon a thorough indoctrination of the rising generation in the teachings of Holy Writ depends the perpetuity of our existence as a separate church body. Failure to conceive of the Lutheran Christian day school as fundamentally a preserver and defender of the church is to shut our eyes to one of its primary functions.[8]

The essayist was quite ready to admit that the Lutheran school could be used as a mission agency, but since Sunday schools, Saturday schools, and vacation Bible schools could accomplish the same thing, the Christian day school had a purpose beyond that. The full-time school had the advantages of more time, regular attendance, and trained teachers and so was better able than part-time agencies to help children "learn to observe *all*

---

[8] Ibid., 3-5. The analogy between the state's interest in education for purposes of self-preservation and the church using schools to do the same is an indicator of the time when the essay was delivered, six months after Japan's surprise attack on Pearl Harbor and the United States' entry into World War II. The country was caught off guard; self-defense was a thought prominent in the minds of Americans. Lange saw the parochial school as an effective agency for the preservation of the Lutheran church.

things God has commanded."[9] One of the objectives endorsed by LEA in its constituting convention of 1942 was the promotion and expansion of the Lutheran Christian day school system. The essay delivered by Paul Lange on the last day of that convention became the first published monograph of the Association and strongly reiterated a long-held position that the Lutheran parochial school was not an institution just loosely connected with the church but was expected to contribute significantly to the carrying out of the mission of the church.

The Lutheran Education Association was intended to be an association of individuals within the Evangelical Lutheran Synodical Conference of North America. The group was independent and not under any synodical sponsorship. A report in the November 1943 issue of the *Lutheran School Journal* suggests, however, that there was some opposition to the organization. The Association membership was 245 at the time, prompting the reporter to comment, "This is not an imposing figure."[10] The writer then mentioned several objections which had allegedly been voiced in opposition to the formation of LEA:

> The negative approaches vary. Some believe that such an organization is a violation of church democracy. . . . Some feel that such an association will become a pressure group. . . . It has been stated that the association is made up of "a bunch of fellows who have an ax to grind."[11]

More than one factor was very likely contributing to the slow growth of the Lutheran Education Association, not the least of which might have been the nature of the times. A war was in progress and conditions were very unsettled, not the best of

---

[9] Ibid., 6.

[10] *Lutheran School Journal*, November 1943, 129.

[11] Ibid.

circumstances under which to try to form a new national education association. It seems that LEA's relationship to the Missouri Synod did need some clarification, however, for at its second convention in 1943 the group adopted the following memorial for presentation to Missouri's 1944 convention:

> The Lutheran Education Association . . . respectfully petitions . . . that the Synod recognize both the need and the possibility of great blessings inherent in an organization such as the Lutheran Education Association and therefore recognize its objectives as being worthy of synodical sanction and endorsement and . . . offer such sanction and endorsement of this organization and encourage the most active and earnest support of all members of our Synod in its programs and plans.[12]

The Missouri Synod responded favorably to LEA's endorsement request and asked that the "association work in cooperation with Synod's Board of Christian Education and that . . . the Executive Secretary of Synod's Board of Christian Education be an advisory member of the Executive Committee of the Lutheran Education Association."[13] The Synod's request that its Board of Christian Education Executive Secretary be made an advisory member of LEA's Executive Committee suggests that there was a concern about how an independent educational association within the Missouri Synod and a synodical board of education were to relate to each other and that the two have a ready avenue of communication with one another. The result in the subsequent history of LEA was that its Executive Committee regularly included among its advisory members not only the Synod's educational executive but

---

[12] *Lutheran School Journal*, April 1944, 371.

[13] *Proceedings of the Thirty-Ninth Regular Convention of the Ev. Lutheran Synod of Missouri, Ohio, and Other States*, 1944, 136.

representatives from synodical colleges, seminaries, and other entities.

The Lutheran Education Association was a dues-paying organization from its very beginning. Within a year, arrangements were made to provide all members with an automatic subscription to the *Lutheran School Journal*. Monographs and yearbooks were also included in the membership fee. Numerous monographs were produced from time to time and yearbooks from 1944 until 1978. The cost of producing the latter began to be a burden on the LEA treasury and was identified as a major cause of the financial difficulties encountered by the organization in the 1970s. As a result, the yearbook enterprise was discontinued, publication activities being restricted to monographs, occasional publications, and materials produced by the departments of the association.

Departments in LEA came into existence over the course of time. These departments are subgroups to accommodate the specialized educational interests of the organization's membership. The first such group to be formed was the Department of Lutheran Elementary School Principals (DLESP), which in the 1990s broadened its membership and took the name Lutheran Education Administrators (LEAD). Special interest groups which followed included Theological Educators in Associated Ministries (TEAM), a department to serve directors of Christian education and pastors, the Department of Early Childhood Education (DECE), and a department for Lutheran Elementary Teachers (LET). The intent of the departmental structure was to make possible the giving of attention to the more specific needs and concerns of smaller groups of educators engaged in very similar activities and still have an umbrella organization to speak in behalf of Lutheran education generally.

During the 35 years that the Lutheran Education Association was engaged in the publication of yearbooks, the authors of the books dealt with a number of topics, ranging from such things as tests and measurements in Lutheran education to a discussion of the child in worship. Three of the yearbooks are worthy of special mention, however, because they touched on matters affecting the Missouri Synod in a broader way. The first of these books appeared in the Synod's centennial year under the title *100 Years of Christian Education*. The multiauthored volume contains a substantial amount of historical information relative to elementary schools in the Missouri Synod. The book also includes a generous supply of footnotes referencing synodical periodicals and convention proceedings and closes with two short helpful indices. Although the volume was an anniversary publication, the promotional overtones which sometimes accompany books of that sort are rare in *100 Years of Christian Education* so that LEA's fourth yearbook continues as a valuable source of information for the study of Lutheran elementary school history prior to 1947.

Nearly 30 years after the publication of its fourth yearbook, the Lutheran Education Association sponsored the writing of an essay which stepped boldly into a conflict which had just erupted in The Lutheran Church—Missouri Synod. Published in 1975 as LEA's 32nd yearbook and written by Paul G. Bretscher, the little volume carried the title *After the Purifying* and was written in response to events taking place in the Missouri Synod at that time. An investigation of the doctrinal stance of the faculty at Concordia Seminary in St. Louis had resulted in a walkout from the institution by most of its faculty and a large majority of its students. The group which left continued to function off campus under the name Concordia Seminary in Exile (Seminex). Bretscher acknowledged that the synodical circumstances of the day were the occasion for his treatise:

The conflict which has been tearing The Lutheran Church—Missouri Synod for the past several years has overwhelming significance for the future of education in our church.

The first focus of that conflict was . . . Concordia Seminary in St. Louis. So intense has the conflict been, that it has yielded two seminaries, one a "Concordia Seminary in Exile" (Seminex), the other a restructured Concordia at the old address. Which of these, if either, is the "real" Concordia Seminary? That question is more than political and constitutional. It involves conflicting understandings of the Word of God, of the church, and thus of Christian understanding.[14]

As Bretscher observed, the synodical crisis had been created by "conflicting understandings of the Word of God." The Missouri Synod had taken up the issues dividing it at its 1973 convention in New Orleans. The yearbook author described the action of that convention in the following manner:

The New Orleans Convention of The Lutheran Church— Missouri Synod was heralded as "a doctrinal crossroads." . . . A dross needed to be purged out so that the Synod might be restored to full doctrinal purity. As the majority of delegates understood the issue, a view of Scripture had entered the church, through the use of the "historical-critical method" of interpretation, which put the Scriptures at the mercy of man's reason. It seemed impossible that men who approved that method could any longer "accept without reservation" the Scriptures as the Word of God (Synod's Constitution, Article II), inspired and inerrant.

---

[14] Paul G. Bretscher, *After the Purifying* (River Forest, IL: Lutheran Education Association, 1975), xi.

The inevitable effect of the method, it seemed, would be to erode the authority of the Scriptures and to undermine the Gospel.[15]

Bretscher was not in accord with the stance of Missouri's 1973 convention. The convention's decisions, however, initiated an investigation of the faculty of Concordia Seminary at St. Louis and eventually resulted in the suspension of Concordia's president by the institution's board of control. The author of *After the Purifying* held that the actions of the convention and the Seminary's board of control were attempts "to purify the Synod of its dross."[16] Bretscher, on the other hand, was not opposed to the use of historical-critical methodology in the study of Holy Scripture and felt that what was called the "Synod's doctrinal position" was what needed refining:

> The dross is *not* the use of the historical-critical method in Bible study. . . . That method of itself is quite external to our doctrine. . . . The real dross lies *within* our doctrine. It is mixed and fused with what we have called "Synod's doctrinal position."[17]

In short, Bretscher subscribed to a method of studying Scripture which the Missouri Synod in convention had officially rejected.

In *After the Purifying*, Bretscher explained how he approached the study of the Bible. He did not wish to be interpreted as saying that Holy Scripture was made up of the Gospel, "the message . . . which God addresses to our hearts out of the cross of Christ" and mere leftovers, "that Biblical

---

[15] Ibid., 7.

[16] Ibid., 8.

[17] Ibid., 62.

content which is 'not a part of the Gospel' "[18] and which could arguably then be ignored. He wanted to be understood as affirming "two pervasive 'realities.' . . . We shall call the one reality 'theological' (of God)," he said, "and the other 'historical' (of men)."[19] The latter dealt with "the authorship of Biblical books, with the formation of the Pentateuch in the Old Testament and of the Gospels in the New, . . . with the understanding of literary forms, with the historicity and facticity of persons and events. . . ."[20] With respect to the study of the Bible on the premise that it is composed of two realities, the author concluded that the Christian exegete

> in terms of the Bible's "theological reality" . . . is a hungry child of God, eager to hear the Word of God and feed on it as his Bread of Life. In terms of the "historical reality" of Scripture, he is a disciplined historian, facing all the hardships and hazards of the historical enterprise, but not afraid to use his mind. . . . It is not his business to worry about consequences.[21]

LEA's 32nd yearbook was an endorsement of the use of historical-critical methodology for the study of Holy Scripture.

The chairman of the editorial committee which attended to the publication of *After the Purifying* for the Lutheran Education Association was Paul W. Lange, the essayist at LEA's 1942 constituting convention. Of the Bretscher treatise Lange said: "The author has provided a lucid and provocative book."[22] And provocative it was! A review article from the pen of Raymond

---

[18] Ibid., 77-78.

[19] Ibid., 78.

[20] Ibid., 87.

[21] Ibid., 92-93.

[22] Ibid., vi.

Surburg, a faculty member at Concordia Theological Seminary in Springfield, Illinois, concluded with the comment:

> Bretscher's views on the Holy Scriptures are not Lutheran and contradict the Biblical position on inspiration and inerrancy and militate against the view that *all* of the Bible is Word of God (the view of historic Christianity). Having read and considered the words of *After the Purifying*, we are forced to say to Bretscher what Luther said to Zwingli: "You have a different spirit."[23]

Bretscher was forthright in setting forth his views in *After the Purifying*; Raymond Surburg was equally direct in his critique of those views. LEA's 1975 yearbook written by Paul Bretscher stepped boldly into a doctrinal controversy which at the time was engaging the entire Lutheran Church—Missouri Synod.

An earlier yearbook of the Lutheran Education Association, the one issued in 1972, also entered into the broader synodical arena. That document, however, did not deal primarily with theology but rather with Missouri Synod church polity. Voting membership in the Synod is given to pastors in congregations and to congregational lay delegates. Teachers—and for that matter, ordained clergymen serving in the seminaries and colleges of the church—do not have the franchise. This has long been an irritant among some educators in the Synod and became a frequent topic of discussion again in the 1960s and early 1970s. LEA's 29th yearbook took up the issue with an interpretive essay written by Stephen Schmidt of Concordia Teachers College in River Forest and entitled *Powerless Pedagogues*. The book was relatively popular, prompting two contributors to the 50th anniversary pamphlet of LEA to single out the document for special mention in connection with some

---

[23] Raymond F. Surburg, *The Springfielder*, March 1976, 215.

of the financial difficulties experienced by the Association in the 1970s. Said one writer: "A bright light appeared when it was announced that the 1972 yearbook, *Powerless Pedagogues*, was the first in nine years to be paid for during the year of production."[24] Reviewing the financial success of the annual publications, the treasurer from 1974 to 1978 observed: "Some of the yearbooks (*Powerless Pedagogues*, *Catalytic Community*) brought some modest income into the LEA coffers," but "most of them were financial disasters."[25] Since the yearbooks were distributed to LEA members as part of their membership fee, the modest financial achievement of *Powerless Pedagogues* would have been obtained from outside sales. The book, with its captivating title and provocative thesis, had created interest beyond LEA's regular membership.

As indicated above, the issue of teacher franchise at synod and district conventions was not new. Back in 1887, for example, a number of teachers submitted an overture to the Synod requesting that teachers be given the franchise in some of the business of the Synod. An area specifically mentioned was the election of officers. The 1887 convention delegates were not convinced that such a move was wise and also felt that extending the franchise in that way required a revision of the synodical constitution, a task which could not have been taken up in that session of the Synod. The request was tabled. Two conventions later, in 1893, a petition for a partial teacher-franchise was again before the Synod. At that convention the Synod resolved to stay with its previous practice of granting voting privileges to parish pastors and congregational delegates only. The decision was based on the premise that "a synod is a voluntary association of congregations with equal rights. . . .

---

[24] Lutheran Education Association, *The First Fifty Years—Touching Lives* (LEA History 1942-92), 25.

[25] Ibid., 42.

According to this principle . . . only congregations belonging to the Synod have voting rights."[26] It was then argued that pastors of congregations and lay delegates were functioning not on their own but as representatives of their congregations. If teachers were granted the franchise, it was reasoned, they would be representing themselves or their profession and would create an imbalance in congregational representation, since all parishes did not have teachers. The concept of a partial franchise for teachers, an arrangement, in other words, which would give teachers voting privileges in only some of the business of the Synod was dismissed, moreover, as a plan which in practical application would result "in a host of arbitrary decisions and endless disputes."[27]

It was the franchise matter which Stephen Schmidt took up in LEA's 29th yearbook, *Powerless Pedagogues*. The author admitted in the preface to his book that his bias was that of a Lutheran teacher. In addition, he was also frank to add:

> This historical essay was written neither as an act of celebration nor always as a happy memory. Rather the pages which follow will appear at times critical, bitter, and often filled with some pain and sadness. This has been a difficult book to write for the history of the Lutheran teacher is not simply a story of success and professional accomplishment. It is a story of struggle, of failure, of frustration and disappointment, as well as dedication, satisfaction, and joy.[28]

---

[26] *Synodal-Bericht der . . . Synode von Missouri, Ohio und andern Staaten* (Synodical Report of the . . . Synod of Missouri, Ohio, and Other States), 1893, 124.

[27] Ibid., 125.

[28] Stephen A. Schmidt, *Powerless Pedagogues* (River Forest, IL: Lutheran Education Association, 1972), iv.

With that the die was cast. The 1972 yearbook of the Lutheran Education Association was a forceful pressing for teacher-franchise in The Lutheran Church—Missouri Synod and a call for a heightened awareness of the significant contributions made by professional Lutheran teachers in the life of the church.

Schmidt's contention was that from the time of the formation of the Missouri Synod the status of the Lutheran teacher was never clearly defined. "Teachers were almost clergy, yet almost laymen," he said.[29] That analysis is also reflected in three of the subheadings of the book's third chapter: "The Teacher: Almost a Hireling"; "The Lutheran Teacher: Almost a Minister"; "Training the Almost Ministry." And where did this leave the teacher in the polity of the church? "Neither lay nor clergy in the eyes of the congregation, the teacher was defranchized by the church at local, district, and national levels of church government. . . . Teachers were not to participate in the governing power of the church."[30] Teachers, in the estimation of Schmidt, were at least partially responsible for the situation in which they found themselves. Looking back at the history, he maintained that when teachers approached the Synod on the question of franchise, "they were careless about their homework" in one case and "lost the issue" in another "because of their political ineptness."[31] The clergy, however, was considered to be the chief contributor to the in-between status of teachers in the Missouri Synod:

> Teachers were the bearers of an inferiority illness, birthed in a lack of ecclesiastical identity and nurtured by decades of careful coaching by the masters of theological gamesmanship. The clergy maintained power by appeal

---

[29] Ibid., 5.

[30] Ibid., 88.

[31] Ibid.

to the theological—to the spirit. The laymen maintained power with pocketbook strength. The teacher was left powerless, deserted by his colleagues, disillusioned by history, and taught by the clergy that he was inferior. The clergy knew the rules of the power game in the church and carefully guarded lay-clergy balance.[32]

Schmidt confessed in the prologue to *Powerless Pedagogues* that some of his lines would be bitter. They were. He wrote a strident appeal in the hope that things could be changed. Twenty years later, a contributor to LEA's 50th anniversary pamphlet recalled Stephen Schmidt's book and commented: "Years of searching for identity through franchise and ordination proved frustrating. . . . Members [of the Lutheran teaching profession] generally concluded that they were 'powerless pedagogues' in a church where politics were best handled by others."[33] Regardless, however, of what position one takes over against the thesis of Stephen Schmidt and the conclusions he draws in *Powerless Pedagogues*, his book cannot be ignored in any study of the history of Lutheran schools. His view was shared, although not necessarily with the same degree of acerbity, by many, not only at the time he wrote his essay but for at least three-quarters of a century before he took pen in hand and in the years that have elapsed as well. In addition, the many citations throughout the work, carefully referenced at the end of each chapter, direct the research scholar to a vast amount of source material pertinent to the study of Lutheran school history.

Although teachers in The Lutheran Church—Missouri Synod have not been successful in obtaining the franchise,

---

[32] Ibid., 89.

[33] Lutheran Education Association, *The First Fifty Years—Touching Lives* (LEA History 1942-92), 25.

teachers in the Wisconsin Evangelical Lutheran Synod have long held that privilege. The first registering of teachers as voting members in that synod came in 1872. When the Wisconsin Synod later federated with the Minnesota and Michigan Synods in 1892, only pastors and lay delegates voted in the assemblies of the federation, although teachers in the Wisconsin Synod itself continued to have the franchise in the business of that body. When the federated synods, including also the Nebraska Synod, merged into the Evangelical Lutheran Joint Synod of Wisconsin and Other States in 1917, the long-established arrangement of the original Wisconsin Synod was taken over by the merged group, a practice which still remains in effect in the Wisconsin Evangelical Lutheran Synod. Male teachers become members of the district in which they are teaching by making application and submitting the necessary credentials. Even as groups of congregations and pastors within the Synod are then represented at synodical conventions by duly elected delegates, so also the Synod's male teachers have representation. The method of determining how many representatives the roster of teachers is to have at synodical conventions has not always been the same. The following formula was in effect in 1975:

> For every ten male teachers in active service in the district . . . the district shall be entitled to one teacher delegate. . . . Members of the faculty, teaching at one of the educational institutions of the Synod or within the Synod, are to be placed on the roster of active pastors, provided they have been ordained as pastors; all others of the respective faculty are to be placed on the roster of active teachers.[34]

---

[34] Wisconsin Ev. Lutheran Synod, *The Constitution and Bylaws*, 1975, 8.

The revised Constitution and Bylaws of the Wisconsin Evangelical Lutheran Synod approved in 1997 does not apportion teacher representation in the above manner but does retain the Synod's historic practice of giving a voice to teachers at synodical conventions. Male teachers become members of synodical districts by making application for such membership and are then granted representation at the conventions of the Wisconsin Synod under the following constitutional provision:

> At conventions of the synod, districts shall be represented by three classes of voting delegates: congregation representatives (lay delegates), pastors, and male synodically certified teachers. . . .

> The distribution of delegates among the districts shall be arranged as follows:
> 1. The number of delegates shall not exceed 400 voting delegates.
> 2. Half of the voting delegates shall be lay delegates.
> 3. In determining the distribution of male teacher and of pastor voting delegates, teachers shall be represented in the same proportion to their total number as pastors are to their total number.[35]

Thus, while teacher-franchise was a controversial twentieth-century issue in The Lutheran Church—Missouri Synod and set off the spark for LEA's 1972 fiery yearbook, *Powerless Pedagogues*, the subject created no stir in the Wisconsin Evangelical Lutheran Synod where Lutheran school teachers had enjoyed voting privileges, in a sense, since 1872.

---

[35] *Constitution and Bylaws of the Wisconsin Evangelical Lutheran Synod* (Milwaukee: Wisconsin Evangelical Lutheran Synod, 1997), 8.

The Lutheran Education Association produced its last yearbook in 1978. To avoid any misunderstanding, it needs to be said that *Powerless Pedagogues* and *After the Purifying* were not typical of the publications of the Association. The authors of these two volumes chose to debate highly contested issues in The Lutheran Church—Missouri Synod. From that point of view, they are historically important. That is especially the case in the context of Lutheran school history with Stephen Schmidt's treatise, dealing, as it does, with the status of the Lutheran school teacher. Debate, however, was not the ordinary approach of the authors of LEA yearbooks. The same can be said of the Association's many monographs and other occasional pieces. A glance at the many titles reveals that the Lutheran Education Association with its publications sought to encourage, inspire, and guide Lutheran educators in their teaching activities.

In 1984, LEA added another feature to its program of services to members when its executive board introduced the concept of a triennial convocation. The intent was to replace the Association's annual conventions, which were lagging in attendance, with a large-scale inspirational kind of gathering to be held in the spring of the year. The idea caught on. Over 600 people attended the first convocation in Indianapolis. More than 2,600 came together for the third in the Chicago area in 1990 and nearly 4,000 for the sixth convention held in Indianapolis in 1999.

Founded in 1942, the Lutheran Education Association organized itself as an independent education society intending to serve members of the Synodical Conference in a variety of ways. The two primary members of the Synodical Conference were The Lutheran Church—Missouri Synod and the Wisconsin Evangelical Lutheran Synod, both of whom had a strong commitment to Lutheran parochial schools. Members of the latter synod showed little interest in the society at the time of its founding and never became involved with it during the years that the Synodical Conference remained in existence. Although membership in LEA is not restricted to members of The Lutheran Church—Missouri Synod, the association is an organization of educators from that church body primarily. Concordia University in River Forest, Illinois, has provided the association with office space over the years, and in 1995, LEA engaged a full-time executive director to work from that office.

Suggested for Further Reading

Lutheran Education Association. *100 Years of Christian Education*. Fourth Yearbook. River Forest, IL: Lutheran Education Association, 1947.

———. *The First Fifty Years—Touching Lives*. River Forest, IL: Lutheran Education Association, 1992.

Schmidt, Stephen A. *Powerless Pedagogues*. River Forest, IL: Lutheran Education Association, 1972.

✤ ✤ ✤ 1947 ✤ ✤ ✤

The United States Supreme Court:
Everson v. Board of Education

In matters pertaining to the separation of church and state in American life, agreement is often more easily reached on a statement of principles than on the application of those principles. That is true whether the issues are being discussed by legal experts and legislative bodies or by theologians and church communities. The United States Supreme Court found this to be the case when it had to render a decision in *Everson v. Board of Education of the Township of Ewing* in February of 1947. The nine men sitting on the bench at that time had little disagreement on the basic principles of separation of church and state under the United States Constitution, and yet, when it came to ruling on a concrete case involving the principles, the Court was sharply divided. The decision was 5-4, with the minority expressing its disagreement in two lengthy dissenting opinions.

The case had come to the United States Supreme Court via New Jersey state courts and involved the payment by Ewing Township of the cost of transporting children to Roman Catholic schools. Twenty-one children were involved; $859.80 had been set aside to pay for their transportation on public carrier, and $357.74 had been paid to the parents in reimbursement for the fares which they paid to get their children to and from school. The United States Supreme Court was to determine whether this was a violation of the Fourteenth Amendment, which forbids the taxation of the private property of one person for the private purposes of another, and of the First Amendment, which forbids the establishment of religion by the federal government, the latter amendment having been made applicable also to the states by a 1940 court ruling (*Cantwell v. Connecticut*).

In arriving at a decision in *Everson v. Board of Education*, the Court had to address two questions. First, there was the issue of whether private schools were being aided directly or only indirectly by the transportation accommodation provided their pupils. If it was determined that the schools were benefitting only indirectly or incidentally, could the New Jersey law really be considered a violation of constitutional provisions guaranteeing the separation of church and state? Second, the Court had to decide whether the New Jersey statute was legislation for the physical well-being of parochial school children or in the interest of their schools. All agreed that the state had the authority to enact compulsory education laws. Was how parochial school children went to and from their schools a matter of schooling or public safety? In the *Everson* case, what is known as the "child-benefit" theory came into play. Although traffic risks were the child-benefit rationale in 1947, the theory would eventually be part of the defense for other kinds of federal assistance to students in both private and public schools. Notable among such laws would be the Elementary and Secondary Education Act of 1965. Title II of that act authorized the making of

> grants for the acquisition of school library resources, textbooks, and other printed and published instructional materials for the use of children and teachers in public and private elementary and secondary schools.[1]

---

[1] Joshua Weinstein, *When Religion Comes to School* (Washington D.C.: University Press of America, 1979), 104.

By and large, states were reluctant to assist the private sector of education on the basis of the child-benefit theory. In some cases state constitutions made such action impossible; in other cases legislators and voters were not convinced of the wisdom of the theory. In the area of higher education, however, the federal government proceeded, as time went on, to provide extensive assistance to students in private and church-related colleges and universities and even to the institutions themselves. Evidence can be seen in the student-loan and work-study programs available not only for general educational purposes but even for students preparing themselves for church vocations and at theological seminaries. The students and society as a whole are seen as the primary beneficiaries of such programs. *Everson v. Board of Education of the Township of Ewing* with its 5-4 Supreme Court decision relative to bus transportation to private common schools made its contribution to that view of government assistance in higher education.

The school bus law contested before the United States Supreme Court in 1947 had come out of the state of New Jersey. That was not the only state, however, which had authorized or had laws which would have permitted the transportation of parochial school children to church and private schools at that time. Arrangements and permissions varied from state to state, but about 20 states had taken positive action relative to the matter.[2] Publicly financed bus transportation for school children became part of the educational scene in the United States when public school districts in rural and small-town areas began consolidating. Such consolidation required a network of buses to transport children from their homes or

---

[2] For a detailed review of the bus situation for private schools children, see R. Freeman Butts, *The American Tradition in Religion and Education* (Boston: Beacon, 1950), 151-153, and John W. Klotz, "Supreme Court on State Aid to Private Schools," *Lutheran School Journal*, April 1947, 378-79.

districts to the centralized elementary and secondary consolidated schools. This practice and the increased public cost attendant upon it contributed to the solicitation of school transportation funds for children attending nonpublic schools. If the safety of children was part of the rationale for busing pupils to consolidated public schools, should not the physical well-being of children attending private schools be of equal public concern?

There is no question that the school bus issue involves a certain amount of mixing of church and state, and that is what made it difficult to resolve the issue. The 5-4 *Everson* decision by nine men well-informed in matters of constitutional law makes that clear. States, too, found themselves caught on the horns of a dilemma and in some cases even made an about-face on the question. Thus, for example, the state supreme court of Kentucky ruled against bus transportation to private schools in 1942 when it said:

> The portion of school law requiring that pupils attending private schools be given the same transportation rights as pupils of public schools violates constitutional provision requiring that taxes be levied and collected for "public purposes" only.[3]

Reversing itself in 1945, the supreme court of the same state ruled that a given school bus act

> . . . constitutes simply what it purports to be—an exercise of police power for the protection of childhood against the inclemency of weather and from the hazards of present-day highway traffic.

---

[3] Quoted in R. Freeman Butts, *The American Tradition in Religion and Education*, 155.

. . . the fact that in a strained and technical sense the school might derive an indirect benefit from the enactment, is not sufficient to defeat the declared purpose and the wholesome effect of the law.[4]

In the state of Wisconsin a reversal also took place but not by the state supreme court and not in a short span of time. Presented with a test case in 1923, the Wisconsin Supreme Court ruled that a district school board had no authority to provide bus transportation to pupils of private schools. The court said:

The contract made by the district board whereby it attempted to provide transportation of pupils to a private school was an act beyond its authority and therefore invalid. . . . The school board is by statute authorized to provide transportation for such children of school age as desire to attend a public school and no others.[5]

An attempt was made in 1946 to amend the Wisconsin constitution by referendum so as to make it constitutionally possible to pass a law affording private school children bus transportation at public expense. The attempt failed but was presented to voters again in 1967. The question on the ballot in that year was:

Shall Section 23 of Article I of the Constitution be created so that the legislature may provide for the safety and welfare of children by providing for the transportation of children to and from any parochial or private school or institution of learning?[6]

---

[4] Ibid., 156.

[5] Ibid., 153.

[6] Quoted in *Legislative Counselor* (Wisconsin Protestant Legislative Council, Incorporated), October 1967.

On April 4, 1967, Wisconsin voters approved the constitutional change by a vote of 494,236 to 377,107. The legislature then proceeded to enact legislation which provided for the transportation costs of pupils attending nonpublic schools and established the conditions under which such transportation was to be made available.[7] What was unconstitutional in 1923 became constitutional in 1967 through a voter-mandated change in the Wisconsin state constitution.

As is obvious from the change of mind in Wisconsin as well as elsewhere, more and more people in the mid-twentieth century were seeing the busing of children to and from school as a matter of safety and not just schooling. Prior to *Everson* the federal government itself had been engaged in a major activity in behalf of the physical health and well-being of children in parochial as well as in public schools. The involvement came in the form of government subsidy for school lunch programs. The National School Lunch Act of 1946 made both cash payments and surplus food commodities available to parochial and private schools as well as to public schools. The act was the culmination of a government subsidy program begun already in the 1930s during the Great Depression. The federal government had two concerns as it involved itself in school lunch programs. One was the nutrition of children; the other was a responsible way in which to use up surplus agricultural commodities. The funds and products for school lunches were to be distributed through state offices, but in states where it was unconstitutional for a public office to disburse aid of any kind to parochial or private schools, the federal assistance went directly to those schools instead of through state agencies. Although bus transportation is more critical to the operation of a school than a noon lunch, it can be argued that a subsidized food service enhances a parochial school program and also reduces the

---

[7] Ibid.

overall cost of education at the school. The Court majority in
Everson drew a parallel between the protection which state-paid
policemen extended to parochial school children and bus
transportation for such children but made no mention of federal
subsidy for school lunches. A reference to the latter was
included, however, in one of the two minority opinions
subscribed to by four justices. The four declared:

> Finally, transportation, where it is needed, is as essential
> to education as any other element. Its cost is as much a
> part of the total expense, except at times in amount, as
> the cost of textbooks, of school lunches, of athletic
> equipment, of writing and other materials; indeed of all
> other items composing the total burden.[8]

Although the Supreme Court did not see a strong connection
between government subsidy for lunches in parochial schools
and tax-supported transportation for pupils in such schools, the
passing reference to the lunch program in the Court's minority
opinion suggests that the kinship between the two practices
was not totally ignored in the bus-issue discussions.

Of greater import for the *Everson* ruling was a Supreme
Court decision rendered 17 years earlier. In 1930, the United
States Supreme Court ruled in *Cochran et al. v. Louisiana State
Board of Education et al.* that the furnishing free of charge of
school textbooks to children in private, both sectarian and
nonsectarian, schools was not in violation of the United States
Constitution. The case in question had arisen as the result of a
1928 act by the Louisiana state legislature which said that

> the Severance Tax Fund of the State . . . shall be devoted
> after allowing funds and appropriations as provided by

---

[8] *Everson v. Board of Education of Ewing Tp. et al.,* in *Supreme Court Reporter,* 67, 527.

the Constitution of the State, first, to supplying school books to the school children of the State of Louisiana, and that thereafter such further sums as remain . . . shall be transferred to the State public school funds.[9]

After a trial court had refused to grant an injunction barring the State Board of Education from supplying textbooks to children in nonpublic schools, the case went before the Louisiana State Supreme Court. That court ruled that the textbook legislation violated neither the state nor the federal constitution.

The state court decision was appealed to the United States Supreme Court where the case was rather quickly decided. The highest court of the land affirmed the Louisiana State Court judgment in a unanimous decision. The case was not argued on the basis of the establishment-clause of the First Amendment but, as in *Meyer* and *Pierce*,[10] on the basis of the Fourteenth which forbade the taking of one person's private property to benefit the private purposes of another. The appellants had argued that under the Louisiana act private schools were the beneficiaries of property supplied by public tax money. The United States Supreme Court disagreed, upholding the opinion of the Louisiana State Supreme Court which had said:

> The schools . . . are not the beneficiaries of these appropriations. They obtain nothing from them, nor are they relieved of a single obligation, because of them. The school children and the state alone are the beneficiaries. . . . What the statutes contemplate is that the same books that are furnished children attending public schools shall be furnished children attending private schools. . . . The legislation does not segregate private schools, or their

---

[9] Louisiana, *Acts Passed by the Legislature* (1928), 114.

[10] See chapters 15 (1923) and 16 (1925) of the present volume.

pupils, as its beneficiaries or attempt to interfere with any matters of exclusively private concern. Its interest is education, broadly; its method, comprehensive. Individual interests are aided only as the common interest is safeguarded.[11]

The "establishment-of-religion" issue raised in *Everson* in 1947 was not debated in the *Cochran* decision of 1930. Children and the state were seen as the beneficiaries of legislation which supplied school textbooks for the use of all children in the state, regardless of the kind of school they attended. The Court held that public money could be used for that purpose and that the Fourteenth Amendment was not violated. The decision was precedent-setting in terms of government assistance to students in nonpublic schools. Looking back at the *Cochran* case nearly 50 years after the decision, a writer concluded:

The concept of "child benefit" which was developed in this case raised a series of profound controversial issues concerning free lunches, medical services, psychological services, free transportation, tuition grants and scientific equipment for nonparochial studies in private and parochial schools. The Cochran decision brought about new interpretations and new definitions of the "wall of separation" between church and state to which Jefferson referred in the early nineteenth century. Many of these issues are still unresolved and await new challenges and new court definitions.[12]

Everson v. the Board of Education was such a new challenge.

---

[11] *Cochran v. Louisiana State Board of Education*, in *Supreme Court Reporter*, 50, 335-36.

[12] Joshua Weinstein, *When Religion Comes to School* (Washington D.C.: University Press of America, 1979), 41.

The New Jersey law which initiated the proceedings was passed on June 9, 1941. The law stipulated that

> whenever in any district there are children living remote from any schoolhouse, the board of education of the district may make rules and contracts for the transportation of such children to and from school, including the transportation of school children to and from school other than a public school, except such school as is operated for profit in whole or in part.[13]

As is apparent, the statute did not mandate bus transportation for school children but permitted school districts to provide it for both public and private school children, unless the private school involved was being operated for profit.

The second paragraph of the Act did include a requirement, however, with respect to nonpublic school children. Such children were to be accorded free bus privileges along routes established for public school pupils if busing was provided for the latter. The law read:

> When any school district provides any transportation for public school children to and from school, transportation from any point in such established school route to any other point in such established school route shall be supplied to school children residing in such school district in going to and from school other than a public school, except such school as is operated for profit in whole or in part.[14]

---

[13] New Jersey, *Acts of the One Hundred and Sixty-fifth Legislature* (1941), 581.

[14] Ibid.

The Board of Education of Ewing Township, located in the vicinity of Trenton, New Jersey, chose to reimburse parents for the fares they paid for their children to ride to school by way of public carrier. Since this was done for public school pupils, it also had to be done for a number of children attending Catholic schools.

When a certain Mr. Everson contested the Ewing Township practice, the case was referred to the New Jersey State Supreme Court. The difficulty of ruling in the case was apparent in that court already. The three justices on the court were divided 2 to 1 on the issue. The majority considered the practice to be in violation of the state constitution and at variance with an earlier state court decision which ruled against giving free state aid to private or sectarian schools. The constitutional paragraphs involved said:

> No donation of land or appropriation of money shall be made by the state or any municipal corporation to or for the use of any society, association or corporation whatever.[15]

The dissenting justice, in a lengthy opinion, argued that the transportation of pupils to private schools on bus routes already established for transporting public school children did not constitute a donation "for the use" of a "society, association or corporation." He maintained that the statute facilitated rather the state's compulsory education laws which permitted parents to choose private schools for the education of their children. He formulated that argument in the following way:

> I cannot find in any of our constitutional prohibitions a purpose to deny such transportation [i.e., transportation

---

[15] New Jersey, *Reports of Cases . . . in the Supreme Court and . . . in the Court of Errors and Appeals*, vol. VII, 101.

on routes established for public school children] to children of non-profit private schools, seeking the education which satisfies the standard of the compulsory education law. If this transportation provision be viewed apart from the institutions themselves, and considered as an aid to parents in making educational facilities of their choice available to their children with a measure of safety, in the service of an essential public interest, it seems to me that constitutional doubts lose their force. As so viewed, the act is an aid of compulsory education, a primary concern of society.[16]

By a vote of 2-1 the New Jersey State Supreme Court had ruled in favor of Everson and against the Board of Education of Ewing Township, but the case was still not over on New Jersey soil. The judgment was appealed to the New Jersey Court of Errors and Appeals.

The Court of Errors and Appeals consisted of nine justices, who arrived at a 6-3 decision to reverse the judgment of the New Jersey State Supreme Court. The Appeals Court ruled that the state school-transportation law and the Ewing Township practice were not in violation of the state constitution but an aid to the compulsory education statutes of New Jersey. The majority reasoned:

> Many situations could arise, where, without regular means of transportation, parents would be placed in a situation which made it practically impossible to comply with the compulsory education requirements and therefore . . . subject to . . . penalties. . . .
>
> It was to meet this mischief that the original statute authorizing the transportation of pupils living remote

---

[16] Ibid., 103.

from the schools was enacted. The statutes looking to transportation became complementary to and in aid of the compulsory education statutes.[17]

A minority opinion, written by one justice and concurred in by two others, not only expressed disagreement with the majority but included an extensive discussion on the so-called "child-benefit" theory and implications of it. The dissenting justices said:

> A major question is whether the furnishing of transportation to private or parochial schools out of public money is in aid or support of such schools. . . . The argument that such disbursements are not in aid of the schools is based upon what is known as the "child-benefit" theory which presents as a distinction that charges are for the benefit of the children rather than of the schools. That theory seems to have first been given judicial sanction in the State of Louisiana where the courts sustained a statute which permitted the use of public funds to purchase school books for distribution, free of cost, apparently as a loan, "to the school children of the state," a classification which by its broad terms included children in attendance at private and parochial schools. . . . *Cochran v. Louisiana State Board of Education.*[18]

After noting that three states, namely, Louisiana, Mississippi, and Maryland, had received judicial support for legislation based on the "child-benefit" theory, the dissenting justices in the New Jersey Court of Errors and Appeals added that the weaknesses of the "child-benefit" theory were

---

[17] New Jersey, *Reports of Cases . . . in the Supreme Court and . . . in the Court of Errors and Appeals*, vol. VIII, 355.

[18] Ibid., 357-58.

. . . its vagueness and the impossibility of satisfactorily distinguishing one item of expense from another in the long process of child education. . . . [and] the almost limitless extent of the "child-benefit" theory.[19]

The minority reasoned further that

every step in the educational process is, presumably, for the benefit of the child and, therefore, theoretically for the benefit of the state. Consequently, if the argument is sound, it is within the discretion of the legislature . . . to provide for practically the entire cost of education in private and parochial as well as in public schools.[20]

The dissenters considered the "child-benefit" theory "an ingenious effort to escape constitutional limitations,"[21] and refused to join their six colleagues in voting to reverse the earlier 2-1 decision of the New Jersey State Supreme Court.

It is not surprising that *Everson v. Board of Education of Ewing Township* was moved on to the United States Supreme Court. The proceedings in New Jersey, with a court of appeals reversing a state supreme court decision and with carefully reasoned dissenting opinions in both tribunals, were ample testimony to the constitutional tensions involved in the school bus law under review. The United States Supreme Court affirmed the ruling of the New Jersey Court of Errors and Appeals and declared that providing publicly funded bus transportation for pupils attending private or parochial schools was not in violation of the United States Constitution. The highest court of the land was also sharply divided on the issue,

---

[19] Ibid., 359.

[20] Ibid., 360.

[21] Ibid., 362.

however, as its 5-4 decision in support of the New Jersey statute shows. Fifteen years later, Justice Douglas, who had voted with the narrow majority in *Everson v. Ewing Township*, had second thoughts on the verdict and said with respect to it: "The *Everson* case seems in retrospect to be out of line with the First Amendment."[22] Had Justice Douglas been convinced of that in 1947, the ruling in *Everson* would have been just the opposite of what it was. Douglas' change of heart is further evidence that issues involving the separation of church and state in American education are exceedingly complex at times and not easily resolved.

The United States Supreme Court was quite frank to admit this in 1947 when it commended state courts for how they had been handling church-school cases but added the comment:

> Their decisions, however, show the difficulty in drawing the line between tax legislation which provides funds for the welfare of the general public and that which is designed to support institutions which teach religion.[23]

That, of course, was precisely the challenge of *Everson* when it came before the Court. It was not for the judiciary to pass judgment on whatever politics might possibly have lurked behind the enactment of the New Jersey law but whether the transporting of pupils to parochial schools was primarily a matter of public safety and so not in conflict with the First and Fourteenth Amendments.

The five-member majority in its written opinion disposed of the "due-process" clause of the Fourteenth Amendment first.

---

[22] *Engel v. Vitale* (1962), in Herbert Kliebard, *Religion and Education in America: A Documentary History* (Scranton, PA: International Textbook Company, 1969), 207.

[23] *Everson v. Board of Education of Ewing Tp. et al.,* in *Supreme Court Reporter,* 67, 511. Also in Kliebard, *Religion and Education,* 135.

It had been argued that the bus law taxed some people to help others carry out their private purposes, a taking away of one person's property for the benefit of another without due process of law, in other words. To this argument the majority on the Court replied:

> The fact that a state law, passed to satisfy a public need, coincides with the personal desires of the individuals most directly affected is certainly an inadequate reason for us to say that a legislature has erroneously appraised the public need.[24]

The majority also took note of the fact that new circumstances sometimes require actions in the interest of public welfare which were not necessary or deemed advisable previously. In that connection the majority opinion asserted:

> Changing local conditions create new local problems which may lead a state's people and its local authorities to believe that laws authorizing new types of public services are necessary to promote the general well-being of the people.[25]

Having said that, the justices directed their attention specifically to the school bus case before them and added that from a safety point of view they considered it within the authority of the states to enact

> . . . legislation to reimburse . . . parents for payment of the fares of their children so that they can ride in public busses to and from schools rather than run the risk of

---

[24] Ibid., 507. Also in Kliebard, *Religion and Education*, 131.

[25] Ibid. Also in Kliebard, 131.

traffic and other hazards incident to walking or "hitchhiking."[26]

As precedent for such state aid to individuals the majority opinion cited past practices of subsidizing farmers, home-owners, transportation systems, and businesses.

The second issue in *Everson*, namely, the "establishment-of-religion" clause of the First Amendment, required lengthier treatment than the "due-process" clause of the Fourteenth. Part of the reason lay in the fact that the Supreme Court had not addressed First Amendment issues in previous education cases such as *Meyer*, *Pierce*, and *Cochran*. To a large extent *Everson* was a pioneer case in this respect. Furthermore, the Court was sharply divided on the relationship between state-subsidized transportation of children to parochial schools and the establishment-of-religion prohibition of the First Amendment. In addition, the issue was highly sensitive nationally and had far-reaching implications. The five-man majority on the Court was aware of this and also had no argument with that interpretation of the First Amendment which maintained that its purpose was to build "a wall of separation between Church and State," as Thomas Jefferson so memorably put it in a letter of 1802.[27] Keeping the Jeffersonian principle in mind, the Court majority opinion concluded:

> The First Amendment has erected a wall between church and state. That wall must be kept high and impregnable. We could not approve the slightest breach. New Jersey has not breached it here.[28]

---

[26] Ibid. Also in Kliebard, 131.

[27] Gordon C. Lee, *Crusade Against Ignorance: Thomas Jefferson on Education* (New York: Teachers College, 1961), 69.

[28] *Everson v. Board of Education*, in *Supreme Court Reporter*, 67, 513. Also in Kliebard, 137.

The majority recognized that the New Jersey school-bus statute helped children to get to church schools and also admitted that some children might not attend such schools without publicly funded bus transportation. The justices were also fully cognizant of the fact that a state was forbidden by the "establishment-of-religion" clause from contributing funds for the support of a church. The majority pointed out, however, that government was also not to hamper citizens in the free exercise of their religion. It was this aspect of the First Amendment which persuaded the five justices to rule that government-subsidized busing of parochial school children to schools approved for the fulfilling of compulsory education laws was not unconstitutional. The Supreme Court majority contended that the First Amendment

> requires the state to be neutral in its relations with groups of religious believers and non-believers; it does not require the state to be their adversary. State power is no more to be used so as to handicap religions than it is to favor them.[29]

The four justices who were unwilling to vote affirmatively on the constitutionality of the New Jersey school bus law submitted two dissenting opinions. All four expressed agreement with the one opinion; two appended their names to the other. The opinion joined in by all four justices included a lengthy discussion of the history leading up to the ratification of the First Amendment and the contributions of James Madison and Thomas Jefferson to the process. That history made it clear, according to the four justices, that the First Amendment

---

[29] Ibid.

forbids any appropriation, large or small, from public funds to aid or support any and all religious exercises.[30]

Since the dissenting justices were not convinced that it was possible to make a distinction between the religious and civil functions of a parochial school, the religious aspect of the institution, in the opinion of these justices, made that type of school ineligible for any kind of government funding. Transportation to parochial schools, moreover, was seen to be an essential part of the total education program. The minority group put it this way:

> Payment of transportation is no more, nor is it any less essential to education, whether religious or secular, than payments for tuitions, for teachers' salaries, for buildings, equipment and necessary materials. Nor is it any the less directly related, in a school giving religious instruction, to the primary religious objective all those essential items of cost are intended to achieve. No rational line can be drawn between payment for such larger, but not more necessary, items and payment for transportation. The only line that can be so drawn is one between more dollars and less. Certainly in this realm such a line can be no valid constitutional measure.[31]

Recognizing that distinctions were being made between aid which benefited the students and was not in support of the schools themselves, the minority statement added:

> State courts have divided upon the issue, some taking the view that only the individual, others that the institution

---

[30] *Everson v. Board of Education*, in *Supreme Court Reporter*, 67, 524.
[31] Ibid., 527.

receives the benefit. A few have recognized that this dichotomy is false, that both in fact are aided.[32]

The minority opinion written by Justice Jackson and joined in by Justice Frankfurter devoted itself particularly to an analysis of the role of the Catholic school as an agency for the teaching of the tenets of the Roman Catholic faith. The opinion cited sections pertaining to Catholic schools from the canon law of the church and concluded that Catholics themselves would very likely not deny that their schools are a vital part of the Roman Catholic Church. For that reason, the two justices expressed the conviction that

> Catholic education is the rock on which the whole structure rests, and to render tax aid to its church school is indistinguishable . . . from rendering the same aid to the Church itself.[33]

It seems that Justice Jackson came to this conclusion during the course of the deliberations on the case, argued in November 1946 and decided in February 1947, for he began his dissent by saying: "I find myself, contrary to first impressions, unable to join in this [the majority] decision."[34] Once he had made up his mind, however, he was uncompromising in his view and chided the majority opinion in no uncertain terms:

> The Court's opinion marshals every argument in favor of state aid and puts the case in its most favorable light, but much of its reasoning confirms any conclusions that there are no good grounds upon which to support the present legislation. In fact, the undertones of the opinion,

---

[32] Ibid., 530-31.

[33] Ibid., 515. Also in Kliebard, 141.

[34] Ibid., 513. Also in Kliebard, 137.

advocating complete and uncompromising separation of Church and State, seem utterly discordant with its conclusion yielding support to their commingling in educational matters. The case which irresistibly comes to mind as the most fitting precedent is that of Julia who, according to Byron's report, "whispering 'I will ne'er consent,'—consented."[35]

Referring in the final sentence of his dissenting opinion to another statement of dissent in the case, Justice Jackson said:

I cannot read the history of the struggle to separate political from ecclesiastical affairs . . . without a conviction that the Court today is unconsciously giving the clock's hands a backward turn.[36]

With that, a minority had its say in *Everson v. Board of Education of the Township of Ewing*. By a vote of 5 to 4, however, the United States Supreme Court had ruled that a 1941 New Jersey law enabling school districts to provide bus transportation at public cost to parochial and nonprofit private schools was not in violation of the United States Constitution. The law was first contested in New Jersey courts in 1943 upon the reimbursement of the Board of Education of Ewing Township to parents of the Roman Catholic faith for the fares these parents paid to have their children transported, by public carrier, to elementary and secondary Catholic schools. Transportation costs for pupils attending public schools had been similarly underwritten. New Jersey courts were divided on the question of church-state entanglement in the matter of assisting children to get to and from parochial schools. The United States Supreme Court in coming to grips with a First

---

[35] Ibid. Also in Kliebard, 138.

[36] Ibid., 517. Also in Kliebard, 144.

Amendment educational issue of this type for the first time was likewise sharply divided, as its final decision and written opinions clearly demonstrate.

A number of other church-state cases and issues in the area of education surfaced in the 1940s. Shortly after the *Everson* decision, for example, the Pennsylvania Supreme Court ruled that bus transportation for parochial school children in that state was unconstitutional. Reporting on the decision, the *Lutheran Standard*, official periodical of the American Lutheran Church, reported:

> In Pennsylvania the state supreme court has upheld the directors of the Kennett Square consolidated school in refusing to provide bus transportation for parochial school children. Suit was brought by a Catholic citizen who contended that the school board was required by law to provide transportation "to the nearest public school," from where his daughter would walk to St. Patrick's parochial school, two blocks away. The state court held that the recent decision of the U.S. Supreme Court in a New Jersey case was not applicable in this instance since the New Jersey school code specifically permits such service.[37]

In addition to the bus issues in the 1940s like those in New Jersey and Pennsylvania, questions arose relative to released-time programs for the religious instruction of children attending public schools. The United States Supreme Court addressed that practice in 1948 (*McCollum v. Board of Education*) and again in 1952 (*Zorach v. Clauson*). Mention might also be made of the church-state issues involved in the flag-salute controversies which did not affect Lutherans particularly or Lutheran parochial schools but do provide

[37] *Lutheran Standard*, June 7, 1947. Also quoted in *Lutheran Education*, September 1947, 56.

evidence of the tensions which sometimes arise in church-state relationships. On the matter of mandating a flag salute by pupils in public schools, the Supreme Court did an about-face in the 1940s. It ruled against the concerns of Jehovah's Witnesses in 1940 (*Minersville v. Gobitis*) and reversed itself in 1943 (*West Virginia Board of Education v. Barnette*).

Because the Missouri and Wisconsin Synods operated comprehensive parochial school systems and as members of the Synodical Conference together espoused a theology which advocated a separation of church and state, the church-state educational issues arising in the 1940s could not be ignored by the two bodies. In their 1941 conventions already both synods deemed it advisable to give attention to the subject of government involvement in matters pertaining to parochial school education. The Wisconsin Synod School Board recommended that the districts of the synod appoint committees "whose duty it shall be to keep an eye on state legislation affecting our church and school."[38] These committees were to keep the synodical School Board informed on pending legislation in the various states. The Missouri Synod was more specific in its approach. The convention instructed the synod's Board of Christian Education to study the question of government aid to churches in the field of education. With that kind of directive, the Board appointed a committee to carry out the study task. That committee submitted an 18-page report in 1944. On the basis of that report the Board for Parish Education, the name by which the group was now known, formulated and presented to the 1944 synodical convention a policy statement which the Missouri Synod adopted and then reaffirmed in 1947.[39]

---

[38] *Proceedings of the . . . Evangelical Lutheran Joint Synod of Wisconsin and Other States*, 1941, 64.

[39] *Reports and Memorials for the Twenty-fourth Delegate Synod*, Ev. Lutheran Synod of Missouri, Ohio, and Other States, 1944, 75.

The policy statement reasserted what Synodical Conference Lutherans had said at other times, namely, that the education of children, according to Holy Scripture, is a responsibility given by God to parents but that the state also has an interest in the education of its citizens. The policy statement then noted that

The modern school program of the state has two aspects:

1. The social service program (library service, lunches, health service, transportation, etc.).

2. The teaching program (curriculum, teaching, philosophy of education).

A vital difference exists between these two programs. They are associated merely as a matter of convenience. The social service program is administered through schools because schools offer the easiest access to the children.

In the social service program character-forming principles are not consciously formulated, discussed, evaluated, and implemented. Neither do these services contribute consciously and directly to the building up, the integration, and implementation of a philosophy of life.

The social service program should in equity be available to all children of school age irrespective of their school association, just as in the case of public library service. The State can grant to children in church schools this program, since rendering this service does not promote the religious tenets of the Church. The social service program can be granted by the State to church schools . . . without sacrifice of sovereignty on the part of the State or sacrifice of principle on the part of the Church. Hence, the Church can accept this program. . . .[40]

With respect to the teaching program of schools, the document made a number of significant observations. It noted first that "the Church may not subject its teaching program to the supervision, control, and direction of the State."[41] Having said that, the statement acknowledged that "when . . . the State contributes tax money, it has the right to control the expenditures, sanctioning both the purpose for which and the manner in which the money is expended."[42] For that reason, it was argued, the church should not seek subsidy from the state for the teaching programs in parochial schools. And even if the state were willing to relinquish all supervisory rights—as it does, for example, in the case of tax exemptions—the church would do well to remember that the State has the right at any time to withdraw its subsidy or to assert its supervisory authority. If the latter should take place in any given situation, the church would have to decline government subsidy, and if the former occurred, school systems which depended on state aid or had expanded because of it stood in danger of collapsing. The caveat had been sounded, lest anyone think that parochial schools could accept government aid for their teaching programs without serious risk or an unacceptable sacrifice of principle.

In concluding its report, the Board of Christian Education added a comment on what are sometimes referred to as the secular subjects in a Lutheran Christian day school. The statement was very likely included to meet any objection that the teaching aspect which the board had identified in schooling

---

[40] Ibid., 75-76.

[41] Ibid., 76.

[42] Ibid.

could be subdivided into religious and nonreligious subjects, the latter being in principle eligible for government assistance. The board contended:

> The argument that the State is not being asked to subsidize the religious teaching of sectarian schools, but only the teaching of the secular branches is specious and invalid, for all teaching in church schools—also the teaching of the secular branches—becomes a part of the teaching program (curriculum, teaching, and philosophy of education of the Church). Secular branches are taught in the light of the religious tenets of the Church.[43]

According to the Board of Parish Education report to the Missouri Synod convention in July of 1947, few had disagreed with the 1944 position. The Synod also was in agreement with the principles set forth, took note of the fact that the majority of the United States Supreme Court had taken a similar position in the Court's February 1947 *Everson* opinion, and resolved "that the provisions of the 1944 report be continued as operative for the next triennium."[44]

The Wisconsin Synod took up the question of government aid to church-related schools at a much later date than did the Missouri Synod. It was not until 1961 that a synodical convention directed the Synod's Conference of Presidents to formulate a statement on federal aid to church-related schools. A brief statement was prepared and presented to the synodical convention of 1963, but it took until 1967 before a more comprehensive document was ready for presentation to a synodical convention. That document was produced by the

---

[43] Ibid., 77.

[44] *Proceedings of the Fortieth Regular Convention of the Ev. Lutheran Synod of Missouri, Ohio, and Other States*, 1947, 315.

Wisconsin Synod's Advisory Committee on Education and discussed at the Synod's 1967 convention. If the Wisconsin Synod School Board report of 1943 is any indication, the Synod was more concerned at that time with the teaching of religion in public schools than with the issue of government aid to parochial schools. The board's report of 1943 said:

> Since various leaders in educational, religious, and government circles are again strongly advocating the teaching of religion in the public schools . . . , we want to emphasize again that we are uncompromisingly opposed to any such practice.
>
> 1. Because it militates against the strict separation of church and state. . . .
>
> 2. Because it involves a unionistic practice. . . .[45]

The School Board at that time had also expressed its misgivings about released-time programs for the religious instruction of pupils in public schools.

The Missouri Synod was equally concerned in the 1940s about religious education in public schools. In fact, a committee had been appointed to study the issue and report on it. The Board of Parish Education presented an opinion on the matter in a detailed report to the 1947 convention of the Missouri Synod. In that report, the board observed:

> The public schools are being severely criticized because of the extremely secular character of their program. Peremptory demands are being made for the inclusion of

---

[45] *Proceedings of the . . . Evangelical Lutheran Joint Synod of Wisconsin and Other States*, 1943, 45-46.

religion in the curriculum. On the other hand, liberals in church and school are clamoring for complete secularization, for a public school program oriented against a wholly naturalistic background. . . . As Christian citizens we dare not stand aloof and passively wait for developments. It is our duty as Christians and as citizens to see that religious freedom is properly safeguarded.[46]

The board report analyzed the problem of religious teaching in public schools, including among other things a concern about how the theory of evolution was presented, and then proposed some solutions. It urged, as its Wisconsin Synod counterpart had, that congregations establish Lutheran parochial schools wherever possible. The Missouri Synod, however, was also ready to endorse arrangements for weekday religious instruction on released time, a practice not recommended by the School Board of the Wisconsin Synod. In both synods, however, the encouragement to establish Lutheran parochial schools remained strong, a well-known and long-time emphasis by those two members of the Synodical Conference.

When the Wisconsin Synod's Advisory Committee on Education issued its statement on government aid to education, the United States Supreme Court decision in the New Jersey *Everson* case was 20 years old. In the meantime, government aid to private schools—particularly on the part of the federal government—was on the rise. In April of 1967, moreover, voters in the state of Wisconsin, where the Wisconsin Synod had its largest membership concentration, had amended their state constitution to permit the busing of children to nonpublic schools at public expense. Federal response to the constitutionality of that practice had been given in *Everson*. It was not expected that a ruling would be sought again, especially

---

[46] *Reports and Memorials, Synodical Centennial Convention* (Missouri Synod), 1947, 227.

in light of the national Elementary and Secondary Education Act of 1965 which provided federal funds for state public school systems and for private schools within the states. Such legislation demonstrated that the United States Congress, too, had subscribed to the "child-benefit" theory underlying the decision of the majority in the 1947 Supreme Court case of *Everson v. Board of Education of Ewing Township.* The Wisconsin Synod's Advisory Committee on Education was keenly aware of the increase of government aid which was coming to nonpublic schools and admitted that in the two-year period between 1965 and 1967 the committee had devoted a good deal of time "to a consideration of the rapidly-increasing programs of government aid to [private] education and their possible effect upon the synodical system of higher education."[47]

The result of the Advisory Committee's study was the submission to the Wisconsin Synod's 1967 convention of a document entitled "Governmental Aid to Education." The document set forth in detail the classic Lutheran position on the role and function of church and state in society and the means which each is to use to accomplish its tasks. Warning against the confusing and mixing of church and state, the document concluded by saying:

> There is not necessarily a mixture of state and church when both participate in one and the same endeavor but each participates in this endeavor only in the sphere of its own function and restricts itself to its own means. We have such examples in the Christian pastor's performance of marriages. We also have such examples in our Christian day schools. Insofar as our Christian day school teachers teach subject matter which also belongs in the realm of the State . . . , the state is pleased to have them perform a

---

[47] *Reports and Memorials for the Thirty-Ninth Convention*, The Wisconsin Evangelical Lutheran Synod, 1967, 1.

function . . . which the state would otherwise carry out. . . . The Christian day school teachers at the same time perform the functions and use the means of the church as they utilize this teaching situation and its entire program to train Christian children with the Gospel and the whole counsel of God in Christian faith and life.[48]

That having been said, the authors of the document came to the conclusion:

. . . we see that there is a wide realm of contacts in church and state relations, which lie in the area of adiaphora and are not in themselves necessarily a confusion of church and state. Nevertheless, it needs to be borne in mind that actions and decisions in just this realm call for very cautious and discerning judgment in order that in the handling of these adiaphora neither the interests of the church or of the state may actually suffer.[49]

The Lutheran Church—Missouri Synod had come to a similar conclusion when it addressed the government-aid issue in the 1940s. Both church bodies recognized that "absolute and complete separation of Church and State does not exist in our land"[50] but warned that in those areas where the work of the two intersects, extreme caution needs always to be exercised.

That kind of intersection was reached when the *Everson* case came before the courts in 1947. In that and similar situations it is not unusual to be reminded that early national leaders like James Madison and Thomas Jefferson warned against the

---

[48] *Proceedings of the . . . Wisconsin Evangelical Lutheran Synod,* 1967, 172.

[49] Ibid., 173.

[50] *Reports and Memorials, Synodical Centennial Convention* (Missouri Synod), 1947, 227.

entanglement between religion and government and that Jefferson himself had lauded the First Amendment for having built "a wall of separation between Church and State." In another education case involving church and state, however, a Supreme Court justice questioned to what extent Jefferson himself, a strong advocate of general schooling, would have applied the separation principle to all educational practices. In a dissenting opinion to the Court's decision in *McCollum v. Board of Education*, Justice Reed remarked that

> the "wall of separation between church and State" that Mr. Jefferson built at the University which he founded [the University of Virginia, a school governed and controlled by the State of Virginia] did not exclude religious education from that school. The difference between the generality of his statement in the separation of church and state and the specificity of his conclusions on education are considerable. A rule of law should not be drawn from a figure of speech.[51]

From the time of Jefferson to *Everson*, of course, common schooling had undergone considerable changes and had taken on dimensions not thought of by men like Jefferson. Parochial schools in 1947 were also markedly different from those of 1847, the year of the founding of The Lutheran Church— Missouri Synod. The programs of all schools had grown and with that growth the expectations of parochial schools had reached the point that made the practical application of the principle of separation of church and state a great deal more complex. The government admitted this and the church realized it. In *Everson* the Supreme Court ratified government assistance programs which had been given to parochial schools prior to

---

[51] *Illinois ex rel. McCollum v. Board of Education of . . . Champaign County, Illinois,* in Kliebard, *Religion and Education in America*, 183.

1947 and with its acceptance of the theory that it is possible to distinguish between government aid to students in church-related schools and support of the schools themselves opened the door for later assistance to students attending private schools at the elementary, secondary, and higher education levels.

Suggested for Further Reading

Butts, R. Freeman. *The American Tradition in Religion and Education*. Boston: Beacon Press, 1950: 146-78.

_____. "The Search for Freedom." Chap. in *Public Education in the United States*. New York: Holt, Rinehart and Winston, 1978: 271-98.

Duker, Sam. *The Public Schools and Religion: The Legal Context*. New York: Harper and Row, 1966: 85-108.

Kliebard, Herbert M. *Religion and Education in America: A Documentary History*. Scranton, PA: International Textbook Company, 1969: 127-49.

Warshaw, Thayer S. *Religion, Education, and the Supreme Court*. Nashville: Abingdon, 1979: 26-29.

Weinstein, Joshua. *When Religion Comes to School*. Washington D.C.: University Press of America, 1979: 49-51.

Zirkell, Perry A. and Sharon Nalbone Richardson. *A Digest of Supreme Court Decisions Affecting Education*. Bloomington, IN: Phi Delta Kappa, 1988: 18-19.

Postscript

The purpose of *The Lutheran Parochial School: Dates, Documents, Events, People* has been to provide a framework within which to view the history of the Lutheran Christian day school in the United States. Political and other kinds of history are regularly marked by key dates, important documents, turning-point events, and prominent people. The assumption behind the annotated calendar of the preceding pages is that the same kind of highlighting is possible in the history of the Lutheran parochial school. That institution has unfolded for the most part without a great deal of attention from the general American public. The much larger and geographically more widely distributed system of Roman Catholic schools, on the other hand, is far better known. In localities where Lutheran schools do exist, however, their presence does not go unnoticed and often has to be taken into account in community life and planning. The story of these schools is a small but not unimportant part of both American Lutheran church history and American educational history and for that reason worthy of being chronicled.

The dates and events selected for commentary in the present volume are not the only ones which could have been chosen, of course, and some readers might even wonder about the rationale behind the selection of this or that date. The year 1872, for example, the year of the founding of the Evangelical Lutheran Synodical Conference of North America, might be a case in point. That date and event were included, however, because the Synodical Conference came to be known for its advocacy of Lutheran Christian day schools. The two most extensive parochial school programs on the contemporary scene are operated, moreover, by congregations in The Lutheran Church—Missouri Synod and the Wisconsin Evangelical Lutheran Synods, both of whom were charter members of the Conference and continued as affiliates of it for a period of approximately 90 years. It seemed that a presentation on Lutheran school history would be incomplete without something of a review of that church alliance which had been associated for so long with the cause of the Lutheran parochial school.

The intent of *The Lutheran Parochial School* has not been just to note that something happened at a given time. Such charting could be done in outline form and would include more dates and events than are taken up in the present treatise. The book also does not pretend to be a comprehensive history of the Lutheran parochial school movement. Such a study would perhaps call for a format different from the present one and possibly even more than one volume. The goal of *The Lutheran Parochial School* has been to bring together in a convenient handbook a selection of various types of documents and events in the history of Lutheran elementary schooling and to examine them in more detail than is customary in a general history. Such a discussion quite naturally invites references to the people involved with the events and documents. Who these people were and what they had to say to the issues and circumstances of their day should not go unnoticed. For that reason, the preceding pages are regularly dotted with quotations from past periodical literature and synodical *Proceedings*. The sources from which such quotations are taken are often not readily available apart from a research library or archival center. It is hoped, therefore, that, the quotations in the present volume will be informative especially for readers who do not have convenient access to the sources and documents cited.

Missing in *The Lutheran Parochial School: Dates, Documents, Events, People* is a section dealing with community or area Lutheran high schools. These schools differ from the high school preparatory departments which were operated for years in conjunction with synodical colleges. Lutheran high schools are owned and operated by associations of local congregations rather than by a synod. From their inception, high schools of this type sought to provide a general secondary school education and did not limit themselves to a curriculum designed only for the purpose of accommodating students who intended eventually to become Lutheran pastors or teachers. Congregations in both the Wisconsin Evangelical Lutheran Synod and The Lutheran Church—Missouri Synod sponsor a not insignificant number of such high schools today.

Although the Lutheran high school movement had its promoters in the nineteenth century, no school begun at that time had a long existence. The first area Lutheran high school which had a continued existence was established in Milwaukee in 1903 by members of the Missouri and Wisconsin Synods. The venture has since branched into more than one school, although joint sponsorship of an individual school by members of both synods is no longer part of the picture. Missouri Synod members in Chicago and Fort Wayne followed Milwaukee's lead and founded Lutheran high schools in 1909 and 1916 respectively. The Winnebago Lutheran Academy in Fond du Lac, Wisconsin, had its beginning among Wisconsin Synod Lutherans in 1925. The 1930s brought no new high schools into existence. In 1943, however, an association of individuals in the Missouri and Wisconsin Synods opened a Lutheran high school in Racine, Wisconsin. From that time onwards, the movement mushroomed with the opening of Lutheran high schools from time to time in various parts of the country. The modest beginnings of Lutheran secondary education in the early part of the twentieth century evolved into a rather energetic movement after World War II, so that by the end of the century the number of Lutheran high schools in the United States was close to 90. Lutheran secondary education was not discussed because of when the movement gained momentum and because its manner of unfolding did not lend itself particularly well to the format of the present book. This area of historical study, however, has a rightful claim to in-depth investigation.

An additional word ought also to be said at this point about Lutheran teacher education. That subject was addressed only in connection with three teachers colleges, namely, the schools at Addison-River Forest (1864, 1913), New Ulm (1884), and Seward (1894). With the post-mid-century emergence of more four-year colleges in The Lutheran Church—Missouri Synod, teacher education programs were added to the curricula of those schools. In the Wisconsin Evangelical Lutheran Synod a second two-year teachers college was operated in Milwaukee for a period of 10 years. The latter program was discontinued in 1969, with the result that teacher education in the Wisconsin Synod was again consolidated on one campus. In the Missouri Synod, however, there has been no such reverting to an earlier practice. Teacher education is conducted on the various campuses of Missouri's Concordia University System. The evolvement of that arrangement was not discussed on the preceding pages because it took place in the last part of the twentieth century and so went beyond the time frame of the present volume.

Another twentieth-century phenomenon not given attention was the emergence of church-related early childhood education programs. As is well known, this type of schooling is sponsored not only by Lutheran parishes but by other denominations as well. It is an area in which the large

Evangelical Lutheran Church in America (ELCA) has also been actively involved, although the traditional graded parochial school was not strongly promoted by the individual Lutheran synods which merged with one another during the course of the twentieth century and eventually combined to form ELCA. Congregations in both the Wisconsin and Missouri Synods have also been engaged in early childhood education. The Missouri Synod, for example, reported a total of 1,234 early childhood centers for the 1997-98 school year, 237 more preschools, in other words, than Lutheran elementary schools.[1] A Wisconsin Synod statistical report for the same year reveals a total of 269 early childhood education programs, 219 of which were operated in conjunction with a Lutheran elementary school.[2] According to the Missouri Synod report for 1997-98, only 30 percent of the teachers in Lutheran early childhood centers held synodical teacher certification. This compares with 70 percent in 1988-89.[3] Staffing early childhood education centers with synodically certified teachers, that is, with teachers who have had formal training in Lutheran theology and educational philosophy, has obviously not kept pace with the rapid increase in the number of early childhood education programs.

The appearance in the last part of the twentieth century of preschools operated by Lutheran churches, the sizable increase in the number of Lutheran high schools after World War II, and the expansion of Lutheran teacher training programs to campuses other than those established for that purpose in the nineteenth century are but samples of topics which might have

---

[1] Department of School Ministry, *Statistical Report Summary 1997-98* (St. Louis: The Lutheran Church—Missouri Synod), 4.

[2] Commission on Parish Schools, *School Statistics 1997-98* (Milwaukee: The Wisconsin Evangelical Lutheran Synod, December 1, 1997), 2.

[3] Department of School Ministry, 7.

been incorporated into the present book. A selection of items had to be made and since these topics did not easily fit into an annotated calendar format, a discussion of them was omitted. Should *The Lutheran Parochial School: Dates, Documents, Events, People* find its way into college or seminary courses in the history of Lutheran education or American Lutheran church history, it is the author's hope that the book has been arranged in such a way that it can be used together with other materials and effectively integrated with them.

INDEX